Scheduling and Automatic Parallelization

Alain Darte   Yves Robert   Frédéric Vivien

Scheduling and Automatic Parallelization

With 94 Figures

Birkhäuser
Boston • Basel • Berlin

Alain Darte
Yves Robert
Laboratoire LIP
École Normale Supérieure
  de Lyon
69364 Lyon Cedex 07
France

Frédéric Vivien
Laboratoire ICPS
Université Louis Pasteur
F67400 Illkich
France

Library of Congress Cataloging-in-Publication Data
Darte, Alain.
    Scheduling and automatic parallelization / Alain Darte, Yves Robert, Frédéric Vivien.
        p. cm.
    Includes bibliographical references.
    ISBN 0-8176-4149-1 (hc. : alk. paper)
        1. Compiling (Electronic computers)   2. Parallel processing (Electronic computers)
    I. Robert, Yves, 1958–   II. Vivien, Frédéric.   III. Title.
    QA76.76.C65 D37 2000
    004′.35—dc21   99-046585

AMS Subject Classifications: 10.15.10, 10.10.20, 10.10

Printed on acid-free paper.
© 2000 Birkhäuser Boston   *Birkhäuser* ®

ISBN 0-8176-4149-1
ISBN 3-7643-4149-1   SPIN 10733875

Typeset by the authors in TeX.
Printed and bound by Edwards Brothers, Inc., Ann Arbor, MI.
Printed in the United States of America.

9 8 7 6 5 4 3 2 1

Contents

Preface

Readership

This book is devoted to the study of compiler transformations that are needed to expose the parallelism hidden in a program. This book is not an introductory book to parallel processing, nor is it an introductory book to parallelizing compilers. We assume that readers are familiar with the books *High Performance Compilers for Parallel Computing* by Wolfe [121] and *Supercompilers for Parallel and Vector Computers* by Zima and Chapman [125], and that they want to know more about scheduling transformations.

In this book we describe both task graph scheduling and loop nest scheduling. Task graph scheduling aims at executing tasks linked by precedence constraints; it is a *run-time* activity. Loop nest scheduling aims at executing statement instances linked by data dependences; it is a *compile-time* activity. We are mostly interested in loop nest scheduling, but we also deal with task graph scheduling for two main reasons: (i) Beautiful algorithms and heuristics have been reported in the literature recently; and (ii) Several techniques used in task graph scheduling, like list scheduling, are the basis of the loop transformations implemented in loop nest scheduling.

As for loop nest scheduling our goal is to capture in a single place the fantastic developments of the last decade or so. Dozens of loop transformations have been introduced (loop interchange, skewing, fusion, distribution, etc.) before a unifying theory emerged. The theory builds upon the pioneering papers of Karp, Miller, and Winograd [65] and of Lamport [75], and it relies on sophisticated mathematical tools (unimodular transformations, parametric integer linear programming, Hermite decomposition, Smith decomposition, etc.).

This book is intended for graduate or postgraduate students who want to understand the foundations of automatic parallelization techniques. It will be very useful to researchers interested in scheduling, compilers, and program transformations.

The book is self-contained, in that all proofs are included. Readers will need some basic mathematical skills and some familiarity with standard graph and linear programming algorithms, all of which can be found in *Introduction to Algorithms* by Cormen, Leiserson, and Rivest [26] and in *Theory of Linear and Integer Programming* by Schrijver [110].

Acknowledgments

This book grew out of several lectures at the DEA Informatique de Lyon, the DEA Algorithmique de Paris, and CS594 of the University of Tennessee at Knoxville. Several people have deeply influenced our view of the field. Even though the following list cannot be exhaustive, we would like to thank:

- our colleagues Paul Feautrier, José Fortes, François Irigoin, Catherine Mongenet, Patrice Quinton, Guy-René Perrin, Sanjay Rajopadhye, and Rob Schreiber.

- our former and current PhD students Pierre Boulet, Pierre-Yves Calland, Michèle Dion, Cyril Randriamaro, Fabrice Rastello, Tanguy Risset, and Georges-André Silber.

Lyon, France   Alain Darte
May 1999   Yves Robert
                                                                          Frédéric Vivien

Introduction

Motivation

Scheduling theory originated from operation research. In a computer science framework, scheduling tasks (or subroutines, processes, or threads) to minimize some optimization criteria (such as the total execution time) is a fundamental problem. See the classic book *Computer and Job-Shop Scheduling Theory* by Coffman [24], the recent book *Task Scheduling in Parallel and Distributed Systems* by El-Rewini, Lewis and Ali [37], and the research oriented survey *Scheduling Theory and Its Applications*, edited by Chrétienne, Coffman, Lenstra, and Liu [22].

To understand what a task system is, consider the following toy example:

```
DO i=1, n
 Task T_{i,i}: x(i) = b(i) / a(i,i)
 DO j = i+1, n
  Task T_{i,j}: b(j) = b(j) - a(j,i) * x(i)
 ENDDO
ENDDO
```

This example will be processed in full detail in Chapter 1. Here we only sketch the techniques that will be explained throughout the book. Building the task graph is not very difficult here. Task $T_{i,i}$, which computes x_i and writes it in memory, must precede task $T_{i,j}$, which reads this value, for all $j > i$. Also, the updating at step i of $b(j)$ must precede the updating at step $i + 1$, which means that task $T_{i,j}$ precedes task $T_{i+1,j}$ for $j \geq i + 1$. If such precedence constraints are not enforced, we cannot guarantee that the semantics of the original program are preserved. We are led to the graph of Figure 1. Nodes are tasks, and edges represent precedence constraints. We

xi

then have to weight nodes according to their estimated duration (for example, consider that all tasks have unit duration time) to derive a task system. Typical questions from scheduling theory are the following: (i) What is the minimal execution time using an unlimited number of processors? (ii) What is the minimal execution time using p processors, where p is fixed? (iii) In both cases, how to assign to each task both a time-step at which its execution is started, and a processor number that is responsible for executing the task? Answering such questions is the object of Chapter 1.

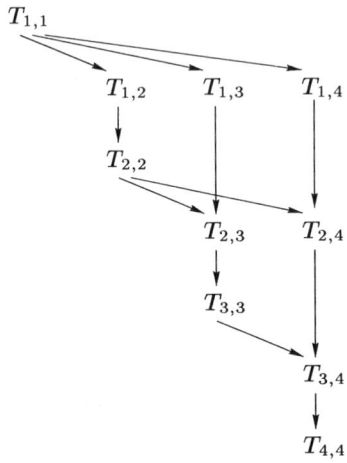

Figure 1: Task graph for the example ($n = 4$).

Current multiprocessor systems have a very efficient memory hierarchy, so that accessing a data item stored in local memory is an order of magnitude faster than accessing a data item stored in the local memory of a remote processor. In other words, communication costs play an important role if we are to accurately model state-of-the-art architectures. Adding communication costs to the story simply amounts to adding edge weights to the task graph; the meaning is that a communication cost along the edge $e : T \longrightarrow T'$ will be paid if and only if T and T' are not executed by the same processor. Adding edge weights dramatically complicates the answer to the previous scheduling questions. Explaining why is the object of Chapter 2.

We are not fully satisfied with task graph systems. First, generating the graph is expensive, and determining the computation and communication costs is difficult. Sometimes both are just unfeasible. Another drawback is that scheduling algorithms can be derived only for fixed values of the program parameters such as n in the preceding code. The result is that the schedules are not generic; changing n from 1000 to 1001, say, will lead to completely different results. And if this is done at compile-time, the value

n may be unknown! What we would like to derive is a generic scheduling that takes the parameter n as input and produces a (compile-time) solution such as the following:

```
DO i=1, n
  Step 2i − 1: x(i) = b(i) / a(i,i)
  DOPAR j = i+1, n
   Step 2i: b(j) = b(j) - a(j,i) * x(i)
  ENDDOPAR
ENDDO
```

Making the parallelism fully explicit is not as easy as the example may lead us to believe. First, we have to identify *data dependences*, i.e., which statement instances must be executed before which other ones to preserve the semantics of the original program. When given a task graph system, we are *given the precedence constraints*; these are the edges of the graph, which the programmer has to provide, as stated earlier. Here the situation is different; we essentially have to implement a technique to automatically derive at compile-time (the equivalent of) these edges. Usually it is impossible to compute the dependences exactly, so we use an approximation. Of course this approximation is conservative; we keep more dependences than actually exist in the program to guarantee the correctness of the result. There are several possible approximations (dependence levels, direction vectors, etc.). For each approximation there is a "best" parallelization, or scheduling, algorithm. This is explained in Chapter 5.

Automatic parallelization techniques aim at extracting the parallelism out of a source program. The extraction is automatic, i.e., by the compiler, and is architecture-independent. To put it in an applicative framework, the idea is to process a Fortran 77 code to generate an HPF program where parallel constructs (i.e., the FORALL construct and the INDEPENDENT directive)

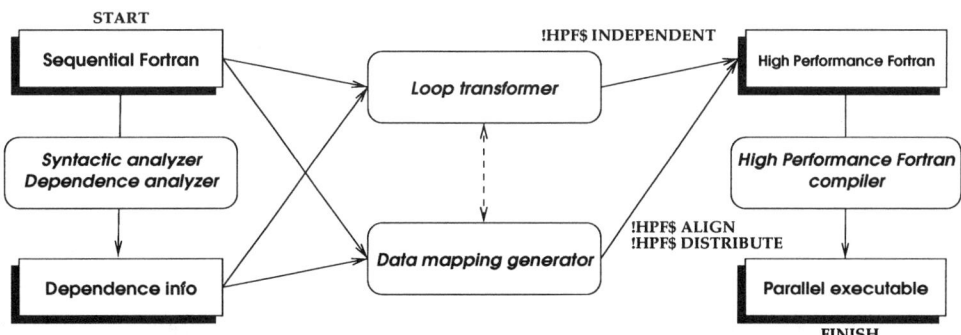

Figure 2: The whole chain of automatic parallelization.

and data distribution (i.e., `ALIGN` and `DISTRIBUTE` directives) have been generated "automagically" without any intervention of the user. Figure 2 depicts the whole chain of transformations needed to convert a Fortran program into an HPF program. Scheduling is only a single piece of the lengthy process!

To be more concrete, consider the following example, which is due to Peir and Cytron [95]:

```
DO i = 0, n
 DO j = 0, n
  a(i,j) = b(i,j-6) + d(i-1,j+3)
  b(i+1,j-1) = c(i+2,j+5)
  c(i+3,j-1) = a(i,j-2)
  d(i,j-1) = a(i,j-1)
 ENDDO
ENDDO
```

The need for compiler transformations is clear in this example. Dependences are not easy to compute by hand. Neither of the two loops can be directly marked parallel, while there is some parallelism hidden in the program. Using Lamport's hyperplane method [75] (see Chapter 5) and alignment directives, we could obtain the following HPF program:

```
 REAL a(n,n),b(n,n),c(n,n),d(n,n)
!HPF$ TEMPLATE Nice_template(n+3,n)
!HPF$ DISTRIBUTE Nice_template(*,BLOCK)
!HPF$ ALIGN a(i1,i2) WITH Nice_template(i1,i2)
!HPF$ ALIGN b(i1,i2) WITH Nice_template(i1-1,i2)
!HPF$ ALIGN c(i1,i2) WITH Nice_template(i1-3,i2)
!HPF$ ALIGN d(i1,i2) WITH Nice_template(i1,i2)
 DO T = 0, 8n
!HPF$ INDEPENDENT
  DO P = max(0, ceiling((T-n)/7)), min(n,floor(n, T/7))
   a(P,T-7P) = b(P,T-7P-6) + d(P-1,T-7P+3)
   b(P+1,T-7P-1) = c(P+2,T-7P+5)
   c(P+3,T-7P-1) = a(P,T-7P-2)
   d(P,T-7P-1) = a(P,T-7P-1)
  ENDDO
 ENDDO
```

Other parallelizations are possible, which are not given here. The most important fact is that the parallelism has been made explicit in the `!HPF$ INDEPENDENT` loop, through the scheduling transformation that has been applied to the original nest. In this book we concentrate on scheduling transformations, those dealing with extracting and exposing the parallelism. Alignment, mapping, and code generation issues are outside the scope of the book. We believe that these issues are not mature enough to be exposed in this book.

Book Overview

The book is divided into two parts. Part I deals with unidimensional problems (task graph systems and decomposed cyclic scheduling), and Part II tackles multidimensional systems (recurrent equations and loop nests).

The first two chapters present results from scheduling theory, both classical and recent, in the framework of task graph systems. These two chapters are not directly related to compile-time transformations. However, they provide useful material (like list-scheduling heuristics) that will be used later in the book. Also, they attempt to summarize state-of-the-art techniques in task graph scheduling.

Chapter 1 deals with basic results on task graph scheduling. We use the original model where only vertices of the task system are weighted; no communication cost is taken into account. Scheduling such task graphs with unlimited resources is not difficult, but the problem with limited resources is NP-complete. We describe list heuristics that are used in that context.

Chapter 2 is the counterpart of Chapter 1 when taking communication costs into account. The problem turns out to be surprisingly difficult; even the problem with unlimited resources is NP-complete. The chapter describes both theoretical results and cost-effective heuristics widely used in software systems.

Chapter 3 is devoted to cyclic scheduling, a basic instance of the software pipelining problem. Cyclic scheduling is a transition from task graphs to loop nests because we operate on a reduced representation of the problem, the *reduced dependence graph* which is manipulated at compile-time. Because the problem is unidimensional, it is conceptually simpler than scheduling general loop nests, and we are able to derive bounds and heuristics in the presence of limited resources. We make use of the Bellman-Ford algorithm and of a retiming technique, due to Leiserson and Saxe [79], that minimizes the "clock-period" of a graph.

Chapter 4 is the most theoretical of the book; it provides mathematical foundations for the next chapter. It addresses scheduling problems related to graphs whose edges are labeled by multidimensional integer vectors. Such graphs come from the computational model introduced by Karp,

Miller, and Winograd [65], and are known as *systems of uniform recurrence equations* (SURE). We study computability issues, linear scheduling, and multi-linear scheduling. It turns out that this study can be used to automatically parallelize codes defined by nested loops.

The last chapter, Chapter 5, deals with loop nests and loop parallelization algorithms. The different dependence representations used in the literature are recalled, and the "optimality" of each parallelism detection algorithm is studied with respect to its underlying dependence representation. The chapter covers most algorithms proposed in the past, from Lamport's hyperplane method and Allen and Kennedy's algorithm to unimodular transformations and general multidimensional affine scheduling techniques such as those developed in Feautrier's algorithm. All the classical loop transformations (loop distribution, loop skewing, general unimodular transformations, etc.) are presented with a uniform scheduling view.

Part I

Unidimensional Problems

Chapter 1

Scheduling DAGs without Communications

1.1 Introduction

This chapter is devoted to a quick overview of elementary results on task graphs scheduling. We start informally with an example in Section 1.2. We introduce basic definitions in Section 1.3. Throughout this chapter, we use a very simple model where communication delays are neglected. When there is no restriction on the number of available resources, optimal scheduling algorithms can be found in polynomial time, as shown in Section 1.4. Section 1.5 deals with limited resources; the scheduling problem becomes NP-complete, and list heuristics are the usual approach.

1.2 Where Do Task Graphs Come From?

Example 1

Consider the following algorithm to solve the linear system $Ax = b$, where A is an $n \times n$ nonsingular lower triangular matrix and b is a vector with n components:

```
DO i=1, n
  Task T_{i,i}: x(i) = b(i) / a(i,i)
  DO j = i+1, n
   Task T_{i,j}: b(j) = b(j) - a(j,i) * x(i)
  ENDDO
ENDDO
```

For a given value of i, $1 \leq i \leq n$, all tasks $T_{i,*}$ represent computations at the ith iteration of the outer loop. The computation of $x(i)$ is performed first (task $T_{i,i}$). Then each component $b(j)$, with $j > i$, of vector b, is updated (task $T_{i,j}$). □

In the original program, there is a total precedence order between tasks. Let us write $T <_{seq} T'$ if task T is executed before task T' in the original sequential code. We have

$$T_{1,1} <_{seq} T_{1,2} <_{seq} T_{1,3} <_{seq} \cdots <_{seq} T_{1,n} <_{seq} T_{2,2} <_{seq} T_{2,3} <_{seq} \cdots <_{seq} T_{n,n}$$

However there are independent tasks that can be executed in parallel. Intuitively, independent tasks are tasks whose execution order can be interchanged without modifying the result of the program execution. A sufficient condition for this is that the tasks do not access the same variable. They can read the same value, but they cannot write into the same memory location (otherwise the result would depend on the identity of the last writing operation). We can express this more formally. Each task T has an input set $\text{In}(T)$ (read values) and an output set $\text{Out}(T)$ (written values). In our example, $\text{In}(T_{i,i}) = \{b(i), a(i,i)\}$ and $\text{Out}(T_{i,i}) = \{x(i)\}$. For $j > i$, $\text{In}(T_{i,j}) = \{b(j), a(j,i), x(i)\}$ and $\text{Out}(T_{i,j}) = \{b(j)\}$. Two tasks T and T' are not independent (we write $T \perp T'$) if they share some written variable:

$$T \perp T' \Leftrightarrow \begin{cases} & \text{In}(T) \cap \text{Out}(T') \neq \emptyset \\ \text{or} & \text{Out}(T) \cap \text{In}(T') \neq \emptyset \\ \text{or} & \text{Out}(T) \cap \text{Out}(T') \neq \emptyset \end{cases}$$

These conditions are known as Bernstein's conditions [16]. We will come back in Chapter 5 and discuss how to determine whether or not these conditions hold. Let us simply try some examples. Task $T_{1,1}$ and task $T_{1,2}$ are not independent because $\text{Out}(T_{1,1}) \cap \text{In}(T_{1,2}) = \{x(1)\}$; therefore $T_{1,1} \perp T_{1,2}$. Similarly, $\text{Out}(T_{1,3}) \cap \text{Out}(T_{2,3}) = \{b(3)\}$, hence $T_{1,3}$ and $T_{2,3}$ are not independent; we write $T_{1,3} \perp T_{2,3}$.

Given the dependence relation $\perp$, we can extract a partial order from the total order $<_{seq}$ induced by the sequential execution of the program. If two tasks T and T' are dependent, i.e., $T \perp T'$, we order them according to the sequential execution; we write $T \prec T'$ if both $T \perp T'$ and $T <_{seq} T'$. The precedence relation $\prec$ represents the dependences that must [1] be satisfied to preserve the semantics of the original program; if $T \prec T'$, then T was executed before T' in the sequential code, and it has to be executed before T' even if we have as many resources as we want, because T and T' share a written variable.

---

[1] Following Bernstein's conditions.

To define $\prec$ more accurately, in terms of order relations, we can write

$$\prec \text{ equals } (<_{seq} \cap \perp)^+$$

where $^+$ denotes the transitive closure. In other words, we take the transitive closure of the intersection of $\perp$ and $<_{seq}$ to derive the set of all constraints that need to be satisfied to preserve the semantics of the original program. In a sense, $\prec$ captures the inherent sequentiality of the original program. The original total ordering $<_{seq}$ was unduly restrictive, only the partial ordering $\prec$ needs to be respected. Why do we need to take the transitive closure of $<_{seq} \cap \perp$ to get a correct definition of $\prec$? In the example, we have $T_{2,4} \perp T_{4,4}$ (which is not a predecessor-ship relation, as there is $T_{3,4}$ in between) and $T_{4,4} \perp T_{4,5}$, hence a path of dependences from $T_{2,4}$ to $T_{4,5}$, while we do not have $T_{2,4} \perp T_{4,5}$. We need to track chains of dependences to correctly define $\prec$.

We can draw a directed multigraph to represent the dependence constraints that need to be satisfied. The vertices of the graph denote the tasks, while the edges express the dependence constraints. An edge $e : T \to T'$ in the graph means that the execution of T' must begin only after the end of the execution of T, whatever the number of available resources. We do not usually draw transitivity edges on the graph, as they represent redundant information; if $T \prec T'$ and $T' \prec T''$ and if there exists a dependence $T \perp T''$, then it will be automatically satisfied. We say that T is a predecessor of T' if $T \prec T'$ and if there is no task T''' in between, i.e., such that $T \prec T'''$ and $T''' \prec T'$. We will give formal definitions in the next section. In our example, the predecessor-ship relations are the following:

- $T_{i,i} \prec T_{i,j}$ for $1 \le i < j \le n$
  (the computation of $x(i)$ must be done before updating $b(j)$ at step i of the outer loop).

- $T_{i,j} \prec T_{i+1,j}$ for $1 \le i < j \le n$
  (updating $b(j)$ at step i of the outer loop must [2] be done before reading it at step $i + 1$).

We end up with the graph drawn in Figure 1.1. We will use this graph throughout this chapter to illustrate the introduced material.

---

[2]Well, "must" is slightly exaggerated, because the addition is an associative and commutative operation. This is true the way the program is written, reusing the same memory location $b(j)$ for all the updates. This is an output dependence that can be removed using standard techniques [94, 121].

1.3   Scheduling DAGs

Definition 1 (Task System) *A task system is a directed vertex-weighted multi-graph* $G = (V, E, w)$ *where:*

- *the set V of vertices represents the tasks (note that V is finite).*

- *the set E of edges represents precedence constraints between tasks:*
  $e = (u, v) \in E$ *iff* $u \prec v$.

- *the weight function $w : V \longrightarrow \mathbb{N}^*$ gives the weight (or duration) of each task. Task weights are assumed to be positive integers.* [3]

Example 1, Continued

For the triangular system (Figure 1.1), we can assume that all tasks have equal weight; let $w(T_{i,j}) = 1$ for $1 \leq i \leq j \leq n$. We could also decide that a division is more costly than a multiply-add and give extra weight to the diagonal tasks $T_{i,i}$.   □

A schedule σ of a task system is a function that assigns a beginning time to each task. We may also have an allocation function alloc that assigns a target processor to each task. We have the following formal definition.

Definition 2 (Schedule) *A schedule of a task system $G = (V, E, w)$ is a function $\sigma : V \longrightarrow \mathbb{N}^*$ such that $\sigma(u) + w(u) \leq \sigma(v)$ whenever $e = (u, v) \in E$.*

In other words, a schedule must preserve the *dependence constraints* induced by the precedence relation $\prec$ and materialized by the edges of the dependence graph; if $u \prec v$, then the execution of u begins at time $\sigma(u)$ and requires $w(u)$ units of time, and the beginning of the execution of v at time step $\sigma(v)$ must be posterior to the end of the execution of u.

Often there are other constraints that must be met by schedules, namely, *resource constraints*. When there is an infinite number of processors [4], we say that we have a problem with unlimited resources, denoted Pb(∞). But when having only a fixed number p of available processors, we speak of a problem with limited resources Pb(p). The resource constraints are expressed as follows; each task $v \in V$ is allocated to a processor alloc(v) using an allocation function alloc : $V \longrightarrow \mathcal{P}$, where $\mathcal{P} = \{1, \ldots, p\}$ denotes the set of available processors. The relationship between the schedule σ and

---

[3]This is not a restriction; tasks weights can be rational numbers. However, because there is a finite number of tasks, we can always scale them up to integers.

[4]In fact we need no more processors than the total number of tasks.

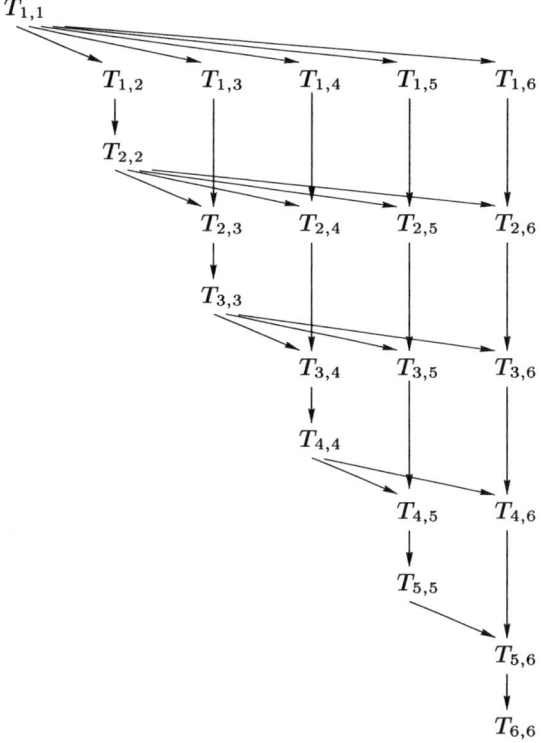

Figure 1.1: Task graph for the triangular system ($n = 6$).

the allocation alloc is that no processor can be allocated more than one task at the same time step. This translates into the following condition:

$$\text{alloc}(T) = \text{alloc}(T') \Rightarrow \left\{ \begin{array}{l} \sigma(T) + w(T) \leq \sigma(T') \\ \text{or} \quad \sigma(T') + w(T') \leq \sigma(T) \end{array} \right.$$

This condition expresses the fact that if two tasks T and T' are allocated to the same processor, then the execution of T must be completed before the execution of T' can begin, or vice versa.

Given a task system, there is a basic condition for a schedule to exist, regardless of resource constraints.

Theorem 1 *Let $G = (V, E, w)$ be a task system. There exists a schedule iff G contains no cycle.*

Proof Clearly, if there is a cycle $v_1 \rightarrow v_2 \ldots \rightarrow \ldots \rightarrow v_k \rightarrow v_1$, then $v_1 \prec v_1$ (v_1 depends on itself), and a schedule σ would satisfy $\sigma(v_1) + w(v_1) \leq \sigma(v_1)$, which is impossible because we assumed $w(v_1) > 0$.

Conversely, if G has no cycle, then there exist vertices with no predecessor (V is finite) and we can thus topologically sort the vertices and schedule them one after the other (i.e., assuming a single processor) according to the topological order. Formally, if $v_{\pi(1)}, v_{\pi(2)}, \dots, v_{\pi(n)}$ is the ordered list of vertices obtained by the topological sort, let $\sigma(v_{\pi(1)}) = 0$ and $\sigma(v_{\pi(i)}) = \sigma(v_{\pi(i-1)}) + w(v_{\pi(i-1)})$ for $2 \le i \le n$. Dependence constraints are respected, because if $v_i \prec v_j$ then the topological sort ensures that $\pi(i) < \pi(j)$. ∎

Theorem 1 explains the name of this chapter; we aim at scheduling *directed acyclic graphs* (or DAGs).

Definition 3 (DAG) *A DAG $G = (V, E, w)$ is a task system (as in Definition 2) where G is a directed acyclic graph.*

Given a task system, the usual objective is to minimize the total execution time of the schedule. We have the following definitions.

Definition 4 (Makespan, $\mathbf{Pb}(\infty)$, $\mathbf{Pb}(p)$) *Let $G = (V, E, w)$ be a DAG.*

1. *Let σ be a schedule for G. Assume σ uses at most p processors (let $p = \infty$ if resources are unlimited). The makespan $MS(\sigma, p)$ of σ is its total execution time:*
$$MS(\sigma, p) = \max_{v \in V}\{\sigma(v) + w(v)\} - \min_{v \in V}\{\sigma(v)\}$$

2. *$Pb(\infty)$ is the problem of determining a schedule σ of minimal makespan $MS(\sigma, \infty)$ assuming unlimited resources. Let $MS_{opt}(\infty)$ be the value of the makespan of an optimal schedule with unlimited resources, in other words, $MS_{opt}(\infty) = \min_{\sigma} MS(\sigma, \infty)$.*

3. *$Pb(p)$ is the problem of determining a schedule σ of minimal makespan $MS(\sigma, p)$ assuming p processors. Let $MS_{opt}(p)$ be the value of the makespan of an optimal schedule with p processors.*

When the first task is scheduled at time 0, the expression of the makespan can be reduced to $MS(\sigma, p) = \max_{v \in V}\{\sigma(v) + w(v)\}$. We extend weights to paths in G as usual; if $\Phi = (T_1, T_2, \dots, T_n)$ denotes a path in G, then $w(\Phi) = \sum_{i=1}^{n} w(T_i)$. Because schedules respect dependences, we have the following easy bound on the makespan.

Proposition 1 *Let $G = (V, E, w)$ be a DAG and σ a schedule for G with p processors. Then $MS(\sigma, p) \ge w(\Phi)$, for all paths Φ in G.*

Proof Consider any path $\Phi = (T_1, T_2, \ldots, T_n)$ in G: $e = (T_i, T_{i+1}) \in E$ for $1 \leq i < n$. Then $\sigma(T_i) + w(T_i) \leq \sigma(T_{i+1})$ for $1 \leq i < n$, and thus $MS(\sigma, p) \geq w(T_n) + \sigma(T_n) - \sigma(T_1) \geq \sum_{i=1}^{n} w(T_i) = w(\Phi)$. ∎

Our last definition introduces the notions of speedup and efficiency for schedules (see [73] for a detailed discussion on speedup and efficiency).

Definition 5 (Speedup, Efficiency) *Let $G = (V, E, w)$ be a DAG, and σ a schedule for G with p processors:*

1. *The speedup is the ratio $s(\sigma, p) = \dfrac{Seq}{MS(\sigma, p)}$, where $Seq = \sum_{v \in V} w(v)$ is the sum of all task weights.*

2. *The efficiency is the ratio $e(\sigma, p) = \dfrac{s(\sigma, p)}{p} = \dfrac{Seq}{p \times MS(\sigma, p)}$.*

Seq is the optimal execution time $MS_{opt}(1)$ of a schedule with a single processor. We have the following well-known result.

Theorem 2 *Let $G = (V, E, w)$ be a task system. For any schedule σ with p processors,*

$$0 \leq e(\sigma, p) \leq 1$$

Proof Consider the execution of σ as illustrated in Figure 1.2 (this is a fictitious example, not related to Example 1). At any time step during execution, some processors are active, and some are idle. At the end all tasks have been processed. Let Idle denote the cumulated idle time of the p processors during the whole execution. Because Seq is the sum of all task weights, the quantity Seq + Idle is equal to the area of the rectangle in Figure 1.2, i.e., the product of the number of processors by the makespan of the schedule: Seq + Idle = $p \times MS(\sigma, p)$. Hence $e(\sigma, p) = \dfrac{Seq}{p \times MS(\sigma, p)} \leq 1$. ∎

Another way to state Theorem 2 is to say that the speedup with p processors is always bounded by p. No superlinear speedup with our model! Here is an easy result to conclude this section: the more resources, the smaller (or equal) the optimal makespan.

Theorem 3 *Let $G = (V, E, w)$ be a task system. We have:*

$$Seq = MS_{opt}(1) \geq \ldots \geq MS_{opt}(p) \geq MS_{opt}(p+1) \geq \ldots \geq MS_{opt}(\infty)$$

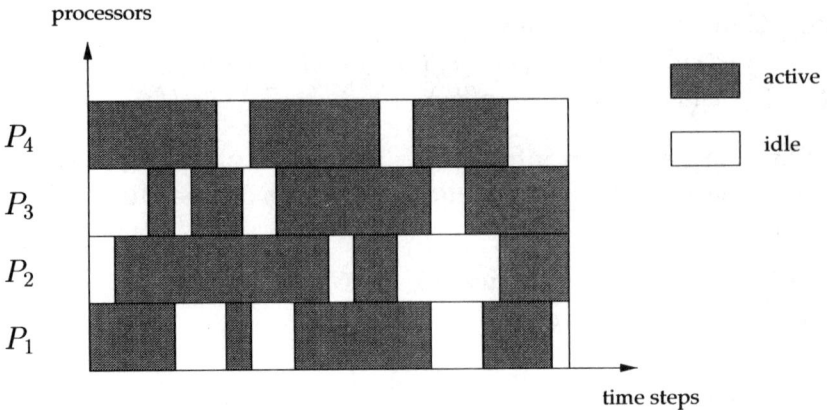

Figure 1.2: Active and idle processors during execution.

Proof   The proof is straightforward. Consider an optimal schedule σ with p processors, and view it as a schedule with $p + 1$ processors where the last processor is kept idle. Then $\mathrm{MS}(\sigma, p + 1) = \mathrm{MS}(\sigma, p) = \mathrm{MS}_{opt}(p)$, hence $\mathrm{MS}_{opt}(p + 1) \leq \mathrm{MS}_{opt}(p)$.   ∎

Theorem 3 can be refined as follows. The number of processors actually used by a schedule σ is $|\mathrm{alloc}(V)|$, i.e., the number of processors that execute at least one task. If we define $\mathrm{MS}'(p)$ as the minimum makespan of all schedules that use exactly p processors, we have $\mathrm{MS}'(p) = \mathrm{MS}_{opt}(p)$ for $1 \leq p \leq |V|$, so that Theorem 3 holds when replacing the $\mathrm{MS}_{opt}(p)$ by the $\mathrm{MS}'(p)$. Intuitively, it cannot hurt to make use of more processors in a model where communication costs are not taken into account! In Chapter 2, we introduce communication costs, and we give an example where $\mathrm{MS}'(p) < \mathrm{MS}'(p')$ while $p < p'$; the refined version of Theorem 3 is no longer true under this new model.

We are now ready to tackle the search of optimal schedules. Not surprisingly, it turns out that the problem $\mathrm{Pb}(p)$ with limited resources is more difficult than $\mathrm{Pb}(\infty)$, whose solution is explained in the next section.

1.4   Solving $\mathrm{Pb}(\infty)$

Let $G = (V, E, w)$ be a given DAG and assume unlimited resources. Remember that a schedule σ for G is said to be *optimal* if its makespan $\mathrm{MS}(\sigma, \infty)$ is minimal, i.e., if $\mathrm{MS}(\sigma, \infty) = \mathrm{MS}_{opt}(\infty)$.

Definition 6 (Entry, Exit, Top Level, Bottom Level) *Let $G = (V, E, w)$ be a directed acyclic graph.*

1. *For $v \in V$, PRED(v) denotes the set of all immediate predecessors of v, and SUCC(v) the set of all its immediate successors.*

2. *$v \in V$ is an entry (top) vertex iff PRED(v) = $\emptyset$.*

3. *$v \in V$ is an exit (bottom) vertex iff SUCC(v) = $\emptyset$.*

4. *For $v \in V$, the top level $tl(v)$ is the largest weight of a path from an entry vertex to v, excluding the weight of v.*

5. *For $v \in V$, the bottom level $bl(v)$ is the largest weight of a path from v to an output vertex, including the weight of v.*

Example 1, Continued

There is a single entry vertex, $T_{1,1}$, and a single exit vertex, $T_{n,n}$. The top level of $T_{1,1}$ is 0, and $tl(T_{1,2}) = tl(T_{1,1}) + w(T_{1,1}) = 1$. We have

$$tl(T_{2,3}) = \max\{w(T_{1,1}) + w(T_{1,2}) + w(T_{2,2}), w(T_{1,1}) + w(T_{1,3})\} = 3$$

because there are two paths from the entry vertex to $T_{2,3}$. □

Note that the top level of a vertex can be computed by a traversal of the DAG; the top level of an entry vertex is 0, while the top level of a nonentry vertex v is

$$tl(v) = \max\{tl(u) + w(u); u \in \text{PRED}(v)\}$$

Similarly, $bl(v) = \max\{bl(u); u \in \text{SUCC}(v)\} + w(v)$ (and $bl(v) = w(v)$ for an exit vertex v). The top level of a vertex is the earliest possible time step at which it can be executed, while its bottom level represents a lower bound of the remaining execution time once starting its execution. This can be stated more formally as follows.

Theorem 4 *Let $G = (V, E, w)$ be a DAG and define σ_{free} as follows:*

$$\sigma_{free}(v) = tl(v), \forall v \in V$$

Then σ_{free} is an optimal schedule for G.

Proof The proof has two parts. First we show that σ_{free} is indeed a schedule, then we derive its optimality. Both are easy:

1. σ_{free} respects all dependence constraints by construction; if $(u, v) \in E$, then $u \in \text{PRED}(v)$ and the constraint $\sigma_{free}(v) \geq \sigma_{free}(u) + w(u)$ is taken into account in the computation of $tl(v) = \sigma_{free}(v)$.

2. To prove that σ_{free} is optimal, use a topological sort order of the vertices of G, and prove by induction that all vertices are scheduled as soon as possible, i.e., as soon as the execution of all their predecessors has been completed.

The free schedule σ_{free} is also known as the as soon as possible (ASAP) schedule.   ∎

From Theorem 4 we have

$$\mathrm{MS}_{opt}(\infty) = \mathrm{MS}(\sigma_{free}, \infty) = \max_{v \in V}\{tl(v) + w(v)\}$$

Hence $\mathrm{MS}_{opt}(\infty)$ is simply the maximal weight of a path in the graph. Note that σ_{free} is not the only optimal schedule. For example the as late as possible (ALAP) schedule σ_{late} is also optimal. We define σ_{late} as follows:

$$\forall v \in V, \sigma_{late}(v) = \mathrm{MS}(\sigma_{free}, \infty) - bl(v)$$

To understand the definition, note that $bl(v)$ is the maximal weight of a path from v to exit nodes, hence the need to start the execution of v no later than $\mathrm{MS}(\sigma_{free}, \infty) - bl(v)$ if we are to terminate all tasks within $\mathrm{MS}(\sigma_{free}, \infty)$ time steps. Both σ_{free} and σ_{late} are important schedules, as it can be shown that any optimal schedule "lies in between;" if σ is an optimal schedule, then $\sigma_{free}(v) \leq \sigma(v) \leq \sigma_{late}(v)$ for all $v \in V$ (see Exercise 1.1).

Corollary 1 *Let $G = (V, E, w)$ be a directed acyclic graph. $Pb(\infty)$ can be solved in time $O(|V| + |E|)$.*

Proof   From Theorem 4 we know that the optimal schedule σ_{free} can be computed using top levels and that $\mathrm{MS}_{opt}(\infty)$ is the maximal weight of a path in the graph. Because G is acyclic, these quantities can be computed by a traversal of the graph, hence the complexity $O(|V| + |E|)$.   ∎

Example 1, Continued

Because all tasks have weight 1, the weight of a path is equal to its length plus 1. The longest path is

$$T_{1,1} \to T_{1,2} \to T_{2,2} \to \ldots \to T_{n-1,n-1} \to T_{n,-1,n} \to T_{n,n},$$

whose weight is $2n - 1$. Note that we do not need as many processors as tasks to achieve execution within $2n - 1$ time steps. For example, we can use only $n - 1$ processors. Let $1 \leq i \leq n$; at time step $2i - 2$, processor P_1 starts the execution of task $T_{i,i}$, while at time step $2i - 1$, the first $n - i$ processors $P_1, P_2, \ldots, P_{n-i}$ execute tasks $T_{i,j}, i + 1 \leq j \leq n$.   □

Ad Hoc Techniques

Although problem Pb(∞) is easy to solve, there remain several open questions. Maybe the most natural one is linked to resources. What is the minimum number of processors required to achieve optimal execution time $MS_{opt}(\infty)$? Rather than stating the difficulty of the problem formally (it is NP-complete, see Exercise 1.2), we discuss in more detail our triangular system example. The key parameters are the size n of the system and the number p of available processors. We just found a schedule σ with $p = n-1$ processors achieving optimal execution time $MS_{opt}(\infty) = 2n - 1$. What is its efficiency? Seq $= \sum_{i=1}^{n} \sum_{j=i}^{n} w(T_{i,j}) = \frac{n \times (n+1)}{2}$, hence the efficiency: $e(\sigma, n-1) = \frac{n(n+1)/2}{(n-1) \times (2n-1)} \approx \frac{1}{4}$. This means that in every time step, only one out of four processors is active in the average. There are two intuitive reasons for this. First, when processing diagonal tasks $T_{i,i}$, only one processor is active. Hence, every second step, $n-1$ processors are idle. This is a fault of our schedule, and we will remedy it. Second, when processing the bottom part of the task graph, the number of executable tasks shrinks, and more processors stay idle. This is inherent to the structure of the DAG (we will quantify this assertion later).

Our aim is to derive a more efficient schedule as far as resources are concerned, i.e., a schedule whose makespan is $2n - 1$ (the absolute minimum), but using fewer processors than $n - 1$. To begin, we execute $T_{1,1}$, because it is the only task without a predecessor. But rather than executing $T_{1,2}, T_{1,3}, \ldots, T_{1,n}$ with $n - 1$ processors in a single time step, we use $\lceil \frac{n}{2} \rceil$ processors and two time steps. The idea is to perform half of the tasks $T_{1,j}$ in the first time step and then the other half together with task $T_{2,2}$ in the second time step. See Table 1.1, where numbers inside brackets represent time steps.

$$T_{1,1}(0)$$

$$
\begin{array}{llll}
T_{1,2}(1) & T_{1,3}(1) & T_{1,4}(1) & T_{1,5}(2) & T_{1,6}(2) \\
T_{2,2}(2) & & & & \\
& T_{2,3}(3) & T_{2,4}(3) & T_{2,5}(3) & T_{2,6}(4) \\
& T_{3,3}(4) & & &
\end{array}
$$

Table 1.1: First execution steps with $n = 6$ and $p = 3$ processors.

We proceed likewise to achieve execution in $2n - 1$ time steps, but using $\lceil \frac{n}{2} \rceil$ rather than $(n - 1)$ processors, hence with efficiency $e(\sigma, \lceil \frac{n}{2} \rceil) \approx \frac{1}{2}$. Can we improve this further? The structure of the DAG gives a lower bound on the minimum number of processors to achieve execution in optimal time. To see this, consider a schedule σ with p processors. During the execution of tasks $T_{n-1,n}$ and $T_{n,n}$ only one processor can be active; there remains $p - 1$ idle processors. In Figure 1.1, we check that no other task can be executed while $T_{5,6}$ and $T_{6,6}$ are being processed. During the execution of tasks $T_{n-2,n-1}$ and $T_{n-1,n-1}$ at most two processors can be active; the one processing these tasks and the other processing one task $T_{*,n}$ in the last column (again, this is clear in Figure 1.1). More generally, during the execution of tasks $T_{n-i-1,n-i}$ and $T_{n-i,n-i}$, $1 \leq i \leq p$, at most i processors can be active. Let Idle be the cumulated idle time of the p processors during the whole execution. The previous discussion shows that Idle $\geq 2(p - 1) + 2(p - 2) + 2(p - 3) + \ldots + 2 = p \times (p - 1)$. From the proof of Theorem 2 we know that Idle $+$ Seq $= p \times \mathrm{MS}(\sigma, p)$, where Seq $= \frac{n(n+1)}{2}$. Therefore, to achieve $\mathrm{MS}(\sigma, p) = \mathrm{MS}_{opt}(\infty) = 2n - 1$, we have the following lower bound on the number of processors:

$$p\mathrm{MS}(\sigma, p) = p(2n - 1) = \mathrm{Seq} + \mathrm{Idle} \geq \frac{n(n + 1)}{2} + p(p - 1)$$

which is equivalent to $p_0 = n - \sqrt{\frac{n(n-1)}{2}} \leq p \leq n + \sqrt{\frac{n(n-1)}{2}}$. Note that p_0 is just a lower bound; we still have to build a schedule with roughly p_0 processors to achieve optimal execution time. We refer to Marrakchi [87] for such a construction. Then the efficiency is, for large n, equivalent to $\frac{n^2}{2} \times \frac{1}{2np_0} \sim \frac{\sqrt{2}+2}{4} \approx 0.85$. To conclude this section, we point out that deriving a bound on the minimal number of processors required to achieve execution in time $\mathrm{MS}_{opt}(\infty)$ can be obtained by reasoning on the structure of the DAG. See [85] for further references.

1.5   Solving Pb(p)

Let $G = (V, E, w)$ be a DAG. It turns out that the problem with limited resources Pb(p) is NP-complete. Hence a polynomial algorithm to determine an optimal schedule is unlikely to exist (unless P $=$ NP!). Therefore we introduce heuristics to compute approximate solutions. The good news is that these heuristics can be guaranteed to achieve at most twice the optimal execution time.

1.5.1   NP-Completeness of Pb(p)

Definition 7 *The decision problem Dec(p) associated with Pb(p) is the following. Given a DAG $G = (V, E, w)$, a number of processors $p \geq 1$, and an execution bound $K \in \mathbb{N}^*$, does there exist a schedule σ for G using at most p processors, such that $MS(\sigma, p) \leq K$?*

Theorem 5 *Dec(p) is NP-complete.*

Proof   First, Dec(p) belongs to NP; if we are given a schedule σ whose makespan is less than or equal to K, we can check in polynomial time that both dependences and resource constraints are satisfied. Indeed, we have to ensure that each dependence constraint (each edge in E) is satisfied and that no more than p processors are needed at any time step. This can be done in polynomial time in the size of the problem instance. Next, consider an arbitrary instance Inst$_1$ of 2-PARTITION, a well-known NP-complete problem [45]: Given n positive integer numbers $\{a_1, a_2, \ldots, a_n\}$, is there a subset I of indices such that $\sum_{i \in I} a_i = \sum_{i \notin I} a_i$? We show that 2-PARTITION can be polynomially reduced to Dec(p). We build an instance Inst$_2$ of Dec(p) as follows. We let $G = (V, E, w)$ with $V = \{v_1, v_2, \ldots, v_n\}$, $E = \emptyset$, and $w(v_i) = a_i, 1 \leq i \leq n$. We also let $p = 2$ and $K = \lfloor \frac{1}{2} \sum_{1 \leq i \leq n} a_i \rfloor$. The construction of Inst$_2$ is polynomial in the size of Inst$_1$. Moreover, Inst$_1$ admits a solution iff there exists a schedule that meets the bound K, hence iff Inst$_2$ admits a solution.   ∎

The previous proof does not establish that Dec(p) is NP-complete in the strong sense. For that, we can use the problem called 3-PARTITION instead of 2-PARTITION.

1.5.2   List Heuristics

Because Pb(p) is NP-complete, we rely on heuristics to schedule DAGs with limited resources. The most natural idea is to use greedy strategies: at each time step, we try to schedule as many tasks as possible onto available processors. Of course there are different possible strategies to decide which tasks are given priority in the (frequent) case where there are more free tasks than available processors. But a key result due to Coffman is that any strategy deciding *not to deliberately keep a processor idle* can be shown to achieve good performance. We express this more formally after giving some definitions.

Definition 8 *Let $G = (V, E, w)$ be a DAG and let σ be a schedule for G. A task $v \in V$ is free at time step t (we note $v \in FREE(\sigma, t)$) iff its execution has not yet started ($\sigma(v) \geq t$) but all its predecessors have been executed at time t ($\forall u \in PRED(v), \sigma(u) + w(u) \leq t$).*

A list schedule is a schedule such that no processor is deliberately left idle; at each time step t, if $|FREE(\sigma, t)| = r \geq 1$, and if q processors are available, then we start the execution of $\min(r, q)$ free tasks.

Theorem 6 *Let $G = (V, E, w)$ be a DAG and assume there are p available processors. Let σ be any list schedule of G. Let $MS_{opt}(p)$ be the makespan of an optimal schedule. Then*

$$MS(\sigma, p) \leq (2 - \frac{1}{p})MS_{opt}(p)$$

It is important to point out that Theorem 6 holds for *any* list schedule, whatever the strategy to choose among free tasks when there are more free tasks than available processors. We first need a lemma.

Lemma 1 *There exists a dependence path Φ in G whose weight $w(\Phi)$ satisfies:*

$$Idle \leq (p - 1) \times w(\Phi)$$

Proof (of Lemma 1) Let T_{i_1} be a task whose execution terminates at the end of the schedule:

$$\sigma(T_{i_1}) + w(T_{i_1}) = MS(\sigma, p)$$

Let t_1 be the largest time step smaller than $\sigma(T_{i_1})$ such that there exists an idle processor during the time interval $[t_1, t_1 + 1[$ (let $t_1 = 0$ if such a time step does not exist). Why is this processor idle? Because σ is a list schedule, no task is free at t_1, otherwise the idle processor would start its execution. Therefore there must be a task T_{i_2} that is an ancestor [5] of T_{i_1} and that is being executed at time t_1; otherwise T_{i_1} would have been started at time t_1 by the idle processor. Because of the definition of t_1 we know that all processors are active between the end of the execution of T_{i_2} and the beginning of the execution of T_{i_1}.

We start the construction again from T_{i_2} so that we obtain a task T_{i_3} such that all processors are active between the end of T_{i_3} and the beginning of T_{i_2}. Iterating the process, we end up with r tasks $T_{i_r}, T_{i_{r-1}}, \ldots, T_{i_1}$ that belong to a dependence path Φ of G and such that all processors are active except perhaps during their execution. In other words, the idleness of some processors can only occur during the execution of these r tasks, during which at least one processor is active (the one that executes the task). Hence Idle $\leq (p - 1) \times \sum_{j=1}^{r} w(T_{i_j}) = (p - 1) \times w(\Phi)$. ∎

Proof (of Theorem 6) Let Idle be the cumulated idle time of the p processors during the whole execution. We know that $p \times MS(\sigma, p) = $ Idle $+$ Seq, where Seq $= \sum_{v \in V} w(v)$ is the sequential time, i.e., the sum of all task

---

[5]The ancestors of a task are its predecessors, the predecessors of its predecessors, and so on.

weights (see Figure 1.2). Now take the dependence path Φ constructed in Lemma 1. We have $w(\Phi) \leq \text{MS}_{opt}(p)$, because the makespan of any schedule is greater than the weight of all dependence paths in G (just because dependence constraints are met). Furthermore, $\text{Seq} \leq p \times \text{MS}_{opt}(p)$ (with equality only if all p processors are active all the time). Putting this together, we get

$$
\begin{aligned}
p \times \text{MS}(\sigma, p) &= \text{Idle} + \text{Seq} \\
&\leq (p-1)w(\Phi) + \text{Seq} &\leq (p-1)\text{MS}_{opt}(p) + p\text{MS}_{opt}(p) \\
&&= (2p-1)\text{MS}_{opt}(p),
\end{aligned}
$$

which establishes the theorem. $\blacksquare$

Theorem 6 basically says that any list schedule is within 50% of the optimum. Therefore the list heuristic is guaranteed to achieve half the best possible performance, whatever the strategy to choose among free tasks. Before presenting the most widely used strategy to perform this choice (in order to get a practical scheduling algorithm), we make a short digression to show that the bound $\frac{2p-1}{p}$ cannot be improved.

Proposition 2 *Let $MS_{list}(p)$ be the smallest possible makespan of a list schedule. The bound*

$$
MS_{list}(p) \leq \frac{2p-1}{p} MS_{opt}(p)
$$

is sharp.

Proof Let K be an arbitrarily large integer. We build a DAG $G = (V, E, w)$, for which any list schedule σ has a makespan $\text{MS}(\sigma, p) \approx \frac{2p-1}{p}\text{MS}_{opt}(p)$ (see Figure 1.3). There are $2p+1$ vertices, whose weights are the following: $w(T_i) = K(p-1)$ for $1 \leq i \leq p-1$; $w(T_p) = 1$; $w(T_i) = K$ for $p+1 \leq i \leq 2p$; and $w(T_{2p+1}) = K(p-1)$. Precedence edges are indicated in the figure. There are exactly p entry vertices, hence $\sigma(T_i) = 0, 1 \leq i \leq p$ for any list schedule σ. At time step 1, the execution of T_p is complete and the free processor (the one having executed T_p) will be successively assigned $p-1$ of the p free tasks $T_{p+1}, T_{p+2}, \ldots, T_{2p}$. Note that this processor starts the execution of the last of its $p-1$ tasks at time $1 + K(p-2)$ and terminates it at time $1 + K(p-1)$. Therefore the remaining pth task will be executed at time $K(p-1)$ by another processor. Only at time $K(p-1) + K = Kp$ will task T_{2p+1} be free, which leads to $\text{MS}(\sigma, p) = Kp + K(p-1) = K(2p-1)$.

However, the DAG can be scheduled in only $Kp + 1$ time steps. The key is to deliberately keep $p-1$ processors idle while executing task T_p at time 0 (which is forbidden to any list schedule). Then at time 1 each processor executes one of the p tasks $T_{p+1}, T_{p+2}, \ldots, T_{2p}$. At time $1 + K$ one

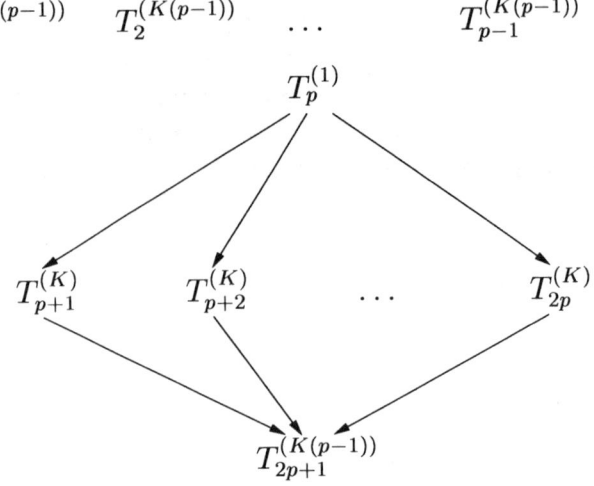

Figure 1.3: The DAG used to bound list scheduling performance; task weights are indicated as exponents inside parentheses.

processor starts executing T_{2p+1} while the other $p-1$ processors execute the tasks $T_1, T_2, \ldots, T_{p-1}$. This defines a schedule with a makespan equal to $1 + K + K(p-1) = Kp + 1$, which is optimal because it is equal to the weight of the path $T_p \to T_{p+1} \to T_{2p+1}$. Hence we obtain the ratio

$$\frac{\mathrm{MS}(\sigma, p)}{\mathrm{MS}_{opt}(p)} \geq \frac{K(2p-1)}{Kp+1} = \frac{2p-1}{p} - \frac{2p-1}{p(Kp+1)} = \frac{2p-1}{p} - \epsilon(K)$$

where $\lim_{K \to +\infty} \epsilon(K) = 0$. ∎

1.5.3 Implementing a List Schedule

In this section, we show how to implement a "generic" list schedule, which means that we do not explicitly show how to handle the priority queue of free tasks, i.e., how to choose among free tasks when there are more free tasks than available processors.

The implementation is not difficult but is somewhat lengthy to describe. The overall scheme can be outlined as follows:

1. *Initialization:*

    (a) Compute the priority level of all tasks.

    (b) Let the priority queue be the list of free tasks (tasks without predecessors) sorted in nondecreasing order of priority.

    (c) Let t denote the current time step: $t = 0$.

2. *While there remain tasks to execute*:

   (a) Add new free tasks, if any, to the queue. If the execution of a task terminates at time step t, suppress this task from the predecessor list of all its successors. Add those tasks whose predecessor list has become empty.

   (b) If there are q available processors and r tasks in the queue, remove the first $\min(q, r)$ tasks from the queue and execute them; if T is one of these tasks, let $\sigma_{cp}(T) = t$.

   (c) Increment t.

Let $G = (V, E, w)$ be a DAG and assume there are p available processors. Let σ be any list schedule of G. Our aim is to derive an implementation whose complexity is $O(|V| \log |V| + |E|)$ for the list schedule. Clearly, the preceding scheme above must be modified because time steps vary from $t = 0$ up to $t = \mathrm{MS}(\sigma, p)$, so that the complexity would depend on task weights. We outline a possible solution in the pseudo-Pascal algorithm of Figure 1.4.

Input:
  the DAG $G = (V, E, w)$, and the number of processors p, $1 \le p \le |V|$.
Output:
  a scheduling time $\sigma(v)$ and a processor number alloc(v) for each task $v \in V$.

  In addition to the data structure representing G store in an array A
    the number of predecessors of each task (its in-degree)
  Initialize the priority heap $\mathcal{Q}$ to tasks without predecessors
  Initialize the processor heap $\mathcal{P}$ to Empty_Heap
  $t = -1$;
  while $\mathcal{Q} \ne$ Empty_Heap do
    $t' =$ Next_event($\mathcal{P}, t$);
    Update(t', A, $\mathcal{Q}$);
    Allocate_Tasks(t', $\mathcal{P}$, $\mathcal{Q}$);
    $t = t'$;
  end while

Figure 1.4: Outline of a list scheduling algorithm.

A few words of explanation are in order for Figure 1.4. We use a heap $\mathcal{Q}$ (see [26]) to store free tasks for two reasons; we can access the task with highest priority in constant time; and we can insert a task in the heap, according to its priority level, in time proportional to the logarithm of the heap size, which is bounded by $|V|$. We use another heap $\mathcal{P}$ to handle active processors; a processor executing a task $v \in V$ is valued by the time step at which the execution of v terminates. Thereby we can compute the next event in constant time, and we can insert a new active processor in the heap in $O(\log |\mathcal{P}|) \leq O(\log |V|)$ time. When we extract a processor from the processor heap, meaning that a task v has terminated, we need to update the in-degree of each successor of v in array A. On the fly, if the in-degree of a given successor v' becomes zero, we insert v' in the priority heap $\mathcal{Q}$. This way, we process each dependence edge of G only once, for a global cost $O(|E|)$. Overall, each task causes two insertions: the first is the insertion of the task itself in heap $\mathcal{Q}$; the second is the insertion of the processor that executes it in heap $\mathcal{P}$. Because each operation costs at most $O(\log |V|)$, we obtain the desired complexity $O(|V| \log |V| + |E|)$ for the list schedule.

1.5.4   Critical Path Scheduling

In this section, we briefly detail a widely used list scheduling technique, known as *critical path scheduling*. We have seen the basic principle of the list scheduling technique and assessed its performance. It remains to explain how to choose among free tasks to get a practical list scheduling algorithm. The most popular selection criterion is based on the value of the bottom level of the tasks. Intuitively, the larger the bottom level, the more "urgent" the task. The *critical path* of a task is defined as its bottom level and is used to assign priority levels to tasks. To summarize in a sentence, critical path scheduling is a list schedule where the priority level of a task is given by the value of its critical path. Ties are broken arbitrarily; see Exercise 1.4.

Example 2

Let us work out a small example. Consider the DAG of Figure 1.5. There are eight tasks, whose weights and critical paths are listed in Table 1.2.

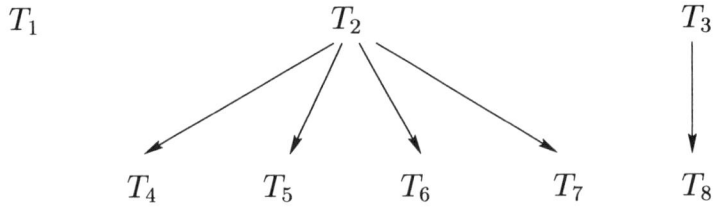

Figure 1.5: A small example.

Assume there are $p = 3$ available processors and let $\mathcal{Q}$ be the priority queue of free tasks. At $t = 0$, $\mathcal{Q}$ is initialized as $\mathcal{Q} = (T_3, T_2, T_1)$. Because

Tasks	T_1	T_2	T_3	T_4	T_5	T_6	T_7	T_8
Weights	3	2	1	3	4	4	3	6
Critical Paths	3	6	7	3	4	4	3	6

Table 1.2: Weights and critical paths.

$q = r = 3$, we execute these three tasks. At $t = 1$, we add T_8 to the queue: $\mathcal{Q} = (T_8)$. There is one processor available, which starts the execution of T_8. At $t = 2$, we add the four successors of T_2 to the queue: $\mathcal{Q} = (T_5, T_6, T_4, T_7)$. Note that we have broken ties arbitrarily (using task numbering). The available processor picks the first task T_5 in $\mathcal{Q}$. Following this scheme, the execution goes on up to $t = 10$, as summarized in Figure 1.6.

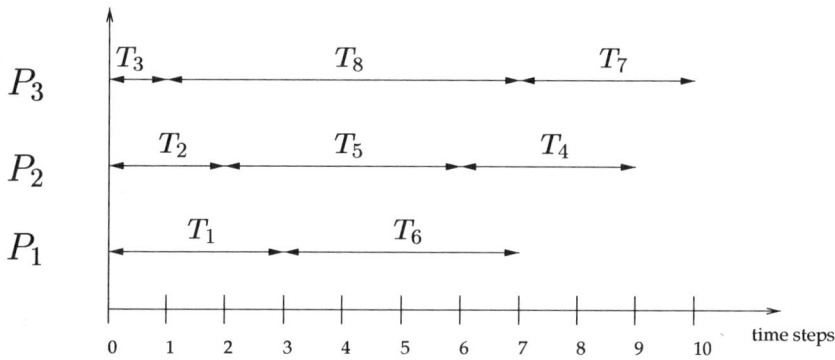

Figure 1.6: Critical path scheduling of Example 2.

Note that it is possible to schedule the DAG in nine time steps only, as shown in Figure 1.7. Again, the trick is to deliberately leave a processor idle

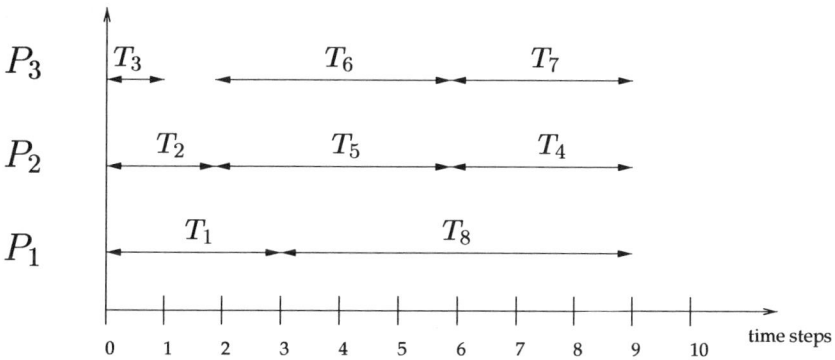

Figure 1.7: Optimal scheduling of Example 2.

at $t = 1$; although it has the highest critical path, T_8 can be delayed by two time steps. T_5 and T_6 are given preference to achieve a better load balance between processors. How do we know that the scheduling of Figure 1.7 is optimal? Because Seq $= 26$, so that three processors require at least $\lceil \frac{26}{3} \rceil =$ nine time steps. This small example aims at providing a concrete basis to better understand the difficulty of scheduling with limited resources. □

1.6 Conclusion

The main results of this introductory chapter are the following:

- Scheduling with unlimited resources is easy (Section 1.4).

- Scheduling with limited resources is an NP-complete problem, but list scheduling heuristics are guaranteed within 50% of the optimum (Section 1.5).

1.7 Bibliographical Notes

All the material covered in this chapter is quite basic. Pioneering work includes the book by Coffman [24]. Chapter 9 of [80] and the IEEE compilation of papers [112] provide additional material. See also the more recent book by El-Rewini, Lewis, and Ali [37]. Finally, note that Appendix A5 of Garey and Johnson [45] proposes a list of NP-complete scheduling problems.

1.8 Exercises

Exercise 1.1

Consider a DAG $G = (V, E, w)$ and assume unlimited processor resources. Show that any optimal schedule σ satisfies:

$$\forall v \in V, \quad \sigma_{free}(v) \leq \sigma(v) \leq \sigma_{late}(v)$$

Exercise 1.2

Consider a DAG $G = (V, E, w)$ and let p_{opt} be the minimum number of processors required to achieve execution in optimal time. Formally,

$$p_{opt} = \min\{p \; ; \; \mathrm{MS}_{opt}(p) = \mathrm{MS}_{opt}(\infty)\}$$

Show that the problem of determining p_{opt} is NP-complete.

Exercise 1.3

Consider the DAG of Figure 1.8. Assume that all tasks have unit weight. What is the optimal execution time $MS_{opt}(\infty)$? How many processors are needed for the ASAP scheduling? For the ALAP scheduling? Determine the minimum number p_{opt} of processors needed to achieve execution in optimal time $MS_{opt}(\infty)$.

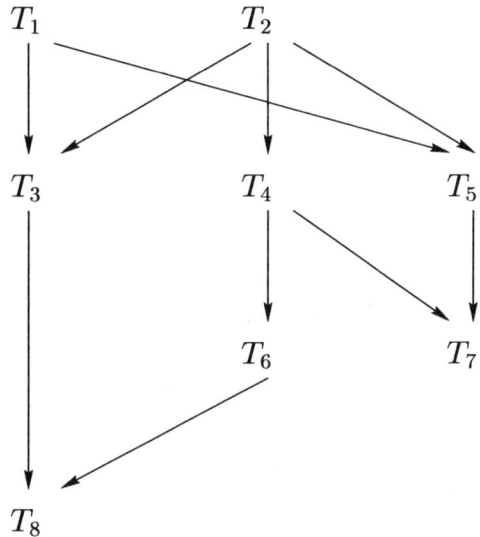

Figure 1.8: The DAG of Exercise 1.3.

Exercise 1.4

How can we break ties in critical path scheduling? If several tasks have the same critical path value, a possibility is to give priority to the one with the largest number of successors. Explain the intuitive idea behind this technique and design an example where it is not optimal.

Exercise 1.5 (Hu's algorithm)

In this exercise, we study the problem of scheduling an intree $G = (V, E, w)$ (DAG where each vertex has at most one successor) for which all vertices have the same execution time; we assume $w(v) = 1$ for all $v \in V$. We denote by level(v) the maximal length of a path starting from v, and we let level$(v) = 0$ if v has no successor. We let $h = \max_{v \in V}$ level(v) be the maximal level in G. We assume there are p identical resources and we denote by $\text{MS}_{opt}(p)$ the minimal makespan of a schedule for p resources and by $\text{MS}(\sigma, p)$ the makespan of a schedule σ for p resources.

- Generalizing Proposition 1 and Theorem 2, show that

$$\forall i,\ 0 \leq i \leq h,\ \text{MS}_{opt}(p) \geq \frac{|V_i|}{p} + i$$

  where $V_i = \{v \in V \mid \text{level}(v) \geq i\}$ is the set of the vertices whose level is at least i.

Let σ be a list schedule with a priority queue ordered by decreasing level. This means that if two tasks u and v are ready to be scheduled at a given time step, then level$(u) \geq$ level(v) implies $\sigma(u) \leq \sigma(v)$. For $0 \leq t < \text{MS}(\sigma, p)$, we denote by S_t the set of tasks executed at time step t by σ: $S_t = \{v \in V \mid \sigma(v) = t\}$.

We first assume that there exists an integer t, $0 \leq t < \text{MS}(\sigma, p)$ such that S_t has exactly p tasks of the same level. We denote by k the largest such integer and by L the (common) level of tasks in S_k. We also assume that $k < \text{MS}(\sigma, p) - 1$ and we denote by L' the maximal level of a task v not yet scheduled at time step k, i.e., such that $\sigma(v) > k$.

- Study the maximal level of a task v in S_t for $k < t < \text{MS}(\sigma, p)$ and show that $\text{MS}(\sigma, p) = k + L' + 2$.

- Show that, for all integers t, $0 \leq t \leq k$, $|S_t| = p$. (Use the fact that G is an intree, i.e., each vertex has at most one successor.)

- Deduce from the previous two questions that $\text{MS}(\sigma, p) = \text{MS}_{opt}(p)$. Show that this optimality result still holds even if $k = \text{MS}(\sigma, p) - 1$ (in which case L' is not defined) or if k does not exist.

This exercise is borrowed from [88], which gives a simpler proof of Hu's algorithm [59].

Chapter 2

Scheduling DAGs with Communications

2.1 Introduction

This chapter deals with task graph scheduling when communication costs are taken into account. First we describe the model that is widely used in the literature, and we comment on its accuracy in Section 2.2. It turns out that introducing communication costs complicates matters a lot. Even the problem of scheduling with unlimited resources becomes NP-complete, as shown in Section 2.3. A guaranteed heuristic to solve Pb(∞) is described in Section 2.4. To solve Pb(p), we discuss two kinds of heuristics. Extensions of the list-scheduling techniques of Chapter 1 are presented in Section 2.5, and two-step clustering heuristics are surveyed in Section 2.6. Finally, some theoretical results are gathered in Section 2.7.

2.2 A Model with Communication Costs

Parallel machines are not kind to the user. Their communication behavior is quite complex to model. The older generation used a primitive store-and-forward mechanism to communicate messages. It was not very efficient, but it could be nicely modeled by a formula like the following: comm(p, p') = dist(p, p') $\times$ ($\beta + L\tau$), where L is the length of the message sent by processor p to processor p'; dist(p, p') is the distance between p and p': dist(p, p') = 1 if p and p' are neighbors (there is a physical link between them), dist(p, p') = 2 if there is an intermediate processor between them, and so on. Finally, β and τ are machine parameters: β is the communication start-up (mainly due to software overhead, but also to hardware configuration delay), and τ is the inverse of the bandwidth. However, current-generation machines do not obey this simple model any longer. Processors are enhanced with communication coprocessors. Messages are split into packets, which are dynamically routed between processors, possibly using different paths. Messages will be routed efficiently if there are no contentions on the communication links (hot-spots). The distance between processors is not that important. Rather, if several processors are to exchange data simultaneously, then the more structured the communication, the more efficient. Therefore locality still plays a role, but indirectly. Anyway, it turns out that the crude communication model that is used in the scheduling community acquires more practical relevance.[1] Indeed, if a task T is to communicate data to a successor task T', the cost is modeled as follows:

$$\text{comm}(T, T') = \begin{cases} 0 & \text{if alloc}(T) = \text{alloc}(T') \\ c(T, T') & \text{otherwise} \end{cases}$$

where alloc(T) denotes the processor that executes task T (see Section 1.3). Intuitively, we consider local memory accesses as negligible, and we pay the same communication cost $c(T, T')$ otherwise. This amounts to assuming that we have a clique of fully connected processors. Our model is so-called *macro-dataflow*: we assume that (i) communication can occur as soon as the data is available, and (ii) there is no resource limitation in terms of communication links. Hypothesis (i) is welcome, as communication can overlap with (independent) computations in modern computers. Hypothesis (ii) is more questionable but it is the price we pay to derive mathematical results. We conclude this discussion by stating the model more formally.

Definition 9 (Communication DAG) *A communication DAG (or cDAG) is a direct acyclic graph $G = (V, E, w, c)$ where vertices represent tasks and edges represent precedence constraints. The weight function is $w : V \longrightarrow \mathbb{N}^*$ and the communication cost is $c : E \longrightarrow \mathbb{N}^*$. Any schedule σ must preserve dependences, which is written as:*

$$\forall e = (v, v') \in E, \begin{cases} \sigma(v) + w(v) \leq \sigma(v') & \text{if alloc}(T) = \text{alloc}(T') \\ \sigma(v) + w(v) + c(T, T') \leq \sigma(v') & \text{otherwise} \end{cases}$$

The expression of resource constraints is the same as in Chapter 1. Throughout this chapter, we keep the same notations as in Chapter 1 for schedules, makespans, problem Pb(∞) with unlimited resources, and problem Pb(p) with p processors, and the like.

---

[1] This is nice for theoreticians! The model was invented before the architectural evolution and it becomes more and more accurate. Who would complain?

2.3   NP-Completeness of Pb(∞)

Including communication costs in the model makes everything difficult, including the solution of Pb(∞). The intuitive reason is that we hesitate between allocating tasks to either many processors (hence balancing workload but communicating intensively) or few processors (less communication but less parallelism too). We illustrate this with a small example, borrowed from [48].

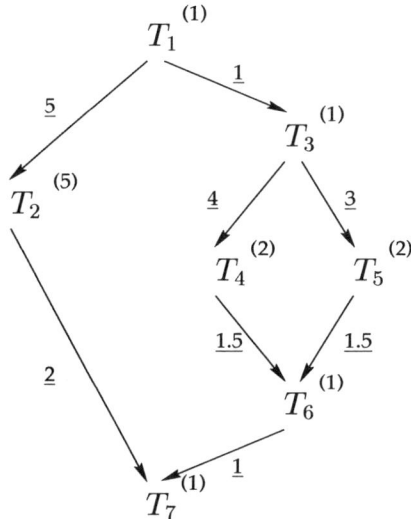

Figure 2.1: Illustrative example for communication costs.

Example 3

Consider the cDAG in Figure 2.1. Task weights are indicated close to the tasks within brackets, and communication costs are represented along the edges, in underline mode. For the sake of drawing nice schedule tables we have assumed two noninteger communication costs: $c(T_4, T_6) = c(T_5, T_6) = 1.5$. Of course, we could scale every weight w and c to have only integer values. We can check the following.

- On one hand, if we allocate all the tasks to the same processor, the makespan will be equal to the sum of all task weights, i.e., 13.

- On the other hand, if we have as many processors as we want (we need no more than seven processors because there are seven tasks), we can allocate one task per processor. Then we can check that the makespan of the ASAP schedule is equal to 14. To see this, it is important to point out that once the allocation of tasks to processors is given, we can compute the makespan easily: for each edge $e : T \to T'$, add a virtual node of weight $c(T, T')$ if the edge links two different processors ($\text{alloc}(T) \neq \text{alloc}(T')$), and do nothing otherwise. Then consider the new graph as a DAG (without communications) and traverse it to compute the length of the longest path, as explained in Chapter 1. In our case, because all tasks are allocated to different processors, we add a virtual node on each edge. The longest path is $T_1 \to T_2 \to T_7$, whose length is $w(T_1) + c(T_1, T_2) + w(T_2) + c(T_2, T_7) + w(T_7) = 14$.

There is a difficult tradeoff between executing tasks in parallel (hence with several distinct processors) and minimizing communication costs. In our example, it turns out that the best solution is to use two processors, according to the schedule in Figure 2.2, whose makespan is equal to 9.

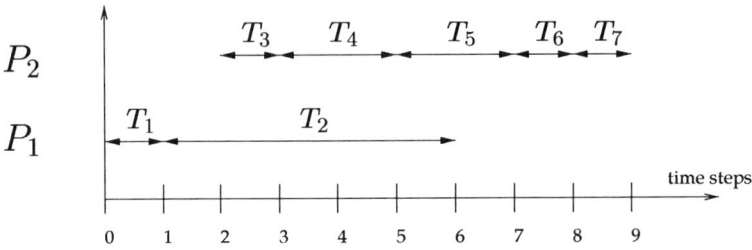

Figure 2.2: An optimal schedule for Example 3.

Note that dependence constraints are satisfied in Figure 2.2. For example, T_2 can start at step 1 on processor P_1 because this processor executes T_1, hence there is no need to pay the communication cost $c(T_1, T_2)$. On the other hand, T_3 is executed on processor P_2, hence we need to wait until step 2 to start it, although P_2 is idle: $\sigma(T_1) + w(T_1) + c(T_1, T_3) = 0 + 1 + 1 = 2$.

How did we find the schedule of Figure 2.2? And how do we know it is optimal? By a tedious case analysis! Exercise 2.1 asks you to prove the optimality of this schedule. □

Example 3 shows that using more processors does not always lead to a shorter execution time. Using the notations of Section 1.3, the minimum makespan of a schedule making actual use of seven processors is $\text{MS}'(7) = 14$ while $\text{MS}'(1) = 13$ (or $\text{MS}'(2) = 9$). In other words, the refined version of Theorem 3 with the MS' is no longer true when communication costs are taken into account. In fact, communication costs even make solving $\text{Pb}(\infty)$, the scheduling problem with unlimited resources, very difficult.

Theorem 7 *Pb(∞) is NP-complete.*

Proof The decision problem Comm(∞) associated with Pb(∞) is the following. Given a cDAG $G = (V, E, w, c)$ and an execution bound $K \in \mathbb{N}^*$, does there exist a schedule σ for G such that MS(σ, ∞) $\leq K$? We want to show that Comm(∞) is NP-complete. First, Comm(∞) belongs to NP. If we are given a schedule σ whose makespan is less than or equal to K, we can check in polynomial time that dependence constraints are satisfied. For each task we know the beginning $\sigma(T)$ of its execution and the processor alloc(T) that executes it, hence we just have to check for constraints.

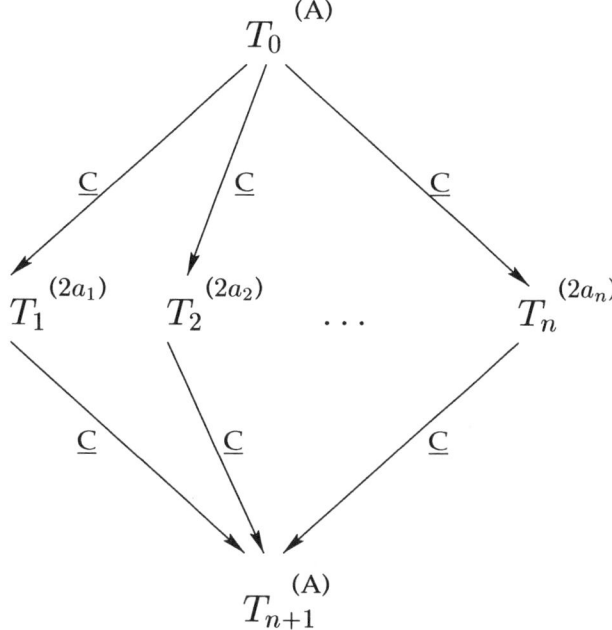

Figure 2.3: Reduction for the NP-completeness proof.

To prove NP-completeness, we use 2-PARTITION as in the proof of Theorem 5, but the reduction is more involved. Consider any instance Inst$_1$ of problem 2-PARTITION. Given n positive integer numbers $\{a_1, \ldots, a_n\}$, is there a subset I of indices such that $\sum_{i \in I} a_i = \sum_{i \notin I} a_i$? We build an instance Inst$_2$ of Comm(∞) as follows; we let $G = (V, E, w, c)$ be a fork-join graph (see Figure 2.3). There are $n + 2$ tasks: $V = \{T_0, T_1, T_2, \ldots, T_n, T_{n+1}\}$. The task weights are defined as follows: $w(T_i) = 2 \times a_i$ for $1 \leq i \leq n$, and $w(T_0) = w(T_{n+1}) = A$, where A is a positive integer. There are $2n$ edges, and the communication costs are all equal: $c(T_0, T_i) = c(T_i, T_{n+1}) = C$ for $1 \leq i \leq n$. Here, C is any integer in the interval $]\alpha - \min_{1 \leq i \leq n} 2a_i, \alpha[$, where $\alpha = \sum_{i=1}^{n} a_i$. Note that this interval does contain an integer, as

$\min_{1 \leq i \leq n} 2a_i \geq 2$. Finally, let $K = 2A + C + \alpha$. The difficult part is to show that Inst$_1$ admits a solution iff there exists a schedule that meets the bound K, hence iff Inst$_2$ admits a solution.

First, assume that Inst$_1$ admits a solution. Let I be a subset of indices such that $\sum_{i \in I} a_i = \sum_{i \notin I} a_i = \frac{\alpha}{2}$. Let $\mathcal{T}_1 = \{T_i, i \in I\}$ and $\mathcal{T}_2 = \{T_i, i \notin I\}$. By hypothesis, $w(\mathcal{T}_1) = w(\mathcal{T}_2) = \alpha$. Consider the schedule in Figure 2.4.

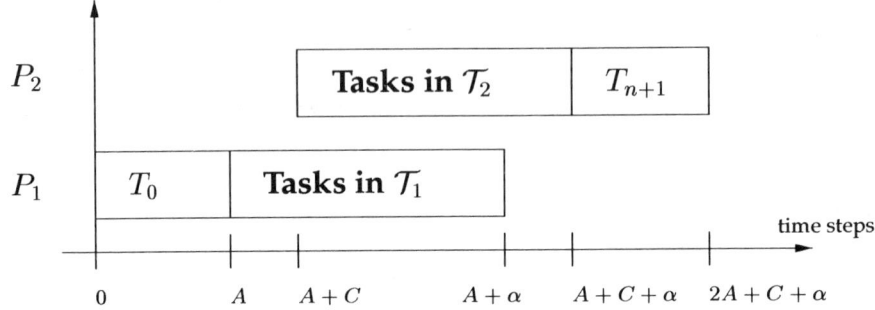

Figure 2.4: A schedule with makespan $K = 2A + C + \alpha$.

The makespan of this schedule is equal to $K = 2A + C + \alpha$. All dependence constraints are satisfied. Indeed:

- Processor P_2 starts executing the tasks in $\mathcal{T}_2$ at step $A + C = w(T_0) + C$.

- Processor P_1 terminates the execution of the tasks in $\mathcal{T}_1$ at step $A + \alpha$. Hence at step $A + \alpha + C$, task T_{n+1} is ready to be executed by processor P_2. Its execution can start right then, as P_2 terminates the tasks in $\mathcal{T}_2$ at step $A + C + \alpha$.

Conversely, assume that Inst$_2$ admits a solution. Let σ be a schedule whose makespan MS(σ) is less than or equal to K. We need the two following lemmas.

Lemma 2 *Tasks T_0 and T_{n+1} are not executed by the same processor in the schedule σ.*

Proof   Assume that the same processor P executes both T_0 and T_{n+1}. Then P executes all the n other tasks T_i, $1 \leq i \leq n$. Otherwise, let T_{i_0} be a task executed by another processor. The makespan of σ is greater than or equal to the length of the path $T_0 \rightarrow T_{i_0} \rightarrow T_{n+1}$:

$$\text{MS}(\sigma) \geq A + C + 2a_{i_0} + C + A = (2A + C) + (2a_{i_0} + C) > (2A + C) + \alpha = K$$

hence a contradiction. Thus P does execute the $n+2$ tasks, which is a contradiction, as the sum of all task weights is $2A + 2\alpha > 2A + \alpha + C = K$.   ∎

Let P_1 be the processor that executes T_0 and P_2 be the processor that executes T_{n+1}.

Lemma 3 *Each task T_i, $1 \leq i \leq n$, is executed by either P_1 or P_2.*

Proof Assume that there exists a task T_{i_0}, $1 \leq i_0 \leq n$, executed by a processor other than P_1 and P_2. Then the makespan of σ is greater than or equal to the length of the path $T_0 \rightarrow T_{i_0} \rightarrow T_{n+1}$: $\mathrm{MS}(\sigma) \geq A + C + 2a_{i_0} + C + A > K$ (as in Lemma 2), hence a contradiction. ∎

Let $\mathcal{T}_1$ be the set of tasks T_i, $1 \leq i \leq n$, executed by P_1. Define similarly $\mathcal{T}_2$ for P_2. The makespan of σ satisfies to:

$$\mathrm{MS}(\sigma) \geq w(T_0) + w(\mathcal{T}_1) + C + w(T_{n+1}) = 2A + C + w(\mathcal{T}_1)$$

To see this, P_1 takes at least $w(T_0) + w(\mathcal{T}_1)$ steps to execute its tasks. Then a communication must occur before P_2 can start T_{n+1}.

Similarly, $\mathrm{MS}(\sigma) \geq 2A + C + w(\mathcal{T}_2)$, because P_2 must wait at least $A + C$ time steps before starting execution. Because $\mathrm{MS}(\sigma) \leq K = 2A + C + \alpha$, we have $w(\mathcal{T}_1) \leq \alpha$ and $w(\mathcal{T}_2) \leq \alpha$. But $w(\mathcal{T}_1) + w(\mathcal{T}_2) = 2\alpha$. Therefore $w(\mathcal{T}_1) = w(\mathcal{T}_2) = \alpha$. Let I denote the set of indices of the tasks in $\mathcal{T}_1$; I is a solution to Inst_1, our instance of 2-PARTITION. ∎

See the bibliographical notes at the end of this chapter for more NP-completeness results.

2.4 A Guaranteed Heuristic for Pb(∞)

In this section, we present a guaranteed heuristic, due to Hanen and Munier [55], to solve Pb(∞). The heuristic is guaranteed within a factor at most $\frac{4}{3}$ of the optimal under the assumption that all communication costs are smaller than all computation costs. Such a task graph is said to be coarse-grain, as stated in the following definition:

Definition 10 (Granularity, Coarse-Grain cDAG) *Let $G = (V, E, w, c)$ be a cDAG. The granularity of G is the computation to communication ratio $g(G) = \frac{\min_{T \in V} w(T)}{\max_{T,T' \in V} c(T,T')}$. G is coarse-grain if $g(G) \geq 1$.*

Granularity issues will play an important role in Section 2.7. Before stating Hanen and Munier's heuristic formally, we motivate it with their idea of favorite successors.

2.4.1 Favorite Successors

Let $G = (V, E, w, c)$ be a cDAG and σ be any schedule for G. Let $T \in V$ be any task. The favorite successor of T, if it exists, is the unique immediate successor T' of T such that

$$\sigma(T') < \sigma(T) + w(T) + c(T, T') \qquad \text{(FS)}$$

If it exists, the favorite successor of T is executed by the same processor as T, otherwise a communication cost would be paid and Condition (FS) would not hold. Now, to see why the favorite successor is unique, assume that two successors T' and T'' of T satisfy condition (FS). T' and T'' are executed by the same processor. Without loss of generality, assume that T' is executed before T''. This implies that $\sigma(T) + w(T) \leq \sigma(T')$, and that $\sigma(T') + w(T') \leq \sigma(T'')$. But, by hypothesis $\sigma(T'') < \sigma(T) + w(T) + c(T, T'')$; hence $w(T') < c(T, T'')$, a result that contradicts the fact that G is coarse-grain. Table 2.1 gives all favorite successors for the optimal schedule for Example 3, which was shown in Figure 2.2.

Task	T_1	T_2	T_3	T_4	T_5	T_6	T_7
Favorite Successor	T_2	—	T_4	—	T_6	T_7	—

Table 2.1: Favorite successors for the schedule of Figure 2.2.

For each edge $e = (T, T') \in E$, we introduce a Boolean variable $x_{T,T'}$: $x_{T,T'} = 0$ if T' is the favorite successor of T, and $x_{T,T'} = 1$ otherwise. The inequality

$$\sigma(T) + w(T) + x_{T,T'} \times c(T, T') \leq \sigma(T')$$

holds for any edge $(T, T') \in E$, whether T' is the favorite successor of T or not. Casting all such inequalities into a linear programming problem is the main idea underlying Hanen and Munier's heuristic.

2.4.2 Hanen and Munier's Heuristic

Given a cDAG, we define the following integer linear program.

Definition 11 *Let $G = (V, E, w, c)$ be a cDAG. We define the integer linear program ILP(G) as follows:*

Minimize M_∞ subject to

$$
\begin{cases}
\forall (T, T') \in E & x_{T,T'} \in \{0, 1\} & (A) \\
\forall T \in V & s(T) \geq 0 & (B) \\
\forall (T, T') \in E & s(T) + w(T) + x_{T,T'} c(T, T') \leq s(T') & (1) \\
\forall T \in V \, s.t. \, SUCC(T) \neq \emptyset & \sum_{T' \in SUCC(T)} x_{T,T'} \geq |SUCC(T)| - 1 & (2) \\
\forall T \in V \, s.t. \, PRED(T) \neq \emptyset & \sum_{T' \in PRED(T)} x_{T',T} \geq |PRED(T)| - 1 & (3) \\
\forall T \in V & s(T) + w(T) \leq M_\infty & (4)
\end{cases}
$$

Lemma 4 *Let $G = (V, E, w, c)$ be a cDAG. The solution M_∞ of the integer linear program $ILP(G)$ is equal to the optimal makespan with unlimited resources $MS_{opt}(\infty)$.*

Proof We show that there is a one-to-one correspondence between valid schedules for G (with unbounded resources) and solutions to the integer linear program $ILP(G)$.

Let σ be a valid schedule for G. Let $s(T) = \sigma(T)$ for each task T, and let $x_{T,T'} = 0$ if T' is the favorite successor of T, and $x_{T,T'} = 1$ otherwise. Then all constraints of $ILP(G)$ are met:

- Constraints (A) and (B) are met by construction.

- Constraint (1) was derived in Section 2.4.1.

- Constraint (2) expresses the fact that each task has at most one favorite successor.

- Constraint (3) expresses the fact that each task is the favorite successor of at most one task, which can be proven quite similarly to Constraint (2).

- The definition of the makespan is $MS(\sigma, \infty) = \max_{T \in V}(\sigma(T) + w(T))$, hence Constraint (4) is met.

Let $M_\infty(\sigma)$ be the value returned by $ILP(G)$ when all variables $s(T)$ and $x_{T,T'}$ are defined as above. Because Constraint (4) is the only constraint on the objective function, we have $M_\infty(\sigma) \geq MS(\sigma, \infty)$.

Reciprocally, consider a solution of the optimization problem $ILP(G)$. To define the induced schedule σ, we need to determine for each task both a starting time and the processor that executes it. For starting times, we simply let $\sigma(T) = s(T)$ for any task $T \in V$. We define the allocation function as follows:

$$
\forall e = (T, T') \in E, \; x_{T,T'} = 0 \Leftrightarrow \text{alloc}(T) = \text{alloc}(T')
$$

To be more precise, we allocate entry tasks to different processors, and we traverse the graph to compute the allocation function as follows: If T' is an immediate successor of T and $x_{T,T'} = 1$, we allocate T' to a new processor, otherwise we allocate T' to the same processor as T. We have no conflict during this traversal. Indeed, due to Condition (2), for each task $T \in V$, there is at most one immediate successor of T allocated to the same processor as T: This is, if it exists, the unique task T' such that $x_{T,T'} = 0$ (T' is then the favorite successor of T). Similarly, due to Condition (3), for each task $T' \in V$, there is at most one predecessor of T' allocated to the same processor as T'. Furthermore, Constraint (1) together with the choice of the allocation function ensures that all dependence constraints are met: σ is a valid schedule for G. Finally, Condition (4) shows that M_∞ is equal to the makespan of σ.   ■

Given a solution to ILP(G), we can interpret $s(T)$ as the top level of T, where bottom and top levels are computed according to the allocation function induced by the variables $x_{T,T'}$. We add the communication cost $c(T, T')$ into the weight of a path going from T to T' iff alloc(T) $\neq$ alloc(T'), i.e., iff $x_{T,T'} = 1$. Condition (4) shows that the solution to ILP(G) is indeed equal to the value of the maximal weight of a path in the dependence graph computed using the previous rules. The difficulty lies in the determination of the allocation function, i.e., on the determination of the $x_{T,T'}$ values. Because these values are integer (and even restricted to 0 or 1), the ILP problem is an integer linear program, which is NP-hard to solve [110]. However, if we relax the condition that the $x_{T,T'}$ are integer, we obtain a linear program to be solved with rational solutions, whose complexity is polynomial [110].

Definition 12 *Let $G = (V, E, w, c)$ be a cDAG:*

- *We define the relaxed linear program RLP(G) as the program obtained by suppressing equation (A) in the definition of ILP(G).*

- *We let $(x_{T,T'}^{rel}, s^{rel}(T), M_\infty^{rel})$ denote the rational solution of the relaxed problem RLP(G).*

Hanen and Munier define their schedule σ^{hm} directly from the solution of the relaxed linear program RLP(G). Let $T \in V$ be any task. Constraint (2) ensures that there is at most one successor T' of T such that $x_{T,T'}^{rel} < \frac{1}{2}$; and constraint (3) ensures that there is at most one predecessor T'' of T such that $x_{T'',T}^{rel} < \frac{1}{2}$. Therefore, let $x_{T,T'}^{hm} = 0$ for any arc $e = (T, T') \in E$ such that $x_{T,T'}^{rel} < \frac{1}{2}$, and $x_{T,T'}^{hm} = 1$ otherwise. For any task $T \in V$, define σ_T^{hm} to be the top level of T, where bottom and top levels are computed according to the allocation function induced by the $x_{T,T'}^{hm}$. We add the communication cost $c(T, T')$ in the weight of a path going from T to T' iff alloc$(T) \neq$ alloc(T'), i.e., iff $x_{T,T'}^{hm} = 1$. As explained earlier, this defines a valid schedule for G.

Theorem 8 *Let $G = (V, E, w, c)$ be a coarse-grain cDAG, with granularity $g(G) \geq 1$. Let σ^{hm} be the schedule defined by Hanen and Munier. Then*

$$MS(\sigma^{hm}, \infty) \leq MS_{opt}(\infty) \times \frac{2g(G) + 2}{2g(G) + 1}$$

Proof For any path in the graph going from a task T to one of its successors T', we have the communication cost $x_{T,T'}^{hm} c(T, T')$ for Hanen and Munier's schedule, instead of $x_{T,T'}^{rel} c(T, T')$ for the solution of RLP(G). Two cases occur:

- $x_{T,T'}^{hm} = 0$: then $w(T) + x_{T,T'}^{hm} c(T, T') \leq w(T) + x_{T,T'}^{rel} c(T, T')$.

- $x_{T,T'}^{hm} = 1$: then $x_{T,T'}^{rel} \geq \frac{1}{2}$. We have

$$\frac{w(T) + x_{T,T'}^{hm} c(T, T')}{w(T) + x_{T,T'}^{rel} c(T, T')} \leq \frac{w(T) + c(T, T')}{w(T) + c(T, T')/2} = \frac{1 + \frac{c(T,T')}{w(T)}}{1 + \frac{c(T,T')}{2w(T)}} \quad \text{and}$$

$$\frac{1 + \frac{c(T,T')}{w(T)}}{1 + \frac{c(T,T')}{2w(T)}} \leq \frac{1 + \frac{1}{g(G)}}{1 + \frac{1}{2g(G)}} = \frac{2g(G) + 2}{2g(G) + 1}$$

In all cases, $w(T) + x_{T,T'}^{hm} c(T, T') \leq \frac{2g(G)+2}{2g(G)+1}(w(T) + x_{T,T'}^{rel} c(T, T'))$, and this inequality extends to all paths in the graph, which leads to the desired result. ∎

An immediate consequence of Theorem 8 is that Hanen and Munier's heuristic is guaranteed with a factor at most $\frac{4}{3}$ for coarse-grain graphs.

2.5 List Heuristics for Pb(p)

Of course the limited resource scheduling problem Pb(p) remains NP-complete when introducing communication costs (see Exercise 2.3). Pb(p) does remain in the NP class. As stated earlier (see Example 3), once the allocation is known, dependence and resource constraints can be checked in linear time. Of course the actual problem is to determine a good allocation. Maybe the most natural idea is to extend the critical path list algorithm introduced in Section 1.5.4. We will explain how to modify it straightforwardly and then how to design a much improved version.

2.5.1   Naive Critical Path

The idea of critical path scheduling remains the same: The algorithm is a list-scheduling algorithm, where priority is given according to the value of the bottom level of each task. The problem is that we do not know how to compute bottom levels. Without knowing the allocation, it is not possible to decide whether some communication costs should be taken into account and whether others should not. A "conservative" approach is to include all communication costs when computing bottom levels (which amounts to assuming one distinct processor per task).

Consider Example 3 again (see Figure 2.1). We report bottom levels in Table 2.2. We check that the critical path of task T_1 is 14, the length of the ASAP schedule with one processor per task.

Task	T_1	T_2	T_3	T_4	T_5	T_6	T_7
Critical Path	14	8	11.5	6.5	6.5	3	1

Table 2.2: Critical paths (bottom levels) for Example 3.

Let us build a list schedule based on the values of these critical paths. The algorithm proceeds as explained in Section 1.5.4. There is an important difference, though. A task is free when all its predecessors have been executed. But a free task cannot start execution as soon as it is free, even if there are available processors; depending on the allocation decision, we may or may not need to wait for some communication delay.

Assume $p = 3$ available processors P_1, P_2, and P_3. When there are more available processors than free tasks, assign the tasks to the processors with (say) lowest numbers. Let $\mathcal{Q}$ be the priority queue of free tasks. In our example, there is $r = 1$ free task at time step $t = 0$: $\mathcal{Q} = (T_1)$. Processor P_1 executes T_1 at $t = 0$. At $t = 1$, we update $\mathcal{Q}$ as $\mathcal{Q} = (T_3, T_2)$ (T_3 is given priority over T_2 because its critical path is larger). All processors are available, so according to our rule we allocate T_3 to P_1 and T_2 to P_2. Note that we are lucky to assign T_3 to P_1: because P_1 has executed T_1, there is no communication delay to pay, hence it can start T_3 at step $t = 1$. On the other hand, P_2 must wait until step $t = 6$ to start T_2. At step $t = 2$, we have $\mathcal{Q} = (T_4, T_5)$ (breaking ties arbitrarily, using task numbers), and two available processors P_1 and P_3. Indeed, although still idle, P_2 has been marked busy until it returns from the execution of T_2. Hence we allocate T_4 to P_1 (execution can start immediately) and T_5 to P_3 (execution cannot start before $t = 5$). Going on, we obtain the execution summarized in Figure 2.5.

We obtain a makespan equal to 14 time steps. Note that the naive critical path (naive CP) scheduling with two processors leads to the same result:

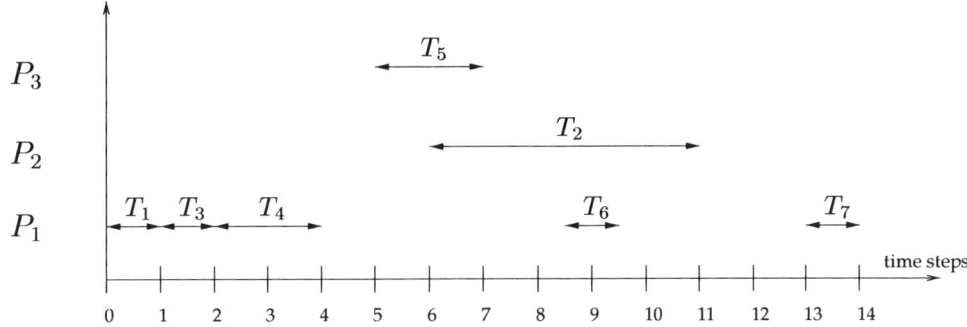

Figure 2.5: Naive critical path scheduling for Example 3.

T_5 would have been executed by P_1 at step $t = 4$ rather than by P_3 at step $t = 5$: this is the only difference. In both cases, we obtain the same make-span, even worse than the execution on a single processor! There must be room for improvement.

2.5.2   Modified Critical Path

If we analyze the execution of naive CP scheduling on our small example, we see that we made a wrong decision when assigning T_2 to P_2. Indeed, at step $t = 1$ we had $Q = (T_3, T_2)$. The first allocation, that of T_3 to P_1, is fine. But the second, that of T_2 to P_2, is not. We should allocate it to P_1 again, even though it is not available. The reason is that P_1 can start T_2 earlier than P_2. The rule of modified critical path (MCP) is: *allocate a free task to the processor that allows its earliest execution, given already-made decisions.* It is important to explain further what "given already made decisions" means. Free tasks from the queue are processed one after the other. At any moment, we know which processors are available and which are busy. Moreover, for the busy processors, we know when they will return from execution. Hence we can always select the processor allowing earliest execution of the task under consideration. It may well be that we select a processor that is currently busy, as discussed earlier for allocating task T_2.

The reader is asked (Exercise 2.5) to write the details of MCP in algorithmic form. Here we run MCP on Example 3 with three processors. We obtain the schedule of Figure 2.6. As already discussed, T_2 is allocated to P_1. Similarly, T_6 is allocated to P_2, because it allows execution at step $t = 8.5$, against 9.5 on P_1 or P_3. The new makespan is 10.5, to be compared with the makespan 14 of naive CP.

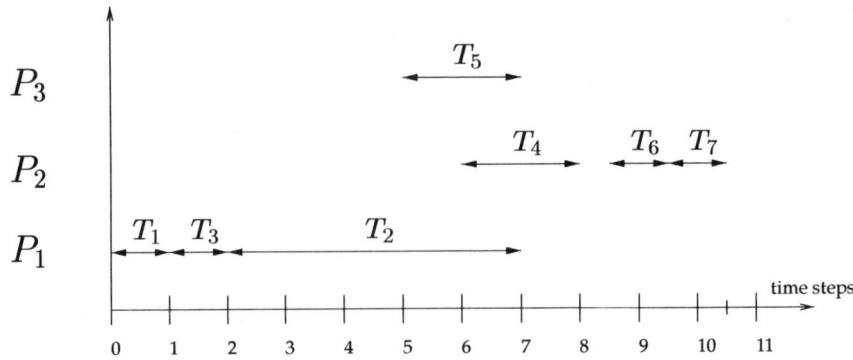

Figure 2.6: Modified critical path scheduling for Example 3.

2.5.3   Hints for Comparison

The comparison of naive CP and MCP for Example 3 should not be overestimated. We are comparing two heuristics; neither of them is always superior to the other (see Exercise 2.6 for an example where naive CP is better than MCP). Our intuition, however, shows that MCP is likely to outperform naive CP in most cases.

To be less specific than in Example 3, let us compare CP and MCP on two very simple graphs: a fork with two nodes and a join with two nodes. In Figures 2.7(a) and 2.7(b), we have three tasks of the same weight w. The communication costs are all equal to c. Assume two processors are available, P_1 and P_2. There are two cases:

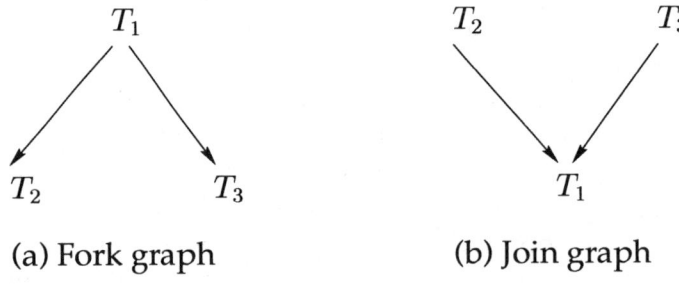

(a) Fork graph   (b) Join graph

Figure 2.7: Elementary graphs for heuristic comparison.

1. **Fork Graph** (Figure 2.7(a)). Naive CP schedules T_1 on P_1 at step $t = 0$. Then it schedules T_2 on P_1 at step $t = w$, and T_3 on P_2 at step $w + c$, hence a makespan equal to $2w + c$. MCP does the same as naive CP if $w > c$. But if $w < c$, the earliest execution time for T_3 is $t = 2w$ on P_1, hence MCP schedules all tasks on P_1, and its makespan is equal

to $3w < 2w + c$. Conclusion: MCP outperforms naive CP if $w < c$ and equals it otherwise.

2. **Join Graph** (Figure 2.7(b)). Naive CP and MCP perform identically. At step $t = 0$, they schedule T_2 on P_1 and T_3 on P_2. At step $t = w + c$, T_1 is scheduled on either P_1 or P_2, and the makespan is $2w + c$. Note that is not optimal if $w < c$; it is better to schedule the three tasks on the same processor! Of course this is forbidden for any list schedule: no processor can be deliberately kept idle.

This short discussion shows how hard it is to draw conclusions. The scheduling problem is NP-complete, and we are only comparing heuristics. Generally speaking, there are three possible directions:

1. **Theoretical:** Prove that the heuristic is guaranteed.

2. **Experimental:** Use random graphs and/or "standard benchmark" graphs to compare heuristics.

3. **Tricky:** Prove that the heuristic is optimal on certain classes of graphs: forks, joins, fork-joins, trees, etc.

The first direction is conceptually the nicest; you are ensured that the heuristic will perform within a certain factor of the optimal in the worst case. The second direction is quite useful in practice. And the third direction helps to tune the heuristics so as to be optimal for certain graph classes. Anyway, list scheduling with limited resources appears so difficult that more sophisticated two-step methods have been introduced. These are discussed in the next section.

2.6 Two-Step Clustering Heuristics

We have seen in Example 3 that it is difficult to trade-off parallelism and communication, even in the presence of unlimited resources. The idea of two-step methods is the following. In the first step, use heuristics to group tasks into clusters. This clustering operation is made assuming unlimited resources, to simplify things. In the second step, clusters will be allocated to available processors, and the final ordering of the tasks will be computed. The basic rule of the game is that all the tasks of a given cluster will be allocated to the same processor. We can think of a virtual processor per cluster in the first phase, while several clusters will be allocated to physical processors in the second phase. Why is clustering a useful heuristic? Sarkar [108] gives the following justification: "If tasks are scheduled on the same processor on the best possible architecture with unbounded number of processors, then they should be scheduled on the same processor in any other architecture." Sarkar's argument, although not true in every case, is very intuitive, and clustering techniques have been widely explored.

In this section, we first present various heuristics for the first step, the *clustering* phase. Then we present heuristics for the second step, namely, allocating and scheduling tasks onto physical processors. We prove no optimality theorem here; please wait until Section 2.7.

2.6.1   Heuristics for the Clustering Phase

We survey three widely studied heuristics for the clustering phase: Kim and Browne's linear clustering [69], Sarkar's greedy clustering [108], and (the underlying principle of) Yang and Gerasoulis's dominant sequence clustering [124].

To be precise in the following discussion, let us restate the definitions of bottom and top levels in the presence of clusters (see Section 1.4 for the definition of $bl(u)$ and $tl(u)$ for a vertex u).

Definition 13 (Clustering, Bottom/Top Level, Estimated Parallel Time)
Let $G = (V, E, w, c)$ be a cDAG.

1. *A clustering is a function $C : V \longrightarrow \mathbb{N}^*$ (each task is assigned a cluster number). We also use C to denote the induced partition of the set of tasks into clusters.*

2. *Given a clustering C, we define top and bottom levels as follows:*
    - *For $v \in V$, $bl(v, C) = w(v) + \max(\max_{in}, \max_{out})$,*
      where $\max_{in} = \max\{bl(u); u \in SUCC(v), C(u) = C(v)\}$
      and $\max_{out} = \max\{bl(u) + c(v, u); u \in SUCC(v), C(u) \neq C(v)\}$.
    - *For $v \in V$, $tl(v, C) = \max(\max_{in}, \max_{out})$,*
      where $\max_{in} = \max\{tl(u) + w(u); u \in PRED(v), C(u) = C(v)\}$
      and $\max_{out} = \max\{tl(u) + w(u) + c(u, v); u \in PRED(v), C(u) \neq C(v)\}$.

3. *Given a clustering C, we define the estimated parallel time as*

$$EPT(C) = \max\{tl(v) + bl(v); v \in V\}$$

In this definition, bottom and top levels are computed according to the clustering; we add communication costs iff the tasks do not belong to the same cluster. The *estimated parallel time* EPT is the length of the longest path in the graph using this rule. In other words, the current clustering indicates which communication costs should be taken into account given already-made decisions: We keep communication costs that link tasks belonging to different clusters so far (and we zero out those that link tasks grouped into the same cluster). Because some clusters will be merged throughout the clustering, this is only an estimation (the current estimation) of the final parallel time. Finally, there remains a problem to solve: What is the ordering of the tasks *inside* a given cluster? All the tasks that belong to the same cluster are executed by the same processor. But if dependences do not induce a total order within the cluster, we must define such a total ordering. For instance, in Example 3, if $\{T_1, T_2, T_3\}$ becomes a cluster at some point, dependences imply to execute task T_1 before the other two tasks T_2 and T_3, which can be executed in any order. Deciding which is executed first may have a tremendous impact on the computation of longest paths in the graph. We will discuss further the scheduling problem inside clusters when we present Sarkar's heuristic.

The three surveyed heuristics are iterative. The initial clustering $\mathcal{C}_0$ is one task per cluster (maximum parallelism), and the initial parallel time is $\text{EPT}(\mathcal{C}_0)$. At step i, we refine the clustering $\mathcal{C}_{i-1}$ to build a new clustering $\mathcal{C}_i$ so that EPT decreases, or at least does not increase: $\text{EPT}(\mathcal{C}_i) \leq \text{EPT}(\mathcal{C}_{i-1})$. Termination obeys different criteria: processing of all vertices, processing of all edges, or stop when the clustering rule leads to an increase of EPT.

Kim and Browne's Linear Clustering

The most natural idea to decrease the EPT is to group all the tasks of a longest path into a single cluster. This is the principle of Kim and Browne's heuristic [69], which can be summarized as follows:

1. Initially, all edges are marked unexamined.

2. Compute top and bottom levels $tl(v, \mathcal{C}_0)$ and $bl(v, \mathcal{C}_0)$ for each $v \in V$. Compute $\text{EPT}(\mathcal{C}_0)$. Select a longest path in the graph (whose length is $\text{EPT}(\mathcal{C}_0)$) and build $\mathcal{C}_1$ from $\mathcal{C}_0$ by grouping all tasks in the selected path into the same cluster. Mark all edges incident to these tasks as examined.

3. While there remain unexamined edges, redo step 2 on the graph of unexamined edges (and incident nodes). Compute $\mathcal{C}_i$ from $\mathcal{C}_{i-1}$ by grouping the tasks of a longest path of $\mathcal{C}_{i-1}$ into a single cluster.

Let us follow Kim and Browne's heuristic on Example 3. Given $\mathcal{C}_0$, we have already computed $\text{EPT}(\mathcal{C}_0) = 14$. $T_1 \rightarrow T_2 \rightarrow T_7$ is the single longest path. Therefore we let $\mathcal{C}_1 = \{\{T_1, T_2, T_7\}, \{T_3\}, \{T_4\}, \{T_5\}, \{T_6\}\}$. We are led to the graph of Figure 2.8. As EPT(C_1) = 13.5, we accept this clustering. The subgraph under consideration for the second step is circled by the dashed line in Figure 2.8: vertices are reduced to $\{T_3, T_4, T_5, T_6\}$. The longest path now is $T_3 \rightarrow T_4 \rightarrow T_6$, therefore $C_2 = \{\{T_1, T_2, T_7\}, \{T_3, T_4, T_6\}, \{T_5\}\}$. Again, we accept this clustering because EPTC_2 = 12.5. There does not remain any unexamined edge, therefore C_2 is the final clustering.

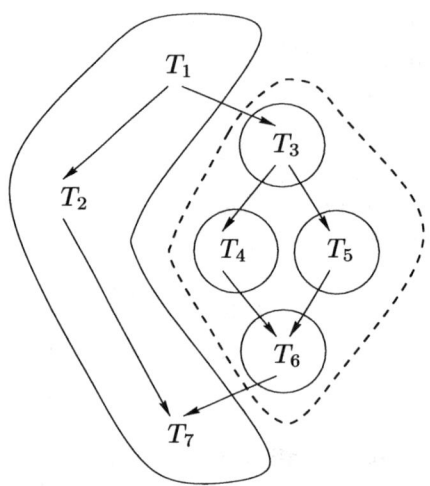
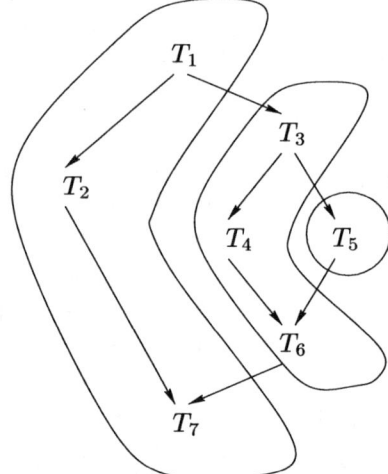

Figure 2.8: Clustering C_1 in Kim and Browne's heuristic.

Figure 2.9: Final clustering in Kim and Browne's heuristic.

We have three clusters at the end (see Figure 2.9). What do we do with these clusters? In other words, how do we move from clustering to scheduling? Assume that we have as many processors as clusters (we need three processors here). The scheduling is easy; each processor executes the tasks of its cluster as soon as possible, as illustrated in Figure 2.10. What makes the scheduling so easy is the *linearity* of the clusters; in each cluster, tasks are totally ordered, because they belong to a path of the dependence graph. Therefore each processor has to process a totally ordered set of tasks, hence the simplicity of scheduling. We will come back to the importance of linear clusters in Section 2.7.

There are at most $|V|$ steps in Kim and Browne's heuristic, and at each step we traverse the graph to compute new top and bottom levels; hence the complexity of the heuristic is $O(|V|(|V| + |E|))$.

Sarkar's Greedy Clustering

Another natural idea to decrease the EPT is to (try to) zero out costly communications. This is the principle of Sarkar's heuristic [108], which can be

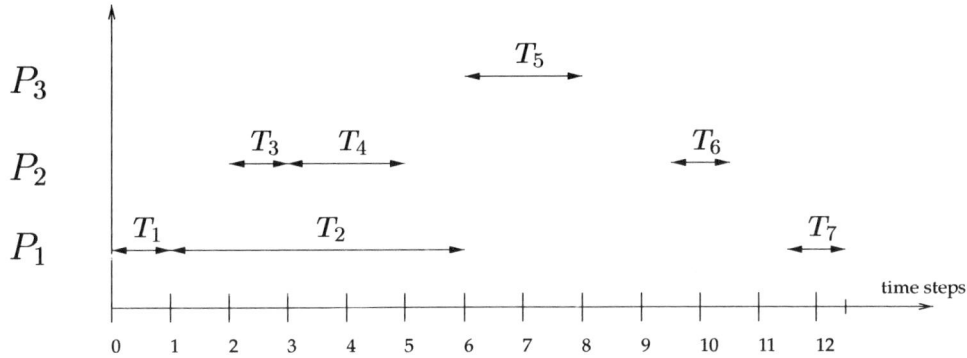

Figure 2.10: Scheduling Kim and Browne's clustering with three processors.

summarized as follows:

1. Sort the edges of the cDAG in descending order of edge (communication) costs.

2. For each edge (in the order above), zero out the edge if the estimated parallel time does not increase. Formally at step i, let $e = (u, v)$ be the edge under consideration: we built $\mathcal{C}_i$ by merging the two clusters $\mathcal{C}_{i-1}(u)$ and $\mathcal{C}_{i-1}(v)$. We do this merging only if $\text{EPT}(\mathcal{C}_i) \leq \text{EPT}(\mathcal{C}_{i-1})$; otherwise we let $\mathcal{C}_i = \mathcal{C}_{i-1}$.

Let us follow Sarkar's heuristic on Example 3. We have $\text{EPT}(\mathcal{C}_0) = 14$. We consider the edges one after the other in the sorted list

$$\{(T_1, T_2), (T_3, T_4), (T_3, T_5), (T_2, T_7), (T_4, T_6), (T_5, T_6), (T_1, T_3), (T_6, T_7)\}$$

1. $w(T_1, T_2) = 5$. If we group T_1 and T_2 in the same cluster, the EPT decreases from 14 to 13.5 ($T_1 \rightarrow T_3 \rightarrow T_4 \rightarrow T_6 \rightarrow T_7$ becomes the longest path). Therefore we do zero out the edge (T_1, T_2). In other words,
$$\mathcal{C}_1 = \{\{T_1, T_2\}, \{T_3\}, \{T_4\}, \{T_5\}, \{T_6\}, \{T_7\}\}$$

2. $w(T_3, T_4) = 4$. If we group T_3 and T_4 in the same cluster, the EPT decreases from 13.5 to 12.5 ($T_1 \rightarrow T_3 \rightarrow T_5 \rightarrow T_6 \rightarrow T_7$ becomes the longest path). Therefore we do zero out the edge (T_3, T_4), and
$$\mathcal{C}_2 = \{\{T_1, T_2\}, \{T_3, T_4\}, \{T_5\}, \{T_6\}, \{T_7\}\}$$

3. $w(T_3, T_5) = 3$. If we group T_3 and T_5 in the same cluster, we have a new cluster $\{T_3, T_4, T_5\}$. How do we schedule it to compute $\text{EPT}(\mathcal{C}_3)$? This cluster is not linear: T_4 and T_5 are independent, hence they can

be ordered in any way. However, we need an ordering to compute longest paths for the current clustering; the same processor will execute sequentially the three tasks $\{T_3, T_4, T_5\}$ in the new cluster, and the ordering of these tasks has an impact on the (estimated) parallel time. The idea is to introduce "a virtual arrow" between T_4 and T_5. To determine which task should be given priority, we can use the values the bottom levels had at the previous step.[2] Here, because $bl(T_4, C_2) = bl(T_5, C_2) = 6.5$, we break the tie by giving priority to T_4 and we draw a virtual arrow $T_4 - - > T_5$. Now that we have ordered tasks inside the new cluster $\{T_3, T_4, T_5\}$, we can compute $EPT(C_3) = 11.5$. Therefore we do zero out the edge (T_3, T_5), and

$$C_3 = \{\{T_1, T_2\}, \{T_3, T_4, T_5\}, \{T_6\}, \{T_7\}\}$$

4. $w(T_2, T_7) = 2$. Merging the two clusters $\{T_1, T_2\}$ and $\{T_7\}$ causes no scheduling problem, as the new cluster remains linear. We obtain $EPT(C_4) = 11.5 = EPT(C_3)$, and we do accept to zero out the edge (T_2, T_7). We have

$$C_4 = \{\{T_1, T_2, T_7\}, \{T_3, T_4, T_5\}, \{T_6\}\}$$

5. $w(T_4, T_6) = 1.5$. Merging the two clusters $\{T_3, T_4, T_5\}$ and $\{T_6\}$ (and scheduling T_6 in last position) leads to $EPT(C_5) = 10$. Therefore

$$C_5 = \{\{T_1, T_2, T_7\}, \{T_3, T_4, T_5, T_6\}\}$$

6. The edge (T_5, T_6) is already zeroed out, $C_6 = C_5$.

7. Finally, zeroing out either the edge (T_1, T_3) or (T_6, T_7) would group all tasks on the same cluster, and EPT would increase to 13. The final clustering C_5 is represented in Figure 2.11. The corresponding scheduling with two processors is illustrated in Figure 2.12.

Let us emphasize an important point (see the discussion at step 3). When merging two clusters, we have a scheduling problem. If the new cluster is not linear, we have to build an ordering of the tasks inside the cluster. To do so, we use a heuristic within the heuristic. We have chosen to order tasks according to the highest bottom level first heuristic, where bottom levels refer to the values computed at the previous step.

There are $|E|$ steps in Sarkar's heuristic, and at each step we traverse the graph to compute new top and bottom levels; hence the complexity of the heuristic is $O(|E|(|V| + |E|))$.

---

[2]This variant of Sarkar's original scheduling strategy is quite natural as it is similar to CP scheduling. It has been proposed by Gerasoulis and Yang [48].

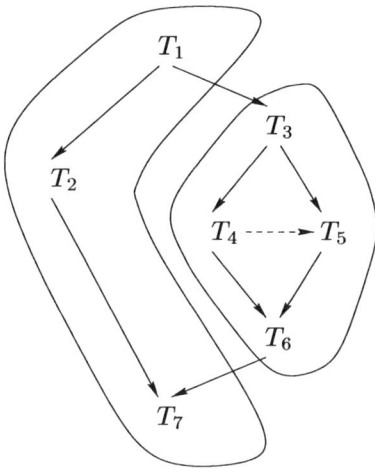

Figure 2.11: Final clustering in Sarkar's heuristic.

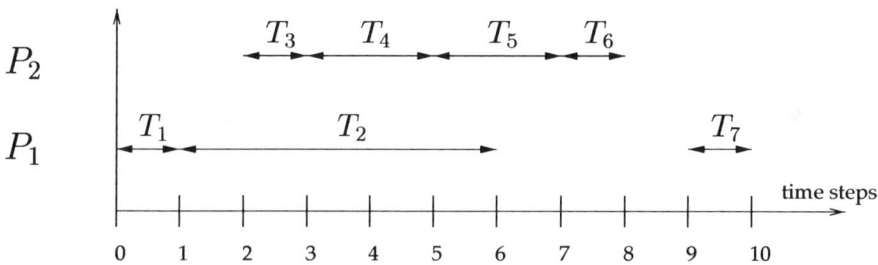

Figure 2.12: Scheduling Sarkar's clustering with two processors.

Dominant Sequence Clustering (DSC)

A third natural idea to decrease the EPT is to zero out one edge of the current longest path, i.e., the *dominant sequence* in the graph (and to accept this zeroing only when EPT does not increase). The iterative scheme for dominant sequence clusterings is the following:

1. Initially, all edges are marked unexamined. Compute top and bottom levels $tl(v, C_0)$ and $bl(v, C_0)$ for each $v \in V$. Determine the dominant sequence DS_0 (a path of length EPT(C_0)). Let $i = 0$.

2. While there remains unexamined edges, do

   - Zero an edge in the dominant sequence DS_i if the estimated parallel time does not increase. Mark this edge examined.

   - Increment i and find a new dominant sequence DS_{i+1}.

Which edge in the DS can we select for the zeroing? There are several possible variants:

1. Select the edge on the current longest path whose zeroing will decrease EPT as much as possible. This is a very costly strategy, as it implies many computations of top and bottom levels per step.

2. Select the edge on the current longest path whose weight is maximal. This is a greedy strategy that trades off complexity and efficiency. It can be viewed as a variant of Sarkar's heuristic.

3. Select the first edge of the longest path. This strategy is cheap and very simple (maybe too simple to produce good results?).

We briefly discuss the second variant. If we select the most costly edge on one of the longest paths, we have a heuristic whose complexity will be the same as Sarkar's heuristic: one traversal per step, hence a worst-case complexity $O(|E|(|V| + |E|))$. For Example 3, we follow the heuristic step by step:

1. With the initial clustering, the longest path is $T_1 \rightarrow T_2 \rightarrow T_7$. If we zero out the maximum weight edge (T_1, T_2), we decrease the EPT to 13.5.

2. The longest path is now $T_1 \rightarrow T_3 \rightarrow T_4 \rightarrow T_6 \rightarrow T_7$. The maximum weight edge is (T_3, T_4). Zeroing it decreases the EPT to 12.5.

3. The longest path is now $T_1 \rightarrow T_3 \rightarrow T_5 \rightarrow T_6 \rightarrow T_7$. The maximum weight edge is (T_3, T_5). Zeroing it decreases the EPT to 11.5, as in Sarkar's heuristic (we add the virtual edge $T_4 -- > T_5$).

4. The longest path is now $T_1 \rightarrow T_3 \rightarrow T_4 \rightarrow T_5 \rightarrow T_6 \rightarrow T_7$. We zero out the maximum weight edge (T_4, T_6) to obtain a longest path of length 10.

5. The longest path remains the same. There are two nonzeroed edges, (T_1, T_3) and (T_6, T_7), with same weight 1. Because the EPT would increase, we refuse to zero out (T_1, T_3) ...

6. ... but we do accept to zero out (T_6, T_7) because the EPT decreases to 9.

7. Finally, we refuse to zero out the last edge (T_2, T_7).

The final clustering is illustrated in Figure 2.13. It turns out that this heuristic is optimal for our example; we obtain the scheduling of Figure 2.2 with two processors. Of course we make the same warning as before. No definitive conclusion can be drawn from this single comparison.

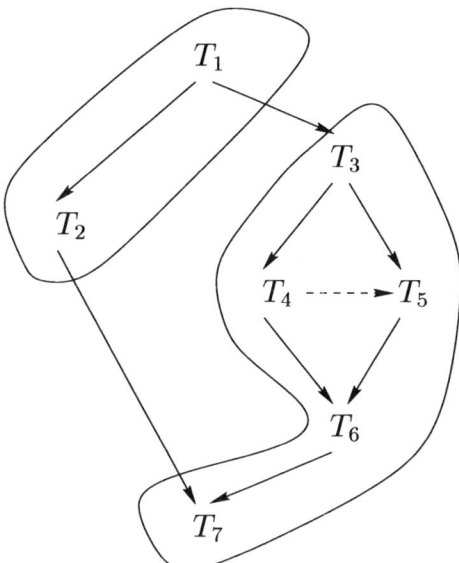

Figure 2.13: Final clustering in the DSC heuristic.

Yang and Gerasoulis's DSC

First we give a short overview of Yang and Gerasoulis's DSC heuristic. Then we present the heuristic in more detail (the reader may want to skip this presentation because it is rather technical).

Overview. As stated earlier, a dominant sequence clustering will cost at most $O(|E|(|V|+|E|))$ operations, which is the same cost as Sarkar's heuristic. For large graphs this is too high a cost. This is why Yang and Gerasoulis [124] have advocated a variant where some edges that do not belong to a DS are still zeroed. Their heuristic cannot be easily described. In a word, the key idea is to relax the zeroing condition: a selected edge is zeroed if the top level of its head decreases (rather than asking for a decrease of EPT). A heap of "free" (to be defined) tasks is maintained to achieve extraction of the highest priority task in logarithmic time. Also, the graph is traversed in a breadth-first order, so as not to recompute bottom levels at each step. Overall, the total complexity of the heuristic is $O((|V| + |E|) \log |V|)$, which makes it very attractive in large-scale applications.

Detailing the Heuristic. Our description of Yang and Gerasoulis's DSC is mainly borrowed from Chrétienne and Picouleau [23]. As with all the previous heuristics, Yang and Gerasoulis's DSC is iterative:

1. The initial clustering C_0 assigns one task per cluster (maximum parallelism), and the initial parallel time is EPT(C_0). Initially, all tasks are marked unexamined.

2. At each step, we have two different types of clusters in the current clustering: the *examined* clusters, whose content may only increase, and the *nonexamined* clusters, which are singletons that may be later merged into an *examined* cluster. Each task of an examined cluster is said to be *inserted*.

3. In the initial clustering C_0, clusters (singletons) that contain an entry task (a task without predecessor) are marked examined, otherwise they are marked nonexamined.

4. At each step, a task may be inserted only if all its predecessors have already been inserted.

5. The algorithm ends when all tasks have been inserted.

Consider the clustering C_i at step i, and let T be a noninserted task. T is said to be *free* if all its predecessors have been inserted. The priority of a free task is the sum of its bottom level $bl(v, C_i)$ and its top level $tl(v, C_i)$. T is said to be *partially free* if at least one of its predecessors has been inserted and at least one other has not. The priority of a partially free task is the sum of its bottom level $bl(v, C_i)$ and its "examined" top level $etl(v, C_i)$ where $etl(v, C_i)$ is defined as the maximum weight of a path leading to T and is composed only of inserted tasks (except T).

As specified earlier, only free tasks can be inserted. We use the previous priorities to decide which free task will be inserted. We determine the following two tasks:

- the free task T_f with highest priority α

- and the partially free task T_{pf} with highest priority β.

Two cases can occur:

1. $\alpha \geq \beta$. The heuristic explores all (inserted) predecessors of T_f until it finds one of them, say T_{pre}, such that adding T_f as the last task of the (examined) cluster that contains T_{pre} allows us to schedule T_f strictly sooner in the resulting new clustering (in other words if the top level of T_f decreases with this insertion). If one of these tests is successful, we adopt the new clustering, otherwise we leave T_f in its singleton cluster, which becomes examined.

2. $\alpha < \beta$. The heuristic explores all inserted predecessors of T_{pf} until it finds one of them, say T_{pre}, such that adding T_{pf} as the last task of the (examined) cluster that contains T_{pre} allows us to decrease the examined top level of T_{pf}. If one of these tests is successful, we "freeze" the cluster containing T_{pre} until T_{pf} becomes free. Using the same procedure as before, except that the cluster containing T_{pre} is no longer a candidate, we try to insert T_f as the last task of an examined cluster.

We do not go further into the description of the heuristic. In fact, rather than choosing any predecessor, Yang and Gerasoulis choose the one that leads to the largest diminution of the current top level. They use a procedure similar to that of Exercise 2.8. The use of the estimated top level is a key point to decrease the complexity of the heuristic. We refer the reader to [124] for a detailed presentation, including several variants and comparisons.

2.6.2   From Clustering to Scheduling with Resources

When we have a clustering, we are not done yet. Clustering is the first step of a two-step process:

1. Cluster the task graph first. All tasks in a cluster will execute in the same processor.

2. (i) Assign the clusters to physical processors.
   (ii) Order the execution of the tasks in each (physical) processor.

We have just dealt with the first step, the clustering. To tackle the second step, the cluster assignment and the final ordering of tasks, we rely on heuristics as before. Indeed, the second step itself is NP-complete too, even if there are as many physical processors as clusters (Exercise 2.4 asks you to show this).

Cluster Assignment

When using a clustering heuristic, we assume the availability of unlimited resource. There is no way to predict the final number of clusters. Most likely, we end up with more clusters than available physical processors. Hence, we have a need to assign many clusters to the same physical processor. A simple strategy is the following;

1. Compute the computational load (the sum of the task weights) for each cluster.

2. Sort the clusters in an increasing order of their loads.

3. Use a load-balancing algorithm so that each processor has approximately the same load. A first algorithm is the wrap mapping[3] of clusters to processors. An alternative suggested by Gerasoulis, Jiao, and Yang [47] is to map all clusters with a load greater than the average load on separate processors, while using a wrap mapping for the remaining clusters and processors.

Another approach is used by Sarkar [108]. The idea is to scan the tasks according to a priority list (bottom levels). At each step, a task (along with all the other tasks of the cluster that it belongs to) is assigned to the processor that minimizes the increase in the estimated parallel time (EPT). The EPT is determined by allocating the already-scheduled clusters on the physical processors and the yet-unscheduled clusters on extra (virtual) processors.

Final Task Scheduling

Finally, we have to schedule all tasks. Note that even if we want to keep a specified ordering inside each cluster (because the cluster is linear or because we computed an ordering during the clustering step), we still have to compute a scheduling, because there are many clusters per processor.

But now each task is assigned a processor number, so those edges that require a communication cost are perfectly known. To order the execution of tasks within each processor such that the total parallel time is minimized, we can use a list-scheduling solution. Each processor has a priority list of tasks based on bottom levels (critical paths). Of course in the computation of bottom levels we include only the communication costs that are not internalized. There are two natural strategies:

- **Free list scheduling.** At each step, we schedule the tasks with highest priority among the free tasks. Remember that a task is free when all its predecessors have been executed.

- **Ready list scheduling.** At each step, we schedule the highest priority tasks among the ready tasks. A task is ready when it can start execution immediately. More precisely, a task is ready at step t if it is free, and if $\sigma(T') + w(t') + c(T', T) \leq t$ for each predecessor T' of T that has not been allocated to the same processor as T.

According to Yang and Gerasoulis [123], ready list scheduling "performs better" than free list scheduling. Few optimality results are known,

---

[3]This means that the cluster ranked in position i is assigned to processor number i mod p, where p is the total number of physical processors.

however. For example, we have to slightly change the priority rule (use a modified bottom level computation where the weight of the task is not included) to prove the optimality of ready list scheduling for fork and join graphs [123].

2.6.3 Clustering Epilogue

At the end of this presentation of clustering techniques, we feel embarrassed. For each step, we have to choose a heuristic. Inside each heuristic, we have to select several subheuristics. Given a task graph, there are very few arguments to help us make the right choice. For the reader who likes theorems and bounds, there are some in the next section.

2.7 Linear Clustering

In this section, we come back to linear clustering (which we informally introduced to describe Kim and Browne's heuristic). We have seen that linear clusters make scheduling much easier. From a theoretical point of view, it is nice to know that there always exists a linear optimal clustering when the task graph is coarse-grain, i.e., when any computation costs more than any communication. This important result is due to Gerasoulis and Yang [49]. We start with the definition of a linear cluster.

Definition 14 (Linear Cluster) *Let $G = (V, E, w, c)$ be a cDAG. A linear cluster is a set of tasks C that belong to a dependence path of G: $C \subset \{T_1, T_2, \ldots, T_m\}$ where $(T_i, T_{i+1}) \in E$ for $1 \leq i < m$. A linear clustering of G is a partition of V into linear clusters.*

Remember that the granularity of a cDAG $G = (V, E, w, c)$ is the computation-to-communication ratio $g(G) = \frac{\min_{T \in V} w(T)}{\max_{T, T' \in V} c(T, T')}$. G is said to be coarse-grain if $g(G) \geq 1$ (see Definition 10). We start with the optimality of linear clusterings for coarse-grain graphs, and we deduce a trivial bound for arbitrary graphs.

Theorem 9 *Let $G = (V, E, w, c)$ be a coarse-grain cDAG. There exists a linear clustering for G that is optimal.*

Proof The proof is iterative. Given an optimal clustering, we make it more and more linear, so to speak, without increasing the makespan. At each step, we take a nonlinear cluster NLC and extract some tasks out of it. The extracted tasks will belong to a dependence path of G. The cluster is then split into two new clusters, a linear one LC (made of the extracted tasks) and a (possibly) nonlinear one NLC', whose size is strictly smaller than that of NLC. Therefore the algorithm terminates. The difficulty is to find an extraction mechanism that guarantees that the makespan does not increase.

We begin with a lemma showing that we can remove all transitivity edges in G.

Lemma 5 *We can assume that G has no transitivity edge.*

Proof   Consider any transitivity edge $(T, T') \in E$; as shown in Figure 2.14 there is also a path $T \to T_1 \to T_2 \ldots \to T_k \to T'$ in E (where $k \geq 1$).

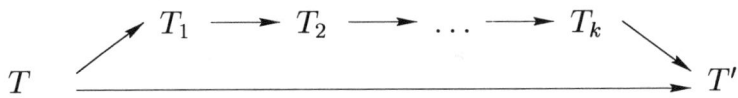

Figure 2.14: Transitivity edges.

Let σ be an arbitrary schedule for G. We claim that the dependence constraint induced by the edge (T, T') is automatically fulfilled, because of the other path. Indeed, we have

$$\sigma(T) + w(T) \leq \sigma(T_1)$$

and

$$\sigma(T_1) + w(T_1) \leq \sigma(T_2) \leq \ldots \leq \sigma(T_k) \leq \sigma(T')$$

By hypothesis, G is coarse-grain and thus $c(T, T') \leq w(T_1)$. Therefore, $\sigma(T) + w(T) + c(T, T') \leq \sigma(T')$.   ■

Initially, we are given an optimal clustering $\mathcal{C}_0$ and a schedule with unlimited resources σ_0 such that $\mathrm{MS}(\sigma_0, \infty) = \mathrm{MS}_{opt}(\infty)$. Note that the task allocation for σ_0 is given by the clustering. The rule of the game is that all tasks of a cluster are executed by the same processor.

The sketch of the proof is the following:

1. *Initialization:*
   $\mathcal{C}_0$ and σ_0 are given.
   Let t denote the current step: $t := 0$;

2. *While (there exists a nonlinear cluster in $\mathcal{C}_t$) do*

   (a) Take a nonlinear cluster NLC in $\mathcal{C}_t$;

   (b) *Extract* a linear cluster LC from NLC: $NLC = LC \cup NLC'$

(c) Construct $\mathcal{C}_{t+1}$ by replacing NLC by the two clusters LC and NLC': $\mathcal{C}_{t+1} = (\mathcal{C}_t \setminus NLC) \cup LC \cup NLC'$.

(d) Construct a new schedule σ_{t+1} such that $\sigma_{t+1}(T) \le \sigma_t(T)\ \forall T \in V$.

(e) Increment t.

Next we explain the extraction procedure. First, we need a definition:

Definition 15 *For $v \in V$, $pred(v)$ denotes the set of immediate predecessors of v that belong to the same cluster as v. Do not confuse with $PRED(v)$, the set of all immediate predecessors of v.*

The extraction procedure at step t takes a nonlinear cluster NLC and extracts a linear cluster LC out of it. The procedure can be sketched as follows:

Extract(NLC, LC, t)

1. Reorder the tasks in NLC according to the execution order. Then $NLC = \{T_{i_1}, \dots, T_{i_m}\}$, where $\sigma_t(T_{i_k}) + w(T_{i_k}) \le \sigma_t(T_{i_{k+1}})$, $1 \le k < m$. Note that all tasks in NLC are executed by the same processor, hence one after the other (no parallelism here).

2. Extract T_{i_m}, the last task of NLC. Let T_c be the last extracted task. Initially, $T_c = T_{i_m}$.
   While (not terminated) do
   if $pred(T_c) = \emptyset$ then *return*
   else

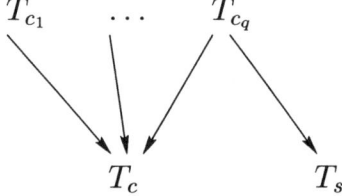

(a) Order the tasks in $pred(T_c)$ according to the execution order: $pred(T_c) = \{T_{c_1}, \dots, T_{c_q}\}$, where $\sigma_t(T_{c_k}) + w(T_{c_k}) \le \sigma_t(T_{c_{k+1}})$, $1 \le k < q$.

(b) If the last task, T_{c_q}, has a successor $T_s \in NLC$ that satisfies:
   $\sigma_t(T_s) + w(T_s) \le \sigma_t(T_c)$
   then *return*
   else extract T_{c_q} and let $T_c = T_{c_q}$.

In other words, the current task is extracted iff its last predecessor in NLC has no other successor scheduled in between. The extracted cluster is clearly linear, because at each step we extract one of the immediate predecessors of the current task. Now comes the hard part: to show that we can construct σ_{t+1} such that $\sigma_{t+1}(T) \leq \sigma_t(T) \ \forall T \in V$. Note that σ_{t+1} uses one more processor than σ_t, because NLC has been split into two clusters LC and NLC'.

We proceed by induction, traversing the graph. For the base case, consider a task T without any predecessor: $\text{PRED}(T) = \emptyset$. Let $\sigma_{t+1}(T) = \sigma_t(T)$ if $T \notin LC$ and $\sigma_{t+1}(T) = 0$ otherwise.

Consider now a task T and assume (by induction) that we have defined σ_{t+1} for all predecessors of T in such a way that

$$\forall T' \in \text{PRED}(T), \sigma_{t+1}(T') \leq \sigma_t(T')$$

We schedule T as soon as possible: we let $\sigma_{t+1}(T) = \max(\max_{in}, \max_{out})$, where

$$\max_{in} = \max\{\sigma_{t+1}(T') + w(T'); T' \in \text{pred}(T)\}$$
$$\max_{out} = \max\{\sigma_{t+1}(T') + w(T') + c(T', T); T' \in (\text{PRED}(T) \setminus \text{pred}(T))\}$$

We have to ensure $\sigma_{t+1}(T) \leq \sigma_t(T)$. The difficulty is that some predecessor T' of T may have changed category, so to speak: moving T' from the set $\text{pred}(T)$ to the set $\text{PRED}(T) \setminus \text{pred}(T)$ (because of the new clustering) implies you should take the communication cost $c(T', T)$ into account, thereby possibly delaying the scheduling of T. However, we will show that we never have to delay T! There are four cases (see Figure 2.15):

(a) $T \notin NLC$. Communication costs have not changed; the set $\text{pred}(T)$ has not been modified. Therefore, by induction, $\sigma_{t+1}(T) \leq \sigma_t(T)$.

(b) $T \in NLC \setminus LC$. T belongs to NLC but has not been extracted. Assume that one predecessor T' of T has been extracted (otherwise we are done as above, $\text{pred}(T)$ has not been modified). Note that this predecessor T', if it exists, is unique because we have removed transitivity edges. Now $T' \in LC$ and $T \in NLC'$; hence we have to take the communication cost $c(T', T)$ into account. We prove that this communication cost is indeed overlapped by other computations.

First, T' is not the last task executed by σ_t in NLC: $T' \neq T_{i_m}$. Indeed, the last executed task has no successor in NLC, while T' does (T is one of its successors). Let T'' be the successor of T' in LC: $T' \to T'' \to \ldots \to T_{i_m}$. Because T' has been extracted in LC, it has no successor in NLC that is executed between itself and T'' (this is the extraction rule). Hence T is executed after T'': $\sigma_t(T'') + w(T'') \leq \sigma_t(T)$. We

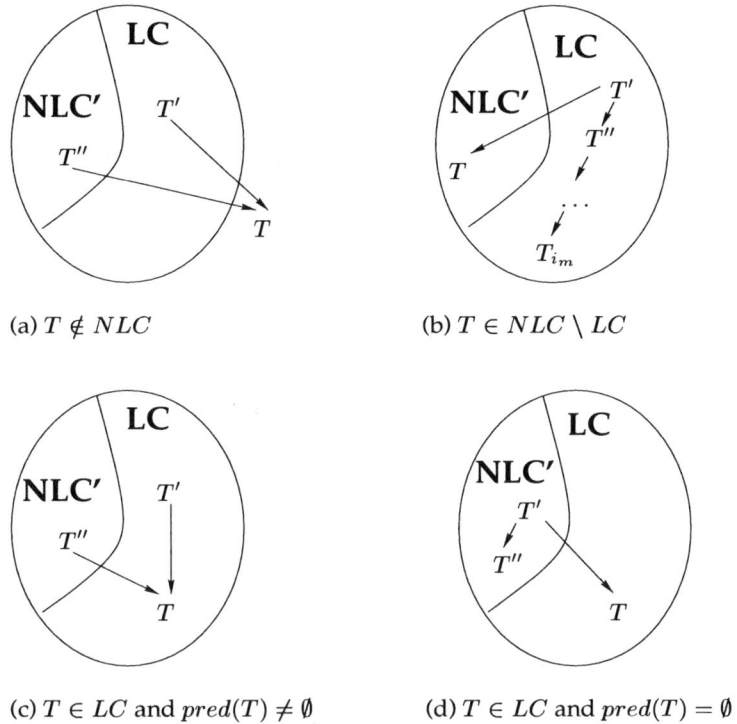

(a) $T \notin NLC$ (b) $T \in NLC \setminus LC$

(c) $T \in LC$ and $pred(T) \neq \emptyset$ (d) $T \in LC$ and $pred(T) = \emptyset$

Figure 2.15: Four cases to define $\sigma_{t+1}(T)$.

know that $\sigma_t(T') + w(T') \leq \sigma_t(T'')$ (T'' is a successor of T') and that $c(T', T) \leq w(T'')$ (the graph is coarse-grain). Therefore

$$\sigma_t(T') + w(T') + c(T', T) \leq \sigma_t(T'') + c(T', T) \leq \sigma_t(T'') + w(T'') \leq \sigma_t(T)$$

By induction, $\sigma_{t+1}(T) \leq \sigma_t(T)$.

(c) $T \in LC$ **and pred**$(T) \neq \emptyset$. T has a predecessor T' in LC. Assume it has another predecessor T'' in NLC'. Because T' has been extracted, the execution order by σ_t is T'', then T', then T. As earlier, the communication cost $c(T'', T)$ is overlapped by the computation cost $w(T')$, hence the result by induction.

(d) $T \in LC$ **and pred**$(T) = \emptyset$. The last case is when T has no predecessor in LC. If T has no predecessor at all in NLC we are done. But T may have a predecessor T' in NLC'. Why has T' not been extracted? Because T' has another successor T'' in NLC scheduled in between: $\sigma_t(T') + w(T') \leq \sigma_t(T'')$ and $\sigma_t(T'') + w(T'') \leq \sigma_t(T)$. Again, the communication cost $c(T', T)$ is overlapped by the computation cost $w(T'')$, hence the result by induction.

This completes the proof of Theorem 9. ∎

A Refinement. A careful reading of the proof of Theorem 9 reveals that the coarse-grain hypothesis is too strong. What is actually needed is a *local* condition. Let T be a fixed task and define

$$\bar{g}(T) = \min \left(\frac{\min_{T' \in \text{PRED}(T)} w(T')}{\max_{T' \in \text{PRED}(T)} c(T', T)}, \frac{\min_{T' \in \text{SUCC}(T)} w(T')}{\max_{T' \in \text{SUCC}(T)} c(T, T')} \right)$$

The condition $\bar{g}(T) \geq 1$, $\forall T \in V$, is enough to derive the same proof (Exercise 2.7 asks you to check this). This condition ensures that each task receives or sends a small amount of communication compared to the computation of its adjacent tasks. We can define $\bar{g}(G) = \max_{T \in V} \bar{g}(T)$ to be the local granularity of G. Of course $g(G) \leq \bar{g}(G)$, hence a coarse-grain graph has a coarse local granularity, so to speak.

Theorem 9 is not constructive; if G is coarse-grain, we know that there exists an optimal linear clustering, but we do not know how to find it. However, there is good news, as *any* linear clustering has a relatively good performance: it is within 50% of the optimal for coarse-grain graphs (the worst-case upper bound $\frac{4}{3}$ obtained by Hanen and Munier is for one particular linear clustering).

Theorem 10 *Let $G = (V, E, w, c)$ be a cDAG. Let $MS_{opt}(\infty)$ be the optimal parallel time. Let PT_{lc} be the parallel time of any linear clustering. Then*

$$PT_{lc} \leq \left(1 + \frac{1}{g(G)}\right) MS_{opt}(\infty)$$

Proof As usual, PT_{lc} is equal to the weight of a path of maximal weight $P : T_{i_1} \to T_{i_2} \to \ldots \to T_{i_k}$ where we take communication costs into account only if they link tasks that belong to different clusters. The desired bound will come from a comparison of the weight of P to the weight of a path without any communication, because the weight of such a path is an absolute lower bound for all schedules. We have $PT_{lc} \leq w(T_{i_1}) + c(T_{i_1}, T_{i_2}) + \ldots + w(T_{i_{k-1}}) + c(T_{i_{k-1}}, T_{i_k}) + w(T_{i_k})$ (on the right-hand side, we have included all communication costs in P). We have $c(T_{i_j}, T_{i_{j+1}}) \leq \frac{1}{g(G)} w(T_{i_j})$ for $1 \leq j \leq k - 1$. As stated before, $\sum_{j=1}^{k} w(T_{i_j}) \leq MS_{opt}(\infty)$, because P is a dependence path of G. Hence we have the result.[4] ∎

---

[4] In fact, we can use the local granularity and prove that $PT_{lc} \leq (1 + \frac{1}{\bar{g}(G)}) MS_{opt}(\infty)$.

2.8 Conclusion

Our main conclusion is that the problem of scheduling with communication delays turns out to be surprisingly difficult. Even the problem with unlimited resources is NP-complete, as was shown in Section 2.3. Fortunately, sophisticated guaranteed heuristics have been derived, both for unlimited resources (Section 2.4) and for limited resources [55]. And for practical problems, clustering heuristics like DSC (Section 2.6) and others have experimentally proven cost-effective [36].

2.9 Bibliographical Notes

Theorem 7 is due to Chrétienne [21]. Picouleau [96, 97] proves that $Pb(\infty)$ remains NP-complete even when we assume all task weights and communication costs to have the same (unit) value – this is the so-called UET-UCT problem (Unit Execution Time-Unit Communication Time) – or even if communication costs are arbitrarily small (but nonzero). Several extensions to Theorem 7 are discussed in the survey paper by Chrétienne and Picouleau [23]. Hanen and Munier's heuristic can be extended to cope with limited resources; see [55].

2.10 Exercises

Exercise 2.1

Prove that the schedule of Figure 2.2 is optimal.

Exercise 2.2

Compute $MS'(3)$ for Example 3. In other words, what is the minimal execution time if actually using three processors?

Exercise 2.3

Prove that $Pb(p)$ (with communication costs) is NP-complete.

Exercise 2.4

In Exercise 2.3, we asked you to show that the problem of determining both the schedule and the allocation of tasks of a cDAG is NP-complete. The two-step clustering heuristic tries to decouple this problem in two subproblems. First find a schedule and an allocation on an unbounded number of processors (clusters), then map the clusters on physical processors and schedule tasks within each processor. Theorem 7 shows that the first step is NP-complete (Pb(∞)). Show that the second step is NP-complete too, even if there are as many physical processors as clusters. In other words, scheduling preallocated tasks is NP-complete.

Exercise 2.5

Express MCP in algorithmic form.

Exercise 2.6

Consider the cDAG of Figure 2.16. Assume $p = 2$ available processors. Show that the naive critical path algorithm overcomes the modified critical path algorithm; the makespan of the former is 14, for the latter 15.

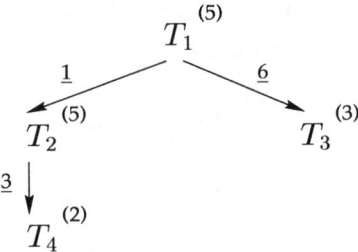

Figure 2.16: The task graph for Exercise 2.6.

Exercise 2.7

Let $G = (V, E, c, w)$ be a cDAG such that $\bar{g}(G) \geq 1$. Prove that there exists an optimal linear clustering for G.

Exercise 2.8

Consider the fork graph of Figure 2.17. Assume that $T_1, \ldots, T_n$ are sorted from left to right such that $w(T_j) + c(T_0, T_j) \geq w(T_{j+1}) + c(T_0, T_{j+1})$ for $1 \leq j < n$.

1. Prove that the following algorithm computes k such that the optimal clustering is given by Figure 2.18.

$i = 1;$
$PT_0 = w(T_0) + c(T_0, T_1) + w(T_1);$

$PT_1 = w(T_0) + \max(w(T_1), c(T_0, T_2) + w(T_2));$
while $PT_i \le PT_{i-1}$ do
   $i = i + 1;$
   $PT_i = w(T_0) + \max(\sum_{j=1}^{i} w(T_j), c(T_0, T_{i+1}) + w(T_{i+1}));$
$k = i - 1;$

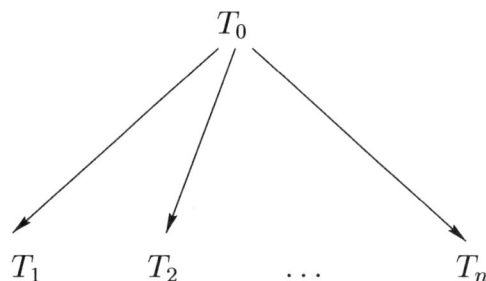

Figure 2.17: Fork graph for Exercise 2.8.

2. Prove that DSC clustering always finds this optimal clustering, but that Sarkar's clustering does not.

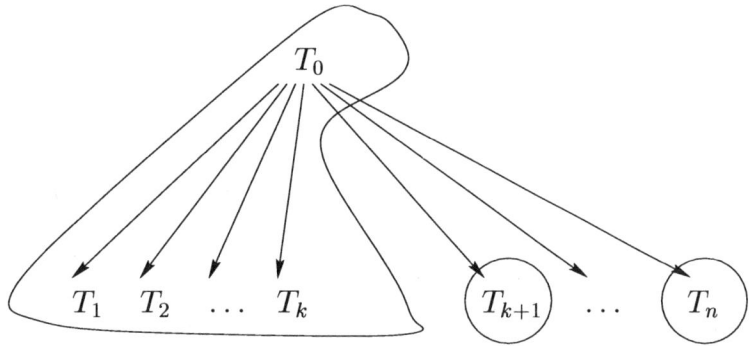

Figure 2.18: Clustering for Exercise 2.8.

Chapter 3

Cyclic Scheduling

3.1 Introduction

In the previous two chapters, we studied the problem of scheduling a finite number of tasks, linked by precedence constraints, with or without resource constraints, with or without communication costs. In all cases, the problem was modeled by an *acyclic* graph, with one vertex per task. In this chapter, we consider the problem of scheduling a set of "generic" tasks that have to be performed infinitely often. This problem, known as the basic cyclic scheduling problem, is the most elementary formulation for studying repetitive applications. It is modeled by a *cyclic* graph, with one vertex per generic task.

We will not give a complete overview of this topic here; we refer to the extended survey by Claire Hanen and Alix Munier in [56]. Our goal here is mainly to show how the techniques developed in Chapter 1 for deriving a heuristic with a performance guarantee for the acyclic case can be adapted to the cyclic case. We will need additional techniques of graph optimization, such as the Bellman-Ford algorithm and a retiming technique, due to Leiserson and Saxe, that minimizes the "clock period" of a graph.

The chapter is organized as follows. In Section 3.2, we define the basic cyclic scheduling problem, first through an example and then more formally. In Section 3.3, we recall a polynomial algorithm for solving the problem with no resource constraints. Finally, in Section 3.4, we study the problem with resource constraints; we show that it is an NP-complete problem, and we give a polynomial heuristic whose performances are guaranteed.

3.2   Problem Formulation

We first illustrate the cyclic scheduling problem, taking the example of loop scheduling. We will use this example throughout this chapter.

3.2.1   An Example

The loop of Example 4 has $n_i = 6$ instructions (A, B, C, D, E, and F) and N iterations; each instruction is executed N times. N is a parameter of unknown value, possibly very large. We call an instruction a *generic task* because it gives rise to a large number of similar instances, called *operations*, one for each value of the loop counter k. We denote by (v, k) the operation that is the instance of the generic task v at iteration k. All instances of a given generic task v are supposed to have the same execution time (or delay) that we denote by $d(v)$.

Example 4

```
DO k=0, N-1
    (A): a(k) = c(k-1)
    (B): b(k) = a(k-2) * d(k-1)
    (C): c(k) = b(k) + 1
    (D): d(k) = f(k-1)/3
    (E): e(k) = sin(f(k-2))
    (F): f(k) = log(b(k) + e(k))
ENDDO
```

There are precedence constraints between the operations of this loop. For example, the computations of A at iteration k writes $a(k)$, hence it must precede the computation of B at iteration $k + 2$, which reads this value. We say that there is a dependence from A to B with distance equal to 2. Dependence distances express the fact that some computations must be executed in a specified order to preserve the semantics of the loop.   □

One way to analyze the task system defined by the operations of the loop and the dependences between them is to completely unroll the loop. Then we can schedule the resulting dependence graph, which is nothing but a DAG, as in Chapter 1. However, this dependence graph is not just any graph, it has a very particular structure. First, its vertices are copies of the instructions of the loop. This is why tasks are not numbered from 1 to $n_i \times N$ (the number of computations within the loop). Rather, they are labeled by a pair of indices: $\{(v, k) \mid v \in V,\ 0 \leq k < N\}$, where V denotes the set of generic tasks, i.e., of instructions in the loop, $V = \{A, B, C, D, E, F\}$ in Example 4.

Second, dependences exhibit a repetitive pattern too. For example, for each value of k, computation (B, k) writes $b(k)$, hence it must precede computation (C, k) that reads this value. Thus there is a dependence edge $(B, k) \to (C, k)$ for $0 \le k < N$. This is a dependence "inside" the same loop iteration, i.e., for the same iteration k. Of course, dependences may also occur between loop iterations. As noticed earlier, the computation (A, k) writes $a(k)$, hence it must precede computation $(B, k + 2)$, which reads this value. This holds for any $0 \le k < N - 2$. A partial representation of the task graph is given in Figure 3.1 (dashed lines represent dependences between different iterations).

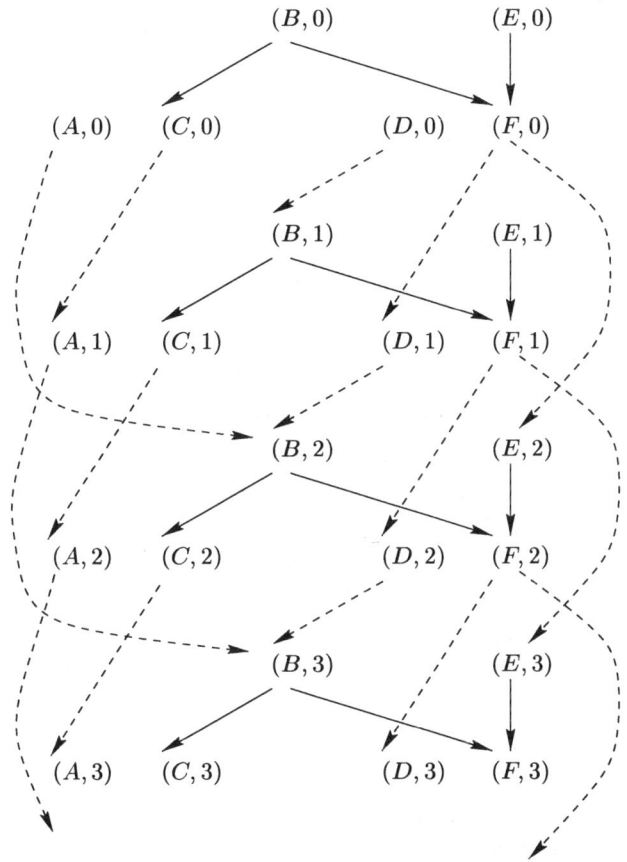

Figure 3.1: Task graph (partial view) for Example 4.

Because of this repetitive structure, we can represent all constraints by a smaller, generally cyclic, graph, called the *reduced dependence graph*, where each vertex corresponds to a generic task, and where the edges are labeled by dependence distances. This graph is a vertex-weighted and edge-weighted directed graph denoted by $G = (V, E, d, w)$, where the function $d : V \rightarrow \mathbb{N}^*$ gives the delay of each vertex (i.e., generic task), and the function $w : E \rightarrow \mathbb{N}$ gives the dependence distance of each edge. This dependence distance means that for any edge $e = (u, v) \in E$, and for any k, $0 \le k < N - w(e)$, the operation $(v, k + w(e))$ cannot start before the operation (u, k) is completed.

The reduced dependence graph of our example is depicted in Figure 3.2. Edge weights are shown close to the arrows. One can check, for example, that there is an edge from vertex A to vertex B with label 2. Delays are shown within square boxes. For example, we assumed that the duration of task E is 10 times greater than the delay of task A.

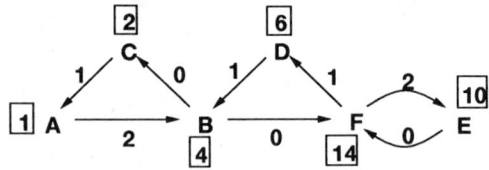

Figure 3.2: Reduced dependence graph.

3.2.2 Average Cycle Time

As in Chapters 1 and 2, the goal is to determine a schedule for all operations $(v, k), v \in V, 0 \le k < N$, of the loop. But we are now looking for a schedule for any value of N. In other words, a schedule is a function $\sigma : V \times \mathbb{N} \rightarrow \mathbb{N}$ that respects the dependence constraints:

$$\forall e = (u, v) \in E, \ \forall k \ge 0, \ \sigma(v, k + w(e)) \ge \sigma(u, k) + d(u) \qquad (3.1)$$

We will measure the performance of a schedule σ by its *average cycle time* λ defined by:

$$\lambda = \liminf_{N \to \infty} \frac{\max\{\sigma(v, k) + d(v) \mid v \in V, \ 0 \le k < N\}}{N}$$

Among all schedules, we will consider some particular schedules that exhibit a cyclic pattern, as the task graph does, the so called cyclic schedules. A *cyclic schedule* σ is a schedule such that $\sigma(v, k) = c_v + \lambda k$ for some $c_v \in \mathbb{N}$ and $\lambda \in \mathbb{N}$. The schedule σ is a periodic schedule with period λ; the same pattern of computations occurs every λ units of time. In other words, it schedules "slices" of length λ. Within each slice, one and only one instance of each generic task is initiated. This is why λ is called the *initiation interval* in the literature. It is also equal to the average cycle time of the schedule; this is why we chose the same notation λ.

3.2.3   Playing with the Example

Consider the reduced dependence graph of Figure 3.2. Delete all edges of nonzero weight. We obtain an acyclic graph $A(G)$ that summarizes all dependences within an iteration of the loop (see Figure 3.3(a)). Why is $A(G)$ acyclic? Because a cycle of zero-weight edges would imply a dependence cycle between task instances (i.e., a cycle in the dependence graph whose vertices are the *operations*), which means that an operation would depend on itself! To say it differently, a zero-weight edge always corresponds to a dependence that goes from a statement to another statement that occurs textually later in the body of the loop. Therefore, the subgraph of zero-weight edges defines a partial order among statements; thus $A(G)$ is acyclic.

Can we schedule $A(G)$ as a usual DAG? No problem; let us apply list-scheduling techniques. Assume we have two (identical) processors. We obtain the critical-path list schedule σ_a depicted in Figure 3.3(b). We have $\sigma_a(B) = \sigma_a(E) = 0, \sigma_a(D) = 4, \sigma_a(C) = \sigma_a(F) = 10$, and $\sigma_a(A) = 12$.

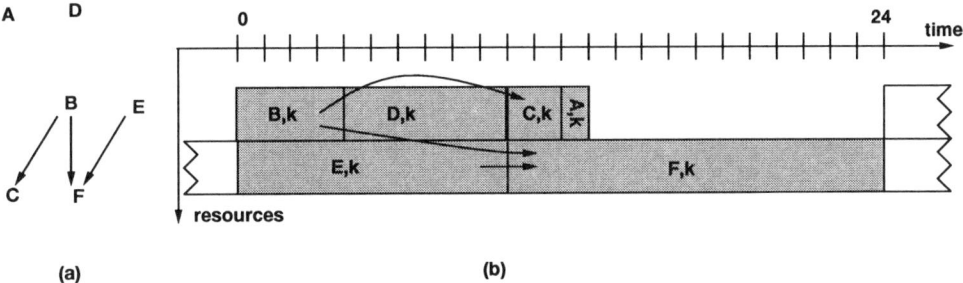

Figure 3.3: (a) The acyclic graph $A(G)$.
            (b) A corresponding list-scheduling allocation: $\lambda = 24$.

Deriving a cyclic schedule σ from the list schedule is easy. We choose the initiation interval λ as the makespan of the list schedule σ_a ($\lambda = 24$ here), and we let $\sigma(v, k) = \sigma_a(v) + \lambda k$ for all $v \in \{A, B, C, D, E, F\}$. This choice guarantees that all dependence constraints are met. Indeed, they are:

- within the same iteration, because they are enforced by σ_a;

- and between iterations, because the choice of λ ensures that any task instance of the next iteration $k + 1$ cannot start before the end of all task instances of iteration k.

Of course the value of λ that we obtain is likewise not the smallest possible one. Consider the following schedule: $\sigma(v, k) = c_v + \lambda k$, where

$\lambda = 20$ and the constants c_v are given in Table 3.1. (We will see that $\lambda = 20$ is not the smallest one either.)

Generic task v	A	B	C	D	E	F
Constant c_v	16	14	18	20	6	20

Table 3.1: Constants c_v for the schedule with $\lambda = 20$.

How we found this schedule will be explained in Section 3.4.4. Let us simply try to understand how it schedules the operations. We can rewrite the constants c_v as $c_v = s_v + \lambda r_v$ where $s_v = c_v \bmod \lambda$ and $r_v = c_v \div \lambda$ (Euclidean division). Then we have $\sigma(v, k) = s_v + \lambda(k + r_v)$. Here all r_v are equal to 0 except $r_D = r_F = 1$. This means that different iteration instances are executed within the same computation slice. To be precise, let slice k denote the time interval $[\lambda k, \lambda(k + 1) - 1]$. Then the computation (v, k) is initiated in slice $k - r_v$. Within a slice (in steady state), we have the execution represented in Figure 3.4. Note that operation instances are not identical in Figure 3.4, as we just explained.

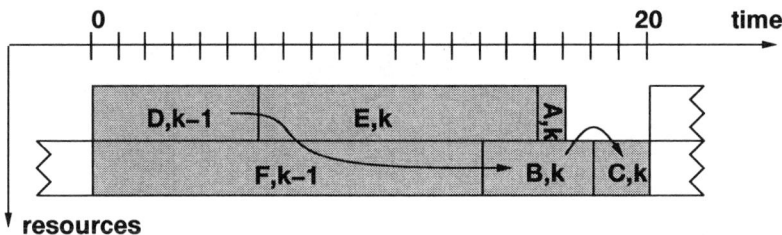

Figure 3.4: A slice of the schedule with $\lambda = 20$.

To check whether the schedule is valid, there are two solutions. Either we directly check that each dependence edge in the reduced dependence graph G is satisfied (8 verifications), or we wait until Section 3.4.3.

3.2.4   Problem Formulation: Summary

Formally, the basic cyclic scheduling (BCS) problem instances are represented by a finite, vertex-weighted, edge-weighted directed multigraph $G = (V, E, d, w)$ where:

- The vertices V of the graph model the generic tasks; each $v \in V$ represents an infinite set of operations $\{(v, k) \mid k \in \mathbb{N}\}$.

- Each generic task v has a positive delay (or duration) $d(v)$; vertex (task) delays d can be rational numbers, but because the graph is finite we can always change the time unit to have integer delays.

- The directed edges E of the graph model dependence constraints. Let $e = (u, v) \in E$ be an edge of G with a nonnegative weight $w(e)$; this means that instance k of generic task u must be completed before the execution of instance $k + w(e)$ of generic task v.

The graph G is the *reduced dependence graph* as introduced in Section 3.2.1. The basic cyclic scheduling problem is to find a schedule σ with minimal average cycle time λ_σ, where

$$\lambda_\sigma = \liminf_{N \to \infty} \frac{\max\{\sigma(v, k) + d(v) \mid v \in V,\ 0 \le k < N\}}{N}$$

that is subject to the following constraints:

- **Dependence Constraints:** Dependences between operations must be preserved, i.e.:

$$\forall e = (u, v) \in E,\ \forall k \le N,\quad \sigma(u, k) + d(u) \le \sigma(v, k + w(e)) \qquad (3.2)$$

- **Resource Constraints:** Each resource is requested by only one operation at a time, and this operation, once started, is performed with no interruption, i.e., if p resources are available:

$$\forall t \in \mathbb{N},\ |\{(v, k) \mid t - d(v) < \sigma(v, k) \le t\}| \le p \qquad (3.3)$$

Remarks:

- The resource constraints given earlier correspond to the simplest case of p identical resources, where operations cannot be cut into smaller pieces. More accurate models can be studied, for example, where resources are of different types, where resources are pipelined (one operation can be *initiated* at each unit of time), etc. However, throughout the chapter, we will keep to the simplest case defined earlier.

- In the preceding definition, we keep to the case where w, the edge weight function, is from E to $\mathbb{N}$ (as in our example Section 3.2.1). We point out, however, that all results presented in this chapter can be extended to the case where w is from E to $\mathbb{Z}$. In both cases, the condition for a schedule to exist is that all cycles $\mathcal{C}$ in G are such that $w(\mathcal{C}) > 0$. Then, all techniques are similar, but the proofs are a bit more complicated in the second case.

Definition 16 (BCS(∞), BCS(p)) *Given a graph $G = (V, E, d, w)$:*

- *BCS(∞) is the problem of finding the minimum possible average cycle time λ_∞ of a schedule using unlimited resources.*

- *BCS(p) is the problem of finding the minimum possible average cycle time λ_p of a schedule using p (identical and nonpipelined) processors.*

3.2.5   Lower Bounds for the Average Cycle Time

In Chapter 1, we gave two lower bounds for the makespan M of a schedule:

- Whatever the number of resources, $M \geq w(\mathcal{P})$ for any path $\mathcal{P}$ in the graph (Proposition 1).

- If p resources are available, $M \geq \dfrac{\text{Seq}}{p}$, where Seq denotes the sequential time, i.e., the sum of all task durations (Theorem 2).

The first bound expresses dependence constraints; the second, resource constraints. Here, we can also derive two lower bounds for the average cycle time as stated by the following theorem. For a cycle $\mathcal{C}$, we denote by $\rho(\mathcal{C})$ the duration to distance ratio $\frac{d(\mathcal{C})}{w(\mathcal{C})}$. We call $\rho(\mathcal{C})$ the *ratio* of $\mathcal{C}$.

Theorem 11 *If a schedule exists for the graph $G = (V, E, d, w)$, then all cycles of G have a positive weight. Furthermore, for any schedule σ with average cycle time λ_σ:*

$$\text{for any cycle } \mathcal{C}, \ \lambda_\sigma \geq \rho(\mathcal{C}) \tag{3.4}$$

$$\text{if } p \text{ resources are available, } p\lambda_\sigma \geq \sum_{v \in V} d(v) \tag{3.5}$$

Proof   Let σ be a schedule and $\mathcal{C}$ a cycle in G: $\mathcal{C} = (v_0, \ldots, v_{r-1}, v_r = v_0)$. Let e_i denote the edge (v_{i-1}, v_i) in this cycle. All constraints (3.2) are satisfied by σ along the cycle. For any $k \in \mathbb{N}$:

$$
\begin{aligned}
\sigma(v_0, k) + d(v_0) &\leq \sigma(v_1, k + w(e_1)) \\
\sigma(v_1, k + w(e_1)) + d(v_1) &\leq \sigma(v_2, k + w(e_1) + w(e_2)) \\
&\ldots \\
\sigma(v_i, k + \textstyle\sum_{j=1}^{i} w(e_j)) + d(v_i) &\leq \sigma(v_{i+1}, k + \textstyle\sum_{j=1}^{i+1} w(e_j))
\end{aligned}
$$

Summing the r inequalities defined for the r edges of $\mathcal{C}$, we get the following inequality:

$$\sigma(v_0, k) + d(\mathcal{C}) \leq \sigma(v_0, k + w(\mathcal{C})) \tag{3.6}$$

This inequality shows that $w(\mathcal{C}) = 0$ is not possible because $d(\mathcal{C}) > 0$. Thus, a necessary condition for the existence of a schedule is that all cycles in the graph have a positive weight. We will see that it is also a sufficient condition. Now, consider a schedule σ (we can thus assume that $w(\mathcal{C}) > 0$). For any $m \in \mathbb{N}$, the inequality (3.6) is true for $k = mw(\mathcal{C})$. By induction on m, we get $\sigma(v_0, 0) + md(\mathcal{C}) \leq \sigma(v_0, mw(\mathcal{C}))$, and because $\sigma(v_0, 0) \geq 0$, $\sigma(v_0, mw(\mathcal{C})) \geq md(\mathcal{C})$.

Let $D(\sigma, n) = \max\{\sigma(v, k) + d(v) \mid v \in V, 0 \leq k < n\}$. $D(\sigma, n)$ is the makespan of σ when considering only the n first iterations. By definition, $\lambda_\sigma = \lim_{N \to \infty} \inf\{\frac{D(\sigma, n)}{n} \mid n \geq N\}$. Assume $N > 1$, and for any $n \geq N$, let $m = \lfloor \frac{n}{w(\mathcal{C})} \rfloor$. Because $D(\sigma, n) \geq D(\sigma, mw(\mathcal{C})) \geq \sigma(v_0, mw(\mathcal{C}))$, we get:

$$\frac{D(\sigma, n)}{n} \geq \frac{md(\mathcal{C})}{n} \geq \left(1 - \frac{w(\mathcal{C})}{n}\right) \rho(\mathcal{C}) \geq \left(1 - \frac{w(\mathcal{C})}{N}\right) \rho(\mathcal{C})$$

This inequality also holds for $\inf\{\frac{D(\sigma, n)}{n} \mid n \geq N\}$, and finally, when N tends toward infinity, we obtain the first lower bound (inequality (3.4)): $\lambda_\sigma \geq \rho(\mathcal{C})$.

To prove the second lower bound, we use Theorem 2 stated in Chapter 1. If p resources are available, then $pD(\sigma, n)$ is greater than the total duration of operations in the set $\{(v, k) \mid v \in V, 0 \leq k < n\}$. Thus, for any $n \in \mathbb{N}$, $pD(\sigma, n) \geq n \sum_{v \in V} d(v)$, and finally, $p\lambda_\sigma \geq \sum_{v \in V} d(v)$. ∎

From now on, we will assume that the graph $G = (V, E, d, w)$ is such that $d(v) > 0$ for all $v \in V$, and $w(\mathcal{C}) > 0$ for all cycles $\mathcal{C}$ in G. Thus, $\rho(\mathcal{C})$ is well-defined, and $\rho(\mathcal{C}) > 0$ for any cycle $\mathcal{C}$.

3.3 Solving BCS(∞)

In this section, we explain how to solve the basic cyclic scheduling problem with unlimited resources. First, we will present two important tools that we will use throughout this chapter: The first tool is the scheduling technique for potential graphs; the second is the well-known Bellman-Ford algorithm.

3.3.1 Scheduling Potential Graphs

We make a short digression to introduce *potential graphs*, which are task graphs with weighted edges and cycles. In the model of Chapter 1, the edges model dependence constraints and are not weighted. Task graphs are acyclic, because a cycle in the graph would imply a task depending on itself.

Consider a task system where each task v has several attributes: a duration (or weight) $p(v)$, a ready time $r(v)$, and a due time (or deadline) $d(v)$. We add a special task s, called a source task. Let $\sigma(v)$ denote the starting time for the execution of v. We assume that the source task starts at time step 0: $\sigma(s) = 0$. All scheduling constraints can be modeled through an edge-weighted graph, with the following meaning. Each vertex of the graph represents a task. An edge $e = (u, v)$ means that we must satisfy the constraint $\sigma(u) + w(e) \leq \sigma(v)$. The edge-weighting function $w : E \longrightarrow \mathbb{Z}$ is defined as follows (note that negative values for w are allowed):

- **Dependences.** If task v depends on u, we introduce the edge $e = (u, v)$ and we let $w(e) = p(u)$. We retrieve the familiar precedence equation $\sigma(u) + p(u) \leq \sigma(v)$.

- **Ready Times.** To express that v cannot start before time step $r(v)$, we introduce an edge $e = (s, v)$ with weight $w(e) = r(v)$. The corresponding constraint is $\sigma(s) + r(v) \leq \sigma(v)$, which is the desired inequality, as $\sigma(s) = 0$.

- **Due Times.** To express that v must complete execution before time step $d(v)$, we introduce an edge $e = (v, s)$ with weight $w(e) = p(v) - d(v)$. We obtain $\sigma(v) + p(v) - d(v) \leq \sigma(s) = 0$, i.e., v completes execution before time step $d(v)$.

We end up with a graph containing cycles (e.g., as soon as a task has both a ready time and a due time) and whose edges have weights, possibly negative. Note that, with the same technique, we can model *relative* deadlines, i.e., constraints that express the fact that a task v must complete execution at most $d(v)$ time steps after the starting time of another task u. We just have to introduce an edge from v to u of weight $p(v) - d(v)$ as we did for absolute deadlines.

Is it always possible to derive a schedule σ that satisfies all constraints (assuming an unlimited number of processors)? The answer turns out to be rather simple. We formalize things before giving the classical result that a schedule exists iff there is no circuit in the graph whose weight is (strictly) positive.

Definition 17 (Potential Graph) *A potential graph $G = (V, E, w)$ is a task graph where $w : E \longrightarrow \mathbb{Z}$ defines edge weights. A schedule σ for G is a function $\sigma : V \longrightarrow \mathbb{N}$ such that all "potential" inequalities are satisfied:*

$$\forall e = (u, v) \in E, \ \sigma(u) + w(e) \leq \sigma(v)$$

Theorem 12 *There exists a schedule for a potential graph $G = (V, E, w)$ iff all simple circuits in G have a nonpositive weight.*

Note that the proof is constructive: if all simple circuits in G have a nonpositive weight, we build a schedule σ satisfying all "potential" inequalities.

Proof Assume first that there exists a simple circuit $\mathcal{C}: \mathcal{C} = v_0 \to v_1 \to \ldots \to v_{p-1} \to v_p = v_0$. Let e_i denote the edge (v_i, v_{i+1}) in this circuit. If a schedule σ exists, then $\sigma(v_j) + w(e_j) \leq \sigma(v_{j+1})$ for $0 \leq j \leq p - 1$. Summing up, we obtain $\sigma(v_0) + \sum_{j=0}^{p-1} w(e_j) \leq \sigma(v_0)$; hence the weight $w(\mathcal{C}) = \sum_{j=0}^{p-1} w(e_j)$ of the circuit $\mathcal{C}$ is nonpositive.

Assume now that each simple circuit in G has a nonpositive weight. We add a source vertex s to G, and we add a zero-weight edge $e = (s, v)$ from s to each vertex v of G. We claim that we can choose the length $t(s, v)$ of the longest path from s to v as schedule; we let $\sigma(v) = t(s, v)$ for each vertex $v \in V$.

Let $v \in V$. First we show that the longest path from s to v is well-defined. Consider the set of all paths from s to v; this set is not empty, as there is an edge from s to v. Consider any path $\mathcal{P}$ from s to v. If $\mathcal{P}$ is not simple, then it contains a simple circuit, whose length is nonpositive. Removing this circuit from $\mathcal{P}$ gives another path whose length is at least that of $\mathcal{P}$. Remove all circuits until obtaining a simple path; its length will be not smaller than that of the original path $\mathcal{P}$. Hence longest paths from s to v can be searched among simple paths from s to v. But the number of such paths is finite, and we can safely let

$$t(s, v) = \max\{w(\mathcal{P}) \mid \mathcal{P} \text{ is a simple path from } s \text{ to } v\}$$

Next let $\sigma(v) = t(s, v)$ for each vertex $v \in V$. To prove that all "potential" inequalities are satisfied, consider an edge $e = (u, v)$. The length of the longest path from s to v is not smaller than the length of the longest path from s to u plus the weight of the edge e; see Figure 3.5. In other words, t satisfies the triangular inequality; $t(s, u) + w(e) \leq t(s, v)$ for each $e = (u, v)$. This can be rewritten as $\sigma(u) + w(e) \leq \sigma(v)$. ∎

3.3.2 The Bellman-Ford Algorithm

In this section, we introduce the Bellman-Ford algorithm, which we use to compute shortest (or longest) paths in graphs with cycles. We refer the reader to the book of Cormen, Leiserson, and Rivest [26] for a detailed presentation of various path-computation algorithms. We present here the algorithm for *longest* paths for consistence with Theorem 12 and our need

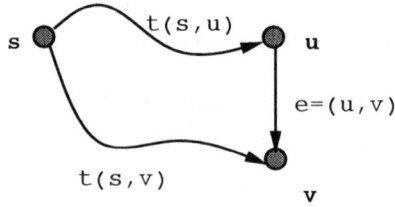

Figure 3.5: Triangular inequality for longest paths.

in the next section. A similar algorithm can be proposed for shortest paths (as in [26]); we just have to change the sign of all edge weights (and the condition is then that all cycles in the graph have a nonnegative weight).

Let $G = (V, E, w)$ be a graph whose edges are weighted by a function $w : E \longrightarrow \mathbb{Z}$, and assume that all cycles have a nonpositive weight. The goal is to compute longest paths from a source vertex $s \in V$ to all vertices of G. As shown in the proof of Theorem 12, we can restrict to simple paths. Still, we need an efficient (polynomial) algorithm, the Bellman-Ford algorithm, which is based on the idea of "relaxing" edges. For each vertex $v \in V$, we update two variables:

1. $d(v)$, which is the length of the current longest path, denoted $LP(v)$, from s to v;

2. $\Pi(v)$, which is the immediate predecessor of v in the current longest path: $LP(v) : s \rightsquigarrow \Pi(v) \to v$.

These variables are initialized with the following procedure:

Initialization

$d(s) \leftarrow 0$
$\forall v \in V$
$\quad d(v) \leftarrow -\infty$
$\quad \Pi(v) \leftarrow \mathrm{NIL}$

To "relax" edge $e = (u, v)$, we use the following procedure:

Relaxation(e=(u,v))

if $d(v) < d(u) + w(e)$ then
$\quad d(v) \leftarrow d(u) + w(e)$
$\quad \Pi(v) \leftarrow u$

The Bellman-Ford algorithm can now be stated:

Bellman-Ford Algorithm

> Initialization
> for $i = 1$ to $|V| - 1$ do
>   for each edge $e \in E$ do Relaxation(e)
> Termination check
> for each edge $e = (u, v) \in E$ do
>   if $d(v) < d(u) + w(e)$ then
>   return "positive weight cycle reachable from s"
>   otherwise return "OK"

For each $v \in V$, let $\delta(s, v)$ denote the length of the longest path from s to v ($\delta(s, v) = -\infty$ if no such path exists). We have the following property.

Lemma 6 *Let $v \in V$. Throughout the algorithm, $d(v) \leq \delta(s, v)$. As soon as $d(v) = \delta(s, v)$, $d(v)$ remains unchanged until the end.*

Proof The property holds at the initialization: $d(s) = 0 = \delta(s, s)$, and $d(v) = -\infty$ for each $v \neq s$.

Assume by contradiction that, at some step of the algorithm, there exists v such that $d(v) > \delta(s, v)$. More precisely, let v be the first vertex for which $d(v)$ becomes strictly larger than $\delta(s, v)$; $d(v)$ has just been updated, through the relaxation of an edge $e = (u, v)$ for some $u \in V$ (after calling **Relaxation(e)**). Then $d(v) = d(u) + w(e)$ and $d(v) > \delta(s, v)$. Because of the triangular inequality, $\delta(s, v) \geq \delta(s, u) + w(e)$. Hence $d(u) > \delta(s, u)$, a contradiction because v is the first vertex that has this property.

Finally, $d(v)$ is never decreased when updated, hence the second part of the assumption. ∎

We now prove the correctness of the Bellman-Ford algorithm. We also show how it can be used to effectively build a positive weight cycle, when one exists.

Proof (of Bellman-Ford Algorithm) If there is no cycle of positive weight in G, then at the end of the algorithm, $d(v) = \delta(s, v), \forall v \in V$. To see this, consider $v \in V$ that can be reached from s by the longest (simple) path $\mathcal{P} : v_0 = s \rightarrow v_1 \rightarrow \ldots \rightarrow v_k = v$. The path is simple, hence $k \leq |V| - 1$. By induction on step i of the outermost loop, it is easy to see that $d(v_i) = \delta(s, v_i)$, and thus, $d_v = \delta(s, v)$ in at most $|V| - 1$ steps. Also, $d(v) = \delta(s, v) \geq \delta(s, u) + w(e) = d(u) + w(e)$ at the end of the algorithm, and all the tests return a negative answer.

On the other hand, assume that there exists a cycle $\mathcal{C}$ denoted by $\mathcal{C} = (v_0, v_1, \ldots, v_{k-1}, v_k = v_0)$ of positive weight. If the algorithm had returned the answer "OK" we would have $d(v_i) \geq d(v_{i-1}) + w(e_i)$ for $1 \leq i \leq k$, where e_i denotes the edge (v_{i-1}, v_i) in C. Summing up, we would get $w(C) \leq 0$, a contradiction. Therefore, there is an edge $e = (u, v)$ such that $d(v) < d(u) + w(e)$.

Let $e_0 = (v_1, v_0)$ be such an edge. Build backwards a *simple* path $\mathcal{P}$, as long as possible, following the father relation Π computed in **Relaxation**: $v_{k+1} = \Pi(v_k)$ for $k \geq 1$. This construction could stop either because $\Pi(v_k) = $ NIL, or because $\Pi(v_k)$ occurs already in $\mathcal{P}$. We claim that only the second case can happen. Indeed, for a vertex v, denote by $I(v)$ the last iteration i where $d(v)$ was modified, and $I(v) = 0$ if $d(v)$ is never modified, i.e., if $\Pi(v) = $ NIL. For any vertex v, $I(\Pi(v)) \geq I(v) - 1$, and because $d(v_0) < d(v_1) + w(e)$, $d(v_1)$ has been modified at the last iteration: $I(v_1) \geq |V| - 1$. Now, if the first vertex of $\mathcal{P}$ is v_k (the path has $k + 1$ vertices), we obtain by summation $I(v_k) \geq I(v_1) - (k - 1) \geq |V| - k$. If the first case occurs, $\Pi(v_k) = (NIL)$, then $I(v_k) = 0$, and thus $k \geq |V|$. The path $\mathcal{P} : v_k \rightsquigarrow v_0$ is not a simple path, a contradiction. Finally, $\Pi(v_k) = v_j$ for some j between 0 and $k - 1$, and this forms a cycle $C : v_j \rightarrow v_{k-1} \rightsquigarrow v_j$.

Now, remember that just after the relaxation of an edge $e = (u, v)$, we have $d(v) = d(u) + w(e)$, and $\Pi(v) = u$. Then, $d(u)$ can only increase. Thus, for each edge of C, $d(v) \leq d(\Pi(v)) + w(e)$. Summing these inequalities along the cycle, we obtain $w(C) \geq 0$. Furthermore, at least one of these inequalities is strict, for example, the edge (v_r, v_{r-1}) where v_r is the last vertex in C that has been modified. Thus, $w(C) > 0$. ∎

The complexity of the Bellman-Ford algorithm is $O(|V||E|) \leq O(|V|^3)$.

3.3.3 Optimal Schedule for Unlimited Resources

We are ready to solve BCS(∞), the basic cyclic scheduling problem with unlimited resources ($p = \infty$). Given a graph $G = (V, E, d, w)$ (d defines the vertex weights, w the edge weights), we search a schedule σ whose average cycle time λ_σ is as small as possible. By Theorem 11, we know that $\lambda_\sigma \geq \rho(C)$ for all cycles C in G. We will show that this lower bound is tight. There is a schedule whose average cycle time is equal to the maximum cycle ratio in the graph.

We assume that all the cycles in G have a positive weight; otherwise no schedule exists (Theorem 11). Then we will build a schedule of the form $\sigma(v, k) = c_v + \lambda k$ where $c_v \in \mathbb{Q}$, and $\lambda \in \mathbb{Q}$. Actually, with this formula, σ is not exactly a schedule as defined in Section 3.2.2 because it does not always take integer values. In this case, we can still consider $\lfloor \sigma \rfloor$ defined by $\lfloor \sigma \rfloor(v, k) = \lfloor c_v + \lambda k \rfloor$; it is also a schedule (if σ satisfies Equation (3.1) then $\lfloor \sigma \rfloor$ also satisfies it) with same average cycle time. This schedule is not a cyclic schedule, but a K-periodic schedule (see [56] to know more about K-periodic schedules). Nevertheless, to make things simpler, we will still call σ a cyclic schedule even if λ is not an integer.

For a cyclic schedule, dependence constraints can be simplified. Indeed, the constraints (3.1)

$$\forall e = (u, v) \in E, \ \forall k \geq 0, \ \sigma(u, k) + d(u)) \leq \sigma(v, k + w(e))$$

reduce to

$$\forall e = (u, v) \in E, \ c_u + d(u) \leq c_v + \lambda w(e) \tag{3.7}$$

There is a simple characterization of all possible values for λ.

Definition 18 *Let $\lambda \in \mathbb{Q}$. We define an edge-weighted graph $G'_\lambda = (V', E', w'_\lambda)$, from G, as follows:*

- *Vertices of G'_λ: add to V a new vertex s: $V' = V \cup \{s\}$.*

- *Edges of G'_λ: for each vertex $v \in V$ add to E an edge from s to v: $E' = E \cup (\{s\} \times V)$.*

- *Weight of the edges of G'_λ: let $w'_\lambda(e) = 0$ if $e = (u, v) \in E' \setminus E$, and let $w'_\lambda(e) = d(u) - \lambda w(e)$ otherwise.*

Lemma 7 *λ is a valid average cycle time (i.e., there is a schedule with average cycle time equal to λ) if and only if G'_λ has no cycle of positive weight.*

Proof Note first that G'_λ and G have the same cycles. Furthermore, for a cycle $\mathcal{C}$, $w'_\lambda(\mathcal{C}) = d(\mathcal{C}) - \lambda w(\mathcal{C})$. Thus, $w'_\lambda(\mathcal{C}) > 0$ if and only if $\lambda < \rho(\mathcal{C})$.

Now, if λ is a valid average cycle time, then $\lambda \geq \rho(\mathcal{C})$ for any cycle $\mathcal{C}$ (Theorem 11). Thus, G'_λ has no cycle of positive weight.

Conversely, if G'_λ has no cycle of positive weight, one can define, for all $v \in V$, the longest path (in G'_λ) from s to v, which we denote by $t(s, v)$. By definition, $t(s, v)$ satisfies the following triangular inequality:

$$\forall e = (u, v) \in E, \ t(s, v) \geq t(s, u) + w'_\lambda(e)$$

i.e.,

$$\forall e = (u, v) \in E, \ t(s, u) + d(u) \leq t(s, v) + \lambda w(e)$$

This proves that $\sigma(v, k) = t(s, v) + \lambda k$ is a valid schedule (or $\lfloor \sigma \rfloor$ if λ is not an integer). ∎

The preceding discussion makes the link with potential graph scheduling clear. From Theorem 11, we know that if there is a cycle $\mathcal{C} \in G$ such that $\lambda < \rho(\mathcal{C})$, then no schedule exists with average cycle time λ. Conversely, if $\lambda \geq \rho(\mathcal{C})$ for all cycles $\mathcal{C}$, then we can restrict to schedules of the form $\sigma(v, k) = c_v + \lambda k$ (or the floor function of it). Then, dependence constraints reduce to the constraints (3.7), which define a potential scheduling problem on G'_λ. The fact that the weights $w'_\lambda(e)$ may not be integral (if λ is not an integer) is not a problem; the Bellman-Ford algorithm can still be used to solve the potential scheduling problem. (We point out that when λ is an integer, the schedule built this way is integral. No need to consider $\lfloor \sigma \rfloor$ because $\lfloor \sigma \rfloor = \sigma$ in this case.)

Lemma 7 has two important consequences:

- Given a value λ, it is easy to determine if λ is a valid initiation interval, and if so, to build a corresponding schedule. We just apply the Bellman-Ford algorithm (Section 3.3.2) on the graph G'_λ.

- The optimal initiation interval λ_∞ is the smallest value λ such that G'_λ has no positive cycle. Therefore, $\lambda_\infty = 0$ if G is an acyclic graph and $\lambda_\infty = \max\{\rho(\mathcal{C}) \mid \mathcal{C} \text{ simple cycle of } G\}$ otherwise. (The reader can check that $\rho(\mathcal{C})$ is maximal for simple cycles; see also the proof of Theorem 13.)

Example 4, Continued

In this example, we have three simple cycles: $\rho(C_1) = \frac{7}{3}$ for $C_1 : A \to B \to C \to A$, $\rho(C_2) = \frac{24}{2}$ for $C_2 : B \to F \to D \to B$, and $\rho(C_3) = \frac{24}{2}$ for $C_3 : E \to F \to E$. Hence $\lambda_\infty = 12$. Note that the proof of Theorem 12 gives the whole schedule; we have to compute longest paths in the graph G'_{12}, which is represented in Figure 3.6. Longest paths $t(s, v)$ from the source

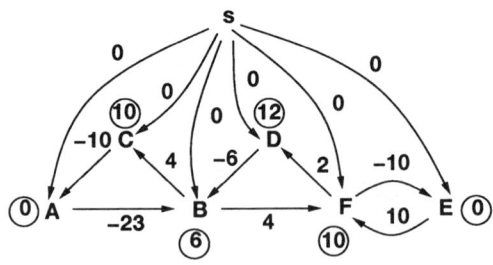

Figure 3.6: The graph G'_{12}.

vertex s to all other vertices v are the circled values in Figure 3.6. For example, $t(s, D) = 12$, the length of the path going from s to D through E

and F. According to Theorem 12 and Lemma 7, we derive a valid schedule $\sigma(v, k) = c_v + \lambda k$ by letting $c_v = t(s, v)$. Two consecutive slices (in steady state) are represented in Figure 3.7. As in Figure 3.4, only dependences within the same iteration are depicted (by arrows). To help the reader, execution times are summarized in Table 3.2.

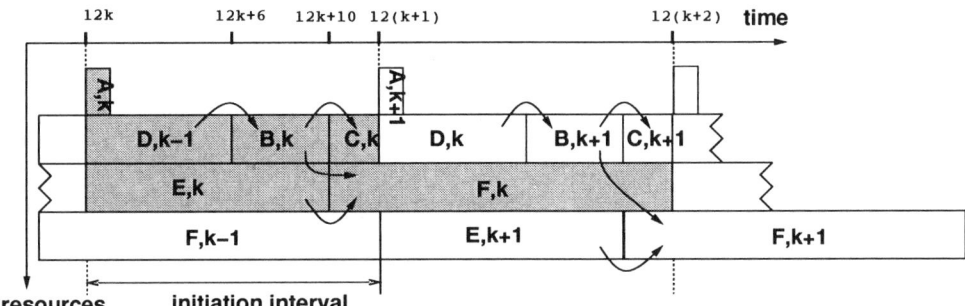

Figure 3.7: The schedule with unlimited resources ($\lambda_\infty = 12$).

Time step	λk	$\lambda k + 6$	$\lambda k + 10$	$\lambda k + 12$	$\lambda k + 18$	$\lambda k + 22$
Processor P_1	(A, k)			$(A, k+1)$		
Processor P_2	$(D, k-1)$	(B, k)	(C, k)	(D, k)	$(B, k+1)$	$(C, k+1)$
Processor P_3	(E, k)		(F, k)			
Processor P_4				$(E, k+1)$		$(F, k+1)$

Table 3.2: Starting times for the schedule with unlimited resources.

We need four processors to achieve this schedule. Note that because we start a new operation instance every λ_∞ steps, we may need more processors than generic tasks. For example, $w(F) = 14 > \lambda_\infty = 12$, hence there are two processors (P_3 and P_4 in Figure 3.7) to alternately compute the successive instances of F. $\qquad\Box$

To conclude this section, we formally state the main result in Theorem 13.

Theorem 13 *Let $G = (V, E, d, w)$ be a graph. The minimum possible average cycle time λ_∞ of a schedule using unlimited resources is $\lambda_\infty = 0$ if G is acyclic and is the maximum cycle ratio ρ in G otherwise.*

Corollary 2 *Given a graph $G = (V, E, d, w)$, BCS(∞) can be solved in time $O(|V||E|\log(|V|\Delta))$, where $\Delta = d_{\max}(w_{\max})^2$, $d_{\max} = \max_{v \in V} d(v)$ and where $w_{\max} = \max_{e \in E} w(e)$.*

Proof   We assume that G has at least one cycle, otherwise $\lambda_\infty = 0$. Thus, λ_∞ is equal to the maximum cycle ratio in G. Let us first check that this maximum is reached for a simple cycle. Consider a nonsimple cycle C, which can be decomposed into two cycles C_1 and C_2 where C_1 is a simple cycle. Now, we use the following simple inequality: Let a, b, c, d be positive numbers and $m = \max(\frac{a}{b}, \frac{c}{d})$. Then, $a \le mb$ and $c \le md$, thus $(a + c) \le m(b + d)$. This proves that:

$$\frac{a+c}{b+d} \le \frac{a}{b} \quad \text{or} \quad \frac{a+c}{b+d} \le \frac{c}{d}$$

Apply this inequality to C: Either $\rho(C) \le \rho(C_1)$ or $\rho(C) \le \rho(C_2)$. In the first case, we are done; in the second case, we can apply the same decomposition to C_2, and finally, we get a simple cycle with better ratio.

In the following we denote by ρ the maximum cycle ratio in G. Note that because $\rho(C)$ is maximal for a simple cycle C, $\rho(C) \le d(C) \le |V| d_{\max}$ (and $\rho(C) > 0$ because we assumed that G has at least one cycle). We first explain how we can compute $\overline{\rho} = \lceil \rho \rceil$. We will then extend the technique to the case where the maximum cycle ratio is not an integer. In both cases, we perform a binary search in an interval $]b_{\inf}, b_{\sup}]$ starting from the interval $]0, |V| d_{\max}]$, and making sure that there is at least one cycle C such that $\rho(C) \in]b_{\inf}, b_{\sup}]$, but no cycle C such $\rho(C) > b_{\sup}$.

In the first case, we look for $\overline{\rho}$ among integer values. While $b_{\sup} - b_{\inf} > 1$, we let $\lambda = \lceil (b_{\inf} + b_{\sup})/2 \rceil$, and we call the Bellman-Ford algorithm in G'_λ. If the algorithm returns the existence of a positive weight cycle, then $\lambda < \rho$, and we continue the search in the interval $]\lambda, b_{\sup}]$. Otherwise, $\lambda \ge \rho$, and we continue the search in the interval $]b_{\inf}, \lambda]$. The algorithm stops when $b_{\sup} = b_{\inf} + 1$, and in this case, $\overline{\rho} = b_{\sup}$. Each step has a cost $O(|V||E|)$, and the number of steps is $O(\log(|V| d_{\max}))$, hence the overall complexity.

In the second case, when ρ is not an integer, we perform a binary search among rational numbers. We first give a lower bound for the minimal difference η between two different cycle ratios; if C_1 and C_2 are two cycles with different ratios, then:

$$|\rho(C_1) - \rho(C_2)| = \frac{|d(C_1)w(C_2) - d(C_2)w(C_1)|}{w(C_1)w(C_2)} \ge \frac{1}{(w_{\max})^2} = \eta$$

We then follow the same technique. While $b_{\sup} - b_{\inf} > \eta$, we let $\lambda = (b_{\inf} + b_{\sup})/2$, and we use the Bellman-Ford algorithm to decide if $\lambda > \rho$. When $b_{\sup} - b_{\inf} \le \eta$, we are sure that there is one and only one value $\rho(C)$ for a cycle C such that $b_{\inf} < \rho(C) \le b_{\sup}$. We conclude with a last call to the Bellman-Ford algorithm with $\lambda = b_{\inf}$. Because $\rho > b_{\inf}$, the algorithm returns the existence of a positive weight cycle. Let C be such a cycle (built, for example, as explained in Section 3.3.2): $w'_\lambda(\mathcal{C}) = d(\mathcal{C}) - \lambda w(\mathcal{C}) > 0$, thus $\rho(\mathcal{C}) > \lambda$, and $\rho(\mathcal{C})$ is the desired value for ρ. The number of steps is now $\log(|V|d_{\max}(w_{\max})^2)$.

The algorithm for computing ρ is borrowed from [51].   ■

3.4 Solving BCS(p)

We first make a short digression to study the NP-completeness of BCS(p). Sorry to break the main thread, but we have to assess the complexity of the problem before introducing heuristics.

3.4.1 NP-Completeness of BCS(p)

The decision problem associated with BCS(p) is to decide, given a number of resources p and a bound $K \in \mathbb{N}^*$, if there exists a schedule with average cycle time at most K. To the best of our knowledge, whether this problem belongs to NP or not is still an open question. The problem is that we don't know if a solution (a certificate) can be coded in polynomial size.

Nevertheless, we can show that restricting to integral cyclic schedules, i.e., schedules of the form $\sigma(v, k) = c_v + \lambda k$ where $\lambda \in \mathbb{N}$, leads to an NP-complete problem.

Definition 19 (Dec-BCS(p)) *The decision problem Dec-BCS(p) associated with BCS(p) is the following. Given a graph $G = (V, E, d, w)$, a number of identical resources $p \geq 1$, and a bound $K \in \mathbb{N}^*$, does there exists an integral cyclic schedule σ whose average cycle time λ_σ is at most K?*

Theorem 14 *Dec-BCS(p) is NP-complete.*

Proof We first show that Dec-BCS(p) belongs to NP. We restrict to graphs $G = (V, E, d, w)$ such that $K \leq \sum_{v \in V} d(v)$; otherwise the answer for G is obviously "YES". Given an integral cyclic schedule σ whose average cycle time λ is at most K (and $\lambda > 0$ because $p\lambda \geq \sum_{v \in V} d(v)$), we can first check in linear time that dependence constraints are satisfied. Indeed, we have to check that each inequality (3.7) is satisfied; there are $|E|$ such inequalities, and each inequality involves only numbers that are polynomially bounded ($\log(\lambda)$ is linear in $\log(d)$ because $\lambda \leq \sum_{v \in V} d(v)$).

To check that no more than p resources are busy at each time step is a bit trickier. The problem is that a verification polynomial in p or λ is not admissible, we need a verification polynomial in $|V|$, $|E|$, possibly in $\log(p)$, $\log(d)$, or $\log(w)$. Because the schedule is periodic with period λ, it is sufficient to check the resource constraint in a time interval $I = [T, T + \lambda[$

where $T \geq \max_{v \in V} c_v$. At a given time step t, the number $\mathcal{A}(v)$ of active operations (v, k) is the number of non negative integers in the interval $](t - c_v)/\lambda - d(v)/\lambda, (t - c_v)/\lambda]$. We write $d(v) - 1 = r(v)\lambda + s(v)$ with $0 \leq s(v) < \lambda$. Then the reader can check that $\mathcal{A}(v) = r(v)$ if $(t - c_v) - \lambda \lfloor (t - c_v)/\lambda \rfloor \geq s(v) + 1$, and $\mathcal{A}(v) = r(v) + 1$ otherwise. Thus, for each $v \in V$, there are at most two important time steps to check: the time step $t_1 \in I$ such that $t_1 - c_v$ is a multiple of λ (and for which $\mathcal{A}(v) = r(v) + 1$), and the time step $t_2 \in I$ (if it exists) such that $(t_2 - c_v) - \lambda \lfloor (t_2 - c_v)/\lambda \rfloor = s(v) + 1$. There are thus only $2 * V$ time steps to check, and the resource constraints can be checked in polynomial time; $O(V)$ additions, each one with $O(V)$ terms involving polynomially bounded numbers.

Next, consider an arbitrary instance Inst_1 of Dec(p), the decision problem associated with Pb(p), the problem of scheduling a DAG with p processors (see Chapter 1). Consider a DAG $G = (V, E, w)$, a number of resources $p \geq 1$, and an execution bound $K \in \mathbb{N}^*$, and ask whether there exists a schedule σ whose makespan is not greater than K: $MS(\sigma, p) \leq K$.

Theorem 5 shows that Dec(p) is NP-complete. We show that Dec(p) can be polynomially reduced to Dec-BCS(p). We build an instance Inst_2 of problem Dec-BCS(p) as follows. We let $G = (V', E', d', w')$ with $V' = V$, $d' = w$ (the vertices have the same duration), and $E' = E \cup E''$, where $E'' = \{(u, v) \mid u \text{ exit vertex of } V, v \text{ entry vertex of } V\}$. In other words, we add an edge from every exit vertex of V to every entry vertex of V. By definition of entry and exit vertices, these edges were not present in E. We let $w'(e) = 0$ for each edge $e \in E$ and $w(e) = 1$ for each edge $e \in E''$. Finally, we let $p' = p$ and $K' = K$ and ask whether there exists a cyclic schedule for G' with p' processors whose average cycle time is at most K'. The construction of Inst_2 is polynomial (and even quadratic, as we add at most $O(|V|^2)$ edges) in the size of Inst_1. Moreover, if Inst_1 admits a solution schedule σ, then the cyclic schedule $\sigma_c(v, k) = \sigma(v) + MS(\sigma, p)k$ is a solution to Inst_2.

Conversely, if there exists a cyclic schedule $\sigma_c(v, k) = c_v + \lambda k$, whose initiation interval λ is not greater than K, then we define the schedule σ for the DAG G by $\sigma(v) = c_v - \min_{u \in V} c_u$, to start execution at time step 0. σ is a valid schedule because the edges in E with zero weight enforce all dependences in G. Also, because of the edges in E'', there is no overlap between two different instances, i.e., the last operation instance (u, k) must be completed before any operation instance $(v, k+1)$ can be started. Therefore $\max_{u \in V}\{\sigma(u) + w(u)\} - \min_{v \in V} \sigma(v) \leq \lambda$, hence $MS(\sigma, p) \leq \lambda \leq K$, and Inst_1 admits a solution. ∎

Note that the second part of the proof could be adapted to noncyclic schedules. Thus, the decision problem for general schedules is at least as complex as Dec-BCS(p). But the first part of the proof, which shows that

Dec-BCS(p) is in NP, does not apply to any schedule because we do not know if such a schedule can be coded in polynomial size.

We now focus on heuristics whose performance can be guaranteed. We denote by λ_p, the minimal achievable average cycle time for a schedule:

$$\lambda_p = \inf\{\lambda_\sigma \mid \sigma \text{ is a schedule, for } p \text{ resources, with average cycle time } \lambda_\sigma\}$$

Remember that by Theorem 11, $p\lambda_p \geq \sum_{v \in V} d(v)$ and for any cycle $\mathcal{C}$ in G, $\lambda_p \geq \rho(\mathcal{C})$, i.e., $\lambda_p \geq \lambda_\infty$.

Many heuristics have been proposed in the literature, but very few are guaranteed, only the heuristic by Gasperoni and Schwiegelshohn [46] and its extension by Calland, Darte, and Robert [18]. We explain this last one; it uses traditional concepts introduced in software pipelining heuristics: modulo scheduling, loop compaction, and loop shifting.

We start by studying loop compaction, the technique used for the example of Section 3.2.3.

3.4.2 Loop Compaction

Loop compaction consists in scheduling the body of the loop without trying to mix up iterations. The general principle is the following. We consider the graph $A(G)$ that captures the dependences lying in the loop body (called *loop-independent* dependences in loop terminology). These are the dependences whose distance is equal to 0. The graph $A(G)$ is acyclic; it can be scheduled using techniques for acyclic graphs, for example, list scheduling. Then, the new pattern built for the loop body is repeated to define a cyclic schedule for the whole loop. See Section 3.2.3 for an example of this technique.

We now formalize loop compaction and study its performances.

Algorithm (Loop Compaction)

Let $G = (V, E, d, w)$ be a dependence graph.

1. Define $A(G) = (V, E', d)$ where $E' = \{e \in E \mid w(e) = 0\}$.

2. Perform a list scheduling σ_a on $A(G)$. Compute the makespan of σ_a:
   $\lambda = \max_{v \in V}(\sigma_a(v) + d(v))$.

3. Define the cyclic schedule σ by:
   $$\forall v \in V, \ \forall k \in \mathbb{N}, \ \sigma(v, k) = \sigma_a(v) + \lambda k$$

Lemma 8 *The schedule σ given by the loop compaction algorithm is a valid cyclic schedule for G. Furthermore, $p\lambda \leq p\lambda_p + (p-1)\Phi(G)$ where $\Phi(G)$ is the maximal weight of a path in $A(G)$.*

Proof First, $A(G)$ is acyclic. Indeed, if $A(G)$ has a cycle $\mathcal{C}$, then the weight $w(\mathcal{C})$ is equal to 0. But $\mathcal{C}$ is also a cycle of G, and we assumed that all cycles of G have a positive weight. The schedule σ_a is thus well-defined, and we can let λ be its makespan. As in Theorem 6, there exists a path $\mathcal{P}$ in $A(G)$ such that $p\lambda \leq \sum_{v\in V} d(v) + (p-1)d(\mathcal{P})$. Because $\sum_{v\in V} d(v) \leq p\lambda_p$ and because $d(\mathcal{P}) \leq \Phi(G)$ by definition of $\Phi(G)$, we get the desired inequality.

It remains to prove that σ is a valid cyclic schedule. Resource constraints are obviously met because of the list scheduling and the definition of λ, which ensures that different iterations do not overlap. To show that dependence constraints are satisfied for each $e = (u,v)$ of E, we need to verify inequalities (3.7):

$$\forall e = (u,v) \in E, \ \sigma_a(u) + d(u) \leq \sigma_a(v) + \lambda w(e)$$

On one hand, suppose that $e \in E'$, i.e., $w(e) = 0$. Because σ_a is a schedule for $A(G)$, $\sigma_a(u) + d(u) \leq \sigma_a(v)$, and the inequality is satisfied. On the other hand, if e was deleted, then $w(e) > 0$, and thus $\lambda w(e) \geq \lambda$. But, by definition of λ, we have $\sigma_a(u) + d(u) - \sigma_a(v) \leq \sigma_a(u) + d(u) \leq \lambda$. Thus, the inequality is also satisfied. ■

Note that we cannot conclude, as in Chapter 1, that we get a guaranteed heuristic. Indeed, in Chapter 1, we were able to bound $\Phi(G)$ because of Proposition 1. Here, $\Phi(G)$ has a priori nothing to do with λ_p. Our goal is now to mix up iterations (through loop shifting; see the following section) so that the resulting acyclic graph $A(G)$ has the smallest possible $\Phi(G)$.

More precisely, we will show how to shift operations such that:

- the maximal weight $\Phi(G)$ of a path in $A(G)$ is as small as possible, because it is tightly linked to the guaranteed bound for the list scheduling; and

- the number of edges in the acyclic graph is minimal, to reduce the number of dependence constraints for the acyclic scheduling problem.

3.4.3 Loop Shifting

We illustrate the concept of loop shifting on the example of Section 3.2.3.

Example 4, Continued

PRELUDE   Where PRELUDE is:

DO k=1, N-1

  (A): a(k) = c(k-1)

  (D): d(k-1) = f(k-2)/3

  (B): b(k) = a(k-2) * d(k-1)

  (C): c(k) = b(k) + 1

  (E): e(k) = sin(f(k-2))

  (F): f(k-1) = log(b(k-1) + e(k-1))

ENDDO

POSTLUDE

a(0) = c(-1)

b(0) = a(-2) * d(-1)

c(0) = b(0) + 1

e(0) = sin(f(-2))

and POSTLUDE is:

d(N-1) = f(N-2)/3

f(N-1) = log(b(N-1) + e(N-1))

The reader can check that this code computes exactly the same as the original code. The computation of (F, k) and (D, k) is delayed by one iteration. Thus, (B, k) and (E, k) are still computed before (F, k), and $(F, k - 1)$ is still computed before (D, k). However, we have to check that (F, k) and (D, k) are not computed after the operations that should use them. (F, k) has to be computed before $(E, k + 2)$, which is still the case (it is now computed one iteration before). However, (D, k) is now computed at the same iteration as $(B, k+1)$; this is why we re-ordered the body of the loop so that (D, k) appears textually before $(B, k + 1)$ (the new dependence distance is 0, i.e., the dependence becomes loop-independent).

The new dependence graph is given in Figure 3.8. We can now apply the loop compaction technique to this new graph, and we retrieve the solution with $\lambda = 20$ given in Section 3.2.3. Note that the maximal weight of a path in the original graph $A(G)$ is 24 (the path $E \rightarrow F$); it is now equal to 14 (the "path" reduced to the vertex F). □

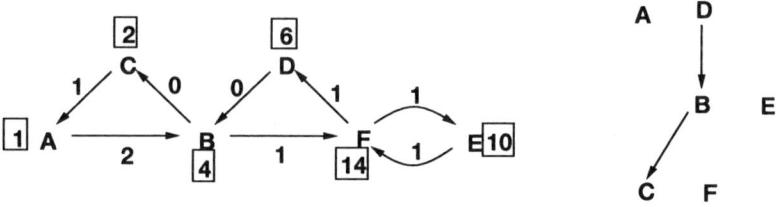

Figure 3.8: Dependence graph after loop shifting and the corresponding acyclic graph.

More formally, loop shifting consists of the following transformation. Instead of considering that the vertex $v \in V$ in the graph G represents all the operations of the form (v, k), we consider that it represents all the operations of the form $(v, k - r(v))$, which means that we delay operation (v, k) by $r(v)$ iterations. In our example $r(A) = r(B) = r(C) = r(E) = 0$ and $r(D) = r(F) = 1$. The new dependence distance $w_r(e)$ for an edge $e = (u, v) \in E$ is now $w_r(e) = w(e) + r(v) - r(u)$ because the dependence is from $(u, k - r(u))$ to $(v, k - r(u) + w(e)) = (v, k - r(v) + w_r(e))$. This defines a transformed graph $G_r = (V, E, d, w_r)$. Note that for any cycle $\mathcal{C}$, $w(\mathcal{C}) = w_r(\mathcal{C})$.

Now, if $w_r(e) \neq 0$, the two operations in dependence are computed in different iterations in the transformed code. If $w_r(e) > 0$, the two operations are computed in the original order and the dependence is now a loop-carried dependence. If $w_r(e) = 0$, both operations are computed in the same iteration, and we place the statement corresponding to u textually before the statement corresponding to v so as to preserve the dependence as a loop-independent dependence. This reordering is always possible because the transformed graph $G_r = (V, E, d, w_r)$ has no zero-weight cycle (G and G_r have the same cycle weights). If $w_r(e) < 0$, the loop shifting is not valid. Note that G_r and G are two representations of the same problem, as shown by the following lemma.

Lemma 9 *There is a one-to-one correspondence between the schedules for G and for G_r.*

Proof   We show that the function σ_r is a schedule for G_r if and only if the function σ, defined by $\sigma(v, k) = \sigma_r(v, k + r(v))$, is a schedule for G. Obviously, resource constraints are satisfied for σ if and only if they are satisfied for σ_r. It remains to check all dependence constraints, i.e., inequalities (3.2):

$$\sigma(u, k) + d(u) \leq \sigma(v, k + w(e)) \qquad\qquad \Leftrightarrow$$
$$\sigma_r(u, k + r(u)) + d(u) \leq \sigma_r(v, k + w(e) + r(v)) \qquad \Leftrightarrow$$
$$\sigma_r(u, k') + d(u) \leq \sigma_r(v, k' + w_r(e)) \text{ where } k' = k + r(u)$$

Thus, G and G_r are two representations of the same problem.   ∎

In other words, reasoning on G_r is just a change of representation. It cannot prevent us finding a schedule. Here, we use loop shifting as a preprocessing step so that G_r is in the most desired form for loop compaction.

Such a function r is called a *retiming* in the context of synchronous VLSI circuits [79]. Each vertex v represents an operator, with a delay $d(v)$. The weight $w(e)$ of an edge e is interpreted as a number of registers. The graph $A(G)$ that we used in loop compaction is the graph of edges "without registers." When $A(G)$ is acyclic (as in our hypotheses), G has no cycle of zero weight; using VLSI terminology, we say that G is synchronous.

Retiming amounts to suppress $r(u)$ registers to the weight of each edge leaving u and to add $r(v)$ registers to each edge entering v. The constraint $w(e) + r(v) - r(u) \geq 0$ means that a negative number of registers is not allowed for retiming.

Using this new formulation, we can state our objectives more precisely in terms of retiming:

Objective 1: Find a retiming r that minimizes the longest path in $A(G_r)$, i.e., in terms of retiming, that minimizes the clock period $\Phi(G_r)$ of the retimed graph (see Section 3.4.4).

Objective 2: Find a retiming r so that the number of edges in $A(G_r)$ is minimal, i.e., distribute registers to leave as few edges without registers as possible (see Section 3.4.5).

3.4.4 The Leiserson-Saxe Retiming Algorithm

In this section, we recall the retiming algorithm proposed by Leiserson and Saxe for minimizing the clock period of a VLSI circuit, i.e., the maximal weight of path with no registers. All missing proofs can be found in [79].

As in the previous sections, we denote by $u \overset{\mathcal{P}}{\rightsquigarrow} v$ a path $\mathcal{P}$ of G from u to v, by $w(\mathcal{P}) = \sum_{e \in \mathcal{P}} w(e)$ the sum of the weights of the edges of $\mathcal{P}$, and by $d(\mathcal{P}) = \sum_{v \in \mathcal{P}} d(v)$ the sum of the delays of the vertices of $\mathcal{P}$. We define W and D as follows:

$$\begin{aligned} W(u,v) &= \min\{w(\mathcal{P}) \mid u \overset{\mathcal{P}}{\rightsquigarrow} v\} \\ D(u,v) &= \max\{d(\mathcal{P}) \mid u \overset{\mathcal{P}}{\rightsquigarrow} v \text{ and } w(\mathcal{P}) = W(u,v)\} \end{aligned}$$

W and D are computed by solving an all-pairs shortest-path algorithm on G where edge $u \overset{e}{\rightarrow} v$ is weighted with the pair $(w(e), -d(u))$. Finally, let

$$\Phi(G) = \max\{d(\mathcal{P}) \mid \mathcal{P} \text{ path of } G, \ w(\mathcal{P}) = 0\}$$

$\Phi(G)$ is the length of the longest path of zero weight in G (and is called the *clock period* of G in VLSI terminology).

Theorem 15 (Theorem 7 in [79]) *Let $G = (V, E, d, w)$ be a synchronous circuit, let c be an arbitrary positive real number, and let r be a function from V to the integers. Then r is a legal retiming of G such that $\Phi(G_r) \leq c$ if and only if*

1. *$r(u) - r(v) \leq w(e)$ for every edge $u \overset{e}{\rightarrow} v$ of G, and*

2. *$r(u) - r(v) \leq W(u,v) - 1$ for all vertices $u, v \in V$ such that $D(u,v) > c$.*

Intuitively, the first inequality means that the retiming leaves a non-negative number of registers on each edge (valid retiming), while the second inequality means that the retiming leaves at least one register on each path $\mathcal{P}$ whose weight $d(\mathcal{P})$ is not less than c (otherwise the clock period is greater than $d(\mathcal{P})$).

Theorem 15 provides the basic tool to establish the following algorithm (Algorithm OPT1) that determines a retiming such that the clock period of the retimed graph is minimized.

Algorithm (Algorithm OPT1 in [79])

1. Compute W and D (see Algorithm WD in [79]).

2. Sort the different values $D(u, v)$.

3. Among the elements $D(u, v)$, perform a binary search for the minimum achievable clock period. To check whether a potential clock period c is feasible, apply the Bellman-Ford algorithm to determine whether the conditions in Theorem 15 can be satisfied.

4. For the minimum achievable clock period found in step 3, use the values for the $r(v)$ found by the Bellman-Ford algorithm as the optimal retiming.

This algorithm runs in $O(|V|^3 \log |V|)$. There is a more efficient algorithm whose complexity is $O(|V||E| \log |V|)$, which is a significant improvement for sparse graphs. It runs similar to the previous algorithm, except in step 3 where the Bellman-Ford algorithm is replaced by the following algorithm:

Algorithm (Algorithm FEAS in [79])

Given a synchronous circuit $G = (V, E, d, w)$ and a desired clock period c, this algorithm produces a retiming r of G such that G_r is a synchronous circuit with clock period $\Phi(G_r) \leq c$, if such a retiming exists.

1. For each vertex $v \in V$, set $r(v)$ to 0.

2. Repeat the following $|V| - 1$ times:

   (a) Compute the graph G_r with the existing values for r.

   (b) for any vertex $v \in V$ compute $\Delta(v)$ the maximum sum $d(\mathcal{P})$ of vertex delays along any zero-weight directed path $\mathcal{P}$ in G_r leading to v. This can be done in $O(|E|)$.

(c) For each vertex v such that $\Delta(v) > c$, set $r(v)$ to $r(v) + 1$.

3. Run the same algorithm used for step 2b to compute $\Phi(G_r)$. If $\Phi(G_r) > c$, then no feasible retiming exists. Otherwise, r is the desired retiming.

In the following, we denote by Φ_{opt} the minimum achievable clock period for G.

Example 4, Continued

For the graph of Figure 3.2, $\Phi_{opt} = 14$ and the retiming r that achieves this clock period is obtained in two steps by Algorithm FEAS (Figures 3.9 (a), (b), and (c) show the successive retimed graphs). This is how we found the solution presented in Figure 3.8. □

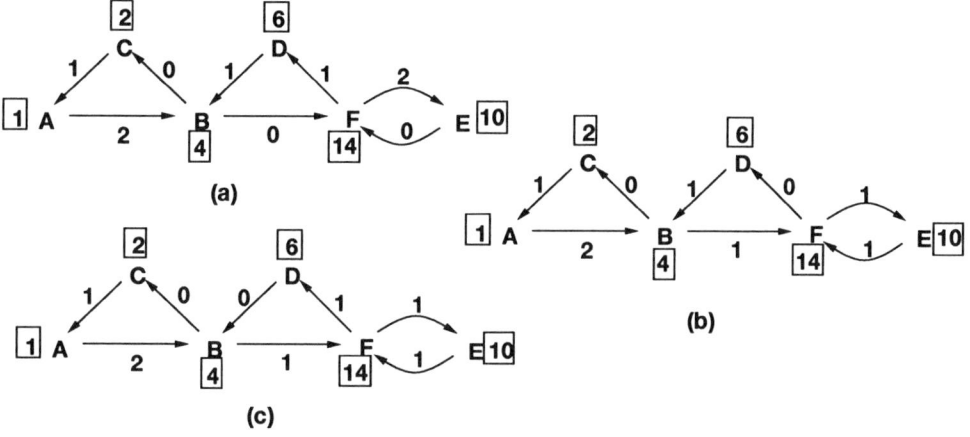

Figure 3.9: (a) Initial dependence graph G. (b) and (c) Successive steps of the Leiserson-Saxe algorithm.

We now come back to the performance bound given in Lemma 8. By loop shifting followed by loop compaction, we can define a cyclic schedule σ whose average cycle time satisfies $p\lambda \leq p\lambda_p + (p - 1)\Phi_{opt}$ where Φ_{opt} is the minimum achievable clock period for G. It remains to establish a link between Φ_{opt} and λ_p to obtain a heuristic for which λ/λ_p is bounded.

Lemma 10 Φ_{opt} *and* λ_∞ *are linked by the inequalities* $\lambda_\infty \leq \Phi_{opt} \leq \lceil \lambda_\infty \rceil + d_{max} - 1$ *where* $d_{max} = \max_{v \in V} d(v)$.

Proof   Let us apply the loop shifting/loop compaction algorithm with unlimited resources. For that, we define a retiming r such that $\Phi(G_r) = \Phi_{opt}$ and we define the graph $A(G_r)$ by deleting from G all edges e such that $w_r(e) > 0$. Then we define a schedule for $A(G_r)$ with unlimited resources by $\sigma_a(v) = \max\{d(\mathcal{P}) : \mathcal{P} \text{ path of } A(G) \text{ leading to } v\}$. The makespan of σ_a is Φ_{opt} by construction. Finally, we get a schedule for G by defining $\sigma(v, k) = \sigma_a(v) + (r(v) + k)\Phi_{opt}$. Because by definition λ_∞ is the smallest possible average cycle time for $p = \infty$, we have $\lambda_\infty \leq \Phi_{opt}$.

Now, consider a schedule σ for unlimited resources and initiation interval equal to $\bar{\rho} = \lceil \lambda_\infty \rceil$, as defined in Section 3.3.3: $\sigma(v, k) = t(s, v) + \bar{\rho}k$. Let $s(v) = t(s, v) \bmod \bar{\rho}$ and $r(v) = \lfloor \frac{t(s,v)}{\bar{\rho}} \rfloor$. Because σ is a schedule, for all edges $e = (u, v)$:

$$t(s, u) + d(u) \leq t(s, v) + \bar{\rho}w(e)$$

which we rewrite into:

$$s(u) + d(u) - s(v) \leq \bar{\rho}\left(w(e) + r(v) - r(u)\right)$$

Because $s(u) + d(u) - s(v) \geq -s(v) > -\bar{\rho}$, we have $w(e) + r(v) - r(u) > -1$, i.e., $w(e) + r(v) - r(u) \geq 0$ because these numbers are integers. Thus, r is a valid retiming. Let us compute $\Phi(G_r)$, i.e., the maximal weight in $A(G_r)$. When $r(v) - r(u) + w(e) = 0$, $d(u) \leq s(v) - s(u)$. Thus, for any path $\mathcal{P}$ in $A(G_r), \mathcal{P} = (v_1, \ldots, v_n)$, we have $d(\mathcal{P}) \leq s(v_n) - s(v_1) + d(v_n) < \bar{\rho} + d_{max}$. By definition, $\Phi(G_r)$ is the maximal weight in $A(G_r)$, thus $\Phi(G_r) \leq \bar{\rho} + d_{max} - 1$. Finally, because $\Phi_{opt} \leq \Phi(G_r)$, we get the desired inequality. ∎

We thus have the following result:

Theorem 16 *A cyclic schedule whose average cycle time λ is such that:*

$$p\lambda \leq p\lambda_p + (p - 1)(\lceil \lambda_\infty \rceil + d_{max} - 1) \quad \text{and} \quad \lambda_\infty \leq \lambda_p$$

can be derived in time $O(|V||E| \log |V|)$.

Proof   The proof is immediate from Lemmas 8 and 10. The complexity of the heuristic is dominated by the Leiserson-Saxe algorithm for retiming. ∎

3.4.5   Minimizing the Number of Constraints in $A(G_r)$

Our purpose in this section is to find a retimed graph with the minimum number of zero-weight edges among all retimed graphs whose clock period is best possible, equal to Φ_{opt}. Removing edges of nonzero weight will give an acyclic graph that matches both objectives stated at the end of Section 3.4.3.

Example 4, Continued

Consider the retimed graph G_r found by the Leiserson-Saxe algorithm (Figure 3.8). G_r does minimize the maximal weight Φ of a path in $A(G_r)$, i.e., it has the minimal clock period, but it does not necessarily minimize the number of zero-weight edges. See again our key example Figure 3.8 for which $\Phi = 14$. We can apply yet another retiming to obtain the graph of Figure 3.10. The length of the longest path of zero weight is still $\Phi = 14$, but the total number of zero-weight edges is smaller. This implies that the corresponding acyclic graph $A(G_r)$ (see Figure 3.10) contains fewer edges than the acyclic graph depicted in Figure 3.8, and therefore is likely to induce a smaller initiation interval when applying loop compaction. (List scheduling a subgraph of a graph will not always produce a smaller execution time; but intuition shows that in most practical cases it will: the fewer constraints, the more freedom.) That is the case in our example; we find an initiation interval equal to 19; see Figure 3.11. It turns out that $\lambda = 19$ is the best possible integer average cycle time with $p = 2$ processors: the sum of all operation delays is 37, and $\lceil \frac{37}{2} \rceil = 19$. However, a schedule with average cycle time equal to 18.5 exists, as we will see at the end of this section. $\square$

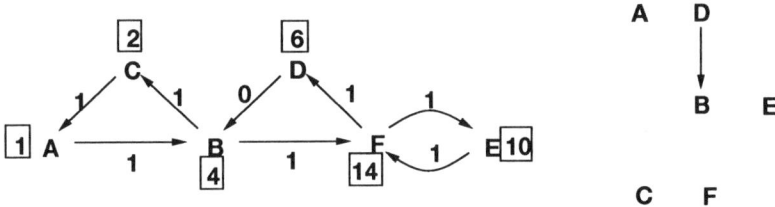

Figure 3.10: The final retimed graph and the corresponding acyclic graph.

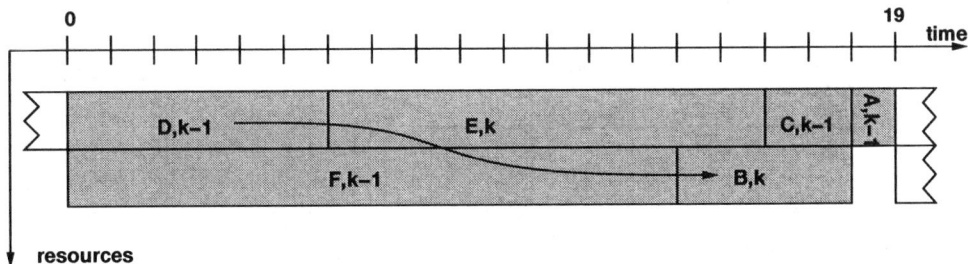

Figure 3.11: A slice of the schedule with $\lambda = 19$.

Recall that a retiming r such that $\Phi(G_r) = \Phi_{\text{opt}}$ is any integral solution to the following system (see formulation of Theorem 15):

$$\begin{cases} r(v)-r(u)+w(e)\geq 0 \text{ for every edge } u \xrightarrow{e} v \in E \\ r(v)-r(u)+W(u,v)\geq 1 \text{ for all vertices } u,v \in V \text{ s.t. } D(u,v)>\Phi_{opt} \end{cases} \quad (3.8)$$

Among these retimings, we want to select one particular retiming r for which the number of zero-weight edges in G_r is minimized. This can be done as follows.

Lemma 11 Let $G = (V, E, d, w)$ be a synchronous circuit. A retiming r such that $\Phi(G_r) = \Phi_{opt}$ and such that the number of zero-weight edges in G_r is minimized can be found in polynomial time by solving the following integer linear program:

$$\begin{cases} \min \sum_{e\in E} v(e) \\ 0 \leq v(e) \leq 1 \\ r(v)-r(u)+w(e)+v(e)\geq 1 \text{ for every edge } u \xrightarrow{e} v \in E \\ r(v)-r(u)+W(u,v)\geq 1 \text{ for all vertices } u,v \in V \text{ s.t. } D(u,v)>\Phi_{opt} \end{cases} \quad (3.9)$$

Proof Consider an optimal integral solution (r, v) of linear system (3.9). r defines a retiming for G with $\Phi(G_r) = \Phi_{opt}$ because system (3.8) is satisfied; indeed $r(v) - r(u) + w(e) + v(e) \geq 1$ and $v(e) \leq 1$ implies $r(v) - r(u) + w(e) \geq 0$.

Note that each $v(e)$ is only constrained by the following equation: $r(v) - r(u) + w(e) + v(e) \geq 1$. There are two cases:

- The edge e in G_r has a zero weight, i.e., $r(v) - r(u) + w(e) = 0$. Then, $v(e) = 1$ is the only possibility.

- The edge e in G_r has a positive weight, i.e., $r(v) - r(u) + w(e) \geq 1$ (recall that r and d are integers). In this case, the minimal value for v is 0.

Therefore, given a retiming r, $\sum_{e\in E} v(e)$ is minimal when it is equal to the number of zero-weight edges in G_r.

It remains to show that such an optimal integer solution can be found in polynomial time. The reader can check that the system (3.9), written in matrix form as $\min\{cx \mid Ax \leq b\}$, is such that A is totally unimodular. Therefore, solving the integer linear programming problem 3.9 is not NP-complete; system (3.9) considered as a (rational) linear programming problem has an integral optimum solution (Corollary 19.1a in [110]), and such an integral solution can be found in polynomial time (Theorem 16.2 in [110]).

We point out that this problem can also be solved as the dual of a minimum-cost flow problem with capacities for which polynomial graph algorithms exist [28]. ∎

A simple optimization that reduces the complexity is to precompute the strongly connected components G_i of G and to solve the problem separately for each component G_i. Then, a retiming that minimizes the number of zero-weight edges in G_r is built by adding suitable constants to each retiming r_i so that all edges that link different components have positive weights.

Concluding Remarks

Let us summarize how the minimization of the number of constraints can be incorporated into our cyclic scheduling heuristic. First, we compute Φ_{opt} the minimum achievable clock period for G; then we solve system (3.9) and obtain a retiming r (loop shifting). We define $A(G_r)$ as the acyclic graph whose edges have zero weight in G_r; the longest path in $A(G_r)$ is minimized and the number of edges in $A(G_r)$ is minimized. Finally, we schedule $A(G_r)$ by list scheduling (loop compaction).

So far we have restricted initiation intervals to *integer* values. Nevertheless, the previous results show that this is sufficient to obtain a performance guarantee. Searching for *rational* initiation intervals might give better results, but at the price of an increase in complexity; searching for $\lambda = \frac{p}{q}$ can be achieved by *loop unrolling* by a factor of q, thereby processing an extended dependence graph with many more vertices and edges. As we just mentioned, a schedule with average cycle time equal to 18.5 exists for our key example; see Figure 3.12. This cannot be improved further; the two processors are always busy, as $\sum_{v \in V} d(v) = 37 = 2\lambda$. We obtained this solution by concatenation of two different list schedules of $A(G_r)$, an ASAP schedule and an ALAP schedule.

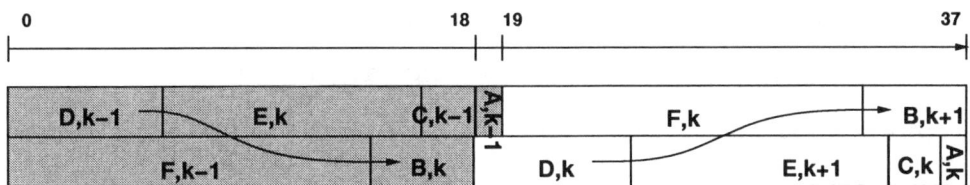

Figure 3.12: A schedule with optimal average cycle time ($\lambda = 18.5$).

Finally, note that all edge-cutting heuristics lead to cyclic schedulings where slices do not overlap (by construction). It would be very interesting to derive methods (more sophisticated than loop unrolling) to synthesize resource-constrained schedulings where slices can overlap.

3.5   Bibliographical Notes

The algorithm presented in this chapter is borrowed from [18], following ideas developed independently by Gasperoni and Schwiegelshohn in [46] and Wang, Eisenbeis, Jourdan, and Su in [114]. The presentation of the NP-complete results is borrowed from Alix Munier's PhD thesis [91] (in French). For more details on theoretical aspects of the cyclic scheduling problem, we refer to the survey by Claire Hanen and Alix Munier in [56].

Our goal here was mainly to make a bridge between classical scheduling problems on acyclic graphs as presented in Chapters 1 and 2, and multidimensional cyclic problems that are addressed in the second part of this book in Chapters 4 and 5. We wanted to gradually introduce the difficulties that arise when scheduling *cyclic* graphs and to present the notion of cyclic scheduling and useful tools such as the Bellman-Ford algorithm. We merged techniques that come from two different fields: circuit synthesis techniques through the Leiserson-Saxe algorithm [79] and compilation-optimization techniques. The cyclic scheduling problem addressed here is indeed a particular case of the software pipelining, which was extensively studied in the past. Seminal papers on software pipelining include those of M. Lam [74], A. Aiken and A. Nicolau [2], and B. R. Rau and C. D. Glaeser [104]. For a comprehensive view on the developments that followed, we refer to the survey by V. H. Allan, R. B. Jones, R. M. Lee, and S. J. Allan [3] and to the huge bibliography proposed by B. R. Rau in [103].

3.6   Exercises

In all exercises, all dependence graphs $G = (V, E, d, w)$ have the following properties. For each vertex $v \in V$, $d(v)$ is a positive integer; for each edge e, $w(e)$ is a nonnegative integer; and there is no cycle C such that $w(C) = 0$.

Exercise 3.1 (Graph with sufficiently many "registers")

In this exercise, all statements have a unitary execution time: $d(v) = 1$, for all $v \in V$.

1. Give a program whose reduced dependence graph is the graph of Figure 3.13.

2. Assume three available identical processors. Compute the initiation intervals λ_{simple} and λ_{super} obtained respectively by scheduling the acyclic graph of zero-weight edges, first with no retiming and then after optimal retiming.

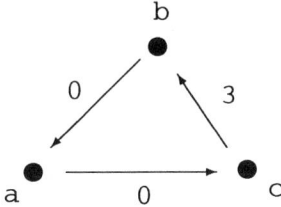

Figure 3.13: Reduced dependence graph.

3. Let K be an arbitrarily large integer. Build a graph $G = (V, E, d, w)$ for which $\frac{\lambda_{\text{simple}}}{\lambda_{\text{super}}} \geq K$ if there are $p = |V|$ identical processors.

4. Let $G = (V, E, d, w)$ be a graph and assume $p = |V|$ identical processors. Give a necessary and sufficient condition for $\lambda_{\text{super}} = 1$.

Exercise 3.2 (Minimizing the number of zero-weight edges)

Consider the following code:

```
DO n=3, N
  b(n) = a(n-1) * a(n-1)
  c(n) = b(n-1) * b(n-1)
  d(n) = c(n-1) * c(n-1)
  a(n) = b(n) + c(n) + d(n)
ENDDO
```

To make things simpler, we assume that the execution time of a multiply is twice the execution time of an addition and that all statements of the code are atomic. Therefore, we can assume that all the instructions have the same delay (equal to 1).

1. Show that the previous code computes the recurrence $a_n = (a_{n-1})^2 + (a_{n-2})^4 + (a_{n-3})^8$ and give the associated reduced dependence graph.

2. What is the clock period of the reduced dependence graph? What is the optimal average cycle time? What average cycle time can be obtained by loop compaction alone? Same question if we assume that only two multiplies at a time can be performed.

3. Find a loop shifting (i.e., a retiming) for which the number of zero-weight edges is minimized. What average cycle time is obtained if loop compaction is then applied (we assume again that there are only

two multipliers)? Give the transformed code with the corresponding prelude and postlude.

Exercise 3.3 (One cycle with self-loops)

Let $G = (V, E, d, w)$ be a graph defined as the cycle $C = (v_1, \ldots, v_{|V|})$ with all self-loops $e = (v_i, v_i)$ (with weight $w(e) = 1$). Assume p identical resources. Let $D_{\max} = \max\{d(v) \mid v \in V\}$ and $M = \max\{D_{\max}, \frac{d(C)}{w(C)}, \frac{d(C)}{p}\}$.

1. Show that M is a lower bound for the average cycle time.

2. Suppose that $p \geq w(C)$. Show that unrolling the graph leads to $w(C)$ independent dependence paths and deduce from this fact a solution whose average cycle time is exactly M.

3. Consider an edge e in G such that $w(e) > 0$. Let $G' = (V, E, d, w')$ be a copy of G except that $w'(e) = w(e) - 1$ for this particular edge e. Show that any cyclic solution for G' is a valid solution for G. Deduce from this property a solution for G whose average cycle time is exactly M even when $p < w(C)$.

Note: This exercise is borrowed from A. Munier's PhD thesis [91].

Exercise 3.4 (Karp's minimum mean-weight cycle algorithm)

In this exercise, we study an algorithm that computes the minimum average cycle time (faster than in Corollary 2) for a graph $G = (V, E, d, w)$ for the particular case where $d(v) = 1$ for all vertices $v \in V$. For a cycle $C = (e_1, \ldots, e_k)$, we let $\mu(C) = \frac{1}{k} \sum_{i=1}^{k} w(e_i)$. The goal is to compute $\mu^* = \min\{\mu(C) \mid C \text{ cycle in } G\}$, which is, according to Theorem 13, the inverse of the minimum average cycle time.

Assume without loss of generality that every vertex $v \in V$ is reachable from a source vertex $s \in V$. Let $\delta(v)$ be the weight of a shortest path from s to v, and let $\delta_k(v)$ be the weight of a shortest path from s to v consisting of exactly k edges (if there is no such path, then $\delta_k(v) = +\infty$). We let $n = |V|$ and we define, in all subsequent computations, $(+\infty) - (+\infty) = 0$.

1. Show that if $\mu^* \geq 0$, then $\delta(v) = \min_{0 \leq k \leq n-1} \delta_k(v)$. Deduce from this that there exists k, $0 \leq k \leq n - 1$, such that $\delta_n(v) - \delta_k(v) \geq 0$.

2. Show that if $\mu^* = 0$, then there exist $v \in V$ and k, $0 \leq k \leq n - 1$, such that $\delta_n(v) - \delta_k(v) = 0$.

3. Deduce from 1 and 2 that if $\mu^* = 0$, then:

$$\min_{v \in V} \max_{0 \le k \le n-1} \frac{\delta_n(v) - \delta_k(v)}{n - k} = \mu^*$$

4. Show that if we add a constant t to the weight of each edge of G, then μ^* is increased by t. Use this to show that

$$\min_{v \in V} \max_{0 \le k \le n-1} \frac{\delta_n(v) - \delta_k(v)}{n - k} = \mu^*$$

5. Give an $O(|V||E|)$-time algorithm to compute μ^*.

Note: This exercise is a modified version of Exercise 25-5 in [26].

Part II

Multidimensional Problems

Chapter 4

Systems of Uniform Recurrence Equations

Note to Reader This chapter is very technical. It can be skipped on first reading if the reader wants only a description of the parallelism detection algorithms presented in the next chapter and does not care about optimality proofs. However, this chapter may be of interest for the reader who is curious to see the link between the seminal paper of Karp, Miller, and Winograd entitled "The Organization of Computations for Uniform Recurrence Equations" [65] and affine loop transformations.

4.1 Introduction

In Chapter 3, we presented some scheduling problems that can be modeled through cyclic graphs whose edges are labeled by integer values. Standard techniques use the Bellman-Ford algorithm or its variants; the key point is to determine if there is a negative weight cycle in the graph. If not, shortest paths can be defined, and, after more or less complicated strategies, schedules can be computed. The reason these techniques work so simply is that the set of integers (that label the edges of the graph) is a totally ordered set. When the weights of the edges are defined on a *partially* ordered set, things get more complicated, if not intractable, and more sophisticated techniques must be used.

This chapter addresses such a case; we consider scheduling problems related to graphs whose edges are labeled by n-dimensional integer vectors instead of one-dimensional vectors, i.e. integer values. Such graphs come from the computational model introduced by Karp, Miller, and Winograd, called a system of uniform recurrence equations (SURE) [65]. We will see in the next chapter how this study can be used to automatically parallelize codes defined by nested loops.

The chapter is divided into three parts:

- In Section 4.2, we study the problem of computability of a system of uniform recurrence equations, in its simplest formulation. Compared to Chapter 3, this part corresponds to the detection of negative weight cycles.

- In Section 4.3, we study more deeply the simplest case of one equation. We explore the link between the computability of the equation and the asymptotic optimality of linear scheduling.

- In Section 4.4, we address the general case of a system of uniform recurrence equations. We study the link between the computability of the system and the asymptotic optimality of multidimensional scheduling.

4.2 Computability of Uniform Recurrence Equations

4.2.1 Definition of a SURE

Systems of uniform recurrence equations were introduced in 1967 by Karp, Miller, and Winograd [65] as a model for understanding the structure of computations in certain repetitive and regular processes.

A *system of uniform recurrence equations* (SURE) is a finite set of equations of the following form:

$$V_i(p) = f_i(\dots, V_{i_k}(p - d_{k,i}), \dots) \text{ for } 1 \leq k \leq m_i \qquad (4.1)$$

where V_i is a data array (or *variable*) to be computed for each integral point p (called an *iteration vector*), included in a subset $\mathcal{P}_i$ of $\mathbb{Z}^n$ (called the *iteration domain* of variable V_i). The vectors $d_{k,i}$ are vectors in $\mathbb{Z}^n$ called *dependence vectors*. The function f_i is a strict function with m_i arguments whose properties (if any) will not be considered.

Looking at Equation (4.1), we say that $V_i(p)$ *depends on* the m_i values $V_{i_k}(p - d_{k,i})$ for $1 \leq k \leq m_i$. If $p - d_{k,i} \notin \mathcal{P}_{i_k}$, the value $V_{i_k}(p - d_{k,i})$ is supposed to be given. Otherwise it must be evaluated before $V_i(p)$. In other words, the left-hand side of each equation can be evaluated only if all arguments of the right-hand side have already been evaluated.

A SURE can be equivalently defined in terms of a multigraph G called a *reduced dependence graph* (RDG). G is naturally defined as follows:

- For each variable V_i, there is a vertex v_i in G.

- For each variable V_i such that $V_i(p)$ depends on $V_{i_k}(p - d_{k,i})$, there is an edge in G, from v_{i_k} to v_i, labeled with vector $d_{k,i}$.

A SURE is then simply defined by a reduced dependence graph G and the definition of the iteration domains $\mathcal{P}_i$.

Example 5

The following set of equations, defined for $\mathcal{P}_1 = \mathcal{P}_2 = \{(i, j, k) | 1 \leq i, j, k \leq N\}$, is a system of two uniform recurrence equations and four dependence vectors:

$$\begin{cases} a(i, \ j, \ k) = b(i, \ j - 1, \ k) + a(i, \ j, \ k - 1) \\ b(i, \ j, \ k) = a(i - 1, \ j, \ k) + b(i, \ j, \ k + 1) \end{cases}$$

Its corresponding reduced dependence graph is depicted on Figure 4.1. □

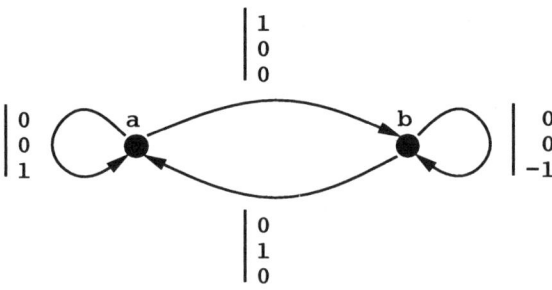

Figure 4.1: Reduced dependence graph for Example 5.

In the following, we use the same graph notations as in the previous chapter; if G is a graph, $V(G)$ denotes its set of vertices and $E(G)$ its set of edges. We denote by $e = (u, v)$ an edge e from vertex u to vertex v and by $w(e)$ the weight that labels e. When there is no ambiguity, x_e and y_e denote the two vertices such that $e = (x_e, y_e)$. We extend the notion of weight to paths of any length: $w(P)$ is the sum of the weights of all edges of P.

We denote by **1** (resp. **0**) the vector whose entries are all equal to 1 (resp. 0). We extend the notation $\leq$ and $\geq$ to vectors; we write $x \geq \mathbf{0}$ if all components of x are nonnegative and $x \geq y$ if $(x - y) \geq \mathbf{0}$.

4.2.2 Computability: Definition and Properties

The precedence relations between evaluations of the variables $V_i(p)$ of a SURE can be captured in a graph called an *expanded dependence graph* (EDG) and denoted by Γ. Γ is defined as follows:

- the set of vertices $V(\Gamma)$ is $(\{1\} \times \mathcal{P}_1) \cup \cdots \cup (\{m\} \times \mathcal{P}_m)$ where m is the number of equations.

- there is an edge from (j, q) to (i, p) if $V_i(p)$ depends on $V_j(q)$, i.e., if the evaluation of $V_j(q)$ must precede the evaluation of $V_i(p)$. We use the notation $(j, q) \xrightarrow{1} (i, p)$.

By induction, we define the relation $\xrightarrow{t}$ for $t > 1$ by $(j, q) \xrightarrow{t} (i, p)$ if Γ has a vertex (k, r) such that $(j, q) \xrightarrow{t-1} (k, r)$ and $(k, r) \xrightarrow{1} (i, p)$. Finally, we write $(j, q) \longrightarrow (i, p)$ if $(j, q) \xrightarrow{t} (i, p)$ for some positive integer t, and $(k, r) \xrightarrow{0} (i, p)$ if and only if $(k, r) = (i, p)$.

A *schedule* is a function T from $V(\Gamma)$ into the nonnegative integers $\mathbb{N}$ such that $T(j, q) < T(i, p)$ whenever $(j, q) \longrightarrow (i, p)$. Such a function T defines an evaluation order for all equations of the SURE that respects the evaluation principle; if this order is followed, all arguments of the right-hand side of an equation are computed before the left-hand side is evaluated. A SURE is said to be *computable* (or explicitly defined) if there exists such a schedule. Note that some SUREs are not computable. If a value $V_i(p)$ depends on itself (possibly through other computations), the SURE is not computable. If a value $V_i(p)$ needs to wait "infinite" time before complete evaluation of the right-hand side, the SURE is also not computable. The following examples illustrate the two cases of noncomputability for a SURE whose iteration domain is $F_n = \mathbb{N}^n$.

Example 6

Consider the following system of uniform recurrence equations, defined for $\mathcal{P}_1 = \mathcal{P}_2 = F_2$:

$$\begin{cases} a(i, \, j) = b(i, \, j - 1) \\ b(i, \, j) = a(i + 1, \, j) + b(i - 1, \, j + 1) \end{cases}$$

To compute $a(i, j)$, we must first compute $b(i, j - 1)$, and $b(i, j - 1)$ depends on $b(i - 1, j)$, which depends on $a(i, j)$. Thus, $a(i, j)$ depends on itself and there is a cycle in the expanded dependence graph associated to this system, which makes it noncomputable. This cycle corresponds to a cycle of zero weight in the reduced dependence graph: $(0, 1) + (1, -1) + (-1, 0) = (0, 0)$. Figure 4.2 depicts a part of the expanded dependence graph.   □

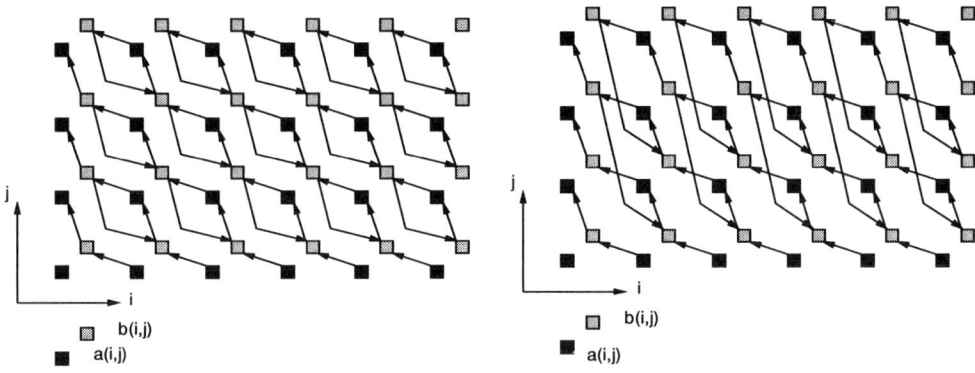

Figure 4.2: EDG for Example 6.   Figure 4.3: EDG for Example 7.

Example 7

Consider the following system of uniform recurrence equations, defined for $\mathcal{P}_1 = \mathcal{P}_2 = F_2$:

$$\begin{cases} a(i,\ j) = b(i,\ j-1) \\ b(i,\ j) = a(i+1,\ j) + b(i-1,\ j+2) \end{cases}$$

There is no self-dependent operation in this example. But to be able to compute $a(i,j)$, we must have computed first $b(i,j-1)$, and $b(i,j-1)$ depends on $b(i-1,j+1)$, which depends on $a(i,j+1)$. Therefore, to be able to compute $a(i,j)$, we must have computed first $a(i,j+1)$, and before that $a(i,j+2)$, etc. Once again, the system is not computable. Infinite time is required to compute $a(i,j)$ because there is an infinite path, directed to $a(i,j)$, in the expanded dependence graph associated to the system. This infinite path corresponds to a cycle of nonpositive weight in the reduced dependence graph: $(0,1) + (1,-2) + (-1,0) = (0,-1)$. Figure 4.3 depicts a part of the expanded dependence graph. $\qquad\square$

The following definitions and lemmas formalize the notion of computability.

Definition 20 (Free Schedule) *The free schedule is the function T_f defined from $V(\Gamma)$ into $\mathbb{N} \cup \{+\infty\}$ by:*

$$T_f(i,p) = \min\{T(i,p) \mid T \text{ is a schedule}\}$$

(by definition, $T_f(i,p) = +\infty$, if there is no schedule).

Lemma 12 *If there is a schedule, T_f is a schedule. It is the "fastest" schedule.*

Proof   Assume that a schedule T exists. Let (i, p) and (j, q) be two vertices of Γ such that $(j, q) \longrightarrow (i, p)$; because T is a schedule, $T(j, q) < T(i, p)$, and because T takes integer values, $T(j, q) + 1 \leq T(i, p)$. Furthermore, by definition of $T_f(j, q)$, $T_f(j, q) \leq T(j, q)$. Thus, $T_f(j, q) + 1 \leq T(i, p)$. Finally, because this holds for any schedule T, we get $T_f(j, q) + 1 \leq T_f(i, p)$, by definition of $T_f(i, p)$. This proves that T_f is a schedule.   ∎

Definition 21 *Let F be defined from $V(\Gamma)$ into $\mathbb{N} \cup \{+\infty\}$ by:*

$$F(i, p) = \max\{t \geq 0 \mid \text{there exists } (j, q) \text{ such that } (j, q) \xrightarrow{t} (i, p)\}$$

$F(i, p)$ is the length of the longest path in Γ directed to (i, p).

Lemma 13 *If for all vertices (i, p) in Γ, $F(i, p) \neq +\infty$, then F is a schedule. Furthermore, if there is a schedule, $F = T_f$.*

Proof   First note that if $F(i, p) \neq +\infty$ for all (i, p), F is a function into $\mathbb{N}$ as required. Let (i, p) and (j, q) be two vertices of Γ such that $(j, q) \xrightarrow{t} (i, p)$, for some $t \geq 1$. By definition of $F(j, q)$, there exists a vertex (k, r) of Γ such that $(k, r) \xrightarrow{t'} (j, q)$ with $t' = F(j, q)$. Thus, $(k, r) \xrightarrow{t'+t} (i, p)$. By definition of $F(i, p)$, $F(i, p) \geq t' + t = F(j, p) + t \geq F(j, p) + 1$. This proves that F is a schedule.

Now, assume that a schedule T exists; by definition of a schedule, $(j, q) \xrightarrow{1} (i, p)$ implies $T(i, p) \geq T(j, q) + 1$ because T takes integer values. By induction on t, we have:

$$(j, q) \xrightarrow{t} (i, p) \Rightarrow T(i, p) \geq T(j, q) + t \geq t$$

and finally, for all (i, p), $F(i, p) \leq T(i, p)$. In particular, $F(i, p) < +\infty$ and, as shown earlier, F is a schedule (and thus T_f is a schedule by Lemma 12). Because $F(i, p) \leq T(i, p)$ holds for any schedule, $F(i, p) \leq T_f(i, p)$. Moreover, by definition of T_f, $T_f(i, p) \leq F(i, p)$, thus, $F = T_f$.   ∎

Corollary 3 *A SURE is computable if and only if whatever the vertex (i, p) in Γ, there is no infinite path in Γ directed to (i, p).*

Proof   Lemmas 12 and 13 show that if a SURE is computable, i.e., if there is a schedule, the free schedule T_f is a schedule and $T_f(i, p)$ is equal to $F(i, p)$, the length of the longest path in Γ directed to (i, p). Thus, for any vertex (i,p), the length of any path directed to (i,p) is bounded by $T_f(i,p)$ and there is no infinite path directed to (i,p).

Conversely, assume that there is no schedule. In particular, the function F is not a schedule, which means (Lemma 13) that there is a vertex (i,p) such that the length of the longest path directed to (i,p) is not bounded:

$$F(i,p) = \max\{t \geq 0 \mid \text{there exists } (j,q) \text{ such that } (j,q) \xrightarrow{t} (i,p)\} = +\infty$$

Note that Γ is a graph with *finite* degree. Thus, at least one direct predecessor (i_1,p_1) of (i,p) satisfies $F(i_1,p_1) = +\infty$. We apply the same argument for (i_1,p_1) and we define (i_2,p_2) such that $F(i_2,p_2) = +\infty$. Finally, by induction, we can build an infinite path directed to (i,p) of the form:
$$\cdots \xrightarrow{1} (i_k,p_k) \xrightarrow{1} \cdots \xrightarrow{1} (i_1,p_1) \xrightarrow{1} (i,p). \qquad \blacksquare$$

If $|V(\Gamma)|$ is finite, i.e., if all iteration domains $\mathcal{P}_i$ are bounded, then there is no infinite path in Γ if and only if Γ is an acyclic graph. Therefore, in this case, the problem of computability of a SURE is decidable, but expensive if the iteration domains are large. We point out that for extensions of the model of SUREs, such as conditional uniform recurrence equations or parameterized affine recurrence equations, the problem of computability becomes undecidable in the general case. We refer to [107] for more details about this topic.

In the following, we recall simpler conditions for computability that are sufficient and necessary for reasonable hypotheses on the iteration domains.

Theorem 17 *Let G be a reduced dependence graph specifying a system $\mathcal{S}$ of uniform recurrence equations defined over the region $F_n = \mathbb{N}^n = \{p \in \mathbb{Z}^n, p \geq 0\}$ (i.e., for all i, $\mathcal{P}_i = F_n$). Then $\mathcal{S}$ is computable if and only if G has no cycle of nonpositive weight, i.e., no cycle $\mathcal{C}$ such that $w(\mathcal{C}) \leq 0$.*

Proof Because of Corollary 3, we just have to show that G has a cycle of nonpositive weight if and only if there an infinite path directed to (i,p) for some vertex (i,p) in Γ.

$\Rightarrow$: Suppose that G has a nonpositive weight cycle $\mathcal{C}$: $\mathcal{C} = (v_i = v_{i_1} \xrightarrow{e_1} v_{i_2} \cdots v_{i_k} \xrightarrow{e_k} v_{i_{k+1}} = v_i)$ and $w(\mathcal{C}) \leq 0$. Define $w_j = \sum_{i=j}^{k} w(e_i)$ for $j \geq 1$: $w_1 = w(\mathcal{C})$ and $w_{k+1} = 0$. Let $p \in F_n$ be such that $p - w_j \in F_n$ for all j, $1 \leq j \leq k$. We have $(i_j, p - w_j) \xrightarrow{1} (i_{j+1}, p - w_{j+1})$ for $1 \leq j < k$, and thus $(i, p - w(\mathcal{C})) = (i_1, p - w_1) \xrightarrow{k} (i_{k+1}, p - w_{k+1}) = (i,p)$. Furthermore, $p - w(\mathcal{C}) \geq p$ because $w(\mathcal{C}) \leq 0$, and we can use the same argument for $p - w(\mathcal{C})$ and we get $(i, p - 2w(\mathcal{C})) \xrightarrow{k} (i, p - w(\mathcal{C}))$ and thus $(i, p - 2w(\mathcal{C})) \xrightarrow{2k}$

(i, p). Finally, by induction on n, we get $(i, p - nw(\mathcal{C})) \xrightarrow{nk} (i, p)$, which proves that there is an infinite path in Γ directed to (i, p).

$\Leftarrow$: Assume that there is an infinite path directed to some vertex (i, p) of Γ: $\ldots \xrightarrow{1} (i_k, p_k) \xrightarrow{1} \ldots \xrightarrow{1} (i_1, p_1) \xrightarrow{1} (i, p)$. Extract from the sequence $(i_k, p_k)_{k \geq 1}$ a subsequence $(i_{k_j}, p_{k_j})_{j \geq 1}$ such that the sequence p_{k_j} is nondecreasing in the first coordinate. For that, let π_k be the first coordinate of p_k. Define by induction for $j \geq 1$, $\pi^j = \min\{\pi_k \mid k > k_{j-1}\}$ and $k_j = \min\{k > k_{j-1} \mid \pi_k = \pi^j\}$ (we let $k_0 = 0$). This construction ensures that the sequence π_{k_j} is nondecreasing because for all j, $k_j > k_{j-1}$ and $\pi_{k_j} = \pi^j \geq \pi^{j-1} = \pi_{k_{j-1}}$. Now, with the same technique, we can extract from the sequence (i_{k_j}, p_{k_j}) a subsequence such that p_{k_j} is nondecreasing in the second coordinate (and in the first coordinate). Recursively, we can define a subsequence of (i_k, p_k) that is nondecreasing in each coordinate of the p_k; denote this sequence by (j_k, q_k).

Now consider the sequence j_k. Because G has a finite number of vertices, some value j must occur infinitely many times in the sequence j_k. Therefore, there exist $k_1 < k_2$ such that $(j, p_{k_2}) \longrightarrow (j, p_{k_1})$. Furthermore, by construction, $p_{k_1} \leq p_{k_2}$. This means that v_j belongs to a cycle of G whose weight is $p_{k_1} - p_{k_2}$, i.e., a nonpositive weight cycle. ∎

Now we give a computability condition for bounded iteration domains. This condition is sufficient whatever the iteration domains $\mathcal{P}_i$ but is necessary only for "sufficiently large" domains. Briefly speaking, a domain is sufficiently large if we can build a cycle in Γ from a zero-weight cycle of the reduced dependence graph G.

Theorem 18 *Let G be a reduced dependence graph. Then all systems of uniform recurrence equations defined from G on bounded iteration domains are computable if and only if G has no cycle of zero weight.*

Proof $\Rightarrow$: We prove that if G has a zero-weight cycle, then some SUREs defined from G are not computable.

Let $\mathcal{C}$ be a zero-weight cycle of G: $\mathcal{C} = (v_i = v_{i_1} \xrightarrow{e_1} v_{i_2} \cdots v_{i_k} \xrightarrow{e_k} v_{i_{k+1}} = v_i)$ and $w(\mathcal{C}) = 0$. Define $w_j = \sum_{i=j}^{k} w(e_i)$ for $j \geq 1$: $w_1 = w(\mathcal{C}) = 0$ and $w_{k+1} = 0$. Suppose that there exists $p \in \mathcal{P}_i$ such that $p - w_j \in \mathcal{P}_{i_j}$ for all $j, 1 \leq j \leq k$. Then, we have $(i_j, p - w_j) \xrightarrow{1} (i_{j+1}, p - w_{j+1})$ for $1 \leq j < k$, and thus $(i, p) = (i_1, p - w_1) \xrightarrow{k} (i_{k+1}, p - w_{k+1}) = (i, p)$. Thus, by induction on n, we obtain $(i, p) \xrightarrow{nk} (i, p)$, which proves that there is an infinite path in Γ directed to (i, p). We conclude with Corollary 3. A SURE defined by G on domains $\mathcal{P}_i$ that include a point p that satisfy $p - w_j \in \mathcal{P}_{i_j}$ for all j, $1 \leq j \leq k$, is not computable.

$\Leftarrow$: Conversely, assume that one of the SUREs S defined from G on bounded iteration domains is not computable. Corollary 3 shows that there is an infinite path (i_k, p_k) in the graph Γ associated to S. Because all iteration domains $\mathcal{P}_i$ are bounded, the number of vertices in Γ is finite. Therefore, some vertex (i, p) occurs infinitely many times in the sequence (i_k, p_k). Thus, $(i, p) \xrightarrow{t} (i, p)$ for some $t \geq 1$, which means that v_i belongs to a cycle of G whose weight is $p - p = 0$. ∎

In the rest of the chapter, we consider this last case; we focus on reduced dependence graphs that define computable SUREs for any bounded iteration domains. Therefore, according to Theorem 18, we study only reduced dependence graphs that have no cycle of zero weight. We show how this property can be checked in polynomial time. Furthermore, we show that it is possible to derive closed forms for schedules that can be proved asymptotically optimal compared to the free schedule (which is not necessarily regular).

The study is divided into two parts. The first part considers the special case of a single equation, i.e., of a reduced dependence graph with a single vertex, while the second part is devoted to the general case of a system of uniform recurrence equations, i.e., of an arbitrary reduced dependence graph.

4.3 URE and Linear Scheduling

4.3.1 Introduction

Section 4.3 aims at studying in more detail the particular case of a single equation whose iteration domain is defined as the set of integer points contained in a polyhedron. The main property that we prove is that the computability of a single equation is linked to the existence of regular schedules, called *linear schedules*. Furthermore, we show that the minimal makespan [1] achieved by a linear schedule is close to the minimal absolute makespan, i.e., the makespan of the free schedule.

This result justifies why linear schedules have been so widely used as a tool in automatic code transformation methodologies, because they provide *regular* near-optimal schedules, which is highly desirable for generating small codes. For example, the space-time method used for the synthesis of systolic arrays [90, 100] or the hyperplane method used in automatic parallelization (see Chapter 5) are based on linear schedules.

---

[1] In the VLSI literature, the word *latency* is often used as a synonym for makespan, i.e., the total execution time.

Section 4.3 is organized as follows. In Section 4.3.2, we study more deeply the structure of dependence paths, first when the iteration domain is $F_n = \{z \in \mathbb{Z}^n \mid z \geq 0\}$, and then for more general domains. In Section 4.3.3, we refine Theorem 18 with a more precise formulation of the problem of computability for the case of a URE, defined on a bounded polyhedron. Finally, in Section 4.3.4, we show how to derive linear schedules that can be proved asymptotically optimal (in a sense to be defined) for a single uniform recurrence equation.

We first simplify the notations we used in Section 4.2.1 to the particular case of a single equation.

Simplified Notations for a Single Equation

A uniform recurrence equation (URE) (sometimes called uniform dependence algorithm (UDA) in the literature) is defined by an iteration domain $J \subset \mathbb{Z}^n$ and a reduced dependence graph with a single vertex, i.e., by an equation of the form:

$$V(p) = f(V(p - d_1), \ldots, V(p - d_m)) \tag{4.2}$$

In other words, the structure of the graph itself is useless (there is only one vertex); only the weights of the edges, i.e., the dependence vectors d_i, are important for defining the URE. We write $E = U(J, D)$ for defining a URE whose iteration domain is J and whose dependence vectors are the column vectors of the matrix D. The matrix D, called the *dependence matrix*, is an $n \times m$ matrix if J is an n-dimensional domain and if m is the number of dependence vectors.

We also simplify the notations we used for Γ, the expanded dependence graph; because we consider a single variable $V = V_1$, we identify the vertices of Γ, $V(\Gamma) = \{1\} \times J$, with J itself; we use the notation p instead of $(1, p)$ to denote a vertex of Γ and the notation $p \longrightarrow q$ instead of $(1, p) \longrightarrow (1, q)$ for denoting a path in Γ.

Dependence Path and Linear Equations

Consider a path in Γ, $p = p_1 \xrightarrow{1} \ldots \xrightarrow{1} p_k = q$. By definition of $\xrightarrow{1}$, for all j, $1 \leq j < k$, $p_{j+1} = p_j + d_{i_j}$ for some dependence vector d_{i_j}. Therefore, one has the vector relation:

$$q = p + \sum_{j=1}^{k} d_{i_j} = p + \sum_{i=1}^{m} \lambda_i d_i$$

where λ_i is the number of occurrences of d_i in the path $p \longrightarrow q$. Therefore, a path in Γ between two points p and q implies that $q - p$ is an integral nonnegative linear combination of the dependence vectors, which can be written in matrix form:

$$p \longrightarrow q \quad \Rightarrow \quad \exists \lambda \in \mathbb{N}^n \text{ such that } q - p = D\lambda \tag{4.3}$$

The goal of Section 4.3.2 is to give conditions for the converse to be true, i.e., conditions to build a path in Γ from p to q when $p - q = D\lambda$ for some nonnegative vector λ.

More Definitions

We use the following notation. If M is an integral $n \times m$ matrix, we denote by $\delta(M)$ the n-dimensional vector whose components are given by:

$$\begin{array}{ll} \delta_i = 0 & \text{if } M_{i,j} = 0 \text{ for all } j, \ 1 \leq j \leq m \\ \delta_i = \sum_{j=1}^{m} |M_{i,j}| - 1 & \text{otherwise} \end{array}$$

From now on, we assume that the iteration domain J is defined as the set of all integer points contained in a polyhedron:

$$J = \{x \in \mathbb{Z}^n \mid Ax \leq b\}$$

We write $J = J(A, b)$ and we say that J is a *polyhedral domain* (even if J is not exactly a polyhedron, but the intersection of $\mathbb{Z}^n$ and a polyhedron). We use the notation $J_{\mathbb{Q}}(A, b)$ to denote the same polyhedron defined in $\mathbb{Q}^n$: $J_{\mathbb{Q}}(A, b) = \{x \in \mathbb{Q}^n \mid Ax \leq b\}$. A is a matrix of size $l \times n$, and b is an l-dimensional vector: A and b define, by l inequalities, a polyhedron in an n-dimensional space.

4.3.2 Construction of Dependence Paths

In this section, we give conditions to transform Equation (4.3) into an equivalence, i.e., we give conditions for the existence of a path in Γ from p to q when p and q are such that $p - q = D\lambda$ for some nonnegative integral vector λ. We first study the case where the iteration domain is F_n; then we show a similar result for the case of an arbitrary polyhedral domain.

Dependence Paths for the First Quadrant F_n

Remember that $F_n = \mathbb{N}^n = \{x \in \mathbb{Z}^n \mid x \geq 0\}$. Let $T = \{x \in \mathbb{Q}^n \mid x \geq \delta(D)\}$. We first need a technical lemma.

Lemma 14 *Let $p \in \mathbb{Z}^n$ and $q \in \mathbb{Z}^n$ such that:*

$$q = y + \sum_{i=1}^{m} \theta_i d_i \text{ with } 0 \le \theta_i < 1 \text{ and } y \in T$$

and

$$q = p + \sum_{i=1}^{m} \beta_i d_i \text{ with } \beta_i \in \{0, 1\} \text{ and } p \in F_n$$

Then $q \in F_n$, and there is a path from p to q in F_n, $p \xrightarrow{N} q$ with $N = \sum_{i=1}^{m} \beta_i$.

Proof   To simplify the notations, we first permute the columns of D (i.e., we renumber the dependence vectors) so that $\beta_i = 1$ for $1 \le i \le l$ and $\beta_i = 0$ for $i > l$. Remember that d_i is the ith column of D and $D_{k,i}$ is its kth component. We let $\delta = \delta(D)$.

Let $t_j = p + \sum_{i=1}^{j} d_i$, $t_0 = p$, $t_l = q$, and $t_{j+1} = t_j + d_j$. We now prove that $t_j \in F_n$, for all j, $1 \le j \le l$. Indeed, consider $(t_j)_k$ the kth component of t_j: $(t_j)_k = p_k + \sum_{i=1}^{j} D_{k,i}$. If $D_{k,i} \ge 0$ for all i, $1 \le i \le j$, then $(t_j)_k \ge p_k \ge 0$ because $p \in F_n$. Otherwise, we write:

$$t_j = p + \sum_{i=1}^{j} d_i = q - \sum_{i=1}^{m} \beta_i d_i + \sum_{i=1}^{j} d_i = q - \sum_{i=1}^{l} d_i + \sum_{i=1}^{j} d_i = q - \sum_{i=j+1}^{l} d_i$$

$$t_j = y + \sum_{i=1}^{m} \theta_i d_i - \sum_{i=j+1}^{l} d_i = y + \sum_{i=1}^{j} \theta_i d_i + \sum_{i=j+1}^{l} (\theta_i - 1) d_i + \sum_{i=l+1}^{m} \theta_i d_i$$

Thus, we have:

$$
\begin{aligned}
(t_j)_k &= y_k + \sum_{i=1}^{j} \theta_i D_{k,i} + \sum_{i=j+1}^{l} (\theta_i - 1) D_{k,i} + \sum_{i=l+1}^{m} \theta_i D_{k,i} \\
&\ge y_k + \sum_{i=1}^{j} \theta_i D_{k,i} - \sum_{i=j+1}^{m} |D_{k,i}| > y_k - \sum_{i=1}^{m} |D_{k,i}|
\end{aligned}
$$

The last inequality is indeed a strict inequality because $D_{k.i} < 0$ for at least one i, $1 \le i \le j$, and $0 \le \theta_i < 1$. Finally, $(t_j)_k > y_k - \delta_k - 1 \ge -1$ because $y \in T$. But $(t_j)_k$ is an integer; thus $(t_j)_k \ge 0$. This proves that $t_j \in F_n$.

Therefore, we have proved that $p = t_0 \xrightarrow{1} \dots \xrightarrow{1} t_l = q$, i.e., $p \xrightarrow{l} q$ with $l = \sum_{i=1}^{m} \beta_i$, with $t_i \in F_n$.   ∎

We are now ready to give a sufficient condition for the existence of a dependence path in F_n when its extremities are not too close to the boundary of F_n.

Lemma 15 *Let p and q be two points in $T \cap F_n$ such that:*

$$q = p + \sum_{i=1}^{m} \alpha_i d_i \text{ with } \alpha_i \geq 0, \ \alpha_i \in \mathbb{Z}$$

Then there is a path from p to q in F_n, which uses exactly α_i times the dependence vector d_i, i.e., $p \xrightarrow{N} q$ with $N = \sum_{i=1}^{m} \alpha_i$.

Proof The idea to build the path $p \longrightarrow q$ is to draw the line (p, q), to define $N + 1$ regularly spaced points y_k on this line (where $N = \sum_{i=1}^{m} \alpha_i$), and to round these $N + 1$ points into integer points r_k that can be proved to belong to F_n. This is done as follows.

Let $y_k = (1 - \frac{k}{N})p + \frac{k}{N}q$, for $0 \leq k \leq N$. Because $p \in T$ and $q \in T$, $y_k \in T$ (T is convex). However, in general, $y_k \notin \mathbb{Z}^n$. Note that $y_k = p + \frac{k}{N}(q - p) = p + \frac{k}{N} \sum_{i=1}^{m} \alpha_i d_i$. Let $r_k = p + \sum_{i=1}^{m} \lceil \frac{k\alpha_i}{N} \rceil d_i$ for $0 \leq k \leq N$: $r_0 = p$ and $r_N = q$.

We have:

$$r_k = y_k + \sum_{i=1}^{m} \theta_i d_i \text{ with } \theta_i = \left\lceil \frac{k\alpha_i}{N} \right\rceil - \frac{k\alpha_i}{N}, \ 0 \leq \theta_i < 1$$

$$r_{k+1} = r_k + \sum_{i=1}^{m} \beta_i d_i \text{ with } \beta_i = \left\lceil \frac{(k+1)\alpha_i}{N} \right\rceil - \left\lceil \frac{k\alpha_i}{N} \right\rceil, \ \beta_i \in \{0, 1\}$$

The points r_k and r_{k+1} satisfy the hypotheses of Lemma 14, except that we do not yet know that $r_k \in F_n$, except for $r_0 = p$. Thus, we apply Lemma 14 to r_k and r_{k+1} successively for k from 0 to $N - 1$ (in this order) and we get:

$$r_{k+1} \in F_n \text{ and } r_k \xrightarrow{L_k} r_{k+1} \text{ with } L_k = \sum_{i=1}^{m} \left(\left\lceil \frac{(k+1)\alpha_i}{N} \right\rceil - \left\lceil \frac{k\alpha_i}{N} \right\rceil \right)$$

Finally, because $r_0 = p$ and $r_N = q$, we get $p \xrightarrow{L} q$ with $L = \sum_{k=0}^{N-1} L_k$, i.e.:

$$L = \sum_{k=0}^{N-1} \sum_{i=1}^{m} \left(\left\lceil \frac{(k+1)\alpha_i}{N} \right\rceil - \left\lceil \frac{k\alpha_i}{N} \right\rceil \right) = \sum_{k=1}^{N} \sum_{i=1}^{m} \left\lceil \frac{k\alpha_i}{N} \right\rceil - \sum_{k=0}^{N-1} \sum_{i=1}^{m} \left\lceil \frac{k\alpha_i}{N} \right\rceil$$

$$\Rightarrow \quad L = \sum_{i=1}^{m} \lceil \alpha_i \rceil = \sum_{i=1}^{m} \alpha_i = N$$

Similarly, in the path $p \longrightarrow q$ built earlier, the dependence vector d_i is used exactly α_i times because $\alpha_i = \sum_{k=0}^{N-1} \left(\left\lceil \frac{(k+1)\alpha_i}{N} \right\rceil - \left\lceil \frac{k\alpha_i}{N} \right\rceil \right)$. This completes the proof.   ∎

In conclusion, as soon as p and q are not too close to the domain boundary (condition $p \geq \delta(D)$), it is possible to build a dependence path in F_n that corresponds to a linear relation $q = p + D\lambda$, $\lambda \in \mathbb{Z}^n$, $\lambda \geq 0$. Figure 4.4 illustrates such a situation, with

$$q = \begin{pmatrix} 18 \\ 6 \end{pmatrix} = \begin{pmatrix} 3 \\ 3 \end{pmatrix} + \begin{pmatrix} 3 & -1 \\ -1 & 3 \end{pmatrix} \begin{pmatrix} 6 \\ 3 \end{pmatrix} = p + D\alpha$$

Note that dependence vectors cannot be considered in any order for building a path from p to q; some bad choices lead to paths that go out of the domain F_n, as depicted by dashed lines in Figure 4.4.

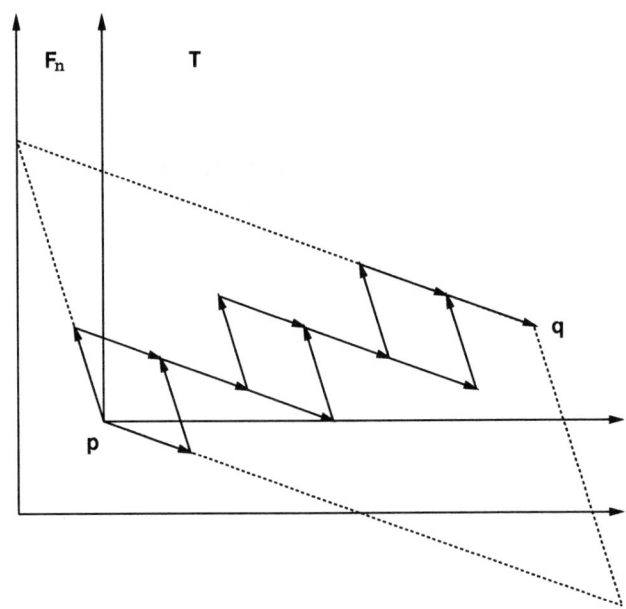

Figure 4.4: Paths in F_n corresponding to a linear relation between p and q.

Dependence Paths for a Polyhedral Domain J

We now consider the case of a polyhedral domain $J = J(A, b)$. We assume that A is an integral matrix whereas vector b may have rational components (the reason for this hypothesis is purely technical; it makes the proof of Theorem 4.6 simpler). We let $\delta = \delta(AD)$, where D is the dependence matrix.

Lemma 16 *Assume that $J(A, b - \delta)$ is not empty and let p and q be two points in $J(A, b - \delta)$ such that:*

$$q = p + D\lambda = p + \sum_{i=1}^{m} \lambda_i d_i \text{ with } \lambda \in \mathbb{Z}^n, \ \lambda \geq 0$$

Then, there is a path from p to q in $J(A, b)$, $p \xrightarrow{N} q$, with $N = \sum_{i=1}^{m} \lambda_i$, which uses exactly λ_i times the dependence vector d_i.

Proof We denote by $\lfloor b \rfloor$ the vector whose components are the floor of the components of b. The proof is based on the following fact: $r \in J(A, b) \Leftrightarrow r \in J(A, \lfloor b \rfloor)$ (r is integral), and $r \in J(A, \lfloor b \rfloor) \Leftrightarrow x = (\lfloor b \rfloor - Ar) \in F_n$. This remark allows us to link paths in J with paths in F_n.

Let $x = \lfloor b \rfloor - Ap$, and $y = \lfloor b \rfloor - Aq$. $y = \lfloor b \rfloor - A(p + D\lambda) = x - AD\lambda$. Furthermore, $x, y \in T \cap F_n$ because $p, q \in J(A, b - \delta) = J(A, \lfloor b \rfloor - \delta)$. Let $D' = -AD$. The points x and y satisfy the hypotheses of Lemma 15: There is a path from x to y in F_n, $x \xrightarrow{N} y$ with $N = \sum_{i=1}^{m} \lambda_i$, which uses exactly λ_i times the dependence vector $d'_i = -(AD)_i = -Ad_i$. This means that we can build a sequence of points x_k, $0 \leq k \leq N$, such that $x_k \in F_n$, $x_0 = x$, $x_N = y$ and $x_{k+1} = x_k + d'_{i_k}$. Actually, $x_k = x + \sum_{j=1}^{k} d'_{i_j} = x - A\sum_{j=1}^{k} d_{i_j}$.

Now, let $p_k = p + \sum_{j=1}^{k} d_{i_j}$. $\lfloor b \rfloor - Ap_k = \lfloor b \rfloor - Ap - A\sum_{j=1}^{k} d_{i_j} = x_k$. Thus, $p_k \in J(A, \lfloor b \rfloor)$. Furthermore, $p_0 = p$ and $p_{k+1} = p_k + d_{i_k}$, i.e., $p \xrightarrow{N} p_N$, with $N = \sum_{i=1}^{m} \lambda_i$. Finally, because the path $x \xrightarrow{N} y$ uses exactly λ_i times the dependence vector d'_i, we have:

$$p_N = p + \sum_{j=1}^{N} d_{i_j} = p + \sum_{i=1}^{m} \lambda_i d_i = q$$

Thus $q = p_N$ and the proof is complete. ∎

4.3.3 Computability Criterion for a Single Equation

From now on, we consider a uniform recurrence equation E defined on a *bounded* polyhedral domain $J = J(A, b)$, with a dependence matrix D: $E = U(J(A, b), D)$. As shown by Corollary 3, E is computable if and only if Γ, its corresponding expanded dependence graph, has no infinite path directed to some vertex of Γ, i.e., (because J is finite) if and only if Γ is acyclic.

We studied in Corollary 18 the link between the cycles in Γ and the zero-weight cycles in the reduced dependence graph; if the reduced dependence graph has a zero-weight cycle and if the domain is "sufficiently large," then there is a cycle in Γ and the URE is not computable. The goal of this section is to define more precisely what we mean by "sufficiently large" and to show the link between the computability and the existence of linear schedules.

We introduce the following sets:

$$S(D) = \{s \in \mathbb{Q}^n \mid sD \geq 1\} \text{ and } V(D) = \{v \in \mathbb{Z}^n \mid v \geq 0, \ v \neq 0, \ Dv = 0\}$$

(To make notations simpler, s is considered as a row vector in $S(D)$ so that sD is well-defined.)

Lemma 17 *For any $s \in S(D)$, the function T_s from J into $\mathbb{N}$ defined by:*

$$T_s(p) = \lfloor sp \rfloor + c_s \text{ where } c_s = -\min_{p \in J} \lfloor sp \rfloor$$

is a schedule for $E = U(J, D)$. Such a schedule is called a linear schedule.

Proof   First, note that c_s is well-defined because J is bounded. Furthermore, for all $p \in J$, $\lfloor sp \rfloor \geq -c_s$. Thus, $T_s(p) \in \mathbb{N}$. T_s is a function from J into $\mathbb{N}$ as required for a schedule. Let $p, q \in J$ such that $p \xrightarrow{1} q$: $q = p + d_k$ for some k, $1 \leq k \leq m$. Then, $sq = s(p + d_k) = sp + sd_k \geq sp + 1 \geq \lfloor sp \rfloor + 1$. Therefore, $\lfloor sq \rfloor \geq \lfloor sp \rfloor + 1$ and consequently, $T_s(q) \geq T_s(p) + 1$. T_s is indeed a schedule. ∎

Lemma 18 *S and V are linked by the equivalence: $S(D) \neq \emptyset \Leftrightarrow V(D) = \emptyset$.*

Proof   Let $V_{\mathbb{Q}}(D) = \{v \in \mathbb{Q}^n \mid v \geq 0, \ v \neq 0, \ Dv = 0\}$. Note that $V_{\mathbb{Q}}(D) = \emptyset$ if and only if $V(D) = \emptyset$, because we can multiply any element of $V_{\mathbb{Q}}(D)$ by a suitable integer (for example, the least common multiple of the denominators of its components) to obtain a vector in $V(D)$.

$S(D) \neq \emptyset$ if and only if $\exists s \in \mathbb{Q}^n$ such that $-sD \leq -1$. By Farkas's lemma (see Corollary 7.1e [110]), this is equivalent to $(-Dy = 0, \ y \geq 0 \Rightarrow -y1 \geq 0)$, i.e., $(Dy = 0, \ y \geq 0 \Rightarrow \sum_{i=1}^n y_i \leq 0)$. Because all the components of y are nonnegative, $\sum_{i=1}^n y_i \leq 0 \Leftrightarrow y = 0$. Therefore, $S(D) \neq \emptyset$ if and only if $\{y \in \mathbb{Q}^n \mid y \geq 0, \ y \neq 0, \ Dy = 0\}$ is empty, which is equivalent to $V(D) = \emptyset$. ∎

Theorem 19 *If $J(A, b - \delta)$ is not empty, with $\delta = \delta(AD)$, then the uniform recurrence equation $E = U(J(A, b), D)$ is computable if and only if there is a linear schedule for E.*

Proof If there is a linear schedule for E, Lemma 17 shows that there is a schedule (because a linear schedule is a schedule), and thus E is computable by definition.

If there is no linear schedule, then $S(D)$ is empty, which by Lemma 18 is equivalent to the fact that $V(D)$ is not empty. Let $\lambda \in V(D)$, and let $p \in J(A, b-\delta): p = p+0 = p+D\lambda$. We apply Lemma 16. There is a path from p to p in $J(A, b)$, which uses λ_i times the dependence vector d_i. Therefore, there is a cycle around p in $J(A, b)$. Γ has a cycle, and by Corollary 3, E is not computable. ∎

4.3.4 Optimal Linear Schedules

Linear schedules are particularly interesting because they provide schedules that are regular, repetitive, and can be coded in a condensed way (only s and c_s need to be stored). Furthermore, among all linear schedules, one often looks for schedules that correspond to the smallest number of iteration steps, i.e., whose makespan is as small as possible.

We first explain how to select $s \in S(D)$ so that the makespan of the corresponding schedule is minimized. Then we compare this minimized makespan to the minimal makespan, i.e., the makespan of the free schedule We show that for large iteration domains, the minimal makespan achieved by a linear schedule is equal, up to a constant independent of the domain size, to the makespan of the free schedule.

Minimizing the Makespan of Linear Schedules

Consider a computable uniform recurrence equation, $E = (J(A, b), D)$, such that $J(A, b)$ is bounded and $J(A, b - \delta)$ is not empty ($\delta = \delta(AD)$). By Theorem 19, we know that $S(D)$ is not empty, i.e., that there is a linear schedule. Let T_s be a linear schedule. The number of steps described by T_s, i.e., the makespan L_s of T_s, is defined by:

$$
\begin{aligned}
L_s &= 1 + \max\{T_s(p) \mid p \in J(A, b)\} - \min\{T_s(p) \mid p \in J(A, b)\} \\
L_s &= 1 + \max\{\lfloor sp \rfloor \mid p \in J(A, b)\} - \min\{\lfloor sq \rfloor \mid q \in J(A, b)\} \\
L_s &= 1 + \max\{\lfloor sp \rfloor - \lfloor sq \rfloor \mid p, q \in J(A, b)\}
\end{aligned}
$$

The optimal linear schedule is the one that minimizes L_s over all rational vectors s such that $s \in S(D)$, i.e., such that $sD \geq 1$. $L_{\min}$ denotes the minimal makespan achieved by a linear schedule: $L_{\min} = \min\{L_s \mid s \in S(D)\}$. Similarly, we denote by L_{free} the makespan of the free schedule, i.e., one plus the length (number of edges) of the longest path in the expanded dependence graph.

To formulate the problem as a rational linear programming optimization, we approximate L_s by removing the floor function and considering all points in $J_{\mathbb{Q}}(A, b)$ instead of $J(A, b)$. We let:

$$L_s^* = \max\{s(p - q) \mid p, q \in J_{\mathbb{Q}}(A, b)\} \text{ and } L_{\min}^* = \min\{L_s^* \mid s \in S(D)\}$$

Lemma 19 $L_{\min} \leq L_{\min}^* + 2$. *Furthermore, if all the vertices of the polyhedron $J_{\mathbb{Q}}(A, b)$ are integer points, then $L_{\min}^* \leq L_{\min}$.*

Proof Let $d(p, q) = \lfloor sp \rfloor - \lfloor sq \rfloor$: $d(p, q) = \lfloor (sq - \lfloor sq \rfloor) + s(p - q) \rfloor$. Because $0 \leq sq - \lfloor sq \rfloor < 1$, we have $s(p - q) \leq (sq - \lfloor sq \rfloor) + s(p - q) < s(p - q) + 1$, and thus $s(p - q) - 1 < d(p, q) < s(p - q) + 1$.

Let $s \in S(D)$. Because $J(A, b)$ is bounded, it contains a finite number of points, therefore L_s, the makespan of T_s (expressed as a minimum among all points in $J(A, b)$), is reached for some points p and q: $L_s = 1 + d(p, q)$. Because $d(p, q) < s(p-q)+1$, we get $L_s < s(p-q)+2 \leq L_s^*+2$. Furthermore, $L_s \geq L_{\min}$. This proves that for all $s \in S(D)$, $L_{\min} < L_s^* + 2$, which implies $L_{\min} \leq L_{\min}^* + 2$.

Consider $L_s^* = \max\{s(p - q) \mid p, q \in J_{\mathbb{Q}}(A, b)\}$. $L_s^* = \max\{sp \mid p \in J_{\mathbb{Q}}(A, b)\} - \min\{sq \mid q \in J_{\mathbb{Q}}(A, b)\}$. The minimum and maximum are both linear programming optimizations, thus L_s^* is reached for some extremal vertices p and q of the polyhedron $J_{\mathbb{Q}}(A, b)$: $L_s^* = s(p-q)$. Because $s(p-q) < d(p, q) + 1$, $L_s^* < d(p, q) + 1$. If all the vertices of $J_{\mathbb{Q}}(A, b)$ are integer points, p and q belong to $J(A, b)$ and thus, $L_s^* < L_s$ because $L_s = \max\{d(p, q) + 1 \mid p, q \in J(A, b)\}$. Finally, we get $L_{\min}^* < L_s$ and $L_{\min}^* \leq L_{\min}$. ■

We now explain how to derive a vector $s \in S(D)$ that minimizes L_s^*. $L_{\min}^*$ is the solution of a min-max problem. However, it can easily be transformed into a simple linear program, as follows:

$$L_s^* = \max\{s(p - q) \mid Ap \leq b, \ Aq \leq b\}$$

Thus, by the duality theorem of linear programming (see Corollary 7.1g in [110]), we have:

$$L_s^* = \min\{(s_1 + s_2)b \mid s_1 \geq \mathbf{0}, \ s_2 \geq \mathbf{0}, \ s_1 A = s, \ s_2 A = -s\}$$

Therefore:

$$L_{\min}^* = \min\{(s_1+s_2)b \mid s_1 \geq \mathbf{0}, \ s_2 \geq \mathbf{0}, \ s_1 A = s, \ s_2 A = -s, \ sD \geq \mathbf{1}\} \quad (4.4)$$

Remark that this problem is linear in b: the search for the optimal vector s over the family of domains $J(A, kb)$ $(k > 0)$ can be reduced to the search on the domain $J(A, b)$ because minimizing $(s_1 + s_2)kb$ is equivalent to minimizing $(s_1 + s_2)b$ if $k > 0$. If $L^*_{\min}(A, b)$ denotes $L^*_{\min}$ for the iteration domain $J(A, b)$, then we have $L^*_{\min}(A, kb) = kL^*_{\min}(A, b)$. This property is fundamental for the rest of our study.

Optimal Linear Schedule Versus Free Schedule

As pointed out before, the simple fact that linear schedules are regular is important for automatic scheduling methodologies. However, a natural question arises. In terms of makespan, how much do we lose compared to the free schedule, which is the fastest schedule?

Karp, Miller, and Winograd answered a similar question by comparing the makespan of the free schedule defined on F_n with the minimal makespan of a piecewise linear schedule (briefly speaking, a piecewise linear schedule is a schedule that is linear on a finite number of subsets of F_n that form a partition of F_n). However, this does not answer our question, because the class of linear schedules is only a subclass of the class of piecewise linear schedules.

Fortes and Parisi-Presicce [44] gave an experimental answer to this question. They computed the difference δ between the makespan of the free schedule and the minimal makespan achieved by a linear schedule for 25 UREs, defined on an n-dimensional cube with $2 \leq n \leq 4$. They report the value $\delta = 0$ for 23 of the 25 algorithms and $\delta = 1$ for the last two algorithms. They also point out that δ remains invariant with changes in the size of the iteration domain of the algorithms.

In this section, we prove that this is indeed a general fact. The difference can be larger than 1 for pathological examples; however, the difference can always be bounded by a constant, independent of the domain size, as soon as the iteration domain is "sufficiently large." Briefly speaking, this comes from the fact that the dual of the linear program from which we compute $L^*_{\min}$ – linear program (4.4) – can be interpreted as the length of a dependence path in the expanded dependence graph, thereby providing a lower bound for the makespan of the free schedule.

Consider a computable uniform recurrence equation $E = (J(A, b), D)$ such that $J(A, b - \delta)$ is not empty ($\delta = \delta(AD)$). By Theorem 19, we know that there is a linear schedule and that a linear schedule that minimizes $L^*_{\min}$ can be built as a solution of the linear program (4.4):

$$L^*_{\min} = \min\{(s_1 + s_2)b \mid s_1 \geq \mathbf{0},\ s_2 \geq \mathbf{0},\ s_1 A = s,\ s_2 A = -s,\ sD \geq \mathbf{1}\}$$

This can be rewritten as:

$$L^*_{\min} = \min\{(s_1 + s_2)b \mid s_1, s_2 \geq \mathbf{0},\ s_1 A - s \geq \mathbf{0},\ -s_1 A + s \geq \mathbf{0},$$
$$s_2 A + s \geq \mathbf{0},\ -s_2 A - s \geq \mathbf{0},\ sD \geq \mathbf{1}\}$$

By the duality theorem of linear programming (see Corollary 7.1g in [110]), this equation is equivalent to:

$$L^*_{\min} = \max\{\mathbf{1}\lambda \mid \ z_q \geq 0, \ z_p \geq 0, \ q_1 \geq 0, \ q_2 \geq 0, \ p_1 \geq 0, \ p_2 \geq 0, \ \lambda \geq 0,$$
$$A(q_1 - q_2) + z_q = b, \ A(p_1 - p_2) + z_p = b,$$
$$(p_1 - p_2) - (q_1 - q_2) + D\lambda = 0\}$$

or, by letting $p = p_1 - p_2$, $q = q_1 - q_2$, and removing the slack variables z_p and z_q, to:

$$L^*_{\min} = \max \left\{ \sum_{i=1}^{m} \lambda_i \mid \lambda \geq 0, \ Aq \leq b, \ Ap \leq b, \ q = p + D\lambda \right\} \qquad (4.5)$$

We first formulate a naive lemma that explains intuitively the link between the minimal makespan of a linear schedule, $L_{\min}$, and the makespan of the free schedule, L_{free}.

Lemma 20 *If the linear program (4.5) has an optimal integral solution p, q, and λ such that the relation $q = p + D\lambda$ corresponds to a dependence path in the domain J, then $L_{\text{free}} \leq L_{\min} \leq L_{\text{free}} + 1$.*

Proof $L_{\text{free}} \leq L_{\min}$ is true by definition of the free schedule.

For the second inequality, consider an optimal solution of linear program (4.5) specified by integral vectors p, q, and λ, such that the relation $q = p + D\lambda$ defines a dependence path in J. This path has exactly $\sum_{i=1}^{m} \lambda_i$ edges. Therefore, $L_{\text{free}} \geq 1 + \sum_{i=1}^{m} \lambda_i = 1 + L^*_{\min}$. Finally, because $L_{\min} \leq L^*_{\min} + 2$ by Lemma 19, we get: $L_{\min} \leq L_{\text{free}} + 1$. ∎

In many practical examples, which are often very simple, the hypotheses of Lemma 20 are satisfied and we retrieve the experimental results of Fortes and Parisi-Presicce. The difference between the makespan of the free schedule and the makespan of the optimal linear schedule is 0 or 1. In general, however, two problems can occur:

- First, the relation $q = p + D\lambda$ may not correspond to a dependence path in $J = J(A, b)$ if p or q lies in a corner of the domain so that it is not possible to build a path from p to q that remains in the domain. To circumvent this problem, we will use Lemma 16 for points p and q in $J(A, b - \delta)$.

- Second, the linear program (4.5) may have only optimal solutions that are not integral solutions. In other words, p, q, and λ are not necessarily integral vectors. This is the general case, even if the dependence matrix D and the constraint matrix A are totally unimodular.

In the following proofs, we will use the following notation: For an $n \times m$ matrix M, we denote by $\tilde{\delta}(M)$ the n-dimensional vector whose ith component is $\sum_{j=1}^{m} |M_{i,j}|$. Note that $\tilde{\delta}(M) \leq \delta(M) + 1$; $\tilde{\delta}$ is a little less accurate than δ, which we used in Lemma 16. We do not claim that the bounds developed hereafter, in Lemma 21 and Theorem 20, are the sharpest bounds. But using $\tilde{\delta}$ makes proofs simpler.

Lemma 21 *Let $\mu = \tilde{\delta}(A) + \delta(2AD)$. Assume that $J(A, b - \mu)$ is not empty and let p and q be two points in $J_{\mathbb{Q}}(A, b - \mu)$ such that:*

$$q = p + D\lambda = p + \sum_{i=1}^{m} \lambda_i d_i \text{ with } \lambda \in \mathbb{Q}^n, \ \lambda \geq 0$$

Then there is a dependence path in $J(A, b)$ of length at least $\sum_{i=1}^{m} \lambda_i$.

Proof Let $\tilde{p} = \lceil p \rceil$ and $\tilde{q} = \tilde{p} + D\lceil \lambda \rceil$. Write $\tilde{p} = p + z_p$ with $0 \leq z_p < 1$, and $\lceil \lambda \rceil = \lambda + z_\lambda$ with $0 \leq z_\lambda < 1$. We have: $A\tilde{p} = Ap + Az_p \leq b - \mu + Az_p \leq b - \mu + \tilde{\delta}(A) = b - \delta(2AD) \leq b - \delta(AD)$.

Similarly, $\tilde{q} = p + z_p + D\lambda + Dz_\lambda = q + z_p + Dz_\lambda$. Thus, $A\tilde{q} \leq b - \mu + \tilde{\delta}(A) + \tilde{\delta}(AD) = b + \tilde{\delta}(AD) - \delta(2AD)$. Finally, because $\tilde{\delta}(AD) + \delta(AD) = \delta(2AD)$, $\tilde{q}$ is in $J(A, b - \delta(AD))$.

The vectors $\tilde{q}$ and $\tilde{p}$ satisfy the hypotheses of Lemma 16, because they both belong to $J(A, b - \delta(AD))$. Therefore, there is a dependence path of length $\sum_{i=1}^{m} \lceil \lambda_i \rceil$ in $J(A, b)$, and $\sum_{i=1}^{m} \lceil \lambda_i \rceil \geq \sum_{i=1}^{m} \lambda_i$. ∎

As claimed before, we are going to prove that, for sufficiently large domains, the difference between the minimal makespan achieved by a linear schedule and the makespan of the free schedule is bounded by a constant. Before proving this result, we must carefully define what we mean by "constant" (constant with respect to what?) and what we mean by "sufficiently large."

For a subset J of $\mathbb{Q}^n$, we define:

- If t is an n-dimensional vector, $J + t = \{q = p + t \mid p \in J\}$; $J + t$ is the translation of J by vector t.

- If k is a nonnegative rational number, $kJ = \{q = kp \mid p \in J\}$; kJ is the homothetic copy of J by factor k.

If J is a polyhedron ($J = J_{\mathbb{Q}}(A, b)$), then $J + t$ and kJ are polyhedra because $J + t = J_{\mathbb{Q}}(A, b + At)$ and $kJ = J_{\mathbb{Q}}(A, kb)$. Furthermore, we have the following properties:

- $L_{\min}^*(A, kb) = kL_{\min}^*(A, b)$; see, for example, linear program (4.4).

- $L^*_{min}(A, b + At) = L^*_{min}(A, b)$, because for example $(s_1 + s_2)A = \mathbf{0}$ in linear program (4.4).

- $L_{free}(A, b + At) = L_{free}(A, b)$ if t is an integral vector, because the translation by vector t of a dependence path in $J(A, b)$ is a dependence path in $J(A, b + At)$.

Definition 22 (Fatness) *Let A be an integral matrix and b a vector, possibly with rational components; let D be an integral matrix and $\nu = 2\tilde{\delta}(A) + \delta(2AD)$. The fatness f of the polyhedral domain $J = J(A, b)$, with respect to D, is defined as the maximal positive number f such that $J_{\mathbb{Q}}(A, \frac{b}{f} - \nu)$ is not empty.*

Note that if $J_{\mathbb{Q}}(A, \frac{b}{f} - \nu)$ is not empty, then $J(A, \frac{b}{f} - \mu)$ is not empty. In other words, we reduce as much as possible the "size" of J, by a homothetic factor f, so that the homothetic copy $J' = \frac{J}{f}$ is large enough, in the sense that Lemma 21 can be applied. The larger the fatness, the "larger" the domain. Remark that if J is not full-dimensional, then the fatness may be undefined, and if J is not bounded then $f = +\infty$ is possible. Moreover, for a domain J with bounded fatness, $f(kJ) = kf(J)$ and $f(J + t) = f(J)$.

Intuitively (modulo the slight difference between δ and $\tilde{\delta}$), a "fat" domain (i.e., with $f \geq 1$) is a domain that contains an integral point p_0 from which dependence vectors and canonical vectors can be safely added. If $Ap_0 \leq b - \nu$, then for each dependence vector d_i and for each rational z_i, $0 \leq z_i \leq 1$, $A(p_0 + z_i d_i) \leq Ap_0 + \tilde{\delta}(AD) \leq b$, and for each canonical vector e_i, $A(p_0 + z_i e_i) \leq Ap_0 + \tilde{\delta}(A) \leq b$. The exact definition of ν defines a similar (and a bit larger) box around p_0 that remains inside the domain.

Example 8

Consider the simplest case of a rectangular domain: $J = \{(i, j) \mid 0 \leq i, j \leq N\}$, with $N \geq 3$, and let D be the 2-by-2 matrix whose columns are the two vectors $(-1, 2)$ and $(2, -1)$. We have:

$$A = \begin{pmatrix} 1 & 0 \\ -1 & 0 \\ 0 & 1 \\ 0 & -1 \end{pmatrix} \quad D = \begin{pmatrix} -1 & 2 \\ 2 & -1 \end{pmatrix}$$

All components of $\delta(2AD)$ are equal to $2 * 3 - 1 = 5$; all components of $\tilde{\delta}(A)$ are equal to 1, thus all components of ν are equal to 7. $J(A, \frac{b}{f} - \nu)$ is the rectangle defined by the inequalities $7 \leq i, j \leq \frac{N}{f} - 7$. The fatness of J is the largest number such that this rectangle is not empty; f is such that $\frac{N}{f} - 7 = 7$, i.e., $f = \frac{N}{14}$. $\qquad\square$

We are now ready to state the final result.

Theorem 20 *Let E be a computable URE defined by a dependence matrix D on an iteration domain $J = J(A, b)$ where A is an integral matrix. Suppose that the fatness f of J is at least 1. Then there is a linear schedule for E, and with $L_{free} = L_{free}(A, b)$, $L_{min}^* = L_{min}^*(A, b)$, and $L_{min} = L_{min}(A, b)$, we have:*

$$L_{free} \geq \frac{f-1}{f} L_{min}^* + 1 \qquad (4.6)$$

which implies $L_{min}^* \sim L_{min} \sim L_{free}$ when $f \to \infty$. We even have

$$L_{free} \leq L_{min} \leq L_{free} + K$$

where K is constant with respect to the fatness of the domain, in the sense that K is the same for all homothetic copies of J and all copies defined by translations.

Proof $J(A, b - \nu)$ is not empty, thus $J(A, b - \delta(AD))$ is not empty because $\nu \geq \delta(AD)$. Therefore, according to Theorem 19, there exists a linear schedule, i.e., a vector s such that $sD \geq \mathbf{1}$.

By definition of f, the fatness of J, $J_{\mathbb{Q}}(A, \frac{b}{f} - \nu)$ is not empty. Thus, $J_{\mathbb{Q}}(A, b - f\nu)$ is not empty (homothetic copy). Then $J(A, b - f\nu + \tilde{\delta}(A))$ is not empty (by rounding any point in the previous set), and finally $J(A, b - f\mu)$ is not empty (because $-f\nu + \tilde{\delta}(A) \leq -f\mu - (f-1)\tilde{\delta}(A) \leq -f\mu$ because $f \geq 1$). Therefore, we can let $p_0 \in J(A, b - f\mu)$, and $b' = \frac{b - Ap_0}{f}$ so that $0 \leq b' - \mu \leq b'$. Then, because $f \geq 1$, $J(A, (f-1)b')$ is not empty (it contains $\mathbf{0}$). Therefore, we can consider the problem of minimizing the makespan of a linear schedule on $J(A, (f-1)b')$, i.e., we can compute $L_{min}^*(A, (f-1)b')$.

By considering the solution of linear program (4.5), we know that there exist p, q, and λ, such that $\sum_{i=1}^m \lambda_i = L_{min}^*(A, (f-1)b')$ and p and q belong to $J_{\mathbb{Q}}(A, (f-1)b')$ with $q = p + D\lambda$. By Lemma 21, there is a dependence path in $J(A, (f-1)b' + \mu)$ of length at least $\sum_{i=1}^m \lambda_i$. Because $b' \geq \mu$, $J(A, (f-1)b' + \mu) \subset J(A, fb')$. Thus, there is a dependence path in $J(A, fb')$ of length at least $L_{min}^*(A, (f-1)b')$. This proves the inequality: $L_{free}(A, fb') \geq L_{min}^*(A, (f-1)b') + 1$.

Remember that $L_{min}^*(A, kb) = kL_{min}^*(A, b)$ for any nonnegative rational k and that L_{free} and L_{min}^* are unchanged by an integral translation (here we use a translation by vector p_0). Thus,

$$L_{free}(A, b) = L_{free}(A, fb') \geq \frac{f-1}{f} L_{min}^*(A, fb') + 1 = \frac{f-1}{f} L_{min}^*(A, b) + 1 \qquad (4.7)$$

This is the first desired inequality:

$$L_{free}(A, b) \geq \frac{f-1}{f} L_{min}^*(A, b) + 1$$

Note that because $0 \in J(A, b' - \mu)$ and $\mu \geq \delta(2AD)$, $d_i \in J(A, b')$ for any dependence vector d_i, $fd_i \in J_\mathbb{Q}(A, fb')$ and $p_0 + fd_i \in J_\mathbb{Q}(A, b)$. Thus, for any linear schedule defined by vector s, $L_s^*(A, b) \geq s(fd_i + p_0 - p_0) \geq f$ (because $sd_i \geq 1$) and similarly, $L_s(A, b) \geq \lfloor s(\lfloor f \rfloor d_i + p_0) \rfloor - \lfloor sp_0 \rfloor \geq \lfloor f \rfloor$. Therefore, $L_{\min}^* \to +\infty$ and $L_{\min} \to +\infty$ when $f \to +\infty$.

Furthermore, by definition of the free schedule, $L_{\text{free}} \leq L_{\min}$ and by Lemma 19, $L_{\min} \leq L_{\min}^* + 2$. Thus, with Equation (4.6), we have:

$$1 + \frac{2}{L_{\min}^*} \geq \frac{L_{\min}}{L_{\min}^*} \geq \frac{L_{\text{free}}}{L_{\min}^*} \geq \frac{f - 1}{f} + \frac{1}{L_{\min}^*} = 1 - \frac{1}{f} + \frac{1}{L_{\min}^*}$$

This proves that $L_{\min}^* \sim L_{\min} \sim L_{\text{free}}$ when $f \to \infty$.

Consider Equation (4.7) again. This equation can be rewritten as the inequality $L_{\text{free}}(A, b) \geq L_{\min}^*(A, fb') - L_{\min}^*(A, b') + 1$, which is equivalent to $L_{\text{free}}(A, b) \geq L_{\min}^*(A, b) - L_{\min}^*(A, b') + 1$. This gives the second desired inequality:

$$L_{\min}(A, b) \geq L_{\text{free}}(A, b) \geq L_{\min}(A, b) - L_{\min}^*(A, b') + 1$$

or written in the opposite order;

$$L_{\text{free}}(A, b) \leq L_{\min}(A, b) \leq L_{\text{free}}(A, b) + K$$

where $K = L_{\min}^*(A, b') - 1$. K depends on the shape of the domain J, i.e., on the link between A and b, but not on the "size" of the domain, i.e., its fatness. K is a constant, in the sense that K is the same for all homothetic copies of J and all copies defined by translations. ∎

Theorem 20 shows that the makespan of the linear schedule found by solving linear program (4.4) is equivalent to the makespan of the free schedule when the fatness of the iteration domain goes to infinity. The difference is even bounded by a constant. In other words, linear scheduling is asymptotically optimal for one uniform recurrence equation.

Example 8, Continued

Consider the triangular domain $J = \{(i, j) \mid i \geq 0, \, j \geq 0, \, i + j \leq N\}$ and the dependence vectors $d_1 = (2, -1)$ and $d_2 = (-1, 2)$. What is the length of the longest dependence path in J? What is the optimal linear schedule (optimal in the sense that L^* is minimized)?

The domain J and the dependence vectors are described in matrix form by:

$$A = \begin{pmatrix} -1 & 0 \\ 0 & -1 \\ 1 & 1 \end{pmatrix} \quad b = \begin{pmatrix} 0 \\ 0 \\ N \end{pmatrix} \quad D = \begin{pmatrix} 2 & -1 \\ -1 & 2 \end{pmatrix}$$

Solving the linear program (4.4) means solving the following program:

$$\min\{N(z_1 + z_2) \mid x_1 \geq 0, \ y_1 \geq 0, \ z_1 \geq 0, \ x_2 \geq 0, \ y_2 \geq 0, \ z_2 \geq 0,$$
$$-x_1 + z_1 = x, \ -y_1 + z_1 = y, \ x_2 - z_2 = x,$$
$$y_2 - z_2 = y, \ 2x - y \geq 1, \ -x + 2y \geq 1\}$$

for which $s_1 = (x_1, y_1, z_1) = (0, 0, 1)$, $s_2 = (x_2, y_2, z_2) = (1, 1, 0)$, and for which $s = (x, y) = (1, 1)$ is an optimal solution, with $L^*_{\min} = N$. Solving the dual program – linear program (4.5) – means solving the following program:

$$\max\{\lambda_1 + \lambda_2 \mid \lambda_1 \geq 0, \ \lambda_2 \geq 0, \ p_1 \geq 0, \ p_2 \geq 0, \ p_1 + p_2 \leq N,$$
$$q_1 \geq 0, \ q_2 \geq 0, \ q_1 + q_2 \leq N,$$
$$q_1 - p_1 = 2\lambda_1 - \lambda_2, \ q_2 - p_2 = -\lambda_1 + 2\lambda_2\}$$

for which $p = (p_1, p_2) = (0, 0)$, $q = (q_1, q_2) = (0, 1)N$, $\lambda = (\lambda_1, \lambda_2) = (\frac{1}{3}, \frac{2}{3})N$ is an optimal solution. See Figure 4.5 for the structure of dependence paths in J. The length of the longest path is equal to N for any $N \geq 2$ (the values in circles in Figure 4.5 are the values of the free schedule). The point (i, j) is scheduled with the linear schedule $(1, 1)$ at step $i + j$. The makespan of this linear schedule is $N + 1$, thus it is close to optimum. Note, however, that the theoretical bound that we derived in Theorem 20 is not very sharp. We find $K = \frac{N}{f} - 1 = 14 - 1 = 13$. Indeed, we did not claim that the bound of Theorem 20 is the sharpest bound; we wanted only to show that such a bound exists. □

Note that the two linear programs involved in the previous example are parameterized by the size parameter N. In this simple case, we just have to let $N = 1$ to solve the programs because optimal solutions for an arbitrary N can be easily deduced from an optimal solution for $N = 1$. The optimal solution given earlier have been computed by the Maple [19] linear programming package.

In general however, the polyhedral domain J can be of the following form: $J = \{x \in \mathbb{Z}^n \mid Ax \leq b_0 + N_1 b_1 + \ldots + N_k b_k\}$, i.e., b can be linearly parameterized by k independent parameters. In this latter case, we need to use a parameterized linear programming package to solve the resulting linear programs. A program like PIP [43] has this capability.

4.3.5 Conclusion

Let us summarize our main results for the case of a single uniform recurrence equation defined on a bounded polyhedral domain:

- A URE defined on a "sufficiently large" domain is computable if and only if there is a linear schedule.

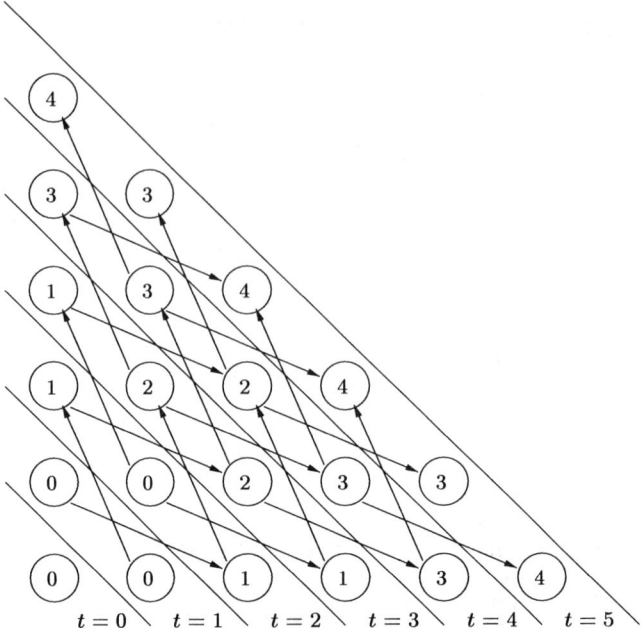

Figure 4.5: Structure of dependence paths in J: free schedule versus linear schedule.

- If there is a linear schedule, a linear programming approach allows us to build a linear schedule that is optimal, up to a constant, for a "sufficiently large" domain.

The main consequence of these two results is that a URE defined on a family of bounded parameterized domains $\{Ax \leq Nb\}$ where $Ax \leq b$ is sufficiently large is either not computable or can be computed in $O(N)$ steps. In other words, a computable URE contains at least $(n-1)$ degrees of parallelism (n if and only if there is no dependence). More precisely, we can build a linear schedule that schedules the URE with a makespan equivalent to kN for some positive rational number k, such that the length of the longest path (i.e., the makespan of the free schedule) is equal to $kN + c_N$ where c_N is bounded: $L_{\text{free}} = kN + O(1)$.

4.4 SURE and Multidimensional Scheduling

4.4.1 Introduction

In this section, we study in more detail the structure of a system of uniform recurrence equations (SURE). We follow the same scheme as in Section 4.3. We first address the problem of computability of a SURE, and then we show the link between the length of the longest dependence path and the minimal makespan of regular schedules.

As summarized in Section 4.3.5, only two cases can occur for a uniform recurrence equation (URE) defined on a family of bounded homothetic domains $\{x \in \mathbb{Z}^n \mid Ax \le Nb\}$ if $\{x \in \mathbb{Z}^n \mid Ax \le b\}$ is sufficiently large. Either the URE is not computable, or there is a linear schedule; and in the latter case, the length $L(N)$ of the longest path is $\Theta(N)$ (except if there is no dependence). To better understand the structure of a URE, we tried to give a more accurate approximation of $L(N)$. This is why we have discussed the computability of a URE for one particular domain J (Theorem 19) and introduced the notion of fatness (Definition 22). Then, within this framework, we were able to prove that the length of the longest path is indeed equal to $kN + O(1)$ for some positive rational k and that a linear schedule with makespan $kN + O(1)$ can be automatically derived.

For a system of uniform recurrence equations (SURE), the situation is much more complicated. First, deciding the computability of a SURE involves a more complex algorithm, first proposed by Karp, Miller, and Winograd. Second, for a computable SURE, the length $L(N)$ of the longest path is not necessarily $\Theta(N)$, but is $\Theta(N^d)$ for some nonnegative integer d. Even if $d = 1$, the length of the longest path is not always of the form $kN + O(1)$. There are examples where the makespan of the free schedule is equal to $kN + \log(N) + O(\log(N))$ or even $kN + \sqrt{N} + O(\sqrt{N})$ (see Exercises).

In this case (when $d = 1$), it is still possible to show that $L(N)$ is equivalent to kN for some positive rational number k and to build a regular schedule with an equivalent makespan. However, the proof is very technical (even more than for a URE); we refer to [77, 76] for more detail. In this section, we focus only on d, the power of N, i.e., we give a less accurate approximation of $L(N)$. We show that the length of the longest path is $\Omega(N^d)$ for some nonnegative integer d and that it is possible to build regular schedules with makespan $O(N^d)$, which are, in this (weaker) sense, asymptotically optimal.

For this discussion, we need a less precise definition of computability and less knowledge on the shape of the iteration domains. The notion of computability that we consider is the computability stated in Theorem 18, i.e., the computability of a dependence graph.

Definition 23 *A reduced dependence graph G is computable if all SUREs defined from G on bounded iteration domains are computable.*

Because a SURE that is not computable for a bounded iteration domain is also not computable for any larger iteration domain, a reduced dependence graph is computable if and only if for all N the SURE defined on the n-dimensional cube of size N is computable. This is why n-dimensional cubes of size N play a particular role in our study. It is sufficient to consider such domains for what we want to prove.

Remember that, as shown in Theorem 18, the noncomputability of a reduced dependence graph (as defined earlier) is only a graph problem; a reduced dependence graph G is computable if and only if G has no cycle of zero weight. This is because we do not address here the problem of computability for a fixed iteration domain, but for a family of domains.

We first recall the decomposition of Karp, Miller, and Winograd that decides the computability of a graph, i.e., that detects zero-weight cycles in a graph whose edges are labeled by integral vectors (Section 4.4.2). This algorithm is based on the construction of a particular subgraph, the subgraph of zero-weight multicycles. We show in Section 4.4.3 how this subgraph can be efficiently built by a linear programming approach. The Karp-Miller-Winograd decomposition is a recursive algorithm whose depth d (the number of recursive calls) plays a fundamental role because it is related to both the length of the longest paths (Section 4.4.2) and the minimal makespan of some regular schedules, called shifted-linear multidimensional schedules (Section 4.4.4).

4.4.2 Detecting Zero-Weight Cycles

This section solves the computability problem stated earlier, i.e., it shows how to decide if there exists a zero-weight cycle in a directed graph $G = (V, E, w)$ where V is the set of vertices, E the set of edges, and w a mapping from E to $\mathbb{Z}^n$ that assigns a weight $w(e)$ to each edge e.

Note first that the problem is not to detect simple cycles of zero weight (which is an NP-complete problem), but cycles of zero weight, i.e., cycles of zero weight that may traverse the same vertex several times and may use an edge more than once. Before going into the computability problem, we recall some results and notations borrowed from graph theory.

Definition 24 (Vector of Cycle) *Given a cycle C in G, the vector of cycle associated to C is a vector q with as many components as edges in G, such that the component associated to an edge e (denoted by q_e) is equal to the number of times edge e is visited in C.*

Definition 25 (Connection Matrix) *The connection matrix for a directed graph $G = (V, E)$ is a $|V| \times |E|$ matrix C such that $C_{v,e} = 1$ if edge e leaves vertex v, $C_{v,e} = -1$ if edge e enters vertex v, and $C_{v,e} = 0$ otherwise (we let $C_{v,e} = 0$ if e is a self-loop for v).*

By definition, if C is a cycle, then its vector of cycle q is such that $q \geq \mathbf{0}$ and $Cq = \mathbf{0}$.

Theorem 21 (Euler's Theorem) *A connected directed graph G contains a Eulerian cycle if and only if each vertex has equal in and out degrees (a Eulerian cycle is a cycle that visits each edge exactly once).*

Theorem 22 *If q is a vector of length $|E|$ such that $q \geq 0$ and $Cq = 0$, then q represents a multicycle, i.e., a union of cycles. Furthermore, if the subgraph of G generated by the edges e such that $q_e > 0$ is connected, then there is a cycle C in G whose vector of cycle is q.*

Proof Build the graph $G_q = (V_q, E_q)$ as follows. V_q is the set of vertices v of V such that at least one edge e incident to v satisfies $q_e > 0$. For each edge $e = (u, v)$ in E such that $q_e > 0$, define q_e edges in G_q from u to v. By construction, each vertex of G_q has equal in and out degrees because $Cq = 0$. According to Euler's theorem, one can define a Eulerian cycle in each connected component of G_q. Each cycle in G_q corresponds to a cycle in G (in which the edge e is traversed exactly q_e times), and the sum of their vectors of cycle is exactly q. Finally, if G_q is connected, q defines only one cycle in G_q that corresponds to a cycle in G. ∎

Theorem 22 shows that multicycles are characterized by linear constraints. This is the key point to solve the problem of zero-weight cycle detection. In the following, we denote by G' *the subgraph of zero-weight multicycles*, i.e., the subgraph of G generated by all edges that belong to at least one multicycle of zero weight. We delay the construction of G' to Section 4.4.3. The following lemmas identify the links between the zero-weight cycles of G and the subgraph G'.

Lemma 22 *A graph G contains a cycle of zero weight if and only if its subgraph G' does.*

Proof The proof is obvious. G' is the subgraph of G generated by the set of edges that belong to a multicycle of zero weight. A cycle is a multicycle; thus G' contains all zero-weight cycles of G. Therefore, if G contains a zero-weight cycle, so does G'. Conversely, any cycle of G' is a cycle of G, too. ∎

Lemma 22 shows that to detect a zero-weight cycle in G, we only need to consider its subgraph G'.

Lemma 23 *A graph G contains a cycle of zero weight if and only if one of its strongly connected components does.*

Proof This is also straightforward as any cycle is contained in a strongly connected component of G. ∎

Lemma 23 shows that to detect a zero-weight cycle in G', we only need to consider each strongly connected component of G'. Lemmas 22 and 23 together give the hint for solving the problem with a recursive search. First, we compute G'. If G' is empty, G has no zero-weight multicycle, thus no zero-weight cycle. If G' has more than one strongly connected component, then G has a zero-weight cycle if at least one of the strongly connected components of G' has a zero-weight cycle. It remains to solve the terminating case, i.e., the case when G' is strongly connected. This is done thanks to the following lemma.

Lemma 24 *If the subgraph G' of a graph G is strongly connected, then G has a zero-weight cycle.*

Proof By construction, each edge e of G' belongs to a multicycle of zero weight represented by the vector q^e. Thus, $q_e^e > 0$. We define q as the sum of these multicycles, i.e., $q = \sum_{e \in G'} q^e$. For all edges e in G', $q_e > 0$; the subgraph of G' generated by the edges e such that $q_e > 0$ is exactly G'. Therefore, according to Theorem 22, there is a cycle (not only a multicycle) in G' whose vector of cycle is q, because G' is strongly connected. Finally, because q is a sum of zero-weight multicycles, the weight of q is also equal to zero. ∎

In their original paper, Karp, Miller, and Winograd proposed a direct proof of this result, with no reference to Euler's theorem. This proof may be more intuitive for the reader. The proof follows.

Proof If G' is strongly connected, there exists in G' a cycle C that passes through all its vertices. Let the successive edges of C be $e_1, e_2, \ldots, e_m$. Each edge e_i of C is contained by definition of G' in a zero-weight multicycle C_i of G, hence of G'. This multicycle can be decomposed into three parts $C_i = e_i + P_i + C_i'$, where C_i' is a multicycle, and $e_i + P_i$ is a cycle of G'. P_i is a path from the vertex to which e_i is directed to the vertex from which e_i is directed.

We can now construct a cycle in G' as follows. The cycle traverses the edges $e_1, e_2, \ldots, e_m$, then returns along the paths $P_m, \ldots, P_2, P_1$. Because each vertex of G' is visited in this process, it is possible to insert the remaining multicycles C_i' at some convenient points. The weight of the resulting cycle is zero because it is the sum of the weights of the zero-weight multicycle C_i. The construction of such a cycle is illustrated in Figure 4.6. ∎

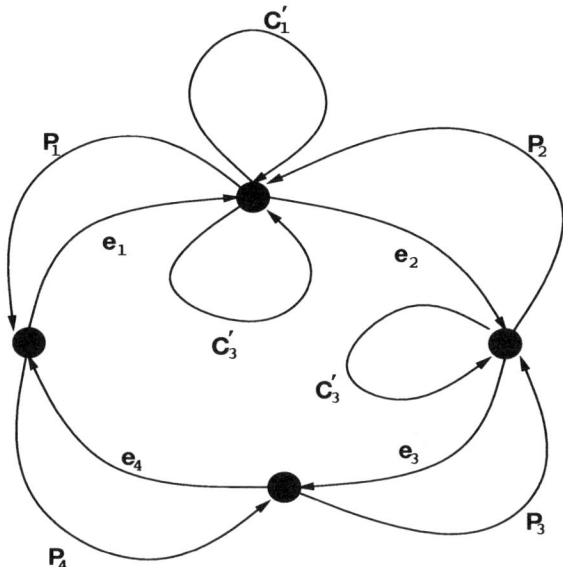

Figure 4.6: Construction of a zero-weight cycle in a strongly connected G'.

We end up with the following algorithm due to Karp, Miller, and Winograd.

Algorithm (Decomposition of Karp, Miller, and Winograd)

Boolean KMW(G)

- Build G' the subgraph of zero-weight multicycles of G.

- Compute $G'_1, G'_2, \ldots, G'_s$, the s strongly connected components of G'.

    - If $s = 0$, G' is empty; return TRUE.
    - If $s = 1$, G' is strongly connected; return FALSE.
    - Otherwise return $\wedge_i$ KMW(G'_i) (logical AND).

Then G is computable (i.e., contains no zero-weight cycle) if and only if KMW(G) returns TRUE.

We define the *depth* of a graph G (denoted by $d(G)$ or simply d) as the maximal number of recursive calls generated by the initial call KMW(G) (counting the first one), except if G is acyclic, in which case we let $d(G) = 0$. We will see in the rest of our study that d is a measure of the degree of parallelism described by G. To make things simpler, we assume, in the rest of the chapter, that the algorithm is not applied directly on G, but *on each strongly connected component of G with at least one edge*. This modification ensures that each recursive call applies to a strongly connected graph with at least one edge, even the first call.

Example 5, Continued

Consider the system of uniform recurrence equations of Example 5 whose dependence graph was depicted on Figure 4.1.

The two edges from a to b and from b to a cannot belong to a zero-weight multicycle, because the first two components of the weight of any multicycle that uses them are positive. The two self-dependences form a zero-weight multicycle, thus G' is the subgraph of G obtained by deleting the two edges from a to b and from b to a (see Figure 4.7).

Figure 4.7: Subgraph of zero-weight multicycles for Example 5.

G' has two strongly connected components. However, for both, the subgraph of zero-weight multicycles is empty, and thus the decomposition stops; both strongly connected components are computable, thus G', and finally G, is computable. Furthermore, the depth of G is 2.   □

Longest Dependence Paths

In this section, we study the structure of dependence paths that correspond to a computable reduced dependence graph G. We show that the length of the longest path is deeply related to the depth of the graph, i.e., to the maximal number of recursive calls in Karp, Miller, and Winograd's decomposition needed for checking that G has no zero-weight cycle.

We have the following preliminary result.

Theorem 23 *Let G be a computable and strongly connected reduced dependence graph and let d be its depth. Consider a SURE defined by G such that all the iteration domains are identical and equal to the n-dimensional cube of size N; $\{p \in \mathbb{Z}^n \mid 0 \le p_i \le N\}$. Then there exists, in the expanded dependence graph Γ associated to the SURE, a dependence path whose length is $\Omega(N^d)$.*

More precisely, the projection of this dependence path onto G visits $\Omega(N^{d_v})$ times each vertex v of G, where d_v is the number of recursive calls for which v still belongs to a cycle.

Proof We first need to introduce some notation.

Remember that the decomposition KMW is a recursive algorithm. We represent its calling sequence as an ordered tree. The root of the tree corresponds to the initial graph G. Each node of the tree corresponds to the decomposition of a subgraph H of G. The number of children of the node corresponding to H is the number of strongly connected components of H', the subgraph of zero-weight multicycles of H. All nodes that are leaves of the calling tree have an empty subgraph of zero-weight multicycles because G is computable.

We denote by $H_{i,j}$ the subgraphs of G that are associated to nodes at depth i in the calling tree. For example, $H_{1,1}$ is equal to G. If G' is not empty, $H_{2,j}$ is the jth strongly connected component of G'. Each $H_{2,j}$ has a corresponding $H'_{2,j}$. If it is not empty, it generates some of the subgraphs $H_{3,k}$, etc.

For all $i < d$, we associate to the graph $H_{i,j}$ a zero-weight multicycle $q_{i,j}$ that defines its corresponding $H'_{i,j}$. As in Lemma 24, $q_{i,j}$ defines for each strongly connected component $H_{i+1,j'}$ of $H'_{i,j}$ a cycle $\mathcal{C}_{i+1,j'}$. By construction, $\sum_{j'} w(\mathcal{C}_{i+1,j'}) = \mathbf{0}$. Furthermore, for $i = 1$ (i.e., for G), we define $\mathcal{C}_{1,1}$ as a cycle passing through all vertices of G (remember that we assumed G to be strongly connected).

We define the starting points $v_{i,j}$ of the cycles $\mathcal{C}_{i,j}$ as follows:

- Start from an arbitrary vertex $v_{1,1}$ of $\mathcal{C}_{1,1}$.

- Follow the edges of $\mathcal{C}_{1,1}$ and let $v_{2,j}$ be the first vertex of $\mathcal{C}_{2,j}$ you reach.

- For $i < d$, define recursively all $v_{i+1,j'}$ in a similar way, starting from $v_{i,j}$ and following $\mathcal{C}_{i,j}$.

We are now ready to build a path $\mathcal{P}(k)$ in G and its corresponding dependence path in Γ of length $\Omega(N^d)$. k is a positive integer, whose value will be fixed later, as a function of N.

We define $\mathcal{P}(k)$ as follows. Traverse k times the cycle $\mathcal{C}_{1,1}$ starting from $v_{1,1}$ and, in each k traversal, the first time the vertex $v_{2,j}$ is reached, traverse, before going further on $\mathcal{C}_{1,1}$, k times the cycle $\mathcal{C}_{2,j}$. Recursively, traverse in the same way, all cycles $\mathcal{C}_{i,j}$. In such a path, $\mathcal{C}_{i,j}$ will be traversed k^i times.

We now build in Γ a path that corresponds to $\mathcal{P}(k)$. For that, we start from a point $p(k)$ in the iteration domain $\mathcal{D}$ (the n-dimensional cube of size N) and we convert the path $\mathcal{P}(k)$ of G into a path in Γ by adding successively the corresponding dependence vectors. It remains to prove that if $p(k)$ is well chosen, all points built this way belong to $\mathcal{D}$.

Consider such a point p. Let $\theta(i, j)$ be the number of times $\mathcal{C}_{i,j}$ has been entirely traversed before reaching p and let $l_{i,j}$ be the remaining part, i.e., a subpath of $C_{i,j}$. We have

$$p = p(k) + w \left(\sum_{i,j} \theta(i,j) C_{i,j} + \sum_{i,j} l_{i,j} \right)$$

For $i > 1$, consider $H_{i-1,j}$ and the strongly connected components $H_{i,j'}$ of $H'_{i-1,j}$; the cycle $C_{i-1,j}$ has been entirely traversed $\theta(i-1,j)$ times. Thus, each cycle $C_{i,j'}$ has been traversed at least $k \times \theta(i-1,j)$ times: thus, $\theta(i,j') \geq k \times \theta(i-1,j)$. Note that $C(i,j')$ may have been traversed more than $k \times \theta(i-1,j)$ times, if cycle $C_{i-1,j}$ is currently being traversed. In this case, during the last traversal of $C_{i-1,j}$, $C_{i,j'}$ has been traversed again a certain number of times between 0 and k, depending on whether p has been reached before, during, or after such a traversal. In all possible cases, $\theta(i,j') \leq k \times \theta(i-1,j) + k$. Furthermore, if there is equality, then $C_{i,j'}$ has been entirely traversed, and thus $l_{i,j'} = \emptyset$.

We let $\theta'(i,j') = \theta(i,j') - k \times \theta(i-1,j)$ for $i > 1$ and $\theta'(1,j) = \theta(1,j)$. From the previous study, we get: $\theta'(i,j') \leq k - 1$ if $l_{i,j'} \neq \emptyset$ and $\theta'(i,j') \leq k$ otherwise.

Recall that for a given $H_{i-1,j}$, we have by construction $\sum_{j'} w(C_{i,j'}) = \mathbf{0}$, thus:

$$w \left(\sum_{j'} \theta'(i,j') C_{i,j'} \right) = w \left(\sum_{j'} (\theta(i,j') - k \times \theta(i-1,j)) C_{i,j'} \right)$$
$$= w \left(\sum_{j'} \theta(i,j') C_{i,j'} \right) - k \times \theta(i-1,j) \times \mathbf{0} = w \left(\sum_{j'} \theta(i,j') C_{i,j'} \right)$$

This holds for all i such that $2 \leq i \leq d$, but also for $i = 1$ by the choice of $\theta'(1,j)$. We add all these equations and we get:

$$w \left(\sum_{i,j} \theta(i,j) C_{i,j} + \sum_{i,j} l_{i,j} \right) = w \left(\sum_{i,j} \theta'(i,j) C_{i,j} + \sum_{i,j} l_{i,j} \right)$$

For a path $\mathcal{P}$ in G, $\mathcal{P} = (e_1, \ldots, e_r)$, we define the two quantities $m(\mathcal{P})$ and $M(\mathcal{P})$ as follows:

$$m(\mathcal{P}) = \max\{t \in \mathbb{Z}^- \mid t\,\mathbf{1} \leq \sum_{i=1}^{k} w(e_i), \forall k, 1 \leq k \leq r\}$$
$$M(\mathcal{P}) = \min\{t \in \mathbb{Z}^+ \mid \sum_{i=1}^{k} w(e_i) \leq t\,\mathbf{1}, \forall k, 1 \leq k \leq r\}$$

These two quantities respectively represent the lower and upper bounds of an n-dimensional cube in which a path in Γ corresponding to $\mathcal{P}$ in G will be easily drawn. We let $m_{i,j} = m(C_{i,j})$ and $M_{i,j} = M(C_{i,j})$, where edges in $C_{i,j}$ are considered in the order defined from $v_{i,j}$. We thus have:

- $m_{i,j}\,\mathbf{1} \leq w(C_{i,j}) \leq M_{i,j}\,\mathbf{1}$.

- $m_{i,j} \mathbf{1} \leq w(l_{i,j}) \leq M_{i,j} \mathbf{1}$.

- $\theta'(i,j') \leq k - 1$ if $l_{i,j'} \neq \emptyset$ and $\theta'(i,j') \leq k$ otherwise.

- $w\left(\sum_{i,j} \theta(i,j)\mathcal{C}_{i,j} + \sum_{i,j} l_{i,j}\right) = w\left(\sum_{i,j} \theta'(i,j)\mathcal{C}_{i,j} + \sum_{i,j} l_{i,j}\right)$.

Finally, we obtain

$$\left(k \sum_{i,j} m_{i,j}\right) \mathbf{1} \leq w\left(\sum_{i,j} \theta(i,j)\mathcal{C}_{i,j} + \sum_{i,j} l_{i,j}\right) \leq \left(k \sum_{i,j} M_{i,j}\right) \mathbf{1}$$

which implies

$$p(k) + \left(k \sum_{i,j} m_{i,j}\right) \mathbf{1} \leq p \leq p(k) + \left(k \sum_{i,j} M_{i,j}\right) \mathbf{1}$$

Finally, let $K = \sum_{i,j}(M_{i,j} - m_{i,j})$, $k = \lfloor \frac{N}{K} \rfloor$, and $p(k) = -(k \sum_{i,j} m_{i,j}) \mathbf{1}$. Therefore, we have built, in the domain $\{p \in \mathbb{Z}^n \mid \mathbf{0} \leq p \leq N \mathbf{1}\}$, an n-dimensional cube of size N a dependence path whose length is $\Omega(N^d)$ because each cycle $\mathcal{C}_{d,j}$ is traversed k^d times (and K does not depend on N, but depends only on G). More precisely, a vertex v that belongs to a cycle, even after d_v recursive calls of the decomposition, belongs to one of the $\mathcal{C}_{d_v,j}$. Thus $\mathcal{P}(k)$ visits $\Omega(k^{d_v})$ times the vertex v, i.e., $\Omega(N^{d_v})$ times. ∎

Remark that Theorem 23 remains true even if the iteration domains are not identical and even if they have more general shapes than cubes, as long as their intersection contains an n-dimensional cube of size $\Omega(N)$.

Example 5, Continued

Consider our main example again. We can build a dependence path of length $\Omega(N^d)$, i.e., $\Omega(N^2)$ as follows. G (depicted in Figure 4.1) is strongly connected; in this particular graph, a cycle that passes through all vertices $(\mathcal{C}_{1,1})$ is, for example, the cycle formed by the edges not in G' (G' was depicted in Figure 4.7). The cycles associated to the two strongly connected components of G' (cycles $\mathcal{C}_{2,1}$ and $\mathcal{C}_{2,2}$) are simply formed by the two self-dependences. Following the proof of Theorem 23, a dependence path of length $\Omega(N^2)$ can be built by following $\Omega(N)$ times the cycle $\mathcal{C}_{1,1}$ while traversing $\Omega(N)$ times the cycles $\mathcal{C}_{2,1}$ and $\mathcal{C}_{2,2}$ during each traversal of $\mathcal{C}_{1,1}$. Such a path is depicted in Figure 4.8. □

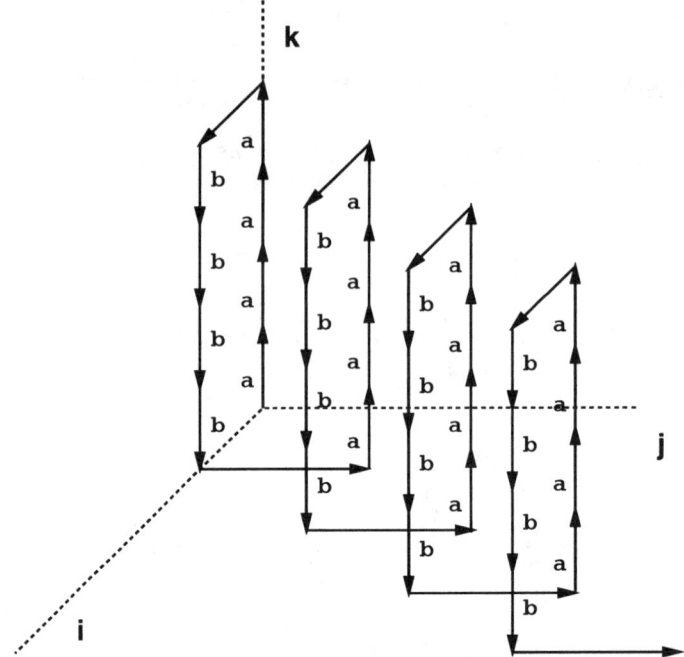

Figure 4.8: A dependence path of length $\Omega(N^2)$ for Example 5.

4.4.3 Construction and Properties of G'

In this section, we return to the construction of the subgraph G'. First, we show how to build G' efficiently (by only one linear programming problem instead of one per edge as in [65]). Second, we show that this construction is closely related to the construction of weakly and strictly separating hyperplanes and thus to a particular class of affine multidimensional schedules, called shifted-linear multidimensional schedules.

Linear Program for Building G'

Remember Theorem 22. A vector q such that $q \geq 0$ and $Cq = 0$ represents a multicycle, where C is the connection matrix; each row of C corresponds to a vertex of G, and each column to an edge of G. Similarly, we define the $n \times |E|$ matrix W as the weight matrix, i.e., the matrix whose columns are the weight of the edges of G, numbered in the same order as in the matrix C. Then a vector q such that $q \geq 0$, $Cq = 0$ and $Wq = 0$ represents a multicycle of zero weight.

Historically, in [65], G' was built by solving $|E|$ linear programs, one per edge of G. We now show (Lemmas 25 and 26) that G' can be built by solving a single linear program. Indeed, the edges of G' are exactly the edges e for which $v_e = 0$ in any optimal solution of the following linear program:

$$\min \left\{ \; \sum_e v_e \; \mid \; q \geq 0, \; v \geq 0, \; q + v \geq 1, \; Cq = 0 \quad Wq = 0 \; \right\} \quad (4.8)$$

Note first that the linear program (4.8) has a finite solution; $q = 0$ with $v = 1$ is indeed a solution. The construction of G' is a consequence of the following lemma.

Lemma 25 *For any optimal solution (q, v) of the linear program (4.8):*

- $q_e \neq 0 \Leftrightarrow v_e = 0$.

- $q_e = 0 \Leftrightarrow v_e = 1$.

Proof Consider an optimal solution (q, v) of the linear program (4.8). Note that the only constraint on v_e is $q_e + v_e \geq 1$. Thus $q_e = 0 \Rightarrow v_e \geq 1 \Rightarrow v_e = 1$ because $\sum_e v_e$ is minimal. Furthermore, $v_e = 0 \Rightarrow q_e \neq 0$. It remains to show that $q_e \neq 0 \Rightarrow v_e = 0$.

Let $q_0 = \min\{q_e \mid q_e \neq 0\}$. We can build another solution (q', v') with $q' = \frac{1}{q_0} q$, $v'_e = 0$ if $q_e \neq 0$ and $v'_e = v_e$ otherwise. By construction, we end up with $\sum_e v'_e \leq \sum_e v_e$ and we have thus found a better solution (which is not possible), except if v has not changed, i.e., if $v_e = 0$ each time $q_e \neq 0$. ∎

Lemma 26 *For any optimal solution (q, v) of program (4.8), $v_e = 0 \Leftrightarrow e \in G'$.*

Proof Any solution (q, v) of the linear program (4.8) corresponds to a zero-weight multicycle ($q \geq 0$, $Cq = 0$, and $Wq = 0$) whose participating edges are the edges e for which $q_e \neq 0$. By Lemma 25, $v_e = 0 \Rightarrow q_e \neq 0$. Thus, if $v_e = 0$, e belongs to the multicycle of zero weight q, i.e., $e \in G'$.

Conversely, let e be an edge of G'. By definition of G', there exists a zero-weight multicycle (i.e., a nonnegative and nonnull vector $\tilde{q}$ with $C\tilde{q} = 0$ and $W\tilde{q} = 0$) such that $\tilde{q}_e \geq 1$. Consider an optimal solution (q, v) of program (4.8). We can form another solution (q', v') with $q' = q + \tilde{q}$, $v'_f = v_f$ if $f \neq e$ and $v'_e = 0$. This solution is a better solution (which is not possible) unless we already had $v_e = 0$. ∎

Lemmas 25 and 26 characterize the edges of G'; the edges of G' are exactly the edges e such that $v_e = 0$ (or equivalently $q_e \neq 0$) in any optimal solution of the linear program (4.8).

Interpretation of the Dual

To better understand what is behind this linear program, let us consider its dual. Program (4.8) can be written in a canonical form as:

$$\min\left\{\sum_e v_e \mid q \geq 0, v \geq 0, w \geq 0, q + v = 1 + w, Cq = 0, Wq = 0\right\} \quad (4.9)$$

Its dual can be written as:

$$\max\left\{\sum_e z_e \mid 0 \leq z \leq 1, \quad Xw(e) + \rho_{y_e} - \rho_{x_e} \geq z_e\right\} \quad (4.10)$$

where the inequality $z_e \geq 0$ corresponds, in the primal, to the variable w_e, where the inequality $z_e \leq 1$ corresponds to the variable v_e, while the inequality $Xw(e) + \rho_{y_e} - \rho_{x_e} \geq z_e$ corresponds to the variable q_e. The dual solution has an interesting property as shown by Lemma 27.

Lemma 27 *For any optimal solution (z, X, ρ) of the dual program (4.10):*

$$e \in G' \Leftrightarrow Xw(e) + \rho_{y_e} - \rho_{x_e} = 0 \quad\quad\quad (4.11)$$
$$e \notin G' \Leftrightarrow Xw(e) + \rho_{y_e} - \rho_{x_e} \geq 1 \quad\quad\quad (4.12)$$

Proof Programs (4.8) and (4.9) are equivalent: we simply replaced the inequality $q + v \geq 1$ by $w \geq 0$ and $q + v = w + 1$. From Lemmas 25 and 26, we know the following.

   If $e \notin G'$, then all optimal solutions of program (4.8) (and thus of program (4.9)) are such that $v_e = 1$ and $q_e = 0$. This implies that any optimal solution of program (4.9) is such that $w_e = 0$.

   Conversely, if $e \in G'$, any optimal solution of programs (4.8) and (4.9) is such that $v_e = 0$ and $q_e \geq 1$. Thus, there exists an optimal solution of program (4.8) with $q_e + v_e > 1$ (simply multiply q by a number $\lambda > 1$), and thus an optimal solution of program (4.9) with $w_e > 0$.

   We are now ready to use the complementary slackness theorem [110], which shows the link between strict inequalities in the dual and null variables in the primal.

- **Variable v:** There is an optimal solution of program (4.10) with $z_e < 1$ if and only if there is no optimal solution of program (4.9) with $v_e > 0$, i.e., if and only if $e \in G'$.

- **Variable w:** There is an optimal solution of program (4.10) with $z_e > 0$ if and only if there is no optimal solution of program (4.9) with $w_e > 0$, i.e., if and only if $e \notin G'$.

- **Variable** q: Among all optimal solutions of linear program (4.10), there is one with $Xw(e) + \rho_{y_e} - \rho_{x_e} > z_e$ if and only if there is no optimal solution of program (4.8) with $q_e > 0$, i.e., if and only if $e \notin G'$.

Summarizing these results, $e \in G'$ if and only if any optimal solution of program (4.10) is such that $z_e = 0$ and $Xw(e) + \rho_{y_e} - \rho_{x_e} = z_e$, and $e \notin G'$ if and only if any optimal solution of program (4.10) is such that $z_e = 1$. This proves the result. This also shows that z_e is equal to either 0 or 1 in any optimal solution (as for v_e in the primal program). ■

Lemma 27 shows how the constraints $sD \geq 1$ that we had for linear scheduling in the case of a URE can be generalized to the case of a SURE. For a URE, the vector s can be interpreted as a vector normal to a hyperplane that separates the space into two half-spaces, all dependence vectors being strictly in the same half-space. We say that s is a strictly separating hyperplane. Here, the vector X defines a hyperplane that is a strictly separating hyperplane for the weights of the cycles not in G' and a weakly separating hyperplane for the weights of the cycles in G'. (To see this, sum inequalities (4.12) and equalities (4.11) along a cycle.) Furthermore, for each subgraph G that appears in the decomposition, X defines a hyperplane that is the "most often strict" i.e., it maximizes the number of the edges for which such a hyperplane is strict (because $\sum_e z_e$ is maximal).

Note that the vector X and the constants ρ are not unique. Once we know which constraints are to be satisfied (Constraints (4.12) and (4.11)), one can choose a particular solution by minimizing some other objective function, the simpler being to minimize the components of X in absolute value (roughly equal to the makespan on a parallelepiped). One can also, as in the case of a URE, minimize the makespan associated to X for any polyhedron. However, as said in Section 4.4.1, these are optimizations that are second-order optimizations; we will not address them here. In the following, we just assume that a vector X and constants ρ have been chosen, satisfying the constraints (4.11) and (4.12).

Note also that choosing the same vector X for all vertices of a strongly connected component is not an arbitrary choice. It comes naturally from the dual formulation, it is an intrinsic property of the model of SURE.

4.4.4 Optimal Multidimensional Schedule for a SURE

During the decomposition algorithm, we associate to each vertex v of G, a sequence of vectors $X_v^1, \ldots, X_v^{d_v}$, and a sequence of constants $\rho_v^1, \ldots, \rho_v^{d_v}$, obtained by considering the dual problem (4.10). d_v is the depth of the decomposition algorithm at which vertex v is removed, i.e., at which v does not belong to a cycle anymore. This sequence of vectors has the following property.

Theorem 24 *The $d_v - 1$ first separating hyperplanes $X_v^1, \ldots, X_v^{d_v-1}$ associated to a vertex v of G are linearly independent. Furthermore, when G is computable, all separating hyperplanes $X_v^1, \ldots, X_v^{d_v}$ associated to v are linearly independent.*

Proof This result is a consequence of Lemma 27. To make the notations simpler, let $G_1 = G$, and G_i be the subgraph of G, generated at depth $i > 1$ of the algorithm, that contains v. For $i > 1$, G_i is the strongly connected component of G'_{i-1} that contains v: $G_i \subset G'_{i-1} \subset G_{i-1}$.

Suppose that for some integer $1 \leq k \leq d_v$, $X_v^1, \ldots, X_v^{k-1}$ are linearly independent and $X_v^1, \ldots, X_v^{k-1}, X_v^k$ are linearly dependent. This means that $X_v^k = 0$ if $k = 1$ or that there exist $\{\lambda_i\}_{1 \leq i \leq k-1}$ such that $X_v^k = \sum_{i=1}^{k-1} \lambda_i X_v^i$ if $k > 1$.

Let $\mathcal{C}$ be a cycle of G_k. Let us show that $X_v^k w(\mathcal{C}) = 0$. If $k = 1$, this is obvious because $X_v^k = 0$. If $k > 1$, we have by construction of the vectors X_v^i, $1 \leq i < k$, and because of Lemma 27:

$$i < k \Rightarrow \forall e \in G_k : \ X_v^i w(e) + \rho_{y_e}^i - \rho_{x_e}^i = 0 \text{ because } G_k \subset G'_i \qquad (4.13)$$

Summing all equations (4.13) for a given i along the edges of $\mathcal{C}$ shows that for all i, $1 \leq i \leq k-1$, $X_v^i w(\mathcal{C}) = 0$. Because X_v^k is a linear combination of the vectors X_v^i, $X_v^k w(\mathcal{C}) = 0$.

However, by construction of X_v^k,

$$\forall e \in G_k : \ X_v^k w(e) + \rho_{y_e}^i - \rho_{x_e}^i \geq z_e \qquad (4.14)$$

where $z_e = 1$ if $e \notin G'_k$ and $z_e = 0$ if $e \in G'_k$. Inequality (4.14) shows that $X_v^k w(\mathcal{C})$ is actually greater than the number of edges in $\mathcal{C}$ that do not belong to G'_k. Thus, every edge of $\mathcal{C}$ belongs to G'_k.

What we just proved is true for any cycle $\mathcal{C}$ of G_k, thus all cycles of G_k are cycles of G'_k. Because G_k is strongly connected by construction, G'_k is also strongly connected. The decomposition algorithm has thus stopped here at level k, with the conclusion that G is not computable.

This proves that $X_v^{(1)}, \ldots, X_v^{(d_v)}$ are linearly independent when G is computable and that $X_v^{(1)}, \ldots, X_v^{(d_v-1)}$ are always linearly independent. ∎

A direct consequence of Theorem 24 is that the depth of the decomposition is small; it is bounded by $n + 1$ when G is not computable and by n when G is computable.

We are now ready to merge all previous results and propose nearly optimal multidimensional schedules for computable SUREs. Remember how we defined a schedule in Section 4.2.2. A schedule is a function T from $V(\Gamma)$ into the nonnegative integers $\mathbb{N}$ such that $T(j,q) < T(i,p)$ whenever $(j,q) \longrightarrow (i,p)$, i.e., a schedule defines an evaluation order of all computations associated to a SURE, through the total order over $\mathbb{N}$. Actually, this evaluation order can be defined through any partial order, as long as the dependences are respected. Any multidimensional schedule defines such an order, the only difference is that the underlying order is no longer the total order over $\mathbb{N}$, but the lexicographic order $<_{lex}$ over $\mathbb{Z}^d$. This lexicographic order $<_{lex}$ is defined for two vectors x and y in $\mathbb{Z}^d$ by induction on d:

- $d = 1$: $x <_{lex} y$ if and only if $x_1 < y_1$.

- $d > 1$: $x = (x_1, x_2, \ldots, x_d) <_{lex} (y_1, y_2, \ldots, y_d) = y$ if and only if

    - $x_1 < y_1$, or
    - $x_1 = y_1$ and $(x_2, \ldots, x_d) <_{lex} (y_2, \ldots, y_d)$.

A multidimensional function defines a schedule if $T(j,q) <_{lex} T(i,p)$ whenever $(j,q) \longrightarrow (i,p)$.

For each vertex v, we complete the sequences of vectors X_v^i and constants ρ_v^i with null vectors and null constants to obtain sequences of same length d. To simplify the notations, we denote by $\mathcal{P}$ a bounded subset of $\mathbb{Z}^n$ that contains all iteration domains of the variables of the SURE.

Lemma 28 *The multidimensional function T:*

$$
\begin{aligned}
V \times \mathcal{P} &\longrightarrow \mathbb{Z}^d \\
(v, p) &\mapsto (\lfloor X_v^1 p + \rho_v^1 \rfloor, \; \ldots, \; \lfloor X_v^{d_v} p + \rho_v^{d_v} \rfloor, 0, \; \ldots, \; 0)
\end{aligned}
$$

defines a multidimensional schedule.

Proof We just have to show that for each edge $e = (x_e, y_e)$, for all $p \in \mathcal{P}$:

$$T(x_e, p - w(e)) <_{lex} T(y_e, p)$$

G is computable, thus the decomposition algorithm ended because all leaves of the calling tree have an empty G'. Thus, at some level of the decomposition, the edge e has been removed. Let k be the level where e has been removed, i.e., $e \in G_k$ but $e \notin G'_k$. By construction, until level k, y_e and

x_e belong to the same subgraph of G, thus their sequences of vectors $X_{x_e}^i$ and $X_{y_e}^i$ are the same until level k:

$$X_{y_e}^1 = X_{x_e}^1 = X^1, \ \ldots \ , \ X_{y_e}^k = X_{x_e}^k = X^k$$

Furthermore, until level $k-1$, each vector X^i is a weakly separating hyperplane for the edge e and, at level k, X^k is a strictly separating hyperplane for e because e has been removed. Thus, for $i < k$:

$$X^i w(e) + \rho_{y_e}^i - \rho_{x_e}^i = 0, \text{ i.e., } \forall p \in \mathcal{P}, \ X^i p + \rho_{y_e}^i = X^i(p - w(e)) + \rho_{x_e}^i$$

and for $i = k$:

$$X^k w(e) + \rho_{y_e}^k - \rho_{x_e}^k \geq 1, \text{ i.e., } \forall p \in \mathcal{P}, \ X^k p + \rho_{y_e}^k \geq X^k(p - w(e)) + \rho_{x_e}^k + 1$$

Thus, whatever the rest of the sequences $X_{y_e}^i$, $X_{x_e}^i$, $\rho_{y_e}^i$, and $\rho_{x_e}^i$ after level k, taking the floor function leads to $T(x_e, p - w(e)) <_{lex} T(y_e, p)$ for all $p \in \mathcal{P}$. ∎

When the dependence graph G has more than one strongly connected component, we first schedule independently each component with a multidimensional schedule built as above. Then, to schedule them together, we simply follow a topological order defined on the strongly connected components of G.

The schedule T belongs to a class of schedules called *shifted-linear multidimensional schedules*. This class is a subclass of the class of affine multidimensional schedules; indeed, each variable is scheduled by a multidimensional affine schedule. Furthermore, at each level of the decomposition, the linear part is the same for all variables that belong to the same strongly connected component.

Note that the makespan of a d-multidimensional schedule T directly depends on its dimension d. If each iteration domain is contained in an n-dimensional cube of size N, then the makespan of the multidimensional schedule is $O(N^d)$. More precisely, if we assume that all the computations count for zero, except the computations associated to variable v, then the makespan of T is $O(N^{d_v})$. This property, related to Theorem 23, leads to the following optimality result.

Theorem 25 *Let G be a computable and strongly connected reduced dependence graph, and let d be its depth. Consider a SURE defined by G, such that the intersection of all iteration domains contains an n-dimensional cube of size $\Omega(N)$ and is contained in an n-dimensional cube of size $O(N)$. Then the multidimensional schedule T defined in Lemma 28 is nearly optimal; if d is the depth of the decomposition algorithm, the makespan of the schedule is $O(N^d)$ and the length of the* *longest dependence path is $\Omega(N^d)$. More precisely, for a given variable v, $O(N^{d_v})$ computations associated to v are sequentialized by T, while there is a dependence path that involves $\Omega(N^{d_v})$ computations associated to v.*

Example 5, Continued

We come back to our main example. G is computable and has depth 2. Theorem 25 shows that there exists a two-dimensional schedule whose makespan is $O(N^2)$ and a dependence path of length $\Omega(N^2)$ (as depicted in Figure 4.8).

Lemma 27 summarizes the constraints that such a schedule has to satisfy. To choose one solution, we can minimize, for example, $\sum_i |X_i|$, the norm of the vector X. Removing absolute values is a well-known technique; we just have to minimize $\sum_i Y_i$ with the additional constraints $Y \geq X$ and $Y \geq -X$. We can also write $X = Y - Z$, with $Y \geq 0$, $Z \geq 0$ and minimize $\sum_i (Y_i + Z_i)$. Note that if the iteration domain is a cube, this corresponds to the minimization of the makespan. If the domain is an arbitrary polyhedron, we can still use techniques similar to those of Section 4.3.4.

Here, for the first level of the decomposition, we have to solve the following linear program (we write $X = (x, y, z)$):

$$\min \left\{ \; |x| + |y| + |z| \; \mid \; x + \rho_b - \rho_a \geq 1, \; y + \rho_a - \rho_b \geq 1, \; -z = 0, \; z = 0 \; \right\}$$

which has infinitely many optimal solutions. The simplest solutions are:

- $X = (2, 0, 0)$, $\rho_a = 1$, $\rho_b = 0$.

- $X = (1, 1, 0)$, $\rho_a = \rho_b = 0$.

- $X = (0, 2, 0)$, $\rho_a = 0$, $\rho_b = 1$.

We start again on each strongly connected component of G' so as to build the second dimension of our schedule. In this example, the second level is straightforward because each component contains only one edge. For the second level, we find $X = (0, 0, 1)$ for variable a and $X = (0, 0, -1)$ for variable b.

Suppose that for the first level, we chose $X = (2, 0, 0)$, $\rho_a = 1$, $\rho_b = 0$. Then the final two-dimensional schedule T schedules $a(i, j, k)$ at step $(2i + 1, k)$ and $b(i, j, k)$ at step $(2i, -k)$. This corresponds to the loop description of Figure 4.9. □

```
DO i=1, N              /* Vector X = (2, 0, 0) */
   /* Constant ρb = 0 */
   DO k=N, 1, -1       /* Vector X = (0, 0, -1) */
      DOPAR j=1, N
        b(i,j,k) = a(i-1,j,k) + b(i,j,k+1)
      ENDDOPAR
   ENDDO
   /* Constant ρa = 1 */
   DO k=1, N           /* Vector X = (0, 0, 1) */
      DOPAR j=1, N
        a(i,j,k) = b(i,j-1,k) + a(i,j,k-1)
      ENDDOPAR
   ENDDO
ENDDO
```

Figure 4.9: Loop description for Example 5.

4.4.5 Conclusion

We now summarize the main results we gave for a system of uniform recurrence equations:

- All SUREs defined from a reduced dependence graph G on bounded iteration domains are computable if and only if G has no cycle of zero weight.

- Detecting if G has no cycle of zero weight can be done by a recursive algorithm based on (rational) linear programming.

- The depth d of this algorithm is a measure of the degree of sequentiality of the SURE; if the intersection of the different iteration domains is contained in a cube of size $O(N)$ and contains a cube of size $\Omega(N)$, then the length $L(N)$ of the longest path is $\Omega(N^d)$ and there is a shifted-linear multidimensional schedule whose makespan is $O(N^d)$.

There remain some open questions related to the approximation of $L(N)$. If $L(N) = \Theta(N^d)$, can we show that $L(N)$ is equivalent to kN^d for some k and can we characterize k? If k is known, can we give an approximation of $L(N) - kN^d$? As said in Section 4.4.1, the answer to the first question is yes for the case $d = 1$ but is unknown for $d \neq 1$. However, the proof is so technical that we did not address this topic here.

4.5 Bibliographical Notes

The model of systems of recurrence equations was originally proposed by Karp, Miller, and Winograd [65]. The different criteria for computability (Section 4.2, Lemmas 12 and 13, Corollary 3, and Theorem 17) are borrowed from their original paper. Concerning the case of a single equation, the path construction technique presented in Lemma 15 is also due to Karp, Miller, and Winograd. For the case of several equations, Theorem 7 in [65] has been decomposed here into three simpler lemmas, Lemmas 22, 23, and 24. Finally, Lemma 6 in [65] is related to Lemma 27 in this chapter, but is weaker.

The detection of zero-weight cycles in cyclic graphs whose edges are labeled by integral vectors has been largely studied again in the 80s by, among others, Kosaraju and Sullivan [72] and then Cohen and Meggido [25], who proposed sophisticated polynomial solutions for fixed dimension (see also the references therein). We chose to present a more elementary (at least conceptually) solution involving a single linear program (Program (4.8)), because this solution emphasize the link between zero-weight multicycles and multidimensional schedules. This last solution is due to Darte and Vivien [31].

The link between the depth of the decomposition of Karp, Miller, and Winograd and the dimension of multidimensional schedules was studied mainly by Rao [102] and Roychowdhury [105]. Theorems 23 and 25 are more accurate formulations of similar results by Rao (Theorems 2.1 and 2.7 in [102]) and Roychowdhury. The structure of longest dependence paths, i.e., of the free schedule, has been deeply studied by Backes in his thesis [10] (see also the paper by Backes, Schwiegelshohn, and Thiele [11]).

For more details on the computability of systems of uniform recurrence equations and of some extensions of this model (such as systems of affine recurrence equations, systems of conditional uniform recurrence equations), we refer to the theses of Joinnault [64] and Saouter [106].

The case of a single uniform equation (developed in Section 4.3) gave rise to many developments in the context of the automatic synthesis of systolic arrays, especially because the existence of a linear schedule makes the scheduling problem very simple. Moldovan [90] and Quinton [100] were the first to introduce the "space-time" mapping transformation, based on the model of uniform recurrence equations, for the automatic design of systolic arrays. It would be impossible to cite all papers issued from the systolic array community. We just mention the following papers that are directly related to the problems presented in Section 4.3: Lisper [84] and Shang and Fortes [111] addressed the problem of deriving a minimal makespan linear schedule. The proof of asymptotical optimality of linear schedules is due to Darte, Khachiyan, and Robert [29].

4.6 Exercises

In the following exercises, we consider only SUREs whose iteration domains $\mathcal{P}_i$ are equal (or equivalently, we study the SUREs restricted to the intersection of all iteration domains). We can then talk about *the* iteration domain of a SURE.

4.6.1 Computability

Exercise 4.1 (On the hypotheses of Theorem 18)

- Give an example of a computable SURE whose corresponding reduced dependence graph has a zero-weight cycle.

- For any N, give an example of a computable SURE whose iteration domain is a square with at least N points and whose corresponding reduced dependence graph has a zero-weight cycle.

Exercise 4.2 (Generalization of Theorem 17)

Explain why the condition of Theorem 17 does not change if the iteration domain is $\{p \in \mathbb{Z}^n \mid p_i \geq n_i\}$ (where n_i is a constant) instead of $\mathbb{N}^n$. More generally, if P is a polyhedron whose characteristic cone K is full-dimensional, show that a SURE defined over P is computable if and only if its corresponding reduced dependence graph G has no cycle $\mathcal{C}$ such that $-w(\mathcal{C})$ belongs to K.

    Hint: Take a Hilbert basis for K, decompose each point in this basis, and extract subsequences of points whose components are nondecreasing. (This exercise is borrowed from an unpublished result by Y. Saouter and H. Leverge.)

4.6.2 URE and Linear Scheduling

Exercise 4.3 (Particular case for Program (4.4))

Let P be an n-dimensional rectangle $P = \{p \in \mathbb{Z}^n \mid l_i \leq p_i \leq u_i\}$ where l_i and u_i are constants such that $l_i \leq u_i$. Show that finding the minimal makespan schedule for a URE with dependence matrix D can be done by solving the following problem:

$$\min\{\textstyle\sum_{i=1}^{n} |s_i|(u_i - l_i) \mid sD \geq 1\}$$

Give two ways for transforming these constraints into a linear program.

    Hint: First way, introduce $s_1 \geq 0$ and $s_2 \geq 0$ such that $s = s_1 - s_2$; second way, introduce t_i such that $t_i \geq s_i$ and $t_i \geq -s_i$.

Exercise 4.4 (Construction of longest dependence paths)

Consider a URE defined over the rectangle $R = \{(i,j) \mid 0 \le i,j \le N\}$ with dependence vectors $(0,1)$, $(1,0)$, $(1,-1)$, and $(3,-4)$. Find the minimal makespan linear schedule. Build a dependence path in R of equivalent length. Show that, in general, the dependence vectors that participate to such a path can be identified by using the complementary slackness theorem [110].

Hint: Use vectors d for which $sd = 1$ where s defines an optimal linear schedule.

Exercise 4.5 (Extremal points of longest dependence paths)

Consider linear program (4.5). When the iteration domain has only integral vertices, one can think that the optimal values for the points p and q are vertices of the iteration domain. Give an example where this is not true.

Hint: Consider, for example, a triangular domain.

Exercise 4.6 (Canonical dependence vectors)

Suppose that the matrix of dependence vectors is equal to the identity matrix. Is it true that, in this case, the optimal linear schedule is given by the vector whose components are all equal to 1?

Hint: The answer is no!

4.6.3 SURE and Multidimensional Scheduling

SUREs of Depth 1

Exercise 4.7 (Schedules: shifted linear on edges and linear on cycles)

When the depth of the decomposition of Karp, Miller, and Winograd is 1, the SURE can be computed by a "shifted linear schedule." A shifted linear schedule is an affine-per-variable schedule whose linear part is the same for all variables. In other words, variable v for iteration vector p is scheduled at time $X.p + \rho_v$, and the vector X does depend on v.

Show that such a function defines a valid schedule as soon as, for any edge $e = (x_e, y_e)$ in the dependence graph, $X.w(e) + \rho_{y_e} - \rho_{x_e} \ge 1$. Show that this condition is equivalent to satisfy $X.w(\mathcal{C}) \ge l(\mathcal{C})$ for each simple cycle $\mathcal{C}$ in the graph, where $l(\mathcal{C})$ is the number of edges in $\mathcal{C}$. Illustrate the technique with an example.

Exercise 4.8 (Theorem 20 is not true for SURE of depth 1)

For a URE, Theorem 20 states that the difference between the makespan of the free schedule and the minimal makespan of a linear schedule is bounded by a constant. Give an example of a SURE (computable by a shifted linear schedule) whose longest dependence path is $O(N)$ but for which the difference between the makespan of the free schedule and the makespan of the minimal shifted linear schedule is $\Omega(\log(N))$. Same question with a difference $\Omega(\sqrt[3]{N})$.

Hint: Consider a dependence graph with two vertices, one cycle C_1 between the two vertices, and two self-loops C_2, C_3. Choose the iteration domain and the dependence vectors so that the longest path goes $\Theta(N)$ times around C_2 and C_3 but has to go through C_1, a nonbounded number of times, $\Omega(\log(N))$ in the first case, $\Omega(\sqrt[3]{N})$ times in the second case.

Exercise 4.9 (Suboptimality for nonstrongly connected graphs)

It can be proved that, for a SURE for which a shifted linear schedule exists, the minimal makespan shifted linear schedule and the free schedule are asymptotically equivalent (the ratio goes to 1 when the length of the longest path goes to infinity) but only when the dependence graph is strongly connected. Build an example where the minimal makespan shifted linear schedule *is not* asymptotically optimal.

SUREs of Depth > 1

Exercise 4.10 (Depth of a SURE)

Give an example of a SURE, defined on a three-dimensional domain, for which the decomposition of Karp, Miller, and Winograd is of depth 1. Same question with depth 2, then depth 3, and finally depth 4.

Exercise 4.11 (Extension to nonbounded polyhedra)

How would it be possible to generalize the technique for the computability problem and the scheduling problem, when the iteration is a nonbounded polyhedron?

Exercise 4.12 (Vector space of all possible solutions)

Consider a solution (X, ρ) used, at a given level, to build a multidimensional schedule (see Lemma 27). Show that for any cycle $\mathcal{C} \in G'$, $X.w(\mathcal{C}) =$

0. What is the dimension of the vector space generated by all possible vectors X at a given level of the decomposition?

Note: When scheduling a SURE in an n-dimensional domain, multidimensional schedules of depth d can be interpreted as d sequential outer loops and $n - d$ parallel inner loops. Here, the analysis of the vector space generated by all possible X is related to the detection of maximal sets of permutable loops and of outermost parallel loops (see Sections 5.4.4 and 5.5.5).

Chapter 5

Parallelism Detection in Nested Loops

5.1 Introduction

Loop transformations have been shown to be useful for extracting parallelism from regular nested loops for a large class of machines, from vector machines and VLIW machines to multiprocessor architectures. Of course, each type of machine corresponds to a different optimized code; depending on the memory hierarchy of the target, the granularity of the generated code must be carefully chosen so that memory access is optimized. Fine-grain parallelism is efficient for vector machines, whereas for distributed-memory machines, coarse-grain parallelism (obtained by tiling or blocking techniques) is preferable and permits the reduction of interprocessor communication.

However, detecting parallelism (i.e., transforming some **DO** loops into **DOPAR** loops) and understanding parallelism (i.e., detecting which dependences are responsible for the sequentiality in the code) is independent of the target architecture. It only depends on the structure of the sequential code to be parallelized. This is certainly one of the reasons why many algorithms have been proposed for detecting DOPAR loops, as a first step in the parallelization process. First, one studies the problem of parallelization on an ideal machine (a PRAM, for example), and then further optimizations are taken into account (depending on the machine for which the code is to be compiled), such as the choice of granularity, the data distribution, and the optimization of communication. This two-step approach is the most often used, not only in the field of automatic nested loops parallelization; this is also the case for general task scheduling or software pipelining, as explained in Chapters 2 and 3.

In this chapter, we study the problem of parallelism detection in imperative codes "a la Fortran," but only in portions of codes that describe repetitive computations through nested loops. As in Chapter 4, this problem is a cyclic scheduling problem. However, some fundamental differences exist between the concept of system of uniform recurrence equations (SURE) and the concept of nested loops.

As we saw in Chapter 4, the order of computations described by a SURE is an *implicit* order; the left-hand side of each equation can be computed only if all arguments on the right-hand side have already been computed. In other words, the order of computations is directed by the semantics of the system. This has two important consequences:

- Dependences are *explicit*; they can be directly read from the system. Each reference on the right-hand side induces a dependence to the left-hand side.

- A SURE is not always computable, i.e., it may happen that there exists no order of computations that respects the semantics.

The first point makes the study of SUREs simpler; the second makes it more complicated.

In sequential imperative codes – in opposition to the model of SUREs that is a model of functional language – there is an *explicit* order of computation. For nested loops, this order is the lexicographic order of iteration vectors, plus the textual order, because the innermost loops are scanned for each instance of the outermost loops. This has two consequences, but with an opposite effect:

- Dependences are *implicit*; they *cannot* be directly read from the code. Dependence analysis algorithms have to be developed to find (in the best cases) or approximate (in the worst cases) the dependences between computations.

- A set of loops is always computable; the semantics of the code is given by the sequential order.

This opposition between sets of nested loops and SUREs is fundamental. However, despite this difference, many similarities exist. Both can be represented by reduced dependence graphs and the scheduling techniques that we developed for SUREs in the previous chapter can be adapted for nested loops.

The chapter is divided into six parts:

- In Section 5.2, we recall classical representation of dependences used for nested loops. We do not describe dependence analysis algorithms.

Excellent books and papers exist on this topic, and we will give pointers to them. Here, we only want to recall here the output of dependence analyzers, i.e., how dependences are represented in reduced dependence graphs.

- In Section 5.3, we recall the first and most famous parallelism detection algorithm: Allen and Kennedy's algorithm. It is the simplest algorithm to understand and implement. Parallelism is revealed using loop distribution.

- In Section 5.4, we recall classical loop transformations, based on unimodular matrices. We briefly present transformations such as Lamport's hyperplane method and Wolf and Lam's algorithm.

- In Section 5.5, we show how the techniques developed for SUREs in Chapter 4 can be adapted, with little effort, to the parallelization of nested loops if dependences are described by a polyhedral approximation of distance vectors. This generalizes both Allen and Kennedy's algorithm and Wolf and Lam's algorithm.

- In Section 5.6, we describe the most general parallelization algorithm developed until now. It is an algorithm based on multidimensional affine-by-statement scheduling, a technique developed by Paul Feautrier.

- Finally, in Section 5.7, we explain how the optimality of these parallelism detection algorithms can be discussed. We show the power of each algorithm and its limitations, and for each algorithm, we state an optimality result. Through examples, we explain what optimality means and does *not* mean.

We think this is the current state of the art in automatic parallelism detection in nested loops. Unfortunately, although this theory is now well established, it only solves the scheduling problem, i.e., the detection of maximal parallelism. It does not solve the mapping problem, i.e., how computations and data are distributed onto physical processors. This last problem is the current hot spot in automatic parallelization and is not yet well-enough understood to be fully addressed in this book. We only mention, in the bibliographical notes, some related problems that start to be well formulated, even if they do not solve the full mapping problem yet.

5.2 Dependence Analysis and Dependence Abstraction

5.2.1 Nested Loops and Dependence Relations

We first introduce the type of codes we will consider in this chapter: codes defined by nested loops, for which the control structure is simple enough to be captured in a sound mathematical framework. We first recall some usual vocabulary related to nested loops, such as iteration vector, iteration domain, and sequential order. Then we will illustrate, through an example, the different types of memory-based dependences. We do not explain how they can be detected; we refer to [125] for more details.

Nested Loops and Sequential Order

Consider the following piece of code:

Example 9

```
DO i=1, N
 DO j=i, N+1
  DO k=j-i, N
   S₁
   S₂
  ENDDO
 ENDDO
 DO r=1, N
  S₃
 ENDDO
ENDDO
```

This small code has four loops and three statements: S_1 and S_2, both surrounded by the loops i, j, and k, and S_3, surrounded by the loops i and r. The loops are *nonperfectly nested*, because all statements are not surrounded by the same loops. However, the two loops j and k are perfectly nested. In other words, nested loops are called *perfectly nested* (or form a *perfect loop nest*) if there is no code, other than a single nested loop, in any loop except the innermost one.   □

Each loop is defined by a loop counter that takes, one after the other, any integral value from the lower bound to the upper bound. [1] The itera-

---

[1] Except if the loops are defined with a *step*. We assume here that all steps are, by default, equal to 1.

tions of n perfectly nested loops are represented by a vector of size n, called the *iteration vector*. The set of all possible values of the iteration vector (defined by the lower and upper bounds of the loops) is called the *iteration domain*. For example, the loops i and r define a two-dimensional iteration vector (i, r) whose iteration domain is the set of integral vectors in the two-dimensional cube $1 \leq i, r \leq N$, whereas the loops i, j, and k define a three-dimensional iteration vector (i, j, k) whose iteration domain is more complicated; it is defined as the set of all integral vectors such that $1 \leq i \leq N$, $i \leq j \leq N + 1$, and $j - i \leq k \leq N$. In both cases, the iteration domain is defined as the set of integral vectors included in a polyhedron.

When running the program, each value of an iteration vector corresponds to a given execution of the code surrounded by the loops; in particular, each statement S is executed for each value I of the iteration vector defined by the loops that surround S. Such an execution is called an *operation* and is denoted by $S(I)$. These operations are carried out in a predefined order, called the *sequential order*, which we denote by the symbol $<_{seq}$.

The sequential order is defined as follows. The different iterations of a set of perfectly nested loops are performed while respecting the strict *lexicographic order* $<_{lex}$ of the iteration vectors. In other words, the operations of a given statement (or block of statements) S are executed as follows:

$$S(I) <_{seq} S(J) \Leftrightarrow I <_{lex} J$$

Furthermore, different statements of a given block of statements are executed by the order given by the text: *the textual order* $<_{text}$. We can now completely define $<_{seq}$, even for nonperfectly nested loops. Indeed, consider two operations $S(I)$ and $T(J)$ corresponding to two statements S and T. Assume that S and T are surrounded by $n_{S,T}$ common nested loops and that S (resp. T) is surrounded by $n_S \geq n_{S,T}$ (resp. $n_T \geq n_{S,T}$) nested loops. Then, I (resp. J) is an iteration vector of size n_S (resp. n_T). We denote by $\tilde{I}$ (resp. $\tilde{J}$) the vector of size $n_{S,T}$ whose components are the first $n_{S,T}$ components of I (resp. J). Consider the code C surrounded by the $n_{S,T}$ outermost loops. C contains the definition of S and T and is associated to an iteration vector of size $n_{S,T}$. Three cases can occur:

- If $\tilde{I} <_{lex} \tilde{J}$, then $C(\tilde{I}) <_{seq} C(\tilde{J})$, and thus $S(I) <_{seq} T(J)$.

- If $\tilde{J} <_{lex} \tilde{I}$, then $C(\tilde{J}) <_{seq} C(\tilde{I})$, and thus $T(J) <_{seq} S(I)$.

- If $\tilde{J} = \tilde{I}$, then $S(I)$ and $T(J)$ are two operations computed for a given iteration of the loops surrounding S and T. These operations are thus executed in the same order as they appear in the code C, i.e., $S(I) <_{seq} T(J)$ if and only if $S <_{text} T$.

In other words, the sequential order is given by the lexicographic order defined on the iteration vectors corresponding to common loops plus the textual order in case of equality for the lexicographic order. To summarize:

$$S(I) <_{seq} T(J) \Leftrightarrow (\tilde{I} <_{lex} \tilde{J}) \text{ or } (\tilde{I} = \tilde{J} \text{ and } S <_{text} T)$$

Note that the lexicographic order is a disjunction of affine inequalities or equalities. If I and J are two vectors of size n, then $I <_{lex} J$ if and only if

$$\begin{aligned}
&\quad\ \{I_1 + 1 \leq J_1\} \\
\text{or} &\quad\ \{I_1 = J_1 \text{ and } I_2 + 1 \leq J_2\} \\
\text{or} &\quad\ \ldots \\
\text{or} &\quad\ \{I_1 = J_1 \text{ and } \ldots \text{ and } I_{n-1} = J_{n-1} \text{ and } I_n + 1 \leq J_n\}
\end{aligned}$$

Example 9, Continued

$S_1(I)$ is carried out before $S_2(J)$ if and only if $I <_{lex} J$ or $I = J$ (because $S_1 <_{text} S_2$ is true), and $S_3(i, r) <_{seq} S_1(i', j, k)$ if and only if $i < i'$ (because $S_3 <_{text} S_1$ is false).   □

In the rest of this chapter, we will consider only the set of nested loops that can be described as just illustrated; each statement S surrounded by n_S nested loops is identified by its position in these loops (textual order $<_{text}$) and by an n_S-dimensional iteration domain, described by a polyhedron $\mathcal{D}_S$. Each integral vector I in the polyhedron $\mathcal{D}_S$ defines a valid iteration vector that corresponds to an instance of S, the operation $S(I)$. All these different operations $S(I)$ (where S is a statement and $I \in \mathcal{D}_S$) are ordered according to the sequential order $<_{seq}$ defined earlier. Loops that fit this model are, for example, Fortran-like loops with unit steps and loop bounds expressed as affine functions of parameters or surrounding indices.

Data Dependences: Flow, Anti, and Output Dependences

Of course, operations cannot be carried out in any order; permuting the evaluation order of two operations may change the final result of the program, and other operations can be performed concurrently. Bernstein [16] identified a partial order (denoted by $\Rightarrow$) defined on the operations that, if respected, leads to semantically equivalent codes, in the following sense: Any execution order (partial or not) that is an extension of the partial order $\Rightarrow$ leads to the same result, the result of the sequential execution. In particular, the sequential order $<_{seq}$ is an extension of $\Rightarrow$.

Operations comparable with respect to this partial order are called dependent. $\Rightarrow$ is defined through the data relations flow, anti, and output dependences. Before defining these types of dependence more precisely, we consider the following piece of code.

Example 10

```
DO i=1, N
 DO j=1, N
  a(i+j) = a(i+j-1) + 1
 ENDDO
ENDDO
```

Let us unroll the loops to better understand the relations between operations carried in Example 10. The different operations are listed in Figure 5.1 for $N = 4$. Dependences (to be defined) are represented by arrows.

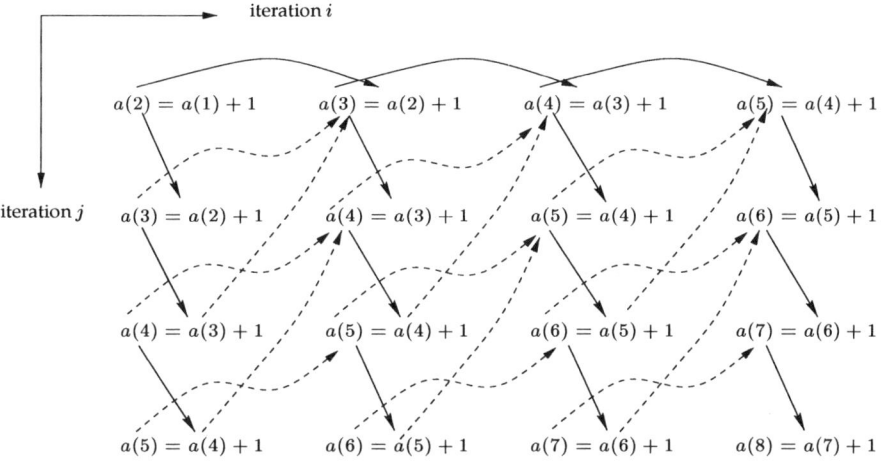

Figure 5.1: Unrolling of Example 10.

Consider the operation at iteration $i = 2$, $j = 2$, i.e., represented by the iteration vector $(2, 2)$. We store in $a(4)$ one plus the value stored in the memory location $a(3)$. This value is the value computed at iteration $(2, 1)$. We say that there is a *flow dependence* from iteration $(2, 1)$ to iteration $(2, 2)$ and that the *dependence distance* is $(0, 1)$ to express the fact that the dependence comes from an operation for the same iteration of loop i and the previous iteration of loop j.

Consider now the operation at iteration $i = 2$ and $j = 1$. $a(2)$ is read, but this time the value of $a(2)$ is the value computed at iteration $(1, 1)$, i.e., for the same iteration of loop j, $j = 1$, but for the previous iteration of loop i. Thus, there is a flow dependence from iteration $(1,1)$ to iteration $(2,1)$ and the dependence distance is $(1,0)$. Remark that this dependence occurs only for iteration vectors of the form $(i,1)$.

Respecting flow dependences is not sufficient to guarantee that the result of the code remains unchanged. Consider, for example, the computation of $a(4)$ and its use at iteration $(1,4)$. If only flow dependences are to be respected then iteration $(1,3)$ has to be carried out before iteration $(1,4)$ because the value of $a(4)$ needed for iteration $(1,4)$ is the value computed at iteration $(1,3)$; same for the operations at iterations $(2,2)$ and $(2,3)$. However, no flow dependence prevents us from carrying out iteration $(2,2)$ before iterations $(1,3)$ and/or $(1,4)$.

However, suppose that the operations are carried out in the following order: $(1,3)$, $(2,2)$, $(1,4)$, and finally $(2,3)$. Then the operation at iteration $(1,4)$ has changed; the value of $a(4)$ is wrong. It should be read at iteration $(1,4)$ before being changed again at iteration $(2,2)$. We say that there is an *anti dependence* from iteration $(1,4)$ to iteration $(2,2)$. The dependence distance here is $(1,-2)$.

Suppose that the operations are carried out in the following order: $(2,2)$, $(1,3)$, $(1,4)$, and finally $(2,3)$. Then the operation at iteration $(1,4)$ is right; however, the operation at iteration $(2,3)$ is no longer correct – the value of $a(4)$ is wrong. In the sequential order, $a(4)$ is written twice before being read at iteration $(2,3)$ – once at iteration $(1,3)$, once at iteration $(2,2)$ – and the desired value is the second one. In this case, we say that there is an *output dependence* from iteration $(1,3)$ to iteration $(2,2)$. The dependence distance here is $(1,-1)$. □

To summarize, we distinguish three types of dependences: flow, anti, and output dependences. These dependences are data dependences (in opposition to control dependences, which will not be considered in this chapter), which means that they are defined by the fact that two operations access the same memory location, either as a read or as a write.

There is a *data dependence* between $S(I)$ and $T(J)$ if both operations access the same memory location and at least one access is a write. The dependence is directed as in the sequential order, i.e., the dependence is a dependence from $S(I)$ to $T(J)$ if $S(I) <_{seq} T(J)$. Furthermore, the dependence is:

- **a flow dependence** if the access to the shared memory location is a write for $S(I)$ and a read for $T(J)$ and if the shared memory location is not accessed as a write between $S(I)$ and $T(J)$, in the sequential order;

- **an anti dependence** if the access to the shared memory location is a read for $S(I)$ and a write for $T(J)$ and if the shared memory location is not accessed as a write between $S(I)$ and $T(J)$, in the sequential order; and

- **an output dependence** if $S(I)$ and $T(J)$ are two consecutive write accesses to a shared memory location.

These three types of dependence are called direct dependences. All other cases correspond to transitive dependences and by extension they may also be called flow, anti, or output dependences, depending on the access types. To summarize:

Flow: write then read.   Anti: read then write.   Output: write then write.

A flow dependence corresponds to the definition of a memory cell and a later reference to it, an anti dependence corresponds to the reference of a memory cell and a later redefinition of it, and an output dependence corresponds to the definition of a memory cell and a later redefinition of it.

Note that two consecutive reads to a shared memory location is sometimes also called dependence. Such a relation is called an input dependence [125].

As said before, $S(I) \Rightarrow T(J)$ denotes a dependence from $S(I)$ to $T(J)$. The relation $\Rightarrow$ defines a partial order on the operations; this partial order is a suborder of the total order $<_{seq}$. Furthermore, any execution order on the operations that respects the partial order $\Rightarrow$ leads to a semantically equivalent code. [2] The topic of the current chapter is to determine such execution orders, especially orders whose longest chains are as small as possible, i.e., orders that reveal maximal parallelism.

5.2.2 Dependence Analysis

Many dependence analysis tests have been developed in the past twenty years, first as sufficient tests for checking the legality of code transformations, then as a basis for more sophisticated parallelism detection algorithms. Different representations (or *abstractions*) of the dependences have been proposed (dependence distance [92], dependence level [5, 4], dependence direction vector [118, 119], dependence polyhedron/cone [61], data flow graph [39], Pressburger formulas [99]), and more accurate tests for dependence analysis have been designed (Banerjee's tests [13], I test [71, 98], Δ test [50], λ test [83, 53], PIP test [39], PIPS test [60], Omega test [99]).

---

[2]As long as data dependences are the only dependences, which will be the case in all codes considered in this chapter.

In general, dependence abstractions and dependence tests have been introduced with some particular loop transformations in mind. For example, the dependence level was designed for Allen and Kennedy's algorithm, but the PIP test is the main tool for Feautrier's method for array expansion [39] and parallelism extraction by affine scheduling [40, 41].

General Problem Formulation

We refer to the original papers for a precise description of dependence tests and to the related chapter of Zima and Chapman's book [125]. We just illustrate here how the dependence analysis problem can be formulated for dependences due to multiple accesses to an array.

Suppose that $S(I)$ and $T(J)$ access to the same array a, for example, S through a write and T through a read:

$$S(I): \quad a(f(I)) \quad = \quad \ldots$$

$$T(J): \quad \ldots \quad = \quad a(g(J))$$

Accessing the same memory location in array a means that:

$$f(I) = g(J) \tag{5.1}$$

which can be checked, when f and g are affine functions with rational components, in polynomial time, as a system of Diophantine equations.

The fact that I and J are two valid iteration vectors is expressed by the relations

$$I \in \mathcal{D}_S \quad \text{and} \quad J \in \mathcal{D}_T \tag{5.2}$$

which can be checked, if $\mathcal{D}_S$ and $\mathcal{D}_T$ are represented as the set of integral vectors in a polyhedron, by integer linear programming techniques in the most general case, or by cheaper algorithms if the iteration domains are simpler (rectangles, triangles, etc.).

Looking for a flow dependence (direct or transitive) means checking if the write occurs before the read in the sequential order, i.e.,

$$S(I) <_{seq} T(J) \tag{5.3}$$

which is a disjunction of inequalities or equalities involving the components of the iteration vectors I and J (see the example hereafter). Equation 5.3 can be rewritten as a disjunction of (in)equalities thanks to the lexicographic and textual orders, as described in the previous section. Looking for anti or output dependences is similar.

Looking for *direct* dependences is more expensive because one has to find, for example, for a flow dependence directed to $T(J)$ the *last* operation that writes the memory location read by $T(J)$. This can be done by linear programming techniques capable of finding lexicographic minima or maxima in polyhedra (see [39, 38]).

Example 10, Continued

Consider the dependences due to the write access $a(i + j)$ and the read access $a(i + j - 1)$. We look for a dependence between a write operation $S(i', j')$ and a read operation $S(i, j)$, where i and j are given. Equation (5.1) implies:

$$i' + j' = i + j - 1$$

Equation $S(i', j') <_{seq} S(i, j)$ implies:

$$(i' \leq i - 1) \text{ or } (i = i' \text{ and } j' \leq j - 1)$$

Therefore, to find the direct flow dependence from $S(i', j')$ to $S(i, j)$ we have to solve the following problem:

$$\max_{<_{seq}}\{(i', j') \mid (i', j') <_{seq} (i, j),\ i' + j' = i + j - 1,\ 1 \leq i, i', j, j' \leq N\}$$

whose solution is:

- $(i, j - 1)$ if $j \geq 2$ and

- $(i - 1, j)$ if $j = 1$.

Similarly, finding a direct anti dependence from $S(i, j)$ to $S(i', j')$ means solving the following problem:

$$\min_{<_{seq}}\{(i', j') \mid (i, j) <_{seq} (i', j'),\ i' + j' = i + j - 1,\ 1 \leq i, i', j, j' \leq N\}$$

whose solution is $(i + 1, j - 2)$ if $j \geq 3$ and $i \leq N - 1$.

We retrieve the two flow dependences with distance vectors $(1, 0)$ and $(0, 1)$ and the anti dependence with distance vector $(1, -2)$. $\qquad\square$

Expanded, Reduced, and Apparent Dependence Graphs

Dependences between operations define a set of precedence constraints (the partial order $\Rightarrow$) that can be represented as a graph called the *expanded dependence graph (EDG)* or sometimes the iteration-level dependence graph.

The vertices of the expanded dependence graph are all possible operations $\{S_i(I) \mid 1 \leq i \leq s$ and $I \in \mathcal{D}_{S_i}\}$ (s is the number of statements in the piece of code that we consider). In the EDG, there is an edge from $S(I)$ to $T(J)$ (denoted by $S(I) \Rightarrow T(J)$) if executing instance $T(J)$ before instance $S(I)$ may change the result of the program, according to Bernstein's conditions.

For each pair p of array references that contains a write (write/read, read/write, or write/write) and induces a dependence from an operation $S(I)$ to an operation $T(J)$ (we write in this case $S(I) \overset{p}{\Rightarrow} T(J)$) we define the set of dependence pairs $R_{S,T}^p$ and the distance set, or set of dependence distances, $E_{S,T}^p$ as follows.

Definition 26 (Set of Dependence Pairs)

$$R_{S,T}^p = \{(I, J) \mid S(I) \overset{p}{\Rightarrow} T(J)\} \qquad R_{S,T}^p \subset (\mathbb{Z}^{n_S} \times \mathbb{Z}^{n_T})$$

where n_S (resp. n_T) is the number of loops that surround S (resp. T).

Definition 27 (Distance Set)

$$E_{S,T}^p = \{(\tilde{J} - \tilde{I}) \mid (I, J) \in R_{S,T}^p\} = \{(\tilde{J} - \tilde{I}) \mid S(I) \overset{p}{\Rightarrow} T(J)\} \quad E_{S,T}^p \subset \mathbb{Z}^{n_{S,T}}$$

where $n_{S,T}$ is the number of loops that surround both S and T and $\tilde{I}$ (resp. $\tilde{J}$) is the vector formed by the first $n_{S,T}$ components of I (resp. J).

Note that a dependence is always directed according to the sequential order. Therefore, if $S(I) \Rightarrow T(J)$, then the distance vector $(\tilde{J} - \tilde{I})$ is lexico-positive: $(\tilde{J} - \tilde{I}) \geq_{lex} \mathbf{0}$. [3] Furthermore, if $S \geq_{text} T$, then $(\tilde{J} - \tilde{I}) \neq \mathbf{0}$.

In general, the EDG, the sets of dependence pairs, and the distance sets cannot be generated at compile-time, either because some information is missing, such as the values of size parameters or, even worse, exact access functions to memory, or because generating the whole graph is too expensive (as large as the number of operations that have to be performed), and may not be needed as such for the optimizations we want to apply.

In [39] however, P. Feautrier showed that for codes with a not-too-complicated structure (the so-called *static control programs*), it is possible to perform an *exact dependence analysis* and to describe exactly the EDG in a condensed way, i.e., with a size proportional to the size of the code, but not to the size of the operations that it describes. Indeed, for such codes, the

---

[3]This is because we assumed the loop steps to be 1. With a loop step equal to -1, the corresponding component of the distance vector would be nonpositive, if the components corresponding to surrounding loops are null.

dependence pair sets $R^p_{S,T}$ can be represented by a finite union of sets of the form:

$$\{(I, f(I)) \mid I \in \mathcal{D}\} \quad \text{(for anti and output dependences)}$$

or

$$\{(f(I), I) \mid I \in \mathcal{D}\} \quad \text{(for flow and output dependences)}$$

where $\mathcal{D}$ is a polyhedron and f is an affine function (or the floor of an affine function). This was the case for Example 10.

Therefore, in this most favorable case, the EDG can be subsumed, in an exact way, by a smaller directed (multi)graph, in general cyclic, with s vertices (one per statement), called the *reduced dependence graph (RDG)* (or statement-level dependence graph). In this graph, there is an edge from S to T for each nonempty $R^p_{S,T}$ and this edge is labeled by a description of $R^p_{S,T}$.

In less favorable cases, the EDG can still be represented by a reduced dependence graph, but in an approximate way. In this case, because the goal is to describe a partial order such that all extensions lead to semantically equivalent executions, this approximation must be an overapproximation. In the RDG, we say that there is a dependence from S to T (and we write $S \to T$) if there exists at least one pair (I, J) such that $S(I) \Rightarrow T(J)$. Furthermore, each dependence $S \overset{e}{\to} T$, i.e., each edge $e = (S, T)$ of the RDG, has a label $w(e)$ that describes a subset D_e of $\mathbb{Z}^{n_{S,T}}$. These labels specify an overapproximation of the distance sets in the following sense:

$$\text{If } S(I) \Rightarrow T(J) \text{ (in the EDG) then}$$
$$\exists e = (S, T) \text{ (in the RDG) such that } (\tilde{J} - \tilde{I}) \in D_e \quad (5.4)$$

Therefore, the RDG describes, in a condensed manner, an iteration-level dependence graph, called (maximal) *apparent dependence graph (ADG)*, which is a superset of the EDG. The ADG and EDG have the same vertices, but the ADG has more edges, defined by:

$$S(I) \Rightarrow T(J) \text{ (in the ADG)} \qquad \Leftrightarrow$$
$$\exists e = (S, T) \text{ (in the RDG) such that } (\tilde{J} - \tilde{I}) \in D_e \quad (5.5)$$

Equations (5.4) and (5.5) ensure that EDG $\subset$ ADG.

To summarize:

- When an exact dependence analysis is feasible, the reduced dependence graph (RDG) gives an exact representation of the sets of dependence pairs $R^p_{S,T}$.

- When the expanded dependence graph (EDG) is captured through an approximation, the RDG gives an overapproximation of the distance sets $E^p_{S,T}$ that defines what we call the apparent dependence graph (ADG).

The notion of ADG will be used in Section 5.7.2 to define the degree of parallelism in an RDG. Examples of EDG, RDG, and ADG are given in the next section, in Example 13.

We now recall classical representations of dependences that give an approximation of sets of dependence distances, with different expressive power: level of dependences, direction vectors, and more general polyhedral approximations.

5.2.3 Approximations of Distance Sets

Classical representations of distance sets (by increasing accuracy) are:

- **level of dependence**, introduced in [5, 4] for Allen and Kennedy's parallelism detection algorithm;

- **direction vector**, introduced by Wolfe in [118, 119] and used in Wolf and Lam's parallelism detection algorithm [117];

- **dependence polyhedron**, introduced in [61] and used in Irigoin and Triolet's supernode partitioning algorithm [63]. For more details on dependence polyhedra, we refer to the PIPS [60] software.

Level of Dependence

Dependences in loops are classified in two categories: *loop-independent* dependences and *loop-carried* dependences. A dependence between two operations $S(I)$ and $T(J)$ is *loop-independent* if it occurs for a given iteration of all loops that surround both S and T, in other words, if $\tilde{I} = \tilde{J}$. Otherwise, the dependence is *loop-carried*; the dependence occurs between two operations that correspond, for at least one common surrounding loop, to different values of the loop counter. In this case, the *level* of the dependence is the depth (one plus the number of surrounding loops) of the outermost loop for which the loop counters of the two operations are different.

More formally, an edge $e = (S, T)$ of the RDG is labeled by a value $l(e) \in [1 \ldots n_{S,T}] \cup \{\infty\}$, where $l(e)$ is defined as follows:

- $l(e) = \infty$ if $S(I) \Rightarrow T(J)$ with $\tilde{J} - \tilde{I} = \mathbf{0}$.

- $l(e) \in [1 \ldots n_{S,T}]$ if $S(I) \Rightarrow T(J)$ and the first nonzero component of $\tilde{J} - \tilde{I}$ is the $l(e)$th component.

When $l(e) \leq n_{S,T}$, the dependence is loop-carried at level $l(e)$, and when $l(e) = \infty$, the dependence is loop-independent. We call *reduced level dependence graph* (RLDG) a reduced dependence graph whose edges are labeled by levels of dependence. We will illustrate the notion of dependence level in Example 11.

Direction Vector

Consider Example 10 again. There are three pairs of array references that induce a dependence, the pair *read* $a(i + j - 1)$-*write* $a(i + j)$, the pair *write* $a(i+j)$-*read* $a(i+j-1)$, and the pair *write* $a(i+j)$-*write* $a(i+j)$. The distance sets are very simple; the distance set associated to the anti dependence is the singleton $\{(1, -2)\}$, the distance set associated to the flow dependence is the pair $\{(1, 0), (0, 1)\}$, and the distance set associated to the output dependence is the singleton $\{(1, -1)\}$.

When the set of distance vectors is finite (as in this case), or more precisely when its size does not depend on the iteration domain size, then the dependence is called *uniform* and each different distance vector is called a *uniform dependence vector*.

Otherwise, a distance set between S and T can still be represented by a vector of dimension $n_{S,T}$, called the *direction vector* whose components belong to $\mathbb{Z} \cup \{*, +, -\} \cup (\mathbb{Z} \times \{+, -\})$. It is defined as follows. The ith component of the direction vector is an approximation of the ith components of all possible distance vectors: it is equal to $z+$ (resp. $z-$) if all ith components are greater (resp. smaller) than or equal to $z \in \mathbb{Z}$. It is equal to $*$ if the ith component may take any value and to z if the dependence is uniform in this dimension with unique value $z \in \mathbb{Z}$. In general, $+$ (resp. $-$) is used as shorthand for $1+$ (resp. $(-1)-$).

Example 11

Consider the following piece of code:

```
DO i=2, N
  S₁ : s(i) = 0
  DO j=1, i-1
    S₂ : s(i) = s(i) + a(j,i) * b(j)
  ENDDO
  S₃ : b(i) = b(i) - s(i)
ENDDO
```

This example is borrowed from the examples proposed with the software Petit; see [66]. The RLDG of this code, i.e., the reduced dependence graph whose edges are labeled by dependence levels, is depicted in Figure 5.2. The RDG labeled by direction vectors is depicted in Figure 5.3. To simplify the figures, only direct dependences are represented, and multi-edges are represented with a single edge with multiple labels.

Indeed, consider first the accesses to the array s. For each iteration of the i-loop, $s(i)$ is initialized by S_1 and read by S_2 in the first iteration of the j-loop, thus there is a loop-independent flow dependence from S_1 to S_2, i.e., a dependence of level ∞ and direction vector $\mathbf{0}$. In the subsequent iterations of the j-loop, $s(i)$ is read and rewritten, thus a flow dependence, an output dependence, and an anti dependence from S_2 to S_2 with direction vector $(0, 1)$, i.e., of level 2. Finally, $s(i)$ is read by S_3 while it was updated for the last time at the last iteration of the j-loop, thus there is a loop-independent flow dependence from S_2 to S_3. Finally, consider the array b: $b(i)$ is written once by the operation $S_3(i)$ but is read for all operations $S_2(i', i)$ provided that $1 \leq i \leq i' - 1$. Because $i' \geq i + 1$, these two array references to b induce only flow dependences with distance $(i' - i) \geq 1$, i.e., the direction vector $(+)$ and level 1. If the dependence analyzer cannot exactly detect direct dependences, then it may consider, for example, that there is a loop-independent dependence from S_1 to S_3. This is the case when the i-loop goes from M to N if M is not known to be equal to 2: The compiler cannot be sure that the j-loop will be executed at least once.   □

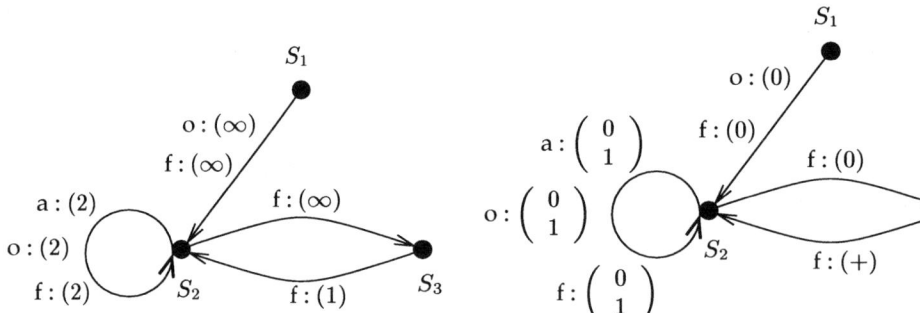

Figure 5.2: RLDG for Example 11.   Figure 5.3: RDG with direction vectors for Example 11.

Polyhedral Approximations

We first recall the mathematical definition of a polyhedron and how it can be decomposed into vertices, rays, and lines.

Definition 28 (Polyhedron, Polytope) *A set P of vectors in $\mathbb{Q}^n$ is called a (convex) polyhedron if there exists an integral matrix A and an integral vector b such that $P = \{x \mid x \in \mathbb{Q}^n, Ax \leq b\}$. A polytope is a bounded polyhedron.*

This definition assumes that the vector b is an integral vector and thus is not parameterized.

A polyhedron can always be decomposed as the sum of a (convex) polytope and a polyhedral cone, called the characteristic cone (for more details, see [110]). A polytope is defined by its vertices, and any point of the polytope is a nonnegative barycentric combination of the polytope vertices. A polyhedral cone is finitely generated and can be defined by its rays and lines. Any point of a polyhedral cone is the sum of a nonnegative combination of its rays and any combination of its lines. Therefore, a convex dependence polyhedron $\mathcal{P}$ can be equivalently defined by a set of *vertices* (denoted by $\{v_1, \dots, v_\omega\}$), a set of *rays* (denoted by $\{r_1, \dots, r_\rho\}$), and a set of *lines* (denoted by $\{l_1, \dots, l_\lambda\}$). Then $\mathcal{P}$ is the set of all vectors p such that

$$p = \sum_{i=1}^{\omega} \mu_i v_i + \sum_{i=1}^{\rho} \nu_i r_i + \sum_{i=1}^{\lambda} \xi_i l_i \qquad (5.6)$$

with $\mu_i \in \mathbb{Q}^+$, $\nu_i \in \mathbb{Q}^+$, $\xi_i \in \mathbb{Q}$, and $\sum_{i=1}^{\omega} \mu_i = 1$.

Remark: To avoid confusion between the vertices of polyhedra and the vertices of graphs, we will sometimes call a graph vertex a *node*.

We now define what we call a polyhedral reduced dependence graph (PRDG), i.e., a reduced dependence graph labeled by dependence polyhedra. Actually, we are interested only in integral vectors that belong to the dependence polyhedra, because dependence distances are always integral vectors.

Definition 29 (Polyhedral Reduced Dependence Graph (PRDG)) *A polyhedral reduced dependence graph (PRDG) is an RDG for which each edge $e : S \to T$ is labeled by a dependence polyhedron $\mathcal{P}(e)$ that approximates the set of distance vectors; the associated ADG contains an edge from instance I of node S to instance J of node T if and only if $(J - I) \in \mathcal{P}(e)$.*

The notion of dependence polyhedron is very close that of *dependence convex hull* [61, 62]. Indeed, a dependence convex hull is a particular dependence polyhedron, the convex hull of the distance vectors. Here we make no assumptions on the dependence polyhedra we handle or on the way they were computed. But as any valid approximation of the EDG, the PRDG must be defined so that the associated ADG is an overapproximation of the EDG. In other words, if $S(I) \Rightarrow T(J)$, then there is an edge $e = (S, T)$ in the PRDG such that the dependence polyhedron $\mathcal{P}(e)$ that labels e contains the distance vector $\tilde{J} - \tilde{I}$.

Links between Dependence Polyhedra, Direction Vectors, and Dependence Levels

Actually, RDGs labeled by direction vectors or levels of dependence are particular approximations of distance sets by polyhedra. Indeed, consider an edge e labeled by an n-dimensional direction vector d. Denote by L^+, L^-, and L^* the sets of components of d that are, respectively, equal to $z+$ (for some integer z), $z-$, and $*$. Denote by d_z the n-dimensional vector whose ith component is equal to z if the ith component of d is equal to z, $z+$, or $z-$ and whose ith component is equal to 0 otherwise. Finally, denote by e_i the ith canonical vector, i.e., tshe n-dimensional vector whose components are all null except the ith component equal to 1. Then, by definition of the symbols $+$, $-$, and $*$, the direction vector d represents exactly all n-dimensional vectors p for which there exist integers λ_i^+, λ_i^-, and λ_i^*, $1 \leq i \leq n$, such that:

$$p = d_z + \sum_{i \in L^+} \lambda_i^+ e_i - \sum_{i \in L^-} \lambda_i^- e_i + \sum_{i \in L^*} \lambda_i^* e_i \qquad (5.7)$$

In other words, the direction vector d represents all integer points that belong to the polyhedron defined by the single vertex d_z, the rays e_i for $i \in L^+$, the rays $-e_i$ for $i \in L^-$, and the lines e_i for $i \in L^*$. For example, the direction vector $(2+, *, -, 3)$ defines the polyhedron with one vertex $(2, 0, -1, 3)$, two rays $(1, 0, 0, 0)$ and $(0, 0, -1, 0)$, and one line $(0, 1, 0, 0)$.

We now consider an edge e labeled by a level $l(e) \neq \infty$. By definition of levels, the first nonzero component of the distance vectors associated to e is the $l(e)$th component, and it may take any positive integer value. Furthermore, we have no knowledge of the remaining components. Therefore, an edge of level $l(e) \neq \infty$ is equivalent to the direction vector: $(0, \ldots, 0, 1+, *, \ldots, *)$ (where the component $1+$ is the $l(e)$th component) and an edge of level ∞ corresponds to the null dependence vector. As any direction vector admits an equivalent polyhedron, so does a representation by level. For example, level 2 in a perfect loop nest of depth 3 means direction vector $(0, 1+, *)$, which corresponds to the polyhedron with one vertex $(0, 1, 0)$, one ray $(0, 1, 0)$, and one line $(0, 0, 1)$. To summarize, levels of dependence and direction vectors are two particular polyhedral approximations of distance sets.

Example 12

The following example illustrates the interest of general polyhedra for approximating distance sets. The weakness of the representation by levels is that after the first nonzero component of the distance vectors, no information is available. The representation by direction vectors tries to solve this problem by giving some information for each dimension. However, the representation by direction vectors cannot express possible relations between different components. This can be done with more general polyhedral approximations.

Code: Dependence relations:

```
DO i=1, N
  DO j=1, N
    S: a(i,j) = a(i,j-1) + a(j,i)
  ENDDO
ENDDO
```

$$\begin{cases} \text{if } 1 \le i, j \le N & S(i,j) \stackrel{\text{flow}}{\Rightarrow} S(i,j+1) \\ \text{if } 1 \le i < j \le N & S(i,j) \stackrel{\text{flow}}{\Rightarrow} S(j,i) \\ \text{if } 1 \le j < i \le N & S(j,i) \stackrel{\text{anti}}{\Rightarrow} S(i,j) \end{cases}$$

The distance set for the first flow dependence is equal to the singleton $\{(0,1)\}$. The distance sets for the two other dependences are equal to

$$\left\{ \begin{pmatrix} k \\ -k \end{pmatrix} \;\middle|\; 1 \le k \le N-1 \right\} \subset \left\{ \begin{pmatrix} 1 \\ -1 \end{pmatrix} + \lambda \begin{pmatrix} 1 \\ -1 \end{pmatrix} \;\middle|\; 0 \le \lambda \right\}$$

Thus, the distance sets can be approximated by a polyhedron independent of N, with one vertex $(1,-1)$ and one ray $(1,-1)$, which exploits the fact that the two components of the distance vectors have related values. □

EDG, RDG, ADG: Illustrating Example

To better understand the links between the three concepts (EDG, RDG, and ADG), let us consider a simple example, the SOR kernel (Figure 5.4), and assume that the dependence abstraction is the dependence level, i.e., assume that the RDG is an RLDG.

```
DO i=1, N
  DO j=1, N
    a(i,j) = a(i,j-1) + a(i-1,j)
  ENDDO
ENDDO
```

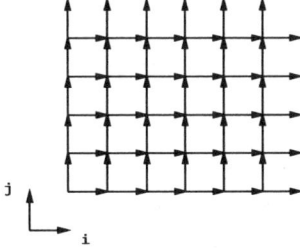

Figure 5.5: EDG for the SOR example.

Figure 5.4: Code for SOR kernel.

Example 13

The EDG for the SOR kernel is given in Figure 5.5. The length of the longest path in the EDG is equal to $2 * N$ (any path in the EDG from the lower-left corner to the upper-right corner). The RDG has only one vertex. It has two edges, one labeled by level 1, corresponding to the uniform dependence vector $(1, 0)$, and one labeled by level 2, corresponding to the uniform dependence vector $(0, 1)$; see Figure 5.6.

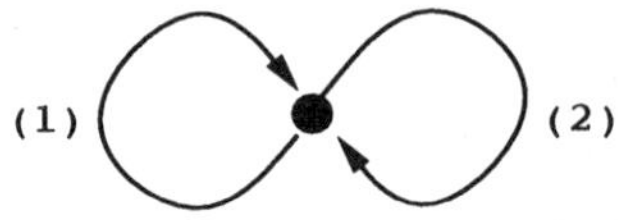

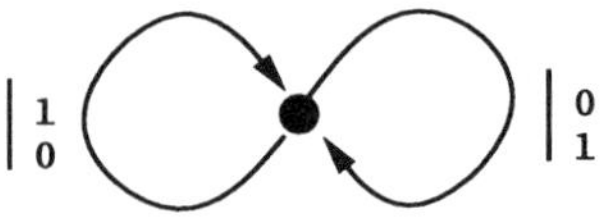

Figure 5.6: RLDG and uniform RDG for the SOR example.

The RLDG for this example is clearly a poor approximation because all dependences are uniform dependence vectors. As said before, levels 1 and 2 are equivalent to the direction vectors $(+, *)$ and $(0, +)$. In other words, the ADG that corresponds to the RLDG is the graph given in Figure 5.7 (in which transitivity edges have not been depicted). This graph is nothing but the graph that describes the sequential order $<_{seq}$ (it has a dependence path of length N^2), and thus the code seems purely sequential, even if the SOR kernel contains some parallelism.

Actually, it is possible to build a set of loops (we call them the apparent loops; see Figure 5.8) that have exactly the same RLDG as the SOR kernel and whose EDG is exactly the same as the ADG depicted in Figure 5.7 (where only direct dependences are represented).

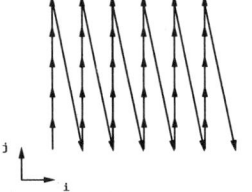

```
DO i=1, N
  DO j=1, N
    a(i,j) = a(i,j-1) + a(i-1,N)
  ENDDO
ENDDO
```

Figure 5.7: ADG for the RLDG of Figure 5.6. This is also the EDG for the code of Figure 5.8.

Figure 5.8: Apparent loops.

The two codes cannot be distinguished by their RLDGs, which are identical. Therefore no parallelism can be detected in the SOR example, as long as the levels of dependence are the only information available, because the apparent loops are purely sequential. The notion of apparent loops will be used to prove the optimality of Allen and Kennedy's algorithm for parallelism detection in an RLDG (Section 5.7.3). □

Limitations of Dependence Approximations

The previous example illustrates the link between the expressive power of a dependence abstraction and the parallelism that can be detected in a set of loops. Indeed, working with an approximation of the dependences limits, by nature, the set of partial orders that are considered as valid and thus limits the parallelism that can be found in the loops. When reasoning on the RDG instead of the EDG, we follow a pessimistic rule: To guarantee the semantics of the code, we guarantee that, in the RDG, the dependence relation $\rightarrow$ between statements describes, in the ADG, a dependence relation $\Rightarrow$ between operations that is an overapproximation of the actual dependence relation $\Rightarrow$ in the EDG. All execution orders considered valid are partial orders that are extensions not only of the EDG, but also of the ADG, thereby limiting the search space.

When exact dependence analysis is feasible and leads to affine dependences, the set of distance vectors is the projection of the integer points of a polyhedron. This set can be approximated by its convex hull or by a more or less accurate description of a larger polyhedron (or a finite union of polyhedra), as we explained before. This approximation is the first limitation for detecting parallelism. Note that a representation by distance sets (the sets $E_{S,T}^p$) is not equivalent to a representation by dependence pairs (the sets $R_{S,T}^p$) because the information concerning the *location* in the EDG of the distance vectors is not provided. This loss of information is the second limitation for detecting parallelism. Nevertheless, the representation by approximation of distance sets remains important, especially when exact dependence analysis is either too expensive or not feasible.

When developing parallelism detection algorithms, one must not forget this fact: By nature, some parallelism cannot be detected because it is hidden by the weaknesses of the dependence abstraction. If we understand this limitation, we may improve the algorithms with the dependence analysis, either by developing ad hoc procedures for particular cases or new methodologies if needed.

The first four algorithms that we discuss – ALLEN-KENNEDY, LAMPORT, WOLF-LAM, and DARTE-VIVIEN algorithms – all work on approximations of the EDG, respectively an RDG labeled by level of dependences (an RLDG) for ALLEN-KENNEDY, an RDG (with a single vertex) labeled by direction vectors for LAMPORT and WOLF-LAM, and an RDG labeled by polyhedral approximations of distance sets (a PRDG) for DARTE-VIVIEN. The capability of these four algorithms to detect parallelism is therefore limited by the more or less expressive power of the dependence abstractions they use.

Furthermore, these four algorithms do not consider the shape of the iteration domains. Therefore, the solution they give is generic, independent of the domains. This is a third limitation for detecting parallelism. For example, if a loop has only a few iterations, it may be desirable to unroll it to reveal more parallelism. This cannot be formulated a posteriori in these three algorithms. However, such a transformation can be done a priori before running the algorithms.

The last algorithm that we discuss, the FEAUTRIER algorithm, does not have these kinds of limitations; in the framework in which it is derived, the EDG and the ADG are equal, i.e., dependence analysis and dependence representations are exact. Furthermore, the shapes of the iteration domains are considered by the algorithm. However, in addition to the fact that exact dependence analysis is not always feasible, it has an intrinsic limitation due to the transformations it looks for. They are not sufficient to reveal the maximal parallelism. Nevertheless, the FEAUTRIER algorithm is the most general algorithm that has been developed until now.

The four first algorithms are also looking for particular transformations, i.e., particular partial orders. However we will see that the limitations due to their restricted transformation choice are hidden by the limitations described earlier as long as parallelism detection is concerned. In other words, looking for more general transformations will not reveal more parallelism: The limitations are due to the dependence approximations and not to the algorithms themselves. In this case, we will say that the algorithms are optimal with respect to the dependence analysis. This notion of optimality is precisely defined in Section 5.7.2.

5.3 Allen and Kennedy's Algorithm

The algorithm developed by Allen and Kennedy [5], then by Allen, Callahan, and Kennedy [4] works with a representation of dependences by levels, i.e., with an RLDG. The initial code is an arbitrary sequence of loops, perfectly or nonperfectly nested. The loops that surround a given statement are not changed. Only the way loops are nested may be changed. Before and after the algorithm, a statement is surrounded by exactly the same loops. The algorithm has two objectives:

- for each statement, to detect the maximal number of parallel loops that surround it, and

- once the first objective has been reached, to minimize the number of synchronization points in the parallelized code.

Because we only consider the detection of parallel loops in this chapter, we only recall how the first objective can be reached. We refer to the original papers [5, 6] and to Zima and Chapman's book [125] for a description of the complete algorithm that includes the second objective.

The key transformations used by the ALLEN-KENNEDY algorithm are the loop distribution (also called loop fission in [121]) and the reverse transformation, loop fusion. The former loop transformation is recalled in Section 5.3.1. Then we present Allen and Kennedy's algorithm in its simpler form in Section 5.3.2. The optimality of this algorithm will be considered in Section 5.7.3.

5.3.1   Loop Distribution

Loop distribution is based on the following remark.

Proposition 3 *All instances of a statement (or block of statements) S can be carried out before any instance of a statement (or block of statements) T if $T(J) \Rightarrow S(I)$ never occurs, i.e., by definition of $T \to S$, if there is no dependence from T to S.*

This is the basis of loop distribution. Figure 5.9 illustrates the simplest case of loop distribution: two statements S_1 and S_2 in a unique loop (Figure 5.9(a)), where S_1 is textually before S_2. Four cases can occur:

- $S_1 \to S_2$ but there is no dependence from S_2 to S_1. Then loop distribution leads to the code in Figure 5.9(b).

- $S_2 \to S_1$ but there is no dependence from S_1 to S_2. Then loop distribution leads to the code in Figure 5.9(c).

- There is no dependence between S_1 and S_2. Then the four codes (Figure 5.9) are valid.

- $S_1 \to S_2$ and $S_2 \to S_1$; then loop distribution is not valid. The initial code (Figure 5.9(a)) is valid, of course, as well as the code of Figure 5.9(d) if there is no loop-independent dependence, i.e., if all dependences are loop carried.

Maximal loop distribution is achieved as follows:

DO i= ... , ...	DO i= ... , ...	DO i= ... , ...	DO i= ... , ...
S_1	S_1	S_2	S_2
S_2	ENDDO	ENDDO	S_1
ENDDO	DO i= ... , ...	DO i= ... , ...	ENDDO
	S_2	S_1	
	ENDDO	ENDDO	
(a)	(b)	(c)	(d)

Figure 5.9: Loop distribution: Basic cases.

1. Compute the strongly connected components (SCCs) of the RDG.

2. Sort the SCCs topologically, i.e., number the SCCs so that $S \to T$ occurs only if S belongs to the strongly connected component C_i and T to the strongly connected component C_j with $i \leq j$. This is always possible because the graph induced by the strongly connected components is acyclic by definition.

3. Distribute the loops around the SCCs, i.e., duplicate the loop structures around each strongly connected component. The statements of a given strongly connected component are kept in the same textual order, and the codes corresponding to the different SCCs are ordered in the same order as the SCCs.

5.3.2 Basic Algorithm

We now present a simplified version of Allen and Kennedy's algorithm that marks "parallel" as many loops as possible for each statement. We first need to define what we call a parallel loop.

Definition 30 (Parallel Loop) *A loop is parallel if all iterations of the loop can be computed concurrently and in any order, i.e., if there is no dependence carried by the loop. In other words, a loop at depth k is parallel if there is no dependence at level k in the RLDG of the code surrounded by the loop.*

In addition to the notation **DOPAR** for parallel loops, we denote by **DOSEQ** a loop with the classical sequential meaning, to make the distinction between a **DO** loop that may be parallel and a **DO** loop that Allen and Kennedy's algorithm has recognized not to be a **DOPAR** loop. Note that what we call **DOPAR** is not the FORALL loop in High Performance Fortran (HPF) [57] but the INDEPENDENT loop in HPF or its correspondence in similar dialects like OPENMP, SUNMP, or CRAY directives.

The main idea of Allen and Kennedy's algorithm is to use loop distribution to reduce the number of statements within a loop and thus the number of potential dependences. The loop distribution principle suggests that the parallelism detection can be done independently in each strongly connected component of the RLDG. Then, Definition 30 is used to mark the outermost loop as a **DOPAR** or **DOSEQ**, and the same technique is used recursively for the inner loops.

Remember that n_S denotes the number of nested loops that surround a statement S (see Section 5.2.1). For an RLDG G, we denote by $l_{\min}(G)$ the minimal level of an edge in G:

$$l_{\min}(G) = \min\{l(e) \mid e \in G\}$$

Here is a sketch of the algorithm in its most basic formulation. The initial call is done with $k = 1$ and G equal to the RLDG of the code to be parallelized:

ALLEN-KENNEDY(G, k)

1. Remove from G all edges of level $< k$.

2. Compute the strongly connected components of G.

3. **For each** strongly connected component C in topological order **do**

   If C is reduced to a single statement S, with no edge,

   Then

   > Generate **DOPAR** loops in all remaining dimensions, i.e., from level k to level n_S, and generate the code for S.

   Else

   > (a) Let $l = l_{\min}(C)$.
   > (b) Generate **DOPAR** loops from level k to level $l - 1$ and a **DOSEQ** loop for level l.
   > (c) Call ALLEN-KENNEDY$(C, l + 1)$.

Example 14

Consider the pseudo-code of Figure 5.10(a) and assume that its corresponding RLDG is the graph depicted in Figure 5.10(b).

The RLDG has two strongly connected components: C_1 with statements S_1, S_2, S_3, and C_2 with statement S_4 only. C_1 has at least one level 1 edge, thus the outermost loop surrounding the statements of C_1 is marked

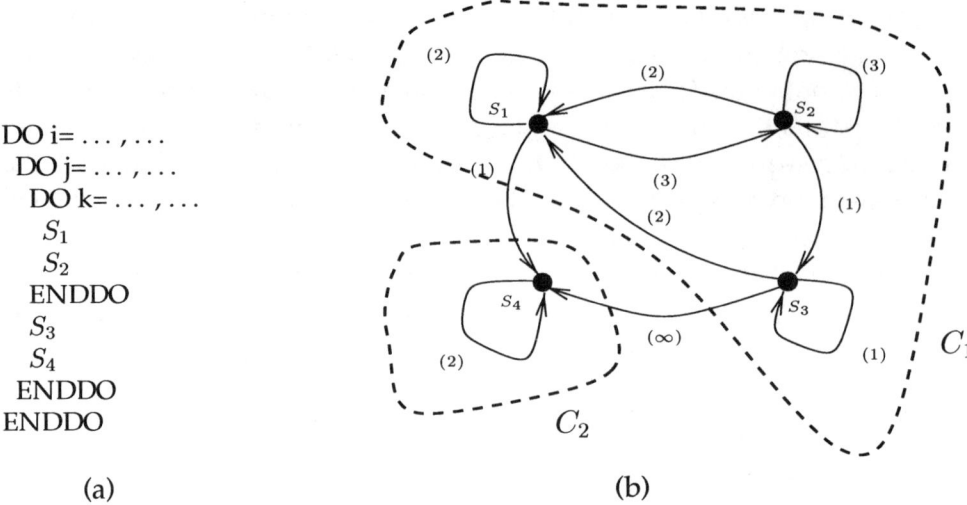

DO i= ... , ...
  DO j= ... , ...
    DO k= ... , ...
     S_1
     S_2
    ENDDO
     S_3
     S_4
    ENDDO
  ENDDO

(a)   (b)

Figure 5.10: Code and RLDG for Example 14.

sequential. C_2 has no level 1 edge but does have a level 2 edge, thus the outermost loop is marked parallel and the second loop is marked sequential. Therefore, the code after the first call is the code of Figure 5.11(a).

The recursion continues. For C_1 we remove all level 1 edges, which means that we now consider the code for a given iteration of the outermost loop. Similarly, for C_2 we remove all edges with level < 3. We get the RLDGs depicted in Figure 5.11(b). S_1 and S_2 are still in the same strongly connected component C_3, which contains a level 2 edge. Thus, one sequential loop is generated and the recursion goes on. S_3 and S_4 form two strongly connected components, with no edge; thus the missing dimensions and the code for the statements are generated. We get the code of Figure 5.12(a). Notice how iterations of S_3 have been moved up before the iterations of S_1 and S_2.

Finally, after three calls, only statements S_1 and S_2 remain in the graph. The level 2 edges are removed and we obtain the RLDG depicted in Figure 5.12(b) with two strongly connected components C_4 and C_5. The last two phases are depicted in Figure 5.13(a,b).   □

Notice that the number of sequential loops that surround a statement S in the parallelized code is exactly the number of recursive calls to ALLEN-KENNEDY that concern S (the initial call excluded). We will use this fact in Section 5.7.3 for reasoning on the degree of parallelism (to be defined) detected by this algorithm.

The algorithm presented is a greedy algorithm. At each level, from the outermost loop to the innermost loop, a maximal distribution of the loops

DOSEQ i= ... , ...

  ALLEN-KENNEDY(C_1, 2)

ENDDOSEQ
DOPAR i= ... , ...
  DOSEQ j= ... , ...

    ALLEN-KENNEDY(C_2, 3)

  ENDDOSEQ
ENDDOPAR

(a)

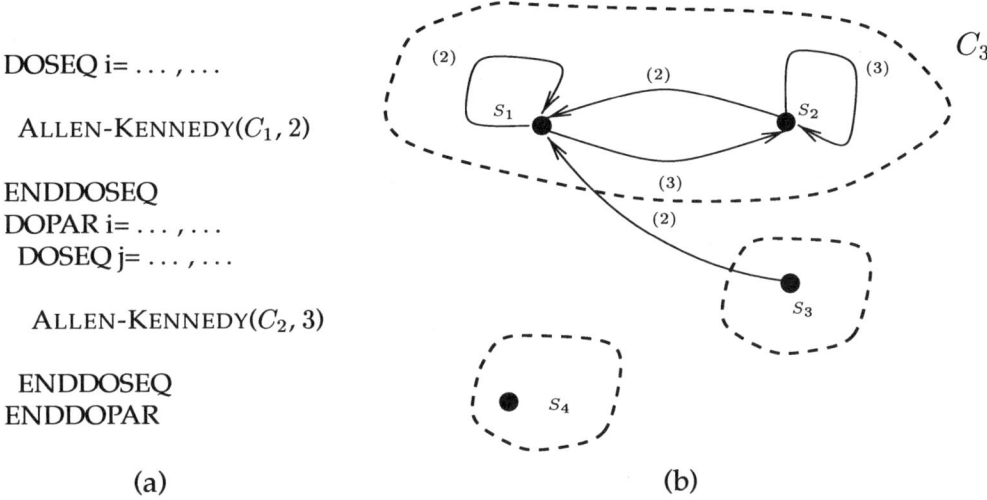

(b)

Figure 5.11: Code and remaining RLDGs for Example 14 before second recursive code generation.

DOSEQ i= ... , ...
  DOPAR j= ... , ...
    S_3
  ENDDOPAR
  DOSEQ j= ... , ...

    ALLEN-KENNEDY(C_3, 3)

  ENDDOSEQ
ENDDOSEQ
DOPAR i= ... , ...
  DOSEQ j= ... , ...
    S_4
  ENDDOSEQ
ENDDOPAR

(a)

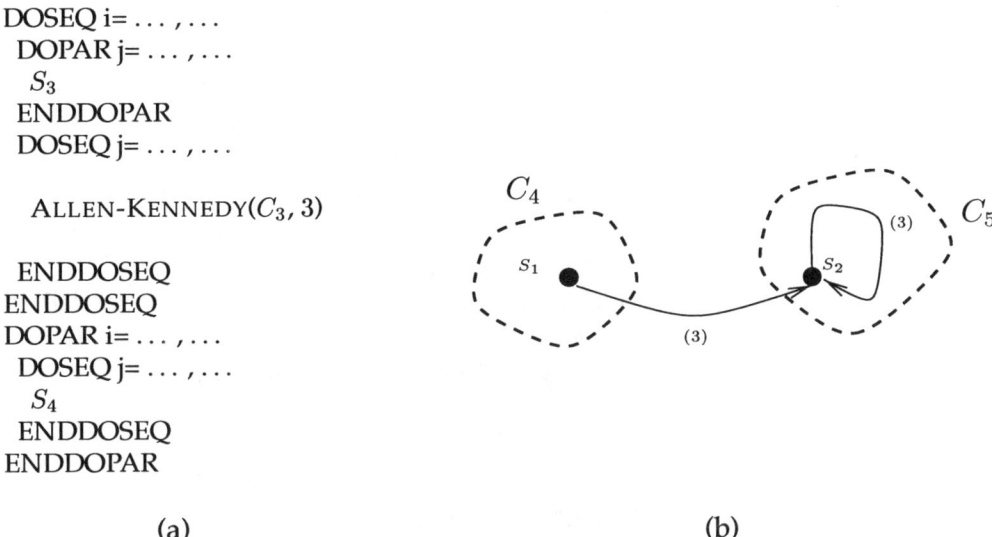

(b)

Figure 5.12: Code and RLDG for Example 14 before third recursive code generation.

```
DOSEQ i= ... , ...          DOSEQ i= ... , ...
  DOPAR j= ... , ...           DOPAR j= ... , ...
  S_3                          S_3
  ENDDOPAR                     ENDDOPAR
  DOSEQ j= ... , ...           DOSEQ j= ... , ...
    DOPAR k= ... , ...           DOPAR k= ... , ...
    S_1                          S_1
    ENDDOPAR                     ENDDOPAR
    DOSEQ k= ... , ...           DOSEQ k= ... , ...
      ALLEN-KENNEDY(C_4, 4)      S_2
    ENDDOSEQ                     ENDDOSEQ
  ENDDOSEQ                     ENDDOSEQ
ENDDOSEQ                     ENDDOSEQ
DOPAR i= ... , ...          DOPAR i= ... , ...
  DOSEQ j= ... , ...           DOSEQ j= ... , ...
  S_4                          S_4
  ENDDOSEQ                     ENDDOSEQ
ENDDOPAR                     ENDDOPAR

       (a)                          (b)
```

Figure 5.13: Code for Example 14 before and after the last recursive code generation.

is applied. This algorithm can be refined to improve secondary goals such as minimizing the number of synchronization barriers, or optimizing data reuse. Indeed, a *partial loop distribution* may be sufficient to reveal the same amount of parallelism while offering better data locality. Statements that belong to different strongly connected components may be kept together when distributing the loops, without changing the nature of the loops, **DOSEQ** or **DOPAR**. The partial loop distribution technique (which is in fact a loop fusion problem once maximal loop distribution is performed) has been mainly studied by McKinley and Kennedy [68, 89] as a particular case of a more general *typed loop fusion* problem. For most proposed optimization objectives, the corresponding problems are unfortunately NP-complete (see also [27]).

5.4   Unimodular Transformations

Unimodular transformations are mainly used for perfectly nested loops. Therefore, in this section, we will restrict our study to the case where all statements are surrounded by the same set of n perfectly nested loops.

In Section 5.4.1, we define unimodular transformations and we show

how to check their validity. In Section 5.4.2, we recall classical results about the hyperplane method for uniform nested loops. Then, in Section 5.4.3, we recall the historical extension of the hyperplane method to direction vectors, proposed by Lamport. Next, we recall in Section 5.4.4 the extension to direction vectors proposed by Wolf and Lam for the simplest case of one statement surrounded by a set of loops.

5.4.1 Definition and Validity

Definition of a Unimodular Transformation

Many loop restructuring transformations have been proposed (see [125], [121], or [12] for a list), among which is the class of the unimodular transformations. A *unimodular transformation* is a transformation that changes the order in which the loop nest enumerates the points of the iteration domain. The iteration domain is scanned by new loop counters, i.e., by a new iteration vector. This new iteration vector, I', is defined from the original one, I, by a *unimodular matrix T : $I' = TI$*. In other words, the iteration domain is no longer enumerated in the lexicographically increasing values of the iteration vector I, but in the lexicographically increasing values of the iteration vector $I' = TI$. A unimodular matrix is an integral square matrix whose determinant is equal to 1 or -1 (unimodular matrices are the regular integral square matrices whose inverses are also integral).

A unimodular transformation changes nothing but the enumeration order. Thus the different operations that belong to a given iteration of the loops after the unimodular transformation were already gathered in an iteration before the transformation. Therefore, when applying a unimodular transformation, we can consider that the loop body is atomic. In other words, we can consider that the nested loops are surrounding only one statement and the corresponding RDG is an RDG with a single node. For the same reason, loop-independent dependences are always respected by unimodular transformations.

A unimodular transformation is fully defined by a unimodular matrix. The following three types of matrices are known as *elementary unimodular matrices*. I_n denotes the identity matrix of size n and $E_{i,j}$ denotes the n-by-n matrix whose components are all null except the component in the ith row and jth column that is equal to 1. $I_n = \sum_{i=1}^{n} E_{i,i}$:

1. $R_i = I_n - 2E_{i,i}$ is integral and equal to its inverse: $(R_i)^{-1} = R_i$.

2. $P_{i,j} = I_n - E_{i,i} - E_{j,j} + E_{i,j} + E_{j,i}$ is integral and equal to its inverse: $(P_{i,j})^{-1} = P_{i,j}$.

3. For $i \neq j$, $S_{i,j}(k) = I_n + kE_{i,j}$ is integral and its inverse is $S_{i,j}(-k)$.

A well-known mathematical result (see, for example, [93]) states that any unimodular matrix can be decomposed as a product of elementary matrices, i.e., matrices of the form R_i, $P_{i,j}$, and $S_{i,j}(k)$. We can even enforce that all matrices of the third type that appear in the decomposition be matrices of the form $S_{i,j}(1)$ with $i \geq j$.

Examples

Three well-known loop transformations are unimodular:

- *Loop permutation.* Originally the iteration domain is scanned by the iteration vector $(I_1, \dots, I_n)$. After transformation by the permutation σ, it is scanned by the iteration vector $(I_{\sigma(1)}, \dots, I_{\sigma(n)})$.

- *Loop reversal.* To reverse the ith loop means to run the ith loop backwards. The new iteration vector is $(I_1, \dots, I_{i-1}, -I_i, I_{i+1}, \dots, I_n)$.

- *Loop skewing.* To skew loop I_j by the integer factor f with respect to loop I_i (with $i < j$) means to scan the domain with the new iteration vector $(I_1, \dots, I_{j-1}, I_j + fI_i, I_{j+1}, \dots, I_n)$.

These loop transformations can be described by elementary unimodular matrices. Indeed, a loop reversal at depth i corresponds to the transformation matrix R_i. A loop interchange of the ith loop and jth loop corresponds to the transformation matrix $P_{i,j}$. A loop skewing of loop i by loop j and factor k corresponds to the transformation matrix $S_{i,j}(k)$.

Example 13, Continued

Consider the SOR example again. The ALLEN-KENNEDY algorithm cannot detect parallelism in this code because the dependence description by level is not accurate enough. However, it is well known that, for this example, a simple loop skewing followed by a loop interchange reveals parallelism (cf. Figure 5.14). □

We are interested in unimodular transformations because ALLEN-KENNEDY is not powerful enough for exploiting a multidimensional knowledge on distance vectors. We also take interest in these transformations because they are easy to use, not only for rewriting the loop nest after transformation, but also for checking their validity.

Loop Nest Rewriting

Applying a unimodular transformation T to a set of perfectly nested loops means computing an operation $S(I)$ at iteration $I' = T(I)$ rather than at

```
DO j=2, 2N
  DOPAR i=max(1,j-N), min(N,j-1)
    a(i,j-i) = a(i-1,j-i) + a(i,j-i-1)
  ENDDOPAR
ENDDO
```

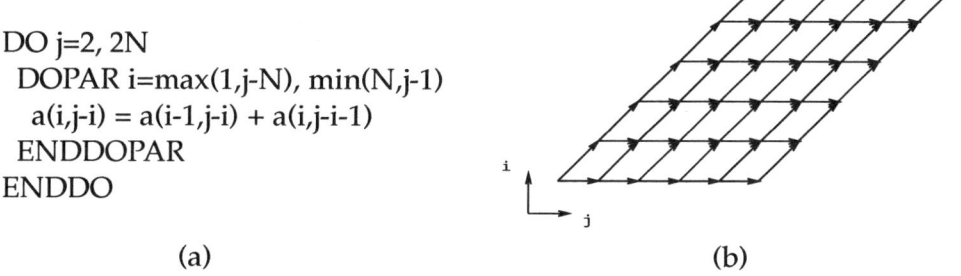

(a)   (b)

Figure 5.14: Parallel code for Example 13 and the transformed EDG ($N=6$).

iteration I, i.e., transforming the code in Figure 5.15(a) into the code in Figure 5.15(b). The latter can be rewritten into the code in Figure 5.15(c). The equivalence with the third code is due to the fact that T is a one-to-one correspondence between integral points in $\mathcal{D}$ and integral points in $T(\mathcal{D})$ when T is unimodular.

```
DO I ∈ D, I integral      DO I' = T(I), I ∈ D, I integral      DO I' ∈ T(D), I' integral
  S(I)                      S(I)                                 S(T⁻¹(I'))
ENDDO                      ENDDO                                 ENDDO
```

$$\text{DO } I \in \mathcal{D}, I \text{ integral} \qquad \text{DO } I'=T(I), I \in \mathcal{D}, I \text{ integral} \qquad \text{DO } I' \in T(\mathcal{D}), I' \text{ integral}$$
$$S(I) \qquad\qquad\qquad S(I) \qquad\qquad\qquad\qquad S(T^{-1}(I'))$$
$$\text{ENDDO} \qquad\qquad\qquad \text{ENDDO} \qquad\qquad\qquad\qquad \text{ENDDO}$$

(a)   (b)   (c)

Figure 5.15: The code before and after a unimodular transformation T.

Validity

Of course, any unimodular transformation is not valid. As explained in Section 5.2, dependences between operations have to be preserved by the transformation. If $S_i(I) \Rightarrow S_j(J)$ in the original code, then we must ensure that $S_i(I) <_{seq} S_j(J)$ in the transformed code. Remember that $S_i(I)$ is now computed at iteration $T(I)$ and $S_j(J)$ at iteration $T(J)$, and that the textual order is left unchanged by a unimodular transformation. Therefore, loop independent dependences ($I = J$ and $S_i <_{text} S_j$) are always respected, as already mentioned. However, a loop carried dependence $S_i(I) \Rightarrow S_j(J)$ is preserved if and only if $T(I) <_{lex} T(J)$, i.e., $T(J - I) >_{lex} \mathbf{0}$ because T is linear. We thus have the following validity condition.

Proposition 4 *A unimodular transformation T is valid if and only if for all nonzero distance vector d, the image $T(d)$ of d by T is strictly lexicographically positive: $d \neq \mathbf{0} \Rightarrow T(d) >_{lex} \mathbf{0}$.*

For any loop transformation T, the validity condition is, of course, that all dependence distances $d' = J' - I' = T(J) - T(I)$ in the new set of loops remain lexicographically positive. However, the fact that T is linear makes things simpler: $d' = T(d)$, where $d = J - I$. We will see in Sections 5.5 and 5.6 that for more complicated transformations such as multi-dimensional affine transformations, the validity condition is more complicated.

The condition of Proposition 4 is particularly easy to check when the number of different distance vectors is constant and bounded (i.e., finite and not parameterized), e.g., for uniform nested loops (see Section 5.2.3). This is why much research has focused on the automatic generation of unimodular transformations for parallelism detection in uniform nested loops. We now present some of this work.

5.4.2   The Hyperplane Method (Uniform Loop Nests)

In this section, we assume that the loop nest to be parallelized only contains uniform dependences; consider the validity condition in Proposition 4. For a unimodular transformation to be valid, we have to ensure that each non-zero uniform dependence vector d satisfies $T(d) >_{lex} 0$. To simplify notation, we identify transformation T with unimodular matrix T; we can thus write $T(d)$ as a matrix-vector product Td. The simpler idea, to make sure that $Td >_{lex} 0$ (the first nonzero component of Td is (strictly) positive), is to apply a greedy strategy, i.e., to choose T so that the *first* component of Td is positive. If such a matrix T exists, then all dependence vectors will be transformed by T into level 1 dependences. In other words, all dependences will be carried by the outermost loop and the transformed code will consist of $n - 1$ parallel loops surrounded by one sequential loop.

This technique is known as the *hyperplane method*, *wave-front method*, or *Lamport method* [75]. This terminology comes from the following interpretation. Denote by s the first row of T. Transforming all dependences into level 1 dependences means that s satisfies the inequality $sd \geq 1$ for all dependence vectors d. For any given constant c, all the operations $S(I)$ such that $sI = c$ can be executed in parallel. These operations belong to an affine hyperplane (or wave-front) normal to s. The flow of computations follows s. This is why s is called either a *strongly separating hyperplane* or a *timing vector*. A vector t is a *weakly separating hyperplane* if its dot product with any distance vector is nonnegative; for all distance vectors d, $td \geq 0$.

Lamport [75] showed that for uniform nested loops, there always exist strongly separating hyperplanes. The proof is constructive and given with Theorem 26. A more intuitive (at least more conceptual) way of understanding this result is given by Theorem 27 and its proof.

Theorem 26 (Hyperplane Concurrency Theorem) *Given a set D of m lexicographically (strictly) positive vectors, there exists an integral vector s such that $sd \geq 1$ for all $d \in D$.*

Proof The proof is constructive. Let D_i be the set of vectors of D whose first nonzero component is the ith component. Because all vectors in D are lexicographically positive, then for all $d \in D_i$, $d(1) = \ldots = d(i-1) = 0$ and $d(i) > 0$. Now, we build the components of s by induction, starting from the last one. Suppose that $s(i+1), \ldots, s(n)$ have already been built such that, for all $k > i$ and for all $d \in D_k$, $sd \geq 1$. If D_i is empty, let $s(i) = 0$; otherwise let $s(i) = \max\left\{ \left\lceil \frac{1 - \sum_{k=i+1}^{n} s(k)d(k)}{d(i)} \right\rceil \,\middle|\, d \in D_i \right\}$. Then, for all $k > i$ and for all $d \in D_k$, the value of sd remains unchanged because $d(i) = 0$. Furthermore, for all $d \in D_i$, $sd = s(i)d(i) + \sum_{k=i+1}^{n} s(k)d(k)$ is, by construction, greater than or equal to 1. ∎

Example 10, Continued

Example 10 contains four different uniform dependence vectors (cf. Figure 5.1): $D_1 = \{(1,-1), (1,-2), (1,0)\}$ and $D_2 = \{(0,1)\}$. With Lamport's procedure, we obtain $s(2) = 1$, and then:

$$s(1) = \max\{(1 - (-1))/1, (1 - (-2))/1, (1 - 0)/1\} = 3$$

Thus, $s = (3, 1)$. □

Once we have a timing vector, we still have to build the unimodular matrix.

Construction of the Unimodular Matrix

Remark that s can always be chosen integral with coprime components. Indeed, suppose that we get a rational vector s such that $sd \geq 1$ for all dependence vectors d. Decompose s under the form $s = \frac{p}{q}s'$ with p and q positive integers and s' integral with coprime components. Then we have

$$sd \geq 1 \Rightarrow sd > 0 \Rightarrow \tfrac{p}{q}s'd > 0 \Rightarrow s'd > 0 \Rightarrow s'd \geq 1$$

because s' and d are integral vectors. Suppose we have a strongly separating hyperplane s, integral with coprime components. What we want is a unimodular matrix T whose first row is s. A simple way to build such a matrix is to use the Hermite normal form (for details see, for example, [110, p. 45]). Let $s = hU$ be the Hermite form of s. By definition, U is a unimodular matrix and h a matrix of the form $[B\ \mathbf{0}]$, where B is a nonsingular, lower triangular, nonnegative matrix. Because s is a row vector, so is h which is thus of the form $[b\ 0 \dots 0]$, where b is a nonnegative integer. Because s is a nonzero integral vector with coprime components, b must be equal to one. Therefore, U is a unimodular matrix whose first row is equal to s.

Example 10, Continued

The Hermite normal form of s is:

$$s = (3,1) = (1,0) \begin{pmatrix} 3 & 1 \\ 1 & 0 \end{pmatrix} \text{ and } T = \begin{pmatrix} 3 & 1 \\ 1 & 0 \end{pmatrix} = \begin{pmatrix} 0 & 1 \\ 1 & 0 \end{pmatrix} \begin{pmatrix} 1 & 0 \\ 3 & 1 \end{pmatrix}$$

The decomposition of T into elementary transformations (as earlier) means that transforming the code with the unimodular transformation T corresponds to a loop skewing by factor 3, followed by a loop interchange. The resulting code follows; one can check that the transformation is valid:

```
DO j=4, 4N
  DOPAR i= max(1, ⌈(j−N)/3⌉), min(N, ⌊(j−1)/3⌋)
    a(j-2i) = a(j-2i-1)+1
  ENDDOPAR
ENDDO
```

□

Here is the more conceptual version of the hyperplane concurrency theorem (Theorem 26).

Theorem 27 *Given a set D of m lexicographically (strictly) positive vectors, the linear program $\{s \mid \forall d \in D, sd \geq 1\}$ has a solution.*

Proof To prove this theorem we use a result established for uniform recurrence equations in Section 4.3.3. There, Lemma 18 shows that this linear program has a solution if and only if a nonnegative and nonnull linear combination of the dependence vectors is never equal to the null vector. But the sum of two lexicographically (strictly) positive vectors is a lexicographically (strictly) positive vector. Therefore, a nonnegative and nonnull linear combination of dependence vectors is always lexicographically (strictly) positive and, thus, not equal to the null vector. In other words, there is no multicycle of null weight in a uniform RDG that comes from a set of loops. ■

Note also that all results obtained in Section 4.3 for a single uniform equation can be reused here. In particular, the linear schedule with minimal makespan gives a hyperplane that leads to the minimal number of sequential iterations for the outermost loop.

5.4.3 The Hyperplane Method (Direction Vectors)

In the previous section we assumed that the loop nest to be parallelized only had uniform dependences. This hypothesis is very restrictive. Here, we only assume that the dependences are represented by direction vectors. Lamport [75] showed how the hyperplane method can be adapted to this more general case, although his technique is not optimal.

Let $D = \{d_1, \dots, d_m\}$ be the set of all direction vectors. Then let $\mathcal{J} = \{j_1, \dots, j_p\}$ be the set of the ranks of the components that are not constant for all the direction vectors, to which we add "1" if it was not already included. In other words, k belongs to $\mathcal{J}$ if $k = 1$ or if there exists $d \in D$ such that $d(k)$ (the kth component of d) is not an integer. Lamport's idea is that $V_k = D_{j_k} \cup \dots \cup D_{j_{k+1}-1}$ is a set of uniform dependences. He builds one strongly separating hyperplane for each of these sets. This way, he proved the following result.

Theorem 28 (Plane Concurrency Theorem) *By a unimodular transformation, the loop nest can be rewritten in a loop nest containing p sequential and $n - p$ parallel nested loops, where $p = |\mathcal{J}|$ (defined earlier).*

Proof Let D_i be the set of vectors of D whose first nonzero component is the ith component.

The desired unimodular matrix T is built such that its kth line, for any $k \in [1, p]$, is a hyperplane that satisfies the dependences in the set $V_k = D_{j_k} \cup \dots \cup D_{j_{k+1}-1}$ (with the notation $j_{m+1} = n+1$). In other words, the kth line of T is a hyperplane that satisfies the direction vectors of dependence levels between j_k and $j_{k+1} - 1$. This property ensures that T defines a valid program transformation.

To prove the existence of such a hyperplane, let us only consider the components of ranks between j_k and $j_{k+1} - 1$. We build a new set V_k' of direction vectors by associating to any vector d of V_k a vector d' of V_k'. d' is a vector of $\mathbb{Z}^{j_{k+1}-j_k}$ that is equal to d when we only consider the components of ranks between j_k and $j_{k+1} - 1$. d' is still a lexicographically (strictly) positive vector. By definition of $\mathcal{J}$ and V_k, d' is a uniform vector, except perhaps for its first component. Indeed, this component can be of the form $z+$, where z is a nonnegative integer (by lexicographic positivity). In such a case, we replace $z+$ by z in $d'(1)$. Then we can use Theorem 26 or 27, which ensures that there exists a strongly separating hyperplane s' of V_k'. Furthermore, we can suppose that this hyperplane is nonnegative (in the proof of Theorem 26 we can add the condition $s(i) \geq 0$), integral, and with coprime components. Let s be the vector of $\mathbb{Z}^n$ that is equal to s' when we only consider the components of ranks between j_k and $j_{k+1} - 1$, and whose other components are null. Then for any vector $d \in V_k$, $sd \geq 1$. Indeed, let d be a vector of V_k. Then $sd = \sum_{i=1}^{n} s(i)d(i) = \sum_{i=j_k}^{j_{k+1}-1} s(i)d(i) = s'(1)d(j_k) + \sum_{i=2}^{j_{k+1}-j_k} s'(i)d'(i) \geq s'd'$, because $s'(1)$ is nonnegative and as $d(j_k)$ is greater than or equal to $d'(1)$.

So far, we have shown that there exist p hyperplanes with the desired properties. We still have to build a unimodular matrix whose first p lines are these p vectors. For $k \in [1, p]$, let s_k be the kth of these vectors, i.e., s_k is the hyperplane that satisfies the vectors in V_k. For any value of k in $[1, p]$, s_k is the only vector among $s_1, \ldots, s_p$ which can have nonzero components between ranks j_k and $j_{k+1} - 1$. Considering s_k as a vector of $\mathbb{Z}^{j_{k+1}-j_k}$, we can complete it into a unimodular matrix T_k (cf. Section 5.4.2). From each line l of T_k not equal to s_k we build a vector of $\mathbb{Z}^n$ by adding $j_k - 1$ zeros at the beginning and $n - j_{k+1} + 1$ at the end of l. The whole set of vectors defines the desired unimodular matrix if, for $k \in [1, p]$, we choose the vector s_k to be the kth line of the matrix. ∎

```
DO i=1, N                                    Direction Vectors
  DO j=1, N
    DO k=1, N
      a(i,j,k)=a(i-1,i,k-1)+a(i,j-1,k+3)
              +a(i,j-1,k+1)
    ENDDO
  ENDDO
ENDDO
```

$$\begin{pmatrix} 1 \\ * \\ 1 \end{pmatrix}, \begin{pmatrix} 0 \\ 1 \\ -3 \end{pmatrix}, \text{ and } \begin{pmatrix} 0 \\ 1 \\ -1 \end{pmatrix}$$

Figure 5.16: Code and direction vectors for Example 15.

Example 15

For the example of Figure 5.16, we have $\mathcal{J} = \{1, 2\}$, $V_1 = \{(1, *, 1)\}$, and $V_2 = \{(0, 1, -3), (0, 1, -1)\}$. To build s_1, we consider the components of ranks between 1 and 1 of the vectors in the set V_1. We end up with the set $\{(1)\}$ and we find $s_1 = (1, 0, 0)$. To build s_2, we consider the components of ranks between 2 and 3 of the vectors in the set V_2. Thus, we end up with the set $\{(1, -3), (1, -1)\}$ and we find $s_2 = (0, 1, 0)$. Then the matrix T is the identity matrix and the parallelized code is identical to the original code except that the innermost loop is known to be parallel. □

In this section, we did not try to extend to direction vectors the results obtained for uniform dependence vectors; we only tried to reuse them. As a consequence, the transformations obtained are not very powerful and we are missing some parallelism. For example, one can find two parallel loops with a unimodular transformation in Example 15, as shown next, when we could only find one. In Section 5.4.4 we present the extension of the hyperplane method to direction vectors proposed by Wolf and Lam.

Example 15, Continued

One can check that the vector $(2, 0, -1)$ has a positive dot product with each direction vector of this example. To find the code

```
DOSEQ i = -n+2, 2n-1
  DOPAR j = 1, n
    DOPAR k = max(⌊ i+2/2 ⌋,1), min(⌊ i+n/2 ⌋,n)
    a(k, j, 2k-i) = a(k-1,k,2k-i-1) + a(k,j-1,2k-i+3) + a(k,j-1,2k-i+1)
    ENDDOPAR
  ENDDOPAR
ENDDOSEQ
```

we transformed the original loop nest using the unimodular matrix:

$$T = \begin{bmatrix} 2 & 0 & -1 \\ 0 & 1 & 0 \\ 1 & 0 & 0 \end{bmatrix}$$

The two innermost loops are now parallel. □

5.4.4 Wolf and Lam's Algorithm

Michael Wolf and Monica Lam proposed a parallelization algorithm that takes as input a representation of the dependences by direction vectors [117, 115]. This algorithm produces unimodular transformations and can be seen as an extension of Lamport's algorithm (Sections 5.4.2 and 5.4.3). However, this algorithm does not produce parallel but fully permutable loops. We first define the notion of permutable loops, and we show how such loops are linked with medium and fine-grain parallelization. Then we give a theoretical interpretation of the algorithm. Finally, we run it on an example.

(Fully) Permutable Loops

Two *permutable loops* are two loops that can be interchanged without violating the semantics of the loop nest. A set of *fully permutable loops* is such that any permutation of loops belonging to the set preserves the semantics of the whole loop nest. To check whether a set of loops is fully permutable, one verifies that the distance vectors are kept lexicographically nonnegative by any permutation of the loops. Notice that the first component of any distance vector is nonnegative. Therefore, if the first and kth loops are permutable, then the kth component of any distance vector is nonnegative. Here is the property for a set of permutable loops.

Theorem 29 *In a perfectly nested set of loops with dependence set D, the loops of ranks between i and j are fully permutable if and only if*

$$\forall d \in D, \ (d(1), \dots, d(i-1)) >_{lex} \mathbf{0} \ \ or \ \ (d(i), \dots, d(j)) \geq \mathbf{0}$$

Proof We first prove that the condition on the distance vectors is sufficient. Let d be a distance vector and σ a permutation of the loops between ranks i and j. σ transforms d into a vector d'. By definition of σ, for all k in $[1, i-1] \cup [j+1, n]$, $d(k) = d'(k)$. d is lexicographically (strictly) positive. We just have to show that this property also holds for d'. If we have $(d(1), \dots, d(i-1)) >_{lex} \mathbf{0}$ (resp. $(d(1), \dots, d(j)) = \mathbf{0}$), d' satisfies the same property and is lexicographically (strictly) positive. If $(d(1), \dots, d(i-1)) = \mathbf{0}$ and $(d(1), \dots, d(j)) \neq \mathbf{0}$, then $(d(i), \dots, d(j)) \geq \mathbf{0}$ and there exists an integer $k \in [i, j]$ such that $d(k) > 0$. Therefore, $(d'(1), \dots, d'(j)) \geq \mathbf{0}$ and there exists an integer $k' \in [i, j]$, $k' = \sigma(k)$, such that $d'(k') > 0$. Then d' is lexicographically (strictly) positive.

We now suppose that the condition on the distance vectors does not hold. Then we show that the loops between ranks i and j are not fully permutable. If the condition does not hold, then there exists a distance vector $d \in D$ such that $(d(1), \dots, d(i-1)) = \mathbf{0}$ and such that there exists k in $[i, j]$ satisfying $d(k) < 0$. Therefore, if we interchange the loops of ranks i and k, d is transformed into a new distance vector whose $i - 1$ first components are null and the ith is strictly negative. Thus, d is transformed into a non-lexicographically positive distance vector, which is forbidden. ∎

```
DO  i=1, N                                Distance Vectors
  DO  j=1, N
    a(i,j) = a(i-1,j+1) + a(i,j-1)
  ENDDO
ENDDO
```
$$\begin{pmatrix} 1 \\ -1 \end{pmatrix}, \ \begin{pmatrix} 0 \\ 1 \end{pmatrix}$$

Figure 5.17: Code and distance vectors for Example 16.

Example 16

In this example, displayed in Figure 5.17, the two loops are not permutable because the first distance vector is not nonnegative. Figure 5.18 presents a unimodular matrix that defines a valid transformation of this example. The associated unimodular transformation changes the two loops into two permutable loops. □

Unimodular Matrix   New Distance Vectors

$$\begin{bmatrix} 1 & 0 \\ 1 & 1 \end{bmatrix} \qquad \begin{pmatrix} 1 \\ 0 \end{pmatrix}, \quad \begin{pmatrix} 0 \\ 1 \end{pmatrix}$$

```
DO i=1, N
  DO j=i+1, i+N
    a(i,j-i)=a(i-1,j-i+1)+a(i,j-i-1)
  ENDDO
ENDDO
```

Figure 5.18: Unimodular transformation for Example 16.

The following theorem shows the link between fully permutable loops and fine-grain parallelism.

Theorem 30 *A set of d consecutive fully permutable loops can always be rewritten as one sequential and $d - 1$ parallel loops.*

Proof We suppose that the set of d consecutive fully permutable loops contains all the loops except the n_1 outermost and the n_2 innermost loops. To prove the result, we apply to the loop nest the unimodular transformation defined by the following matrix:

$$\begin{bmatrix} I_{n_1} & 0 & 0 \\ 0 & T & 0 \\ 0 & 0 & I_{n_2} \end{bmatrix} \text{ where } T = \begin{bmatrix} 1 & 1 & \cdots & 1 & 1 \\ 1 & 0 & \cdots & 0 & 0 \\ 0 & 1 & \cdots & 0 & 0 \\ \vdots & & \ddots & & \vdots \\ 0 & 0 & \cdots & 1 & 0 \end{bmatrix}$$

One can easily check that a dependence that was carried before transformation by one of the n_1 outermost (resp. n_2 innermost) loops is still carried after transformation by the same loop. Furthermore, a dependence that was carried before transformation by one of the d fully permutable loops is carried after transformation by the $(n_1 + 1)$th loop because the components of ranks between $(n_1 + 1)$ and $(n_1 + d)$ of the dependence were all nonnegative before transformation (cf. Theorem 29) and at least one of them was positive. Therefore, the $(d-1)$ loops of ranks between $(n_1 + 2)$ and $(n_1 + d)$ carry no dependences and thus are parallel. ∎

Although fully permutable loops are also linked to fine-grain parallelization, permutable loops are mainly used for medium-grain parallelization. Indeed, the fully permutable loops are required by loop tiling. *Tiling*, also known as *blocking* or *supernode partitioning*, is a technique used to group elemental computation points to increase the granularity of computation and thereby reduce communication time. This technique was introduced by François Irigoin and Rémy Triolet [63] and was discussed by many authors and in many different contexts (see the bibliographical notes). Loop tiling is decomposed in two steps. First a strip-mining is applied to one or several loops; second loops are permuted. Strip-mining decomposes a single loop into two loops: the outer loop (the sectioning loop), which steps between strips of consecutive iterations and the inner loop (the strip loop), which steps between single iterations within a strip. Strip-mining is always legal; its meaning is to group small sets of iterations. Once strip-mining is done, loops are permuted to place the strip loops innermost. This is also done to group computations; see Example 16. When the original loops are permutable, this last transformation is valid. So far we have obtained a tiled loop nest. To obtain a loop nest containing medium-grain parallelism, (some of) the sectioning loops will be parallelized, which can always be done due to Theorem 30.

Example 16, Continued

We come back to Example 16 after a unimodular transformation made its two loops permutable (cf. Figure 5.18). We now apply a strip-mining of length n_1 on the outer loop and of length n_2 on the inner loop. Once strip-mining is applied on the two loops, the second and third loops are permuted. This way, we obtain a loop nest whose two innermost loops are strip loops. This is exactly a tiled loop nest. For our example, a possibility is to generate the code of Figure 5.19. See also [121, pages 352-355] or [122] for more details on validity conditions and code generation for tiling. See also the bibliographical notes at the end of this chapter.   □

Theoretical Interpretation

Wolf and Lam's algorithm is greedy. First, it outputs a set of outermost fully permutable loops that contains as many loops as possible. Some of the dependences may not be satisfied by these loops. Thus, the algorithm calls itself recursively to satisfy the possibly remaining dependences. To produce the largest possible set of outermost fully permutable loops using unimodular transformations, this algorithm looks for the largest set of in-

```
DO i=1, N, n₁
  DO j=i+1, i+N+n₁-1, n₂
    DO I=i, min(N,i+n₁-1)
      DO J=max(I+1,j), min(I+N,j+n₂-1)
        a(I,J-I) = a(I-1,J-I+1) + a(I,J-I-1)
      ENDDO
    ENDDO
  ENDDO
ENDDO
```

Figure 5.19: Tiled code for Example 16.

dependent vectors that have a nonnegative dot product with each direction vector.

Let D be the set of direction vectors. Let $\Gamma(D)$ be the closure[4] of the cone generated by D. Let $\Gamma^+(D) = \{Y \mid \forall X \in \Gamma(D), YX \geq 0\}$. These sets satisfy the following properties. (For definitions and properties on cones and related notions, see [110].)

Lemma 29 $\Gamma(D)$ *is a polyhedral cone.* $\Gamma^+(D)$ *is the set of the weakly separating hyperplanes for D.* $\Gamma^+(D)$ *is also the opposite of the polar cone of $\Gamma(D)$.*

Proof Let $D = \{d_1, \ldots, d_m\}$. For each integer i in $[1, m]$, d_i is a direction vector. Thus, there are some vectors $v_i, r_{i,1}, \ldots, r_{i,p_i}$ such that

$$d_i = \{v_i + \sum_{j=1}^{p_i} \lambda_j r_{i,j} \mid \forall j \in [1, p_i], \lambda_j \geq 0\} \text{ (see Section 5.2.3)}$$

Let $\Gamma'(D) = \{y \mid \forall i \, \forall j \, \mu_i \geq 0, \lambda_{i,j} \geq 0, y = \sum_i \mu_i v_i + \sum_{i,j} \lambda_{i,j} r_{i,j}\}$. $\Gamma'(D)$ is a polyhedral cone by definition. We want to show that $\Gamma(D) = \Gamma'(D)$. Notice first that $\Gamma'(D)$ contains D, the cone generated by D, and therefore contains $\Gamma(D)$ (a polyhedron is always closed). Thus, we only have to prove that $\Gamma'(D)$ is contained in $\Gamma(D)$. Let us take a point y of $\Gamma'(D)$:

$$\begin{aligned} y &= \sum_i \mu_i v_i + \sum_{i,j} \lambda_{i,j} r_{i,j} \\ &= \sum_{i,\mu_i \neq 0} \mu_i (v_i + \sum_j \frac{\lambda_{i,j}}{\mu_i} r_{i,j}) + \sum_{i,\mu_i=0} \sum_j \lambda_{i,j} r_{i,j} \\ &= \lim_{n \to \infty} (\sum_{i,\mu_i \neq 0} \mu_i (v_i + \sum_j \frac{\lambda_{i,j}}{\mu_i} r_{i,j}) + \frac{1}{n} * (\sum_{i,\mu_i=0} (v_i + \sum_j n\lambda_{i,j} r_{i,j}))) \end{aligned}$$

---

[4]The closure of a set E is the set of the points that are the limit of a sequence of elements of E. For example, consider the direction vector $(1, *)$. This direction vector is equal to the set $\beta = \{(1, y) \mid y \in \mathbb{Z}\}$. Thus, it generates the cone $\gamma = \{(x, y) \mid x > 0 \text{ or } x = y = 0\}$. The closure of this cone is the cone $\Gamma = \{(x, y) \mid x \geq 0\}$.

Thus, y belongs to $\Gamma(D)$.

Elements of $\Gamma^+(D)$ are obviously weakly separating hyperplanes for D. Conversely, let Y be a weakly separating hyperplane for D. Y has a non-negative dot products with the points of D, and thus with the points of the cone generated by D, and thus with the points that are limits of points of the cone generated by D.

The polar cone of $\Gamma(D)$ is by definition (see [110] for details) the set $\{Y \mid \forall X \in \Gamma(D), YX \leq 0\}$.   ■

If $\Gamma^+(D)$ is full-dimensional, i.e., of dimension n, we can build a matrix T from n independent vectors of $\Gamma^+(D)$. With this matrix the original loops can be transformed in n fully permutable loops. Furthermore, if $\Gamma^+(D)$ is full-dimensional, $\Gamma(D)$ is a pointed cone (in other words, $\Gamma(D)$ contains no affine space of nonzero dimension). In such a case, there exists a strongly separating hyperplane X: For any vector $d \in D$, $Xd > 0$. Therefore, using X for the first line, one can build a unimodular matrix that transforms the original loop nest in a loop nest whose outermost loop is sequential and the $(n - 1)$ others are parallel.

The notion of strongly separating hyperplane, or timing vector, is particularly interesting for exposing fine-grain parallelism. The notion of fully permutable loops is the basis of all tiling techniques. The two notions are strongly linked by the set $\Gamma^+(D)$ and its properties.

When the cone $\Gamma(D)$ is not pointed, $\Gamma^+(D)$ has a dimension r, $1 \leq r < n$, $r = n - s$ where s is the dimension of the lineality space[5] of $\Gamma(D)$. With r linearly independent vectors of $\Gamma^+(D)$, one can transform the loop nest in a new loop nest whose r outermost loops are fully permutable. Then one can recursively apply the same technique to transform the $n - r$ innermost loops, by only considering the direction vectors not already carried by one of the r outermost loops, i.e., by only considering the direction vectors included in the lineality space of $\Gamma(D)$. This is the general idea of Wolf and Lam's algorithm, even if they did not express it in such terms in [117].

When the vector space generated by the direction vectors has a dimension $m < n$, we can also choose $m - n$ vectors in the orthogonal of this space. These vectors will correspond to $m - n$ outer parallel loops.

General Algorithm

The theoretical discussion can be summarized by the WOLF-LAM algorithm given next. This algorithm takes as input a set of direction vectors

---

[5]The lineality space of a polyhedron P is the vector space associated to the largest affine space included in the polyhedron. If $P = \{x \mid Ax \leq b\}$, the lineality space of P is the set $\{x \mid Ax = 0\}$ (cf. [110]).

Δ and a sequence of linearly independent vectors E (initialized to void). It outputs a sequence E' of linearly independent vectors. The transformation matrix is built from the set E'; the ith line-vector of the matrix is the ith vector of E'. The initial call is WOLF-LAM $(D, \emptyset)$, where D is the set of the direction vectors.

WOLF-LAM(Δ, E)

1. Let $\Gamma(\Delta)$ be the closure of the cone generated by the direction vectors of Δ.

2. Let $\Gamma^+(\Delta) = \{y \mid \forall x \in \Gamma(\Delta), y.x \geq 0\}$ and let r be the dimension of $\Gamma^+(\Delta)$.

3. Add $r - |E|$ vectors to the end of E to build a sequence E' of r linearly independent vectors of $\Gamma^+(\Delta)$ (by construction, $E \subset \Gamma^+(\Delta)$).

4. Let Δ' be the subset of Δ defined by $d \in \Delta' \Leftrightarrow \forall v \in E', v.d = 0$, i.e., $\Delta' = \Delta \cap E'^\perp = \Delta \cap \text{Vect}(\Gamma^+(\Delta))^\perp = \Delta \cap \text{lin.space}(\Gamma(\Delta))$.

5. Call WOLF-LAM (Δ', E').

The heuristic part of the algorithm originally presented by Wolf and Lam concerns the computation of $\Gamma(\Delta)$ and $\Gamma^+(\Delta)$ (steps 1 and 2). We do not describe in detail the computation of $\Gamma^+(\Delta)$ (for the computation of $\Gamma(\Delta)$, see the proof of Lemma 29). Because of step 3 of the algorithm, we must check that E' is a subset of $\Gamma^+(\Delta')$, but $E' \subset \Gamma^+(\Delta) \subset \Gamma^+(\Delta')$.

Actually, this process may lead to a nonunimodular matrix. Building the desired unimodular matrix T can be done as follows:

- Let D be the set of direction vectors. Call WOLF-LAM $(D, \emptyset)$.

- Build a nonsingular matrix U whose first rows are the vectors of E' taken in the order WOLF-LAM produced them. Let $V = pU^{-1}$, where p is a positive integer such that V is an integral matrix.

- Compute the left Hermite form of V: $V = QH$, where H is nonnegative and lower triangular and Q is unimodular.

- $T = Q^{-1}$ is the desired transformation matrix.

To prove it, let us suppose that U transforms the original loop nest in a loop nest whose loops between ranks i and j are fully permutable. Then Theorem 29 states that, for any vector d of D, we have: $(U_1 d, \dots, U_{i-1} d) >_{lex} \mathbf{0}$ or $(U_i d, \dots, U_j d) \geq \mathbf{0}$. We must show that T satisfies the same properties. Let d be a vector of D. We first suppose that $(U_1 d, \dots, U_{i-1} d) >_{lex}$

0. Then, because H is a nonsingular, nonnegative, and lower triangular matrix, we have $((HU)_1 d, \ldots , (HU)_{i-1} d) >_{lex}$ **0.** We now suppose that $(U_1 d, \ldots , U_{i-1} d) = $ **0** and $(U_i d, \ldots , U_j d) \geq $ **0.** Then, for the same reason, $((HU)_1 d, \ldots , (HU)_{i-1} d) = $ **0** and $((HU)_i d, \ldots , (HU)_j d) \geq $ **0.** Finally, because $pTd = pQ^{-1} d = HUd$, we have proved the desired result in both cases.

Example 17

Consider the code of Figure 5.20. The set of direction vectors is the set $D = \{(1, -, 0), (0, 0, 1), (0, 1, -1)\}$. Then, following the proof of Lemma 29, $\Gamma(D)$ is the cone generated by the vectors $(1, -1, 0)$, $(0, -1, 0)$, $(0, 0, 1)$, and $(0, 1, -1)$. The lineality space of $\Gamma(D)$ is bidimensional and generated by $(0, 1, 0)$ and $(0, 0, 1)$, i.e., if $(x, y, z) \in \Gamma(D)$ then for any value of λ and μ $(x, y + \lambda, z + \mu) \in \Gamma(D)$. Therefore $\Gamma^+(D)$ is unidimensional and generated by $E_1 = \{(1, 0, 0)\}$. The first set of fully permutable loops will only contain one loop, which is the original outermost loop.

```
DO i=1, n
  DO j=1, n
    DO k=1, n
      a(i, j, k) = a(i-1, j+i, k) + a(i, j, k-1) + a(i, j-1, k+1)
    ENDDO
  ENDDO
ENDDO
```

Figure 5.20: Example 17 and its RDG.

If we want to directly compute a weakly separating hyperplane X, $X = (x, y, z)$, we solve the system: $x + \text{``} - \text{''} y \geq 0, z \geq 0, y - z \geq 0$. From the first inequality, y is nonpositive. From the last two inequalities, y must be nonnegative. Then $y = 0$. The last two inequalities then become $z \geq 0$, $-z \geq 0$. Therefore, we end up with: $x \geq 0, y = 0, z = 0$.

To build the remaining two loops we now call recursively the algorithm. The set of remaining direction vectors is: $D' = \{(0, 0, 1), (0, 1, -1)\}$. $\Gamma(D')$ is generated by the two vectors $(0, 0, 1)$ and $(0, 1, -1)$ and $\Gamma(D')$ is pointed (the only vector space included in $\Gamma(D')$ is $\{0\}$). Then $\Gamma^+(D')$ is full dimensional. $\Gamma^+(D') = \{(x, y, z) \mid z \geq 0, y \geq z\}$. We complete E_1 with two vectors of $\Gamma^+(D')$, for example, with $E_2 = \{(0, 1, 0), (0, 1, 1)\}$. In this particular example, the transformation matrix T whose rows are the vectors in E_1 and E_2 is already unimodular. This matrix corresponds to a simple loop skewing. For exposing a **DOPAR** loop, we choose the first vector of E_2 in the relative interior of Γ^+ (a vector is in the relative interior of a polyhedron if all vectors close to it and in the polyhedron's affine hull also belong to the polyhedron; see [110]). For example, we take $E_2 = \{(0, 2, 1), (0, 1, 0)\}$. In terms of loop transformations, this amounts to skewing the loop k by factor 2 and then interchanging loops j and k. This way, we obtain the following code:

```
DOSEQ i=1, n
  DOSEQ k=3, 3n
    DOPAR j=max(1,⌈k−n/2⌉), min(n, ⌊k−1/2⌋)
      a(i, j, k-2j) = a(i-1, j+i, k-2j) + a(i, j, k-2j-1) + a(i, j-1, k-2j+1)
    ENDDOPAR
  ENDDOSEQ
ENDDOSEQ
```

whose innermost loop is parallel.   □

5.5   Darte and Vivien's Algorithm

We now present the algorithm proposed by Darte and Vivien [33] that schedules polyhedral reduced dependence graphs. We will first motivate the interest of this dependence representation by considering an example (Section 5.5.1). Then we will show in Section 5.5.2 how to "uniformize" a PRDG, i.e., how to transform it into an equivalent graph that looks like the dependence graph of a system of uniform recurrence equations. This uniformization process will enable us to reuse the results established for SUREs to check the computability of PRDGs (Section 5.5.3) and to schedule them (Section 5.5.4). We then briefly show how to extend it to extract medium-grain parallelism (Section 5.5.5). Finally, we compare it to ALLEN-KENNEDY and WOLF-LAM (Section 5.5.6).

5.5.1   Motivation

In this section we motivate the interest for polyhedral reduced dependence graphs and give the general principle of the DARTE-VIVIEN algorithm.

Example 12, Continued

We recall the code and data dependences for Example 12.

Code   Dependence Relations

DO i=1, N
  DO j=1, N
    a(i,j) = a(i,j-1) + a(j,i)
  ENDDO
ENDDO

$$\begin{cases} \text{if } 1 \leq i, j \leq N & S(i,j) \Rightarrow S(i,j+1) & \text{(flow)} \\ \text{if } 1 \leq i < j \leq N & S(i,j) \Rightarrow S(j,i) & \text{(flow)} \\ \text{if } 1 \leq j < i \leq N & S(j,i) \Rightarrow S(i,j) & \text{(anti)} \end{cases}$$

We consider the parallelization of this example by the algorithms of Allen and Kennedy, Wolf and Lam, and Feautrier (to be presented in Section 5.6).

- ALLEN-KENNEDY The three dependences are respectively of levels 2, 1, and 1. There is a dependence cycle of level 1 and one of level 2. Therefore, no parallelism is detected.

- WOLF-LAM The three direction vectors are, respectively, equal to $(0,1)$, $(+,-)$, and $(+,-)$. In the second dimension, the "1" and the "$-$" are incompatible and prevent the detection of two permutable loops. The code is left unchanged and no parallelism is found.

- FEAUTRIER This algorithm, described in Section 5.6, finds the affine schedule $\Theta(i,j) = 2i + j - 3$ and one degree of parallelism. The corresponding parallelized code is the following:

```
DO j = 3, 3n
  DOPAR i=max(1,⌈(j-n)/2⌉), min(n, ⌊(j-1)/2⌋)
    a(i,j-2i) = a(j-2i,i) + a(i,j-2i-1)
  ENDDOPAR
ENDDO
```

In this particular example, the dependence representation by levels or direction vectors is not accurate enough to reveal parallelism. This is why ALLEN-KENNEDY and WOLF-LAM cannot detect any parallelism. For FEAUTRIER, exact dependence analysis, associated to linear programming methods that require solving (sometimes large[6]) parametric linear programs, enables us to reveal one degree of parallelism.

However, in Example 12, an exact representation of the dependences is not necessary to reveal the hidden parallelism. Indeed, one can notice that there is one uniform dependence $u = (0,1)$ and a set of distance vectors

---

[6]The number of inequalities and variables is related to the number of constraints that define the validity domain of each dependence relation.

$\{(j - i, i - j) = (j - i)(1, -1) \mid 1 \leq j - i \leq n - 1\}$ that can be (over)-approximated by the set $\mathcal{P} = \{(1, -1) + \lambda(1, -1) \mid \lambda \geq 0\}$. $\mathcal{P}$ is a polyhedron with one vertex $v = (1, -1)$ and one ray $r = (1, -1)$. Now, suppose that, as in Feautrier's or Lamport's algorithm, we are looking for a linear schedule $T(i, j) = x_1 i + x_2 j$. Let $X = (x_1, x_2)$. For T to be a valid schedule, we look for X such that $Xd \geq 1$ for any dependence vector d. Thus, $X(0, 1) \geq 1$ and $Xp \geq 1$ for all $p \in \mathcal{P}$. The latter inequality is equal to $X(1, -1) + \lambda X(1, -1) \geq 1$ with $\lambda \geq 0$, which is equivalent to $X(1, -1) \geq 1$ and $X(1, -1) \geq 0$, i.e., $Xv \geq 1$ and $Xr \geq 0$. Therefore, a valid linear schedule is defined by a vector X that satisfies the three following inequalities:

$$Xu \geq 1 \; Xv \geq 1 \; Xr \geq 0 \text{ i.e., } X \begin{pmatrix} 0 \\ 1 \end{pmatrix} \geq 1 \; X \begin{pmatrix} 1 \\ -1 \end{pmatrix} \geq 1 \; X \begin{pmatrix} 1 \\ -1 \end{pmatrix} \geq 0$$

which leads, as earlier, to $X = (2, 1)$, when minimizing the norm of the vector X. $\qquad\qquad\square$

Thus, for the example, an approximation of the dependences by levels or even direction vectors is not sufficient for the detection of parallelism. However, with an approximation of the dependences by polyhedra, we find as much parallelism as with exact dependence analysis, but while solving a simpler set of inequalities.

What is important here is the "uniformization," which enables us to go from the inequality on the set $\mathcal{P}$ to uniform inequalities on v and r. Thanks to this uniformization, the affine constraints disappear, and unlike Feautrier's algorithm, we do not need to use Farkas's lemma. To better understand the "uniformization" principle, think in terms of dependence path. The idea is to consider an edge e, from a statement S to a statement T, labeled by the distance vector $p = v + \lambda r$, as a path ϕ that uses the "uniform" dependence vector v once and the "uniform" dependence vector r λ times. This simulation is summarized in Figure 5.21; we introduce a new node S' that enables to simulating ϕ and a zero-weight edge to go from S' back to the initial node T. This "uniformization" principle is the underlying idea of the loop parallelization algorithm presented in this section.

By uniformizing the dependences, we have in fact "uniformized" the constraints and transformed the underlying affine scheduling problem into a simple scheduling problem where all dependences are uniform ($\mathbf{0}$, v, and r in Figure 5.21). However, there are two fundamental differences between this framework and the classical framework of uniform loop nests:

- The dependence vectors are not necessarily lexico-positive (for example, a ray can be equal to $(0, -1)$). Therefore, the scheduling problem is more difficult. The uniformized dependence graph looks more like

Figure 5.21: Simulation of an edge labeled by a polyhedron with one vertex and one ray.

the dependence graph of a system of uniform recurrence equations than to the dependence graph of a uniform loop nest. Therefore, to schedule our PRDGs, we naturally reuse the techniques developed to check the computability of SUREs and to schedule them. These techniques were presented in Chapter 4.

- The constraint imposed on a ray r is weaker than the classical constraint; the constraint is indeed $Xr \geq 0$ instead of $Xr \geq 1$. This freedom must be taken into account in the parallelization algorithm.

5.5.2 Uniformization

We first show how polyhedral reduced dependence graphs can be captured into an equivalent (but simpler-to-manipulate) structure, the structure of uniform dependence graphs, i.e., graphs whose edges are labeled by constant dependence vectors. This uniformization is nothing but a simple generalization of what we have done with Example 12 in Section 5.5.1. Our aim is to transform all the dependences into uniform dependences. Although in the framework of systolic arrays, to uniformize implies transforming the program itself, here we only transform its reduced dependence graph.

Uniformization Algorithm

To avoid possible confusion, the initial PRDG that describes the dependences in the code to be parallelized is called the *original graph* and is denoted by $G_o = (V, E)$. The uniform RDG, equivalent to G_o and built by the uniformization algorithm, is called the *uniform graph* and is denoted by $G_u = (W, F)$.

The uniformization algorithm builds G_u by scanning all edges of G_o. It starts from $G_u = (W, F) = (V, \emptyset)$, and, for each edge e of E, it adds to G_u new nodes and new edges depending on $\mathcal{P}(e)$, the dependence polyhedron associated to e. We call *virtual nodes* the nodes created by the uniformization process, as opposed to the nodes of G_o, which are called *actual* nodes.

Let $\mathcal{P}(e)$ be a polyhedron. We denote its vertices by $\{v_1, \ldots, v_\omega\}$, its rays by $\{r_1, \ldots, r_\rho\}$, and its lines by $\{l_1, \ldots, l_\lambda\})$. Then $\mathcal{P}(e)$ is the set of all vectors p satisfying:

$$p = \sum_{i=1}^{\omega} \mu_i v_i + \sum_{i=1}^{\rho} \nu_i r_i + \sum_{i=1}^{\lambda} \xi_i l_i \tag{5.8}$$

where $\mu_i \in \mathbb{Q}^+$, $\nu_i \in \mathbb{Q}^+$, $\xi_i \in \mathbb{Q}$, and $\sum_{i=1}^{\omega} \mu_i = 1$.

Algorithm (Uniformization of a PRDG)

UNIFORMIZATION(PRDG G)

1. Let $W = V$ and $F = \emptyset$.

2. For $e : x_e \rightarrow y_e \in E$ do

   (a) If $\rho = 0$, $\lambda = 0$ and $\omega = 1$ (the polyhedron is a singleton, the dependence is uniform)

      - add to F an edge of weight v_1 directed from x_e to y_e.

   (b) If $\rho \neq 0$ or $\lambda \neq 0$ or $\omega > 1$

      - add to W a new virtual node n_e,
      - add to F ω edges of weights $v_1, v_2, \ldots, v_\omega$ from x_e to n_e,
      - add to F ρ self-loops around n_e of weights $r_1, r_2, \ldots, r_\rho$,
      - add to F λ self-loops around n_e of weights $l_1, l_2, \ldots, l_\lambda$,
      - add to F λ self-loops around n_e of weights $-l_1, -l_2, \ldots, -l_\lambda$,
      - add to F a zero weight edge directed from n_e to y_e.

Figure 5.22 shows the uniformization of a dependence polyhedron containing no lines.

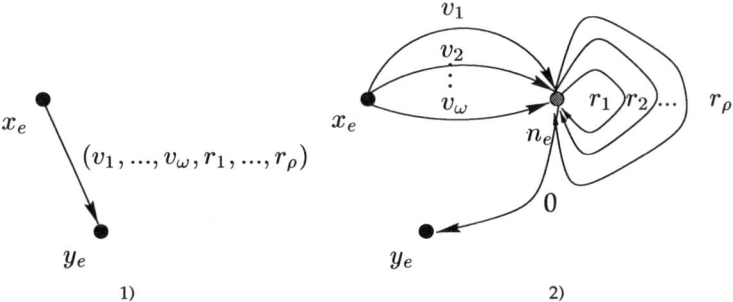

Figure 5.22: Uniformization: (1) original graph; (2) uniformized graph.

Example 18

Consider the following code:

```
DO i = 1, n
  DO j = 1, n
    DO k = 1, j
      a(i,j,k) = c(i,j,k-1) + 1
      b(i,j,k) = a(i-1,j+i,k) + b(i,j-1,k)
      c(i,j,k+1) = c(i,j,k) + b(i,j-1,k+i) + a(i,j-k,k+1)
    ENDDO
  ENDDO
ENDDO
```

The polyhedral reduced dependence graph for Example 18 is presented in Figure 5.23. The dependences were obtained with the dependence analyzer Tiny [120], which approaches them by some particular dependence polyhedra; the direction vectors whose components exclusively belong to the set $\mathbb{Z} \cup \{+, 0+, -, 0-, *\}$. The uniformized dependence graph is drawn in Figure 5.24. The virtual nodes are depicted in gray and the actual nodes in black. This graph contains three virtual nodes that correspond to the symbol "+" and the two symbols "−" of the direction vectors. □

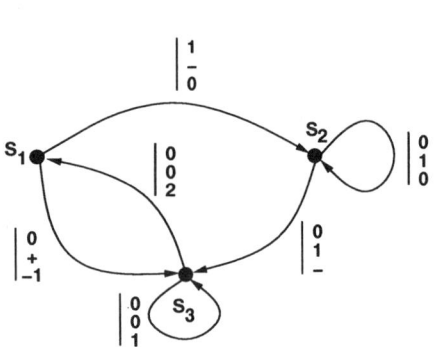

Figure 5.23: RDG with direction vectors.

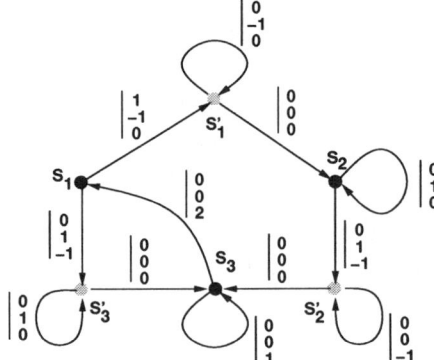

Figure 5.24: Uniformized dependence graph.

Correspondence between a PRDG G_o and Its Translated G_u

In this section we study the structures of the graphs G_o and G_u and show that the two graphs are equivalent in terms of dependence paths. Therefore, instead of manipulating G_o, we will be able to content ourselves with working on G_u, which is a much more classical graph. We suppose here that the original graph G_o is strongly connected (then G_u is also strongly connected). If this is not the case, the results we present in this section are only true for the strongly connected components of G_o.

Remember that edges in G_o are not labeled by a single vector, as in G_u, but by a polyhedron, i.e., a set of vectors. There is a risk of confusion between an edge labeled by a polyhedron and one of its instances, i.e., an edge with the same extremities and whose weight is one of the polyhedron's points. Therefore, we decide to call *polyhedral edge*, the edge e of G_o labeled by the polyhedron $\mathcal{P}(e)$, and to call *dependence edge* one of its instances, f, whose associated weight $w(f)$ is an integral point of the polyhedron: $w(f) \in \mathcal{P}(e)$. In other words, a polyhedral edge e corresponds to as many dependence edges as there are integral vectors in $\mathcal{P}(e)$. A *dependence path* is defined as a sequence of dependence edges whose associated polyhedral edges define a path of G_o. The weight of a dependence path is the sum of the weights of its constitutive edges.

We can now show the links between the paths of G_u and the dependence paths of G_o.

From the graph G_u to the graph G_o. Note first a particularity of the structure of G_u. There is no edge linking two distinct virtual nodes. Therefore, any path between two actual nodes whose intermediate nodes are all virtual nodes visits at most one virtual node, possibly many times. Such a path is called an *atomic path*. Remark that an atomic path can contain no virtual nodes. Also, any path between two distinct virtual nodes has to pass through an actual node. The link between atomic paths in G_u and dependence edges in G_o is straightforward.

Lemma 30 *An atomic path Π_u of G_u corresponds to a unique polyhedral edge e of G_o and the total weight of Π_u is an integer point of the polyhedron associated to e: $w(\Pi_u) \in \mathcal{P}(e)$.*

Proof As we have already seen, the path Π_u visits at most one virtual node, possibly many times. Two cases can occur, depending on whether Π_u contains a virtual node:

- Π_u *contains a virtual node.* This virtual node, denoted by n_e, has been created during the uniformization of a polyhedral edge e. The structure of Π_u is illustrated by the following:

$$\Pi_u = x_e \xrightarrow{v_i} n_e \ldots n_e \xrightarrow{r_i} n_e \ldots n_e \xrightarrow{l_j} n_e \ldots n_e \xrightarrow{-l_k} n_e \ldots n_e \xrightarrow{0} y_e$$

The first edge of Π_u leaves x_e to enter n_e. It corresponds to a vertex of the polyhedron $\mathcal{P}(e)$. The last edge of Π_u starts from n_e to end at y_e; its weight is zero. All the other edges belonging to Π_u are self-edges of n_e whose weight is either a ray of $\mathcal{P}(e)$ or a line (or its opposite). Therefore, the weight of Π_u is the sum of a vertex, a nonnegative integral linear combination of rays, and an integral linear combination of lines of the polyhedron $\mathcal{P}(e)$. By definition of the vertices, rays, and lines of a polyhedron (cf. Equation (5.8)), the weight of Π_u is a point of $\mathcal{P}(e)$.

- Π_u *contains no virtual node.* Because Π_u is an atomic path, all its intermediate nodes are virtual. Therefore, Π_u contains a single edge that links two actual nodes. This edge corresponds to the vertex of a polyhedron that has a unique vertex and neither rays nor lines (case 2a of UNIFORMIZATION). The weight of Π_u is thus a point of $\mathcal{P}(e)$.

In both cases, $w(\Pi_u) \in \mathcal{P}(e)$.   ■

Lemma 30 is easily generalized to any path.

Corollary 4 *A path Π_u of G_u, from an actual node to an actual node, defines an equivalent dependence path Π_o of G_o: each atomic subpath of Π_u corresponds exactly to a polyhedral edge e of G_o whose dependence polyhedron contains the weight of the atomic subpath.*

From the graph G_o to the graph G_u.   Lemma 30 (and a fortiori Corollary 4) is in general not a strict equivalence; it is not always possible to build an atomic path of G_u equivalent to a given dependence edge of G_o. Indeed, an integral vector in $\mathcal{P}(e)$ may be a rational (but not integral) linear combination of vertices, rays, and/or lines of $\mathcal{P}(e)$. However, when the dependence path of G_o considered is a cycle, there is still a correspondence as stated in Lemma 31. In the rest of this section, if $\mathcal{C}$ is a cycle, $m\mathcal{C}$ denotes the cycle formed by m times the cycle $\mathcal{C}$.

Lemma 31 *Let $\mathcal{C}$ be a dependence cycle of G_o, i.e., a cycle of dependence edges. Then there exist an integer m and a cycle $\mathcal{C}_u$ of G_u such that the cycles $m\mathcal{C}$ and $\mathcal{C}_u$ are equivalent, i.e., have same weight and structure.*

Proof   Let e be a dependence edge of $\mathcal{C}$. By definition, $w(e)$ belongs to $\mathcal{P}(e)$ and thus, according to Equation (5.8), satisfies:

$$w(e) = \sum_{i=1}^{\omega(e)} \mu(e,i)v(e,i) + \sum_{i=1}^{\rho(e)} \nu(e,i)r(e,i) + \sum_{i=1}^{\lambda(e)} \xi(e,i)l(e,i)$$

with $\mu(e, i) \in \mathbb{Q}^+$, $\nu(e, i) \in \mathbb{Q}^+$, $\xi(e, i) \in \mathbb{Q}$, and $\sum_{i=1}^{\omega(e)} \mu(e, i) = 1$ and where the $v(e, i)$, $r(e, i)$, and $l(e, i)$ denote the $\omega(e)$ vertices, $\rho(e)$ rays, and $\lambda(e)$ lines of $\mathcal{P}(e)$.

Let Δ be the least common multiple of the denominators of all the $\mu(e, i)$, $\nu(e, i)$, and $\xi(e, i)$ that appear in the decomposition of all the weights $w(e)$. By construction, for each edge e in $\mathcal{C}$, we now have:

$$\Delta w(e) = \sum_{i=1}^{\Delta} v(e, k_i) + \sum_{i=1}^{\rho(e)} \nu'(e, i) r(e, i) + \sum_{i=1}^{\lambda(e)} \xi'(e, i) l(e, i)$$

with $1 \leq k_i \leq \omega(e)$, $\nu'(e, i) \in \mathbb{N}$, and $\xi'(e, i) \in \mathbb{Z}$. We can now build the desired cycle $\mathcal{C}_u$, equivalent to the cycle $\Delta \mathcal{C}$. Let $e_1, \ldots, e_n$ be the dependence edges of $\mathcal{C}$. For each i, $1 \leq i \leq \Delta$, we define the cycle $\mathcal{C}_u^i$ as:

$$\mathcal{C}_u^i = x_{e_1} \overset{v(e_1, k_i)}{\longrightarrow} n_{e_1} \overset{0}{\longrightarrow} y_{e_1} = x_{e_2} \overset{v(e_2, k_i)}{\longrightarrow} n_{e_2} \overset{0}{\longrightarrow} y_{e_2} \cdots$$
$$\cdots y_{e_{n-1}} = x_{e_n} \overset{v(e_n, k_i)}{\longrightarrow} n_{e_n} \overset{0}{\longrightarrow} y_{e_n} = x_{e_1}$$

In fact, if the edge e_j was introduced by the uniformization of a polyhedron containing a unique vertex and neither rays nor lines (case 2a of UNIFORMIZATION), there is no virtual node n_{e_j} and the path element of the form $x_{e_j} \overset{v(e_j, k_i)}{\longrightarrow} n_{e_j} \overset{0}{\longrightarrow} y_{e_j}$ is simply $x_{e_j} \overset{v(e_j, k_i)}{\longrightarrow} y_{e_j}$.

We concatenate all the cycles $\mathcal{C}_u^i$. Finally, we add to the cycle built this way, for each edge e of $\mathcal{C}$, $\nu'(e, i)$ times the self-loop around n_e of weight $r(e, i)$ and $\xi'(e, i)$ times (resp. $-\xi'(e, i)$ times) the self-loop around n_e of weight $l(e, i)$ (resp. $-l(e, i)$) if $\xi'(e, i)$ is nonnegative (resp. negative). This defines a cycle that is equivalent to $\Delta \mathcal{C}$ because of its weight and the edges it contains. ∎

Corollary 4 and Lemma 31 enable us to go from the cycles of G_u to the (dependence) cycles of G_o and reciprocally, up to a multiplicative factor. We will now study G_u. We will apply the results obtained for systems of uniform recurrence equations to the graphs generated by uniformization of polyhedral reduced dependence graphs. The lemmata we just proved will help us to transpose to the original graphs the results we will obtain for the uniformized graphs.

5.5.3 Computability of a PRDG

We look at the problem of computability of polyhedral reduced dependence graphs as we did in the previous chapter for systems of uniform recurrence equations. Contrary to the case of recurrence equations, the edge weights in PRDGs cannot take any value. Indeed, the PRDGs come from sets of nested loops, and the weights are approximations of distance vectors. (For example, as we have already stated, the distance vectors are always lexicographically nonnegative.) Therefore, we could expect that the original execution order of the operations in the loop nest satisfies the dependences represented by the PRDG, and thus that the PRDGs are always computable. This is the case when the PRDG describes exactly and uniquely the dependences of the original loop nest. But most of the time, the dependences are approximated. We made only one hypothesis on this approximation; we supposed that it is conservative. Therefore, we cannot state a priori the computability of our dependence graphs. For example, the PRDG of Figure 5.25(a) is computable (even if the direction vector $(0, *)$ could be refined in the case of nested loops), whereas the PRDG of Figure 5.25(b) is not computable, i.e., cannot be scheduled. This comes from the fact that

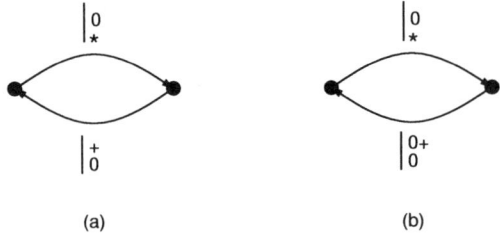

(a)   (b)

Figure 5.25: Two different PRDGs: (a) computable; (b) not computable.

there is a dependence cycle of zero weight in the second PRDG, but not in the first.

In practice, however, the dependence analyzers are clever enough to produce only computable dependence graphs; the dependence polyhedra are included in the polyhedra generated by the dependence levels or all the points of the polyhedra are lexicographically nonnegative, and the original execution order defines a valid schedule. Nevertheless, the computability remains an important problem because its study will show us how to build a scheduling algorithm.

We first define the computability condition and propose two algorithms to check it. Then we study the longest dependence paths of our dependence graphs.

Computability Condition

A reduced dependence graph is said to be *computable* if and only if it describes a well-defined computation. For systems with bounded domains, a reduced dependence graph is computable if and only if its apparent dependence graph (see Sections 5.2.2 and 5.2.3) contains no cycles, i.e., an instance of a statement never depends on itself. As for systems of uniform recurrence equations (cf. Chapter 4), this property is equivalent, for sufficiently large domains, to the fact that there is no zero-weight cycle in the reduced dependence graph. This characterization of the computability of a PRDG, and thus of G_o, can be transposed to the uniformized graph G_u with the help of Corollary 4 and Lemma 31.

Theorem 31 G_o *is computable if and only if* G_u *contains no zero-weight cycle including at least one actual node.*

Decomposition Algorithm (DA)

Theorem 31 moved the computability problem from the original graph G_o to the uniformized graph G_u. Checking the existence of zero-weight cycles in G_u is simpler than in G_o because G_u looks like the reduced dependence graph of a system of uniform recurrence equations. The main difference between the two types of graph is that the graph obtained by uniformization of a PRDG contains two types of nodes: actual nodes and virtual nodes. Here, the computability does not forbid all the zero-weight cycles, but only those that include at least one actual node. We only have to slightly modify the algorithm of Karp, Miller, and Winograd, presented in Section 4.4.2, to enable it to check the computability of our uniformized graphs. The correctness of the new algorithm is a direct consequence of the correctness of the original one (cf. Section 4.4.2).

Algorithm (Checking the Computability of a PRDG)

Boolean DA (Uniformized Graph G)

1. Build G' the subgraph of G generated by all the edges that belong to a zero-weight multicycle of G.

2. Compute the strongly connected components of G' and let G'_1, G'_2, ..., G'_s be the s components that have at least one actual node:

   - If G' is empty or has only virtual nodes, return TRUE.
   - If G' is strongly connected and has at least one actual node, return FALSE.
   - Otherwise, return $\bigwedge_{i=1}^{s} \mathrm{DA}(G'_i)$, where $\bigwedge$ is the logical AND.

Then, G_u has no cycle of zero weight containing an actual node if and only if $\mathrm{DA}(G_u) = \text{TRUE}$. Therefore, a PRDG G_o is computable if and only if $\mathrm{DA}(G_u) = \text{TRUE}$.

The algorithm DA can be called on either a whole uniformized graph or each of its strongly connected components. Nevertheless, for reasons that will become clear in the scheduling section (Section 5.5.4), from now on we suppose that algorithm DA is never called directly on G_u but always on its strongly connected components.

Example 18, Continued

We now illustrate the decomposition algorithm. We consider the uniformized graph presented in Figure 5.24. It contains two elementary cycles, of respective weights $(1,0,1)$ and $(0,1,1)$, and five self-dependences, of respective weights $(0,0,1)$, $(0,0,-1)$, $(0,1,0)$ (twice), and $(0,-1,0)$. The cycle of weight $(0,0,1)$ and the cycle of weight $(0,0,-1)$ define a zero-weight multicycle, as do the cycles of weight $(0,1,0)$ and $(0,-1,0)$, and as do the cycles of weight $(0,1,1)$, $(0,0,-1)$, and $(0,-1,0)$. Therefore, all the edges belong to a zero-weight multicycle except those that only belong to the cycle of weight $(1,0,1)$. The subgraph G' is shown in Figure 5.26.   □

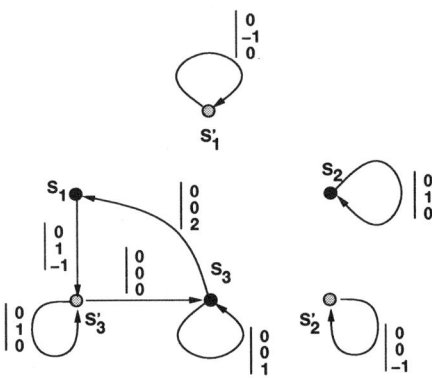

Figure 5.26: Subgraph G' of the edges belonging to a zero-weight multicycle (Example 18).

As we have done for systems of uniform recurrence equations, we define a notion of depth of decomposition for a uniformized graph G_u and for its nodes (cf. Sections 4.4.2 and 4.4.4). The depth of decomposition of a node of a PRDG G_o is equal to the depth of its associated node in G_u. The depth of a graph G_o is equal to the maximum of the depths of its nodes. As for systems of uniform recurrence equations, we will link the notions of depth of decomposition, length of longest dependence paths, and degree of parallelism.

Variant of the Decomposition Algorithm: Algorithm DA*

For technical reasons that will become clear in the scheduling section (Section 5.5.4), we need, in the general case, to slightly modify the algorithm DA. The two algorithms are equivalent in that they output the same answer.

During the decomposition, we want to keep together all the edges of the uniformized graph that were created by the uniformization of a same polyhedral edge, as long as at least one of the edges corresponding to a *vertex* [7] of this polyhedron belongs to a zero-weight multicycle. Then for each polyhedral edge e, if G' contains an edge corresponding to a vertex of $\mathcal{P}(e)$, we add to G' all the edges generated by the uniformization of $\mathcal{P}(e)$ that are not already included in G'. This way we obtain the following algorithm.

Algorithm (Checking the Computability of a PRDG)

Boolean DA* (Uniformized Graph G)

1. Build G' the subgraph of G generated by all the edges that belong to a zero-weight multicycle of G.

2. Initialize G'' to G'. For each polyhedral edge e, if G' contains an edge corresponding to a vertex of $\mathcal{P}(e)$, we add to G'' all the edges generated by the uniformization of $\mathcal{P}(e)$ that are not already included in G''.

3. Compute the strongly connected components of G'' and let G''_1, G''_2, ... , G''_s be the s components that have at least one actual node:

   - If G'' is empty or has only virtual nodes, return TRUE.
   - If G'' is strongly connected and has at least one actual node, return FALSE.
   - Otherwise, return $\bigwedge\limits_{i=1}^{s} \mathrm{DA}(G''_i)$, where $\bigwedge$ is the logical AND.

Note that the edges we add to G'' do not change the structure of the strongly connected components of G'', because we add edges only between nodes that already belong to the same strongly connected component of G''. In particular, the zero-weight edge, which links the nodes n_e and y_e of a polyhedral edge $x_e \xrightarrow{e} y_e$, belongs to G' if and only if one of the edges corresponding to a vertex of $\mathcal{P}(e)$ belongs to G'. Indeed, the only edges entering n_e that are not self-loops correspond to vertices of $\mathcal{P}(e)$ and the only edge leaving n_e that is not a self-loop is the zero-weight edge heading

---

[7]Note: Do not confuse the vertex of a polyhedron with the vertex or node of a graph!

toward y_e. Therefore, because G' is strongly connected by construction, G' includes an edge corresponding to a vertex of $\mathcal{P}(e)$ if and only if it contains the zero-weight edge from n_e to y_e. Thus the edges we add to G'' do not change the structure of strongly connected components of G''. Then there is no risk to connect disjoint strongly connected components and the behavior of the decomposition algorithm is unchanged. Furthermore, the added edges do not belong to a zero-weight multicycle of G. Thus, they cannot change the structure of the zero-weight multicycles appearing in the recursive decomposition of G. Consequently, the algorithms DA and DA* have the same behavior for nodes and zero-weight multicycles. Especially, a node has the same depth of decomposition for both algorithms. (In the case of Example 18, $G' = G''$.)

5.5.4   Scheduling a PRDG

Thanks to the uniformization process we were able to adapt to the PRDGs the computability results obtained for SUREs. Here, we follow the same approach for the scheduling problem. We first show why the results obtained for SUREs need to be adapted and how to adapt them. Then we present the algorithm and prove its correctness.

How to Adapt the Results Obtained for SUREs

A simple idea is to consider the uniformized graph G_u as the dependence graph of a system of uniform recurrence equations and to schedule it with the schedules presented in Section 4.4.4. The problem is that this scheme will not always produce a valid schedule of G_o. In Section 5.5.2 we saw that any path of G_o cannot be simulated by a path of G_u because of the barycentric combinations of vertices of polyhedra and because of the nonintegral combinations of rays and lines. This is the same property that forbids us to simply reuse the results of Section 4.4.4. We now explain the problem in an example.

Suppose that G_o contains a polyhedral edge e whose dependence polyhedron contains at least two vertices denoted by σ_1 and σ_2. Suppose also that f_1 and f_2, the two edges of G_u associated to these two vertices, are not satisfied at the same depth by a schedule found following the results of Section 4.4.4. For example, f_1 is satisfied by the first dimension of the schedule and f_2 by the second. $\mathcal{P}(e)$ contains the dependence edge f of weight $(\sigma_1 + \sigma_2)/2$. The first dimension of the schedule induces on f_1 a delay greater than or equal to 1, but only induces a nonnegative delay on f_2. Therefore, we are only ensured that the first dimension of the schedule induces on f a delay greater than or equal to one-half. Thus, edge f is not satisfied by the first dimension of the schedule (the delay must be at least equal to 1 for an edge to be satisfied). The edge f_1 is satisfied by the first dimension of the schedule and thus was not considered for the computation of the second dimension of this schedule. Consequently, we have *no* information on the delay induced by the second dimension of the schedule on f_1 a fortiori on f. To summarize, we do not know whether the dependence edge f is satisfied, which is quite annoying! Because $\mathcal{P}(e)$ contains all weights $(\lambda\sigma_1 + (1 - \lambda)\sigma_2)$ for any value of λ in $[0, 1]$, we cannot solve our problem by increasing the delay induced on f_1 by the first dimension of the schedule.

We can encounter exactly the same problem with the nonintegral combinations of rays and lines. In fact, each polyhedron has a representation, called *Hilbert basis* [110], in which each integral point of the polyhedron can be decomposed into an integral combination of vertices, rays, and lines. For example, the direction vectors are represented, by definition, on a Hilbert basis (see Section 5.2.3). If we are sure that all the polyhedra we will have to manipulate are represented by an Hilbert basis, then we can simply reuse the results obtained for systems of uniform recurrence equations. The problem also disappears if all the scheduling functions that we consider are integral. We do not want to make this hypothesis, partly because Hilbert basis can be huge and also because we want to give here a general theoretical solution for the scheduling of PRDGs. In practice, however, limiting the algorithm to integral schedules can be sufficient.

To solve our problem, we only need one dimension of the schedule to induce *simultaneously* a positive delay on all the vertices of a polyhedron and the previous dimensions a nonnegative delay on these vertices. Because we do not have this property in the general case, we have to enforce it. The algorithm DA* enables us to ensure this property. Therefore we build the scheduling algorithm on top of this decomposition algorithm. The scheduling algorithm we present is slightly different from the simple fusion of the algorithm DA* and the scheduling algorithm for SUREs. Indeed, we use the freedom we have on rays; we only need to induce a nonnegative delay on rays, not a positive one (cf. the final remark of Section 5.5.1).

The Scheduling Algorithm

The algorithm builds for each actual node S of G_u a sequence of vectors $(X_S^1, \ldots, X_S^k, \ldots, X_S^{d_S})$ and a sequence of constants $(\rho_S^1, \ldots, \rho_S^k, \ldots, \rho_S^{d_S})$. These two sequences define a valid multidimensional schedule, as we will prove. The algorithm is initially called on the uniformized graph G_u if G_u is strongly connected and contains at least one edge. If this is not the case, the algorithm is first called on each strongly connected component of G_u

including an edge. In both cases, the second argument of this initial call is 1. Then the possibly remaining dependences are satisfied by a topological sort of the strongly connected components. The detailed algorithm is the following.

Algorithm (Scheduling of a PRDG)

Boolean DARTE-VIVIEN(Uniformized Graph G, integer k)

1. Build G' the subgraph of G generated by all the edges that belong to a zero-weight multicycle of G.

2. Initialize G'' to G'. For each polyhedral edge e, if G' contains an edge corresponding to a vertex of $\mathcal{P}(e)$, we add to G'' all the edges generated by the uniformization of $\mathcal{P}(e)$ that are not already included in G''.

3. Choose a vector X and, for each node S of G'', a constant ρ_S such that:

$$\begin{cases} \text{if } e \in G'' \text{ or } x_e \text{ is a virtual node, } Xw(e) + \rho_{y_e} - \rho_{x_e} \geq 0 \\ \text{if } e \notin G'' \text{ and } x_e \text{ is an actual node, } Xw(e) + \rho_{y_e} - \rho_{x_e} \geq 1 \end{cases} \quad (5.9)$$

For each actual node S of G let $\rho_S^k = \rho_S$ and $X_S^k = X$.

4. Compute the strongly connected components of G'' and let G_1'', G_2'', ..., G_s'' be the s components that have at least one actual node:

   - If G'' is empty or has only virtual nodes, return TRUE.

   - If G'' is strongly connected and has at least one actual node, return FALSE.

   - Otherwise, return $\bigwedge_{i=1}^{s} \text{DARTE-VIVIEN}(G_i'', k+1)$, where $\bigwedge$ is the logical AND.

Remarks

- Linear program (5.9) can be solved in rational numbers, and thus its resolution has a polynomial cost (cf. [110]).

- We will see that step 2 is needed only for general PRDGs. In particular, it can be ignored for representation of dependences by direction vectors or when the vector X and the constants ρ_S are integral. When step 2 is superfluous, steps 1 and 3 can be solved by a single linear program.

- Voluntarily, we did not explain how to choose the vector X and the constants ρ_S in step 3. The objective function can, for example, minimize the norm of the vector X, $\sum_{i=1}^{n} |X_i|$, thanks to a new variable Y, to two new constraints, $X \leq Y$ and $-X \leq Y$, and to the objective function: $\min \sum_{i=1}^{n} Y_i$. We can also minimize the makespan induced by X on the domain, as we did in Chapter 4.

Example 18, Continued

For this example the sets G' and G'' are equal and were given in Figure 5.26. Linear program (5.9) is then equivalent to:

$$
\begin{cases}
X(0,1,-1) + \rho_{S'_3} - \rho_{S_1} \geq 0 & X(0,1,0) + \rho_{S'_3} - \rho_{S'_3} \geq 0 \\
X(0,0,0) + \rho_{S_3} - \rho_{S'_3} \geq 0 & X(0,0,1) + \rho_{S_3} - \rho_{S_3} \geq 0 \\
X(0,0,2) + \rho_{S_1} - \rho_{S_3} \geq 0 & X(0,0,-1) + \rho_{S'_2} - \rho_{S'_2} \geq 0 \\
X(0,1,0) + \rho_{S_2} - \rho_{S_2} \geq 0 & X(0,-1,0) + \rho_{S'_1} - \rho_{S'_1} \geq 0 \\
X(1,-1,0) + \rho_{S'_1} - \rho_{S_1} \geq 1 & X(0,0,0) + \rho_{S_2} - \rho_{S'_1} \geq 0 \\
X(0,1,-1) + \rho_{S'_2} - \rho_{S_2} \geq 1 & X(0,0,0) + \rho_{S_3} - \rho_{S'_2} \geq 0
\end{cases}
$$

From the previous system, we deduce that the last two components of the vector $X = (x, y, z)$ are null: $y = z = 0$ (because of the self-loops around S_2, S_3, S'_1, S'_2, and S'_3). Looking at all the constraints, we can find, for example, the solution $X = (2,0,0)$, $\rho_{S_1} = \rho_{S_3} = 1$ and $\rho_{S_2} = 0$.

G' contains four strongly connected components. Two of them only include virtual nodes, and we ignore them. The two others do not contain zero-weight multicycles. The component that only contains the node S_2 can be scheduled with the vector $X = (0,1,0)$.

For the other component, linear program (5.9) is equivalent to:

$$
\begin{cases}
X(0,1,-1) + \rho_{S'_3} - \rho_{S_1} \geq 1 & X(0,1,0) + \rho_{S'_3} - \rho_{S'_3} \geq 0 \\
X(0,0,0) + \rho_{S_3} - \rho_{S'_3} \geq 0 & X(0,0,1) + \rho_{S_3} - \rho_{S_3} \geq 1 \\
X(0,0,2) + \rho_{S_1} - \rho_{S_3} \geq 1
\end{cases}
$$

A possible solution is $X = (0,0,2)$, $\rho_{S_1} = 0$, and $\rho_{S_3} = 3$.

To summarize, we find the multidimensional schedule: $(2i, j)$ for S_2, $(2i+1, 2k)$ for S_1, and $(2i+1, 2k+3)$ for S_3. Using the procedure *codegen* of the *Omega Calculator* delivered with the software *Petit* [66], we obtained the parallel code presented in Figure 5.27. The reader can check that neither ALLEN-KENNEDY nor WOLF-LAM can find all the parallelism for this example. Statement S_3 seems to be purely sequential for these two algorithms. □

```
DOSEQ i=1, n
 DOSEQ j=1, n
  DOPAR k=1, j
   b(i,j,k) = a(i-1,j+i,k) + b(i,j-1,k)
  ENDDOPAR
 ENDDOSEQ
 DOSEQ k = 1, n+1
  IF (k ≤ n) THEN
   DOPAR j=k, n
    a(i,j,k) = c(i,j,k-1) + 1
   ENDDOPAR
  ENDIF
  IF (k ≥ 2) THEN
   DOPAR j=k-1, n
    c(i,j,k) = c(i,j,k-1) + b(i,j-1,k+i-1) + a(i,j-k+1,k)
   ENDDOPAR
  ENDIF
 ENDDOSEQ
ENDDOSEQ
```

Figure 5.27: Parallelized version of Example 18.

Algorithm Correctness

We must show that the DARTE-VIVIEN algorithm is correct, i.e., that all its steps are feasible, that the algorithm ends, and that it outputs a correct result. The skeleton of this algorithm is nothing but algorithm DA*. The correctness of the latter was proved in Section 5.5.3. Therefore, we only have to prove that:

- step 3 is feasible, i.e., that there always exist a vector X and some constants ρ_S satisfying linear program (5.9);

- the sequences of vectors and constants define a valid schedule.

The first point is clear; Lemma 27 ensures us that there always exist a vector X and some constants ρ_S that satisfy the system:

$$\begin{cases} \forall e \in G' & Xw(e) + \rho_{y_e} - \rho_{x_e} = 0 \\ \forall e \notin G' & Xw(e) + \rho_{y_e} - \rho_{x_e} \geq 1 \end{cases}$$

Therefore, the weaker constraints of linear system (5.9) can always be satisfied; some ≥ 1 constraints were weakened into ≥ 0 constraints.

To ease the proof of the second point, we complete any sequence of vectors X_S^i with zero vectors and any sequence of constants ρ_S^i with zeros, to only have sequences of length d, the decomposition depth of G_u.

Lemma 32 *If $G_o = (V, E)$ is computable, then the affine multidimensional function Θ produced by* DARTE-VIVIEN:

$$
\begin{aligned}
V \times \mathcal{D} &\rightarrow \mathbb{Z}^d \\
(S, i) &\mapsto (\lfloor X_S^1 i + \rho_S^1 \rfloor, \ldots, \lfloor X_S^{d_S} i + \rho_S^{d_S} \rfloor, 0, \ldots, 0)
\end{aligned}
$$

defines a multidimensional schedule of G_o.

Proof To prove that the function Θ actually defines a schedule, we must show that it satisfies all the dependences represented by the PRDG G_o. In other words, we must prove that, for each polyhedral edge $e = (x_e, y_e)$ of G_o, for each point $w(e)$ of the polyhedron $\mathcal{P}(e)$, and for each point i of the domain $\mathcal{D}$, we have: $\Theta(x_e, i - w(e)) <_{lex} \Theta(y_e, i)$, where $<_{lex}$ is the strict lexicographic order (cf. Section 4.4.4). To achieve this goal, we will establish the existence of an integer k, $k \in [1, d]$, such that:

$$
\begin{cases}
X_{x_e}^i(i - w(e)) + \rho_{x_e}^i & \leq & X_{y_e}^i i + \rho_{y_e}^i & \forall i, \ 1 \leq i \leq k - 1 \\
X_{x_e}^k(i - w(e)) + \rho_{x_e}^k + 1 & \leq & X_{y_e}^k i + \rho_{y_e}^k
\end{cases} \tag{5.10}
$$

which will prove the desired result.

The possible values of the weight $w(e)$ are given by the following equation:

$$
w(e) = \sum_{j=1}^{\omega} \mu_j v_j + \sum_{j=1}^{\rho} \nu_j r_j + \sum_{j=1}^{\lambda} \xi_j l_j \tag{5.11}
$$

with $\mu, \nu, \xi) \in \mathbb{Q}^{+\omega} \times \mathbb{Q}^{+\rho} \times \mathbb{Q}^{\lambda}$ and $\sum_{j=1}^{\omega} \mu_j = 1$.

In the rest of this proof we suppose that the considered polyhedral edge e generates a virtual node during the uniformization. In the other case, the proof is similar to the one that follows.

If G_o is computable, all the recursive calls to DA* end. Furthermore, each of them ends with a call on a subgraph G' that is either empty or only includes virtual nodes. Thus, for each edge that corresponds to a polyhedron's vertex there is a depth at which it no longer belongs to a zero-weight multicycle. Step 2 of the algorithm keeps together in the graph all the edges coming from the uniformization of a same polyhedral edge e, until a minimal depth k where none of the edges corresponding to a vertex of $\mathcal{P}(e)$ belong to a zero-weight multicycle. Thus, the edges coming from the uniformization of $\mathcal{P}(e)$ are always in the same strongly connected component and the sequences of vectors $X_{y_e}^i$, $X_{x_e}^i$, and $X_{n_e}^i$ are equal until the level k (included). Therefore, we forget the index and simply write X^i. Then the system (5.10) can be rewritten:

$$
\begin{cases}
X^i w(e) + \rho^i_{y_e} - \rho^i_{x_e} \geq 0 & \forall i,\ 1 \leq i \leq k-1 \\
X^k w(e) + \rho^k_{y_e} - \rho^k_{x_e} \geq 1
\end{cases}
\tag{5.12}
$$

Step 3 ensures us of the validity, for any i, $1 \leq i \leq k$, of the following inequalities:

$$
\begin{cases}
X^i l_j = X^i l_j + \rho^i_{n_e} - \rho^i_{n_e} \geq 0 \text{ and } X^i(-l_j) \geq 0,\ \text{i.e.,}\ X^i l_j = 0 \\
X^i r_j = X^i r_j + \rho^i_{n_e} - \rho^i_{n_e} \geq 0 \\
X^i v_j + \rho^i_{n_e} - \rho^i_{x_e} \geq 0 \text{ if } i \leq k-1 \text{ and } X^k v_j + \rho^k_{n_e} - \rho^k_{x_e} \geq 1 \\
X^i 0 + \rho_{y_e} - \rho_{n_e} \geq 0
\end{cases}
$$

By the right summation of these inequalities, and using the definition of $w(e)$, we prove that system (5.12) is satisfied. ∎

Example 19

We illustrate once again the DARTE-VIVIEN algorithm. Here we consider a loop nest whose implicit parallelism cannot be fully detected with an approximation of dependences by direction vectors; we need a more precise approximation.

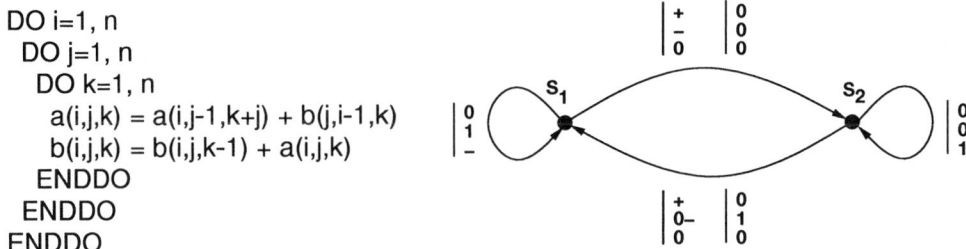

```
DO i=1, n
  DO j=1, n
    DO k=1, n
      a(i,j,k) = a(i,j-1,k+j) + b(j,i-1,k)
      b(i,j,k) = b(i,j,k-1) + a(i,j,k)
    ENDDO
  ENDDO
ENDDO
```

Figure 5.28: Example 19 and its RDG with direction vectors.

The code is displayed in Figure 5.28 along with its reduced dependence graph G_o when its dependences are approximated by direction vectors. This dependence graph was found by the loop analyzer *Tiny* [120]. The uniformization algorithm gives us the uniformized graph G_u in Figure 5.29.

The uniformized graph contains a zero-weight multicycle that includes all the edges whose weight is orthogonal to $(1, 0, 0)$ (cf. Figure 5.29). In G', statements S_1 and S_2 are included in the same strongly connected component. This component also contains a zero-weight multicycle that includes S_2 but not S_1 (this multicycle contains the cycles of weights $(0, 0, 1)$ and

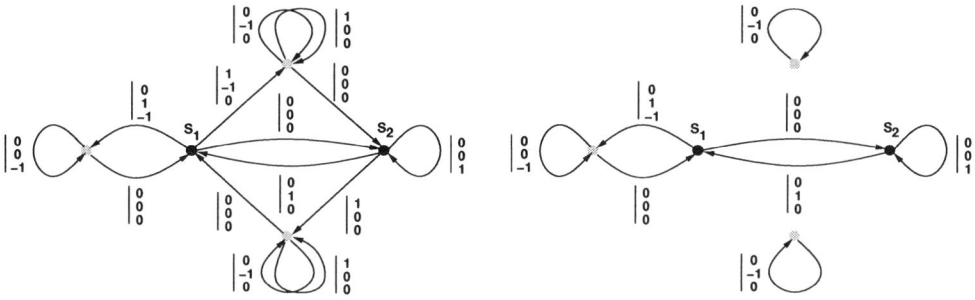

Figure 5.29: Uniformized graph for Example 19 and its subgraph of zero-weight multicycles.

$(0,0,-1))$. Therefore, the decomposition depth of S_1 is equal to 2, and the depth of S_2 is equal to 3. S_2 is thus found to be purely sequential when one parallel loop can be built around S_1. A possible multidimensional schedule is: $(i,2j)$ for S_1 and $(i,2j+1,k)$ for S_2. The resulting code is presented in Figure 5.30.

```
DOSEQ i=1, n
 DOSEQ j=1, n
  DOPAR k=1, n
   a(i,j,k) = a(i,j-1,k+j) + b(j,i-1,k)
  ENDDOPAR
  DOSEQ k=1, n
   b(i,j,k) = b(i,j,k-1) + a(i,j,k)
  ENDDOSEQ
 ENDDOSEQ
ENDDOSEQ
```

Figure 5.30: Parallelized version of Example 19.

One can remark that this is exactly the code that ALLEN-KENNEDY would have found or a version of WOLF-LAM with a step of loop distribution between the construction of two sets of fully permutable loops. However, a more precise analysis of the dependences of this example shows that the uniformized PRDG of Figure 5.31 is a conservative approximation of these dependences. This new approximation contains more parallelism than the old one. Here, the reference to array b in the right-hand side of assignment S_1 generates two dependences: a flow dependence whose dependence polyhedron contains the unique vertex $(0,1,0)$ and a unique ray, $(1,-1,0)$; an anti dependence whose dependence polyhedron contains the unique vertex $(1, -2, 0)$ and a unique ray, equal to the ray of the other dependence polyhedron: $(1, -1, 0)$.

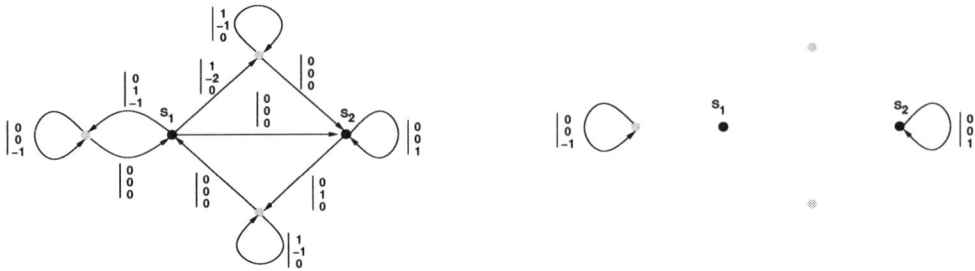

Figure 5.31: Uniformized PRDG G_u for Example 19 and its subgraph of zero-weight multicycles.

One can see in Figure 5.31 how the precision we gain on dependences changed the structure of G', the subgraph of the zero-weight multicycles. The decomposition depth is now equal to 1 for S_1 and 2 for S_2. Thus, we find one more parallel loop around each of the two statements. One possible scheduling is now: $(4i + 2j)$ for S_1 and $(4i + 2j + 1, k)$ for S_2. The new parallelized code is presented in Figure 5.32. S_1 is now surrounded by two parallel loops and S_2 by one.   □

5.5.5 Extension to Medium-Grain Parallelization

DARTE-VIVIEN is a scheduling algorithm. Thus, it is aimed at producing fine-grain parallelism. In fact, it can easily produce the fully permutable loops needed by tiling techniques and thus can be extended to generate medium-grain parallelism. This extension of DARTE-VIVIEN is nothing but a reuse of the principles used in WOLF-LAM. Here we only give a schematic presentation. The curious reader can find a more precise description in [30, 113]; see also Exercise 4.12 in Chapter 4.

We consider a call DARTE-VIVIEN(G, k). At step (3), we originally look for a unique solution $(X, \rho_{S_1}, \ldots, \rho_{S_s})$ of the linear program (5.9). To generate fully permutable loops we look for a set $H = \{(X_1, \rho_{S_1,1}, \ldots, \rho_{S_s,1}), \ldots, (X_m, \rho_{S_1,m}, \ldots, \rho_{S_s,m})\}$ of these solutions. We want this set to be the largest possible (m to be maximal) such that the vectors $X_1, \ldots, X_m$ are linearly independent. Let g be the dimension of the vector space generated by the weights of the cycles of G'. Then the largest set of solutions with the desired properties is of size $m = n - g$. Each of these solutions induces a nonnegative delay on all the edges of G. Thus two of these solutions define two permutable loops. However, some loops have already been generated

```
DOSEQ j=3, 3n
 DOPAR k=1, n
  DOPAR i=max(1,⌈ (j−n)/2 ⌉), min(n,⌊ (j−1)/2 ⌋)
   a(i,j-2i,k) = a(i,j-2i-1,k+j-2i) + b(j-2i,i-1,k)
  ENDDOPAR
 ENDDOPAR
 DOSEQ k=1, n
  DOPAR i=max(1,⌈ (j−n)/2 ⌉), min(n,⌊ (j−1)/2 ⌋)
   b(i,j-2i,k) = b(i,j-2i,k-1) + a(i,j-2i,k)
  ENDDOPAR
 ENDDOSEQ
ENDDOSEQ
```

Figure 5.32: Second parallelized version of Example 19.

by the $k - 1$ first calls to DARTE-VIVIEN, say, m_{k-1} loops. Therefore we cannot produce a set of m fully permutable loops, but only of $m - m_{k-1}$ loops. To produce this set we simply choose among H a set of $m - m_{k-1}$ solutions whose linear parts are linearly independent with the linear parts already generated for the first m_{k-1} loops. Then we proceed recursively. It is possible that, after the last recursive call to DARTE-VIVIEN ends, the total number of loops generated is strictly smaller than n (the dimension of the iteration space). In this case we complete the set of generated loops. The set of added loops is once again a set of fully permutable loops because the added loops are all parallel.

The scheme we presented here enables us to produce fully permutable loops. However, it can be refined. For example, we look for weakly separating hyperplanes that are strictly separating on $G \setminus G'$. We can in fact use weaker hyperplanes, as explained in [30].

5.5.6   Link with ALLEN-KENNEDY and WOLF-LAM

Comparison with ALLEN-KENNEDY

The ALLEN-KENNEDY and DARTE-VIVIEN algorithms have the same behavior on reduced dependence graphs where dependences are approximated by dependence levels. To see it, we just have to consider the representation of a dependence level by a direction vector (cf. Section 5.2.3). Let l be the smallest level of an edge of the RDG by levels, denoted by G, that we consider. A dependence at level $l < \infty$ is equivalent to the di-

$$\overbrace{}^{l-1} \qquad \overbrace{}^{n-l}$$

rection vector: $(0,\ldots,0,1+,*,\ldots,*)$. Thus, the last $n-l$ components of any hyperplane are equal to zero. Therefore, a cycle whose edges are all of levels strictly greater than l is included in G'. Thus the ALLEN-KENNEDY and DARTE-VIVIEN algorithms apply the same loop distribution and mark the same loops as sequential. The only difference is that the parallel loops generated by DARTE-VIVIEN are always inner loops and none of them surround a sequential loop. We can easily adapt this algorithm to generate first all the possible parallel loops and then a sequential loop, and finally apply the algorithm recursively.

Thus, DARTE-VIVIEN can be seen as a generalization of ALLEN-KENNEDY.

Comparison with WOLF-LAM

To compare the two algorithms we look at loop nests with a single statement since WOLF-LAM does not exploit the structure of the dependence graph. We must also compare WOLF-LAM with the extension of DARTE-VIVIEN that generates sets of fully permutable loops. The two algorithms have the same behavior; the sets of fully permutable loops they respectively generate have the same size. Indeed $\Gamma^+(D)$ and $(\Gamma(D))^\perp$ (cf. Section 5.4.4) have the same dimension, equal to the dimension of the vector space that is orthogonal to the vector space generated by the weights of the cycles of G' (see [30] for more details).

Thus, DARTE-VIVIEN can be seen as a generalization of WOLF-LAM.

5.6   Feautrier's Algorithm

So far, all the algorithms we have presented were designed to work with an approximation of the dependences. Paul Feautrier has designed [40, 41] a loop parallelizing algorithm in a framework where an exact data dependence analysis is feasible: the framework of static control flow programs. The solution proposed by Feautrier is in fact a very general scheduling algorithm. Indeed, it can be used to find schedules for loop nests whose dependences are described by any of the main existing representations: levels, direction vectors, polyhedra, and/or affine functions.

In Section 5.6.1, we will describe the problem considered by Paul Feautrier and his solution in the monodimensional case. We then show how his algorithm can be adapted to generate multidimensional schedules (Section 5.6.2) or to process other representation of dependences (Section 5.6.3). Finally we compare this algorithm with DARTE-VIVIEN in Section 5.6.4.

5.6.1 Monodimensional Algorithm

Dependence Representation

In the framework of "static control flow programs," an exact dependence analysis is feasible and each exact dependence relation e from statement S to statement T is defined by a polyhedron $\mathcal{D}_e$, the domain of existence of the dependence relation, and a quasi-affine [8] function h_e as follows:

$$j \in \mathcal{D}_e \quad \Rightarrow \quad S(h_e(j, N)) \rightarrow T(j)$$

where N is the vector of structural parameters. Obviously, the description of the exact dependence between two statements may involve the union of many such dependence relations. Following Paul Feautrier [40], we suppose that all the quasi-affine functions we have to handle are in fact affine functions (at the possible cost of a conservative approximation of the dependences).

We illustrate the exact dependence analysis and representation with the following example.

Example 20

Consider the following example:

```
DO i=0, N
  S₁: s(i) = 0
  DO j=0, N
    S₂: s(i) = s(i) + a(i,j) x(j)
  ENDDO
ENDDO
```

There are two statements whose domains are, respectively:

$$\mathcal{D}_{S_1} = \{i \mid 0 \leq i \leq N\} = \{i \mid i \geq 0, N - i \geq 0\}$$
$$\mathcal{D}_{S_2} = \{i, j \mid 0 \leq i, j \leq N\} = \{i, j \mid i \geq 0, N - i \geq 0, j \geq 0, N - j \geq 0\}$$

There are also two dependences in this loop nest, one from S_1 to S_2 and the other between iterations of S_2:

$$\{i, j \mid 0 \leq i \leq N, j = 0\} \qquad S_1(i) \rightarrow S_2(i, j)$$
$$\{i, j \mid 0 \leq i \leq N, 1 \leq j \leq N\} \quad S_2(i, j - 1) \rightarrow S_2(i, j)$$

Thus each dependence is affine and has a validity domain described by a polyhedron. $\qquad \square$

---

[8] See the original paper [39] for more details.

Searched Schedules

Paul Feautrier does not look for any type of function to schedule affine dependences. He only considers nonnegative functions with rational values that are affine functions in the iteration vector and in the parameter vector. Therefore he only handles (affine) schedules of the form:

$$\Theta(S, j, N) = X_S j + Y_S N + \rho_S$$

where X_S and Y_S are vectors and ρ_S is a constant. The hypothesis of nonnegativity of the schedules is not restrictive because all schedules must be lower bounded.

Problem Statement

Once we have chosen a dependence representation and the form of the schedules, the scheduling problem seems to be simple. For each statement S we just have to find a vector X_S, a vector Y_S, and a constant ρ_S such that, for all dependence relations e the schedule satisfies:

$$j \in \mathcal{D}_e \quad \Rightarrow \quad \Theta(S, h_e(j, N), N) + 1 \leq \Theta(T, j, N) \qquad (5.13)$$

Moreover, the set of constraints is linear, and one can imagine using linear system solvers, as the DARTE-VIVIEN algorithm does. Actually, there are now two difficulties to solve. First, there does not always exist a solution for such a set of constraints. We will see in Section 5.6.2 how the use of multidimensional schedules can overcome this problem. Second, Equation (5.13) must be satisfied for any possible value of the vector of the structural parameters. But polyhedron $\mathcal{D}_e$ may be parameterized. In such a case, Equation (5.13) corresponds to an infinite set of constraints, which cannot be enumerated. There are two means to overcome this problem: the polyhedron vertices and the affine form of Farkas's lemma. A (monodimensional) affine function considered on a polyhedron always takes its extremal values on the vertices of this polyhedron. Therefore, one only needs to consider the constraints

$$X_S h_e(j, N) + Y_S N + \rho_S \leq 1 + X_T j + Y_T N + \rho_T$$

when j corresponds to one of the finitely many vertices of $\mathcal{D}_e$. Even if there is always a finite number of vertices per polyhedron, the whole number of constraints obtained this way can be very huge. Vertices can also be parameterized. This is why Paul Feautrier prefers to use Farkas's lemma.

The Affine Form of Farkas's Lemma and Its Use

This lemma [40, 110] predicts the shape of certain affine forms.

Theorem 32 (Affine Form of Farkas's Lemma) *Let $\mathcal{D}$ be a nonempty polyhedron defined by p inequalities: $a_k x + b_k \geq 0$, for any $k \in \{1, \ldots, p\}$. An affine form Φ is nonnegative over $\mathcal{D}$ if and only if it is a nonnegative affine combination of the affine forms used to define $\mathcal{D}$:*

$$\Phi(x) \equiv \lambda_0 + \sum_{k=1}^{p} \lambda_k(a_k x + b_k), \ \forall k \in [0, p] \ \lambda_k \geq 0$$

The nonnegative values λ_k are called Farkas's multipliers.

This theorem is used to predict the shape of the schedules and to simplify the set of constraints:

- **Schedules.** By hypothesis, the schedule $\Theta(S, j, N)$ is a nonnegative affine form defined on a polyhedron $\mathcal{D}_S$. Therefore, the affine form of Farkas's lemma states that $\Theta(S, j, N)$ is a nonnegative affine combination of the affine forms used to define $\mathcal{D}_S$.

  Let $\mathcal{D}_S = \{x \mid \forall i \in [1, p_S], \ A_{S,i} x + B_{S,i} N + c_{S,i} \geq 0\}$ ($\mathcal{D}_S$ is thus defined by p_S inequalities). Then Theorem 32 states that there exist some nonnegative values $\mu_{S,0}, \ldots, \mu_{S,p_S}$ such that:

  $$\Theta(S, j, N) \equiv \mu_{S,0} + \sum_{i=1}^{p_S} \mu_{S,i}(A_{S,i} j + B_{S,i} N + c_{S,i}) \qquad (5.14)$$

- **Dependence Constraints.** Equation (5.13) can be rewritten as an affine function that is nonnegative over a polyhedron because the schedules are affine functions:

  $$j \in \mathcal{D}_e \quad \Rightarrow \quad \Theta(T, j, N) - \Theta(S, h_e(j, N), N) - 1 \geq 0$$

  Then one can again apply the affine form of Farkas's lemma. Let $\mathcal{D}_e = \{x \mid \forall i \in [1, p_e], \ A_{e,i} x + B_{e,i} N + c_{e,i} \geq 0\}$ ($\mathcal{D}_e$ is thus defined by p_e inequalities). Then Theorem 32 states that there exist some nonnegative values $\lambda_{e,0}, \ldots, \lambda_{e,p_e}$ such that:

  $$\Theta(T, j, N) - \Theta(S, h_e(j, N), N) - 1 \equiv \lambda_{e,0} + \sum_{i=1}^{p_e} \lambda_{e,i}(A_{e,i} j + B_{e,i} N + c_{e,i})$$

Using Equation (5.14), we rewrite the left-hand side of this equation:

$$\mu_{T,0} + \sum_{i=1}^{p_T} \mu_{T,i}(A(T)_i j + B_{T,i} N + c_{T,i})$$

$$-\left(\mu_{S,0} + \sum_{i=1}^{p_S} \mu_{S,i}(A_{S,i} h_e(j, N) + B_{S,i} N + c_{S,i}) - 1\right)$$

$$\equiv \lambda_{e,0} + \sum_{i=1}^{p_e} \lambda_{e,i}(A_{e,i} j + B_{e,i} N + c_{e,i}). \tag{5.15}$$

Actually, Equation 5.15 is a formal equality ($\equiv$); the coefficients of a given component of either of these two vectors must be the same in both sides. The constant terms on both sides of this equation must also be equal. This identification process leads to a set of $(n + q + 1)$ equations equivalent to Equation (5.15), where n is the size of the iteration vector j and q the size of the parameter vector N.

The way we used the affine form of Farkas's lemma enabled us to obtain a finite set of linear equations and inequalities, equivalent to the original scheduling problem, and that can easily be solved using any solver of linear systems. We illustrate the whole process in Example 20.

Example 20, Continued

Schedules

- $\mathcal{D}_{S_1} = \{i \mid i \geq 0, N - i \geq 0\}$. Thus, there exist some nonnegative values $\mu_{1,0}, \mu_{1,1}$, and $\mu_{1,2}$, such that:

$$\Theta(S_1, i, N) \equiv \mu_{1,0} + \mu_{1,1} i + \mu_{1,2}(N - i) \tag{5.16}$$

- $\mathcal{D}_{S_2} = \{i, j \mid i \geq 0, N - i \geq 0, j \geq 0, N - j \geq 0\}$. Thus, there exist some nonnegative values $\mu_{2,0}, \mu_{2,1}, \mu_{2,2}, \mu_{2,3}$, and $\mu_{2,4}$, such that:

$$\Theta(S_2, i, j, N) \equiv \mu_{2,0} + \mu_{2,1} i + \mu_{2,2}(N - i) + \mu_{2,3} j + \mu_{2,4}(N - j) \tag{5.17}$$

Dependence Constraints

- *First dependence:* $S_1(i) \Rightarrow S_2(i, j)$ if $0 \leq i \leq N$ and $j = 0$. Thus the schedules must satisfy the constraint:

$$i \geq 0, N - i \geq 0, j \geq 0, -j \geq 0 \Rightarrow \Theta(S_2, i, j, N) - \Theta(S_1, i, N) - 1 \geq 0$$

and there exist some nonnegative values $\lambda_{1,0}, \lambda_{1,1}, \lambda_{1,2}, \lambda_{1,3}, \lambda_{1,4}$ such that:

$$\Theta(S_2, i, j, N) - \Theta(S_1, i, N) - 1 \equiv \lambda_{1,0} + \lambda_{1,1} i + \lambda_{1,2} (N-i) + \lambda_{1,3} j + \lambda_{1,4}(-j)$$

To rewrite this equation we use Equations (5.16) and (5.17), and we obtain:

$$
\begin{aligned}
& \mu_{2,0} + \mu_{2,1} i + \mu_{2,2}(N-i) + \mu_{2,3} j + \mu_{2,4}(N-j) \\
- \ & (\mu_{1,0} + \mu_{1,1} i + \mu_{1,2}(N-i)) - 1 \\
\equiv \ & \lambda_{1,0} + \lambda_{1,1} i + \lambda_{1,2}(N-i) + \lambda_{1,3} j + \lambda_{1,4}(-j) \qquad (5.18)
\end{aligned}
$$

This equation is a formal equation. Therefore, the coefficient of i must be the same in the two members of the equation, and so on. Thus, Equation (5.18) is satisfied if and only if the following four equations are satisfied:

$$
\begin{aligned}
\mu_{2,1} - \mu_{2,2} - \mu_{1,1} + \mu_{1,2} &= \lambda_{1,1} - \lambda_{1,2} \\
\mu_{2,3} - \mu_{2,4} &= \lambda_{1,3} - \lambda_{1,4} \\
\mu_{2,2} + \mu_{2,4} - \mu_{1,2} &= \lambda_{1,2} \\
\mu_{2,0} - \mu_{1,0} - 1 &= \lambda_{1,0}
\end{aligned}
$$

- *Second dependence:* $S_2(i, j-1) \Rightarrow S_2(i, j)$ if $0 \le i \le N, 1 \le j \le N$. Thus the schedules must satisfy the constraint:

$$i \ge 0, N \ge i, j \ge 1, N \ge j \Rightarrow \Theta(S_2, i, j, N) - \Theta(S_2, i, j-1, N) - 1 \ge 0$$

But $\Theta(S_2, i, j, N) - \Theta(S_2, i, j-1, N) = \mu_{2,3} - \mu_{2,4}$, because of Equation (5.17). There is no need to use Farkas's lemma; we directly obtain the linear inequality:

$$\mu_{2,3} - \mu_{2,4} - 1 \ge 0$$

Simplification To simplify the whole set of equations, one can eliminate as many unknowns as possible. One possible result is:

$$
\begin{aligned}
\lambda_{1,0} &= \mu_{2,0} - \mu_{1,0} - 1 \ge 0 \\
\lambda_{1,1} &= \mu_{2,1} - \mu_{1,1} + \mu_{2,4} \ge 0 \\
\lambda_{1,3} &= \mu_{2,3} - \mu_{2,4} + \lambda_{1,4} \ge 0 \\
\lambda_{1,2} &= \mu_{2,2} + \mu_{2,4} - \mu_{1,2} \ge 0 \\
& \quad \ \mu_{2,3} - \mu_{2,4} - 1 \ge 0
\end{aligned}
$$

The third inequality is meaningless because this is the only one that includes $\lambda_{1,4}$ and $\lambda_{1,4}$ has a positive coefficient. This system can then be rewritten:

$$
\begin{aligned}
\mu_{2,0} &\geq \mu_{1,0} + 1 \\
\mu_{2,1} + \mu_{2,4} &\geq \mu_{1,1} \\
\mu_{2,2} + \mu_{2,4} &\geq \mu_{1,2} \\
\mu_{2,3} &\geq \mu_{2,4} + 1
\end{aligned}
$$

Its simplest solution is then obtained for $\mu_{1,0} = \mu_{1,1} = \mu_{1,2} = \mu_{2,1} = \mu_{2,2} = \mu_{2,4} = 0$, and $\mu_{2,0} = \mu_{2,3} = 1$. The corresponding schedules are:

$$
\begin{aligned}
\Theta(S_1, i, N) &= 0 \\
\Theta(S_2, i, j, N) &= 1 + j
\end{aligned}
$$

which leads to the following parallel code:

```
DOPAR i=0, N
  S₁: s(i) = 0
ENDDOPAR
DOSEQ j=0, N
  DOPAR i=0, N
    S₂: s(i) = s(i) + a(i,j) x(j)
  ENDDOPAR
ENDDOSEQ
```

This code can be obtained by a distribution of loop i followed by an interchange of loops i and j.   □

5.6.2   Extension to Multidimensional Scheduling

There exist some static control flow programs that cannot be scheduled with (monodimensional) affine schedules. For example, the two-deep loop nests that are purely sequential. Therefore, we need to have multidimensional schedules. The solution proposed by Feautrier is simple and greedy. For the first dimension of the schedules one looks for affine functions that induce a nonnegative delay on all dependences, and a delay greater than one on as many dependences as possible. The algorithm is then recursively called on the unsatisfied dependences. Formally speaking, one replaces the inequality (5.13) by the two inequalities:

$$
j \in \mathcal{D}_e \;\Rightarrow\; \Theta(S, h_e(j, N), N) + z_e \leq \Theta(T, j, N) \text{ and } 0 \leq z_e \leq 1 \quad (5.19)
$$

and one looks for an affine function that maximizes the sum $\sum_e z_e$. The search for the affine function is performed again using the affine form of Farkas's lemma. This, plus a strongly connected component distribution that reminds us of ALLEN-KENNEDY, defines the following algorithm.

Algorithm (Feautrier's Multidimensional Algorithm)

FEAUTRIER(G)

1. Compute the strongly connected components of G.

2. **For each** strongly connected component G_i of G **do** in topological order;

   (a) Find, using the method exposed in Section 5.6.1, an affine schedule that induces a nonnegative delay on all the dependences and satisfies Equation (5.13) for as many dependences as possible.

   (b) Build the subgraph G'_i generated by the unsatisfied dependences. If G'_i is not empty, recursively call FEAUTRIER (G'_i).

5.6.3 Extension to Other Dependence Representations

We show here that FEAUTRIER can be extended to process a representation of the dependences by levels, direction vectors, and/or polyhedra. We focus on the latter type because it is a generalization of the two others. Let us consider a perfect loop nest, two instructions S and T of same domain $\mathcal{D}$, with T depending on S by a dependence e described by the polyhedron $\mathcal{P}_e$. The schedule must respect this dependence. Therefore, it must satisfy the equation:

$$\forall j \in \mathcal{D}, \forall d \in \mathcal{P}_e, (j - d) \in \mathcal{D} \quad \Rightarrow \quad \Theta(T, j, n) >_{lex} \Theta(S, j - d, n) \quad (5.20)$$

The set of values of the couple (j, d) satisfying the conditions on the left-hand side of the implication is a polyhedron as $\mathcal{D}$ and $\mathcal{P}_e$ are polyhedra. Indeed, if $\mathcal{D} = \{x \mid Ax + b \geq 0\}$ and $\mathcal{P}_e = \{x \mid Cx + d \geq 0\}$ then:

$$\{(j, d) \mid j \in \mathcal{D}, d \in \mathcal{P}_e, j - d \in \mathcal{D}\} = \left\{ (j, d) \; \middle| \; \begin{bmatrix} A & 0 \\ 0 & C \\ A & -A \end{bmatrix} \begin{bmatrix} j \\ d \end{bmatrix} + \begin{bmatrix} b \\ d \\ b \end{bmatrix} \geq 0 \right\}$$

which is a polyhedron. Then we can apply the affine form of Farkas's lemma to Equation (5.20), as we did for Equation (5.13). Hence we can schedule a loop nest whose dependences are described by levels, direction vectors, and/or polyhedra using the affine form of Farkas's lemma.

5.6.4   Comparison with DARTE-VIVIEN

We can only compare the results of the DARTE-VIVIEN and FEAUTRIER algorithms on the same object. Thus, we compare DARTE-VIVIEN with the version of FEAUTRIER dealing with PRDGs. We show that, even if FEAUTRIER looks for more general schedules, the two algorithms have exactly the same behavior on PRDGs. They produce multidimensional schedules that satisfy the same dependences by the same dimensions.

Theorem 33 (FEAUTRIER Generalizes DARTE-VIVIEN) *Consider a set of perfectly nested loops whose dependences are represented by a strongly connected PRDG denoted by G_o. We suppose that the iteration domain $\mathcal{D}$ contains a hypercube of dimension n and of $\Omega(N)$. Then any schedule proposed by FEAUTRIER satisfies the dependences described by G_o the same way as any schedule built by DARTE-VIVIEN: The first dimension of the two schedules satisfies exactly the same subset of the edges of G_o; the second dimension of the two schedules satisfies exactly the same subset of the edges of G_o not satisfied by the first dimension of these schedules; and so on.*

Proof   Let us consider a strongly connected PRDG, denoted by G_o, of iteration domain $\mathcal{D}$. We show that the first component of the multidimensional schedule built by FEAUTRIER satisfies exactly the same polyhedral edges as any schedule produced by DARTE-VIVIEN. This will prove the desired result. Indeed, both algorithms will have to recursively handle the same set of unsatisfied edges, and they will call themselves recursively on the strongly connected components of the graph generated by the unsatisfied edges; hence they will call themselves on exactly the same subgraphs.

   FEAUTRIER tries to satisfy as many polyhedral edges as possible at each step of the recursion. It looks for an affine schedule that for any edge e of G_o, satisfies the equation:

$$\forall j \in \mathcal{D}, \ \forall d \in \mathcal{P}_e, \ j - d \in \mathcal{D} \ \Rightarrow \ \Theta(S, N, j) \geq \Theta(T, N, j - d) + \delta_e \quad (5.21)$$

where δ_e is always nonnegative ($\delta_e \geq 0$) and satisfies the inequality $\delta_e \geq 1$ for as many edges as possible. Let $\Theta(T, N, j) = X_i j + Y_i N + \rho_i$, where N is the vector of the structural parameters.

   By hypothesis, G_o is strongly connected. Thus, there exists a dependence cycle $\mathcal{C}$ that contains all the nodes of G_u. Let $q_1, \ldots, q_l$ be a set of l simple cycles whose union is a zero-weight multicycle of G_u. If we ignore the iteration domain, we can plug in q_i on $\mathcal{C}$ as many times as we want, because $\mathcal{C}$ includes all the nodes of G_u. But here, in Feautrier's algorithm, we consider the domains. Nevertheless, because the iteration domain contains a hypercube of size $f(N) = \Omega(N)$, such a construction will be possible.

Indeed, let $H(e)$ denote the maximal (in absolute value) component of the weight of a dependence edge e, i.e., $H(e) = \max\{|w(e)_i|$ for $1 \le i \le n\}$. We extend this notation from edges to paths as follows. If $p = e_1, \ldots, e_l$, $H(p) = \sum_{i=1}^l H(e_i)$. From these notations, it immediately follows that if $H(\mathcal{C}) + \lambda H(q_i) \le f(N)$, there exists in the apparent dependence graph of G_o, *when considering the domain* $\mathcal{D}$, a path corresponding to $\mathcal{C}$ on which λ occurrences of the cycle q_i are plugged in. This is possible as soon as

$$\lambda \le \frac{f(N) - H(\mathcal{C})}{\max_i H(q_i)} \tag{5.22}$$

Therefore, the apparent dependence graph of G_o bounded by the domain $\mathcal{D}$ includes, for some iteration vector j, a dependence from $S(j)$ to $S(j + w(\mathcal{C}) + \lambda w(q_i))$ for any cycle q_i. The delay induced on these dependences by the first component of the schedule must be nonnegative (δ_e is always nonnegative in Equation (5.21)). Therefore we have, for any value of i, $X_S(j) + Y_j N + \rho_S \le X_S(j + w(\mathcal{C}) + \lambda w(q_i)) + Y_j N + \rho_S$, i.e., $0 \le X_S(w(\mathcal{C}) + \lambda w(q_i))$. Because a sum of nonnegative terms is always greater than any of its constitutive terms, we have:

$$\forall i, \ 0 \le X_S(w(\mathcal{C}) + \lambda w(q_i)) \le \sum_{i=1}^l X_S(w(\mathcal{C}) + \lambda w(q_i))$$

and, because $\sum_{i=1}^l X_S \lambda w(q_i) = \lambda X_S \sum_{i=1}^l w(q_i) = 0$ (the union of the cycles q_i is a zero-weight multicycle), we obtain:

$$\forall i, \ -X_S w(\mathcal{C}) \le \lambda X_S w(q_i)) \le (l-1) X_S w(\mathcal{C})$$

The term $X_S w(\mathcal{C})$ does not depend on the domain size (which can be parameterized). Therefore, we have bounded the product $\lambda X_S w(q_i)$ by constant terms. But this product includes the factor λ, which can be as large as we want when N grows (Equation 5.22). Therefore, $X_S w(q_i) = 0$. Then, for any instruction S, the linear part X_S of its schedule has a null dot product with the weight of any cycle belonging to a zero-weight multicycle.

Let $q = e_1, \ldots, e_k$ be a simple cycle of dependence edges that is included in a zero-weight multicycle. Let us suppose that the domain is large enough to contain an instance of q. Then it follows from Equation (5.21) that

$$X_{y(e_i)} \left(j + \sum_{j=1}^i w(e_j) \right) + \rho_{y(e_i)} \ge X_{x(e_i)} \left(j + \sum_{j=1}^{i-1} w(e_j) \right) + \rho_{x(e_i)} + \delta_{e(e_i)}$$

where the dependence edge e_i is an instance of the polyhedral edge $e(e_i)$ from $x(e_i)$ to $y(e_i)$. By adding these equations for all values of i we obtain:

$$X_{y(e_k)} \sum_{i=1}^{k} w(e_i) \geq \sum_{i=1}^{k} \delta_{e(e_i)}$$

The right-hand side of this equation is nonnegative by definition. The left-hand side of this equation is null from what precedes; this is the dot product of the linear part of a schedule with the weight of a simple cycle belonging to a zero-weight multicycle. Therefore, for each i, $\delta_{e(e_i)} = 0$ and none of the polyhedral edges visited by a zero-weight multicycle is satisfied. These polyhedral edges are exactly those not satisfied by DARTE-VIVIEN. Indeed, if a polyhedral edge (in G_o) is visited by a simple cycle belonging to a zero-weight multicycle, then at least one of the edges of G_u that correspond to a vertex of a polyhedron is included in a zero-weight multicycle. Therefore, the first component of the schedule produced by FEAUTRIER satisfies none of the polyhedral edges that is not satisfied by the first component of the schedules produced by DARTE-VIVIEN. Conversely, Feautrier's algorithm succeeds in satisfying all the polyhedral edges satisfied by DARTE-VIVIEN as it tries to satisfy as many polyhedral edges as possible with schedules more general than the ones manipulated by DARTE-VIVIEN.   ■

FEAUTRIER is thus a generalization of DARTE-VIVIEN. We will come back to this result in Section 5.7.6.

5.7   Optimality

In this section we study the theoretical efficiency of the algorithms we have presented in this chapter. First, we show in Section 5.7.1 the need of a formal definition for the notion of "optimality," and we propose such a definition in Section 5.7.2. Then we establish optimality and suboptimality results for all the algorithms presented: ALLEN-KENNEDY in Section 5.7.3, WOLF-LAM in Section 5.7.4, DARTE-VIVIEN in Section 5.7.5, and FEAUTRIER in Section 5.7.6.

5.7.1   The Difficulty of Defining an "Optimality" Notion

Intuitively, an algorithm is optimal if it is not possible to do better than it does! The measure of the efficiency of a parallelization algorithm is the (theoretical) execution time of the parallelized program. Thus, one would like to say that a parallelization algorithm is optimal if and only if it optimally parallelizes any program (in the class considered). The problem with such a definition is that many algorithms only have a partial knowledge of the program they parallelize. For example, the only information on the original program known by ALLEN-KENNEDY is a representation of its dependences by dependence levels. Thus ALLEN-KENNEDY cannot see any difference between two different programs that have the same representation of their dependences by levels. The problem is not whether more parallelism can be found if we use another dependence representation. In our point of view, what really matters is whether ALLEN-KENNEDY can detect all the parallelism included in a representation by levels. Therefore, we consider the *optimality with respect to the dependence representation*. This way, we disconnect the problem of parallelism detection with an underlying dependence representation from the problem of the dependence analysis and representation. Using several examples, we now illustrate and clarify the notion of optimality we will formally define in the next section.

Two Loop Nests with the Same RDG

Consider the two codes of Figure 5.33. The dependence relations in both

Example 21

DO i=1, N
  DO j=1, N
    a(i,j) = a(i,j-1) + a(i-1,j)
  ENDDO
ENDDO

Example 22

DO i=1, N
  DO j=1, N
    a(i,j) = a(i,j-1) + a(i-1,N)
  ENDDO
ENDDO

Figure 5.33: Two codes with the same RLDG.

codes are obviously different, but the two codes are identical for ALLEN-KENNEDY because they have the same RLDG (depicted in Figure 5.34).

Figure 5.35 shows the expanded dependence graph, i.e., the exact dependences, for Example 22 (transitivity edges are not depicted). It obviously contains a dependence path including all operations. Therefore, Example 22 contains no parallelism at all, its RLDG cannot contain parallelism (because it describes a superset of the EDG), and thus ALLEN-KENNEDY parallelizes it optimally. Therefore, because ALLEN-KENNEDY see no difference between the two programs, we also say that ALLEN-KENNEDY optimally parallelizes Example 21, with respect to the dependence representation. We did not even look at the actual dependences of Example 21 or at the parallelism it implicitly contains, to state this optimality result. We only look at the RLDG.

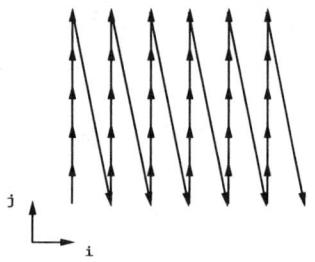

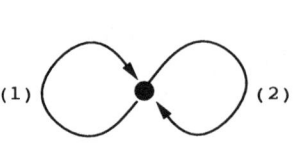

Figure 5.34: RLDG for Examples 21 and 22.

Figure 5.35: EDG for Example 22.

The Dependence Representation Is Fixed

We have just shown that ALLEN-KENNEDY optimally parallelizes Example 21. In Section 5.7.3 we will prove that ALLEN-KENNEDY is optimal *with respect to its underlying dependence representation*, i.e., when dependences are represented by dependence levels. To explain the meaning of our optimality notion, we come back to Example 21, whose exact EDG and RDG with direction vectors are drawn in Figure 5.36. As we have seen, ALLEN-KENNEDY finds no parallelism in this example. However, Lamport's hyperplane method works on this example because the dependences are all uniform (see the RDG with direction vectors shown in Figure 5.36). Thus Example 21 can be rewritten with one sequential and one parallel loop. Therefore, it contains some parallelism even if ALLEN-KENNEDY cannot find it. This is not contradictory to our optimality result because we had to use a sharper representation of the dependences than the one used by ALLEN-KENNEDY to find some parallelism in this example.

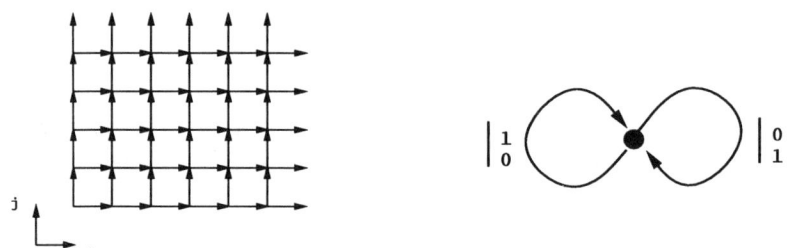

Figure 5.36: EDG and RDG with direction vectors for Example 21.

No Knowledge on the Domain

We now consider the code example given in Figure 5.37. Its reduced dependence graph is strongly connected and contains a level 1 dependence. Thus

ALLEN-KENNEDY finds that the outer loop is sequential. The level 1 dependence is removed and the remaining RDG contains three strongly connected components, each of them containing a single statement and none of them containing a dependence. Thus ALLEN-KENNEDY distributes the second loop and marks "parallel" each of its three occurrences. We end up with the code presented in Figure 5.37.

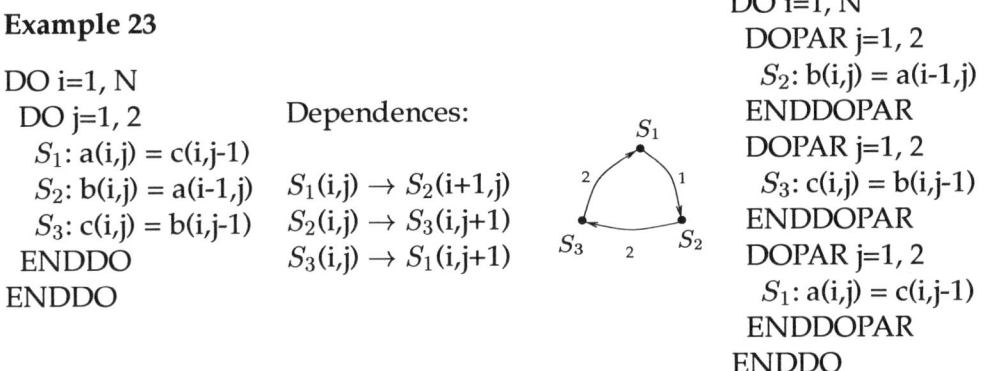

Example 23

```
DO i=1, N
  DO j=1, 2
    S₁: a(i,j) = c(i,j-1)
    S₂: b(i,j) = a(i-1,j)
    S₃: c(i,j) = b(i,j-1)
  ENDDO
ENDDO
```

Dependences:

$S_1(i,j) \rightarrow S_2(i+1,j)$
$S_2(i,j) \rightarrow S_3(i,j+1)$
$S_3(i,j) \rightarrow S_1(i,j+1)$

```
DO i=1, N
  DOPAR j=1, 2
    S₂: b(i,j) = a(i-1,j)
  ENDDOPAR
  DOPAR j=1, 2
    S₃: c(i,j) = b(i,j-1)
  ENDDOPAR
  DOPAR j=1, 2
    S₁: a(i,j) = c(i,j-1)
  ENDDOPAR
ENDDO
```

Figure 5.37: Code, dependence relations, RLDG, and the code parallelized by ALLEN-KENNEDY.

This parallelized code exhibits some parallelism as the three loops at depth 2 are parallel. But each of these loops only describes two iterations! We have indeed discovered very little parallelism! In fact, we could have done a "smarter" parallelization. Knowing that the second loop of Example 23 only describes two iterations, we could unroll it and obtain the code of Figure 5.38.

The RDG of the code of Figure 5.38 contains no cycles. Therefore, AL-LEN-KENNEDY applies a loop distribution and finds that all the loops are parallel. We end up with the program in Figure 5.39. Each of its loops is parallel and describes N iterations instead of the two iterations of the parallel loops found by the first parallelization scheme. Therefore we have found far more parallelism by first unrolling the inner loop. But to do so, we used knowledge ALLEN-KENNEDY does not have: the exact value of the iteration domain. Because we are mainly interested in parallelizing parameterized programs, we consider parallelizations that do not depend on the iteration domain, i.e., that are valid whatever the iteration domain. ALLEN-KENNEDY, WOLF-LAM, and DARTE-VIVIEN produce such parallelization. Thus, when looking for the optimality, we suppose that the parallelization algorithm has no knowledge of the iteration domain.

DO i=1, N
  S_1: a(i,1) = c(i,0)
  S_2: b(i,1) = a(i-1,1)
  S_3: c(i,1) = b(i,0)
  T_1: a(i,2) = c(i,1)
  T_2: b(i,2) = a(i-1,2)
  T_3: c(i,2) = b(i,1)
ENDDO

Dependences:

S_1(i) → S_2(i+1)
S_2(i) → T_3(i)
S_3(i) → T_1(i)
T_1(i) → T_2(i+1)

Figure 5.38: Example 23 with its inner loop unrolled, and its dependence relations.

DOPAR i=1, N
  S_1: a(i,1) = c(i,0)
ENDDOPAR
DOPAR i=1, N
  S_2: b(i,1) = a(i-1,1)
ENDDOPAR
DOPAR i=1, N
  S_3: c(i,1) = b(i,0)
ENDDOPAR
DOPAR i=1, N
  T_1: a(i,2) = c(i,1)
ENDDOPAR
DOPAR i=1, N
  T_2: b(i,2) = a(i-1,2)
ENDDOPAR
DOPAR i=1, N
  T_3: c(i,2) = b(i,1)
ENDDOPAR

Figure 5.39: Unrolled code parallelized by ALLEN-KENNEDY.

How to Measure the Parallelism Found?

So far, we have stressed that, for us, optimality depends on the underlying dependence representation and is defined from this representation but neither from the original code nor from the iteration domain. But to prove an optimality result we need to measure in some way the parallelism found. How can we do this? This question has a simple and intuitive answer: count the number of parallel loops found! But, as shown by the following two codes, this is not possible:

```
DOPAR i=1, 1000
  DOPAR j=1, 100                DOPAR I=0, 99999
    a(i,j) = 0                    a((I div 100) + 1, (I mod 100) + 1) = 0
  ENDDOPAR                      ENDDOPAR
ENDDOPAR
```

Indeed, these two codes are equivalent; to transform one code into the other, we just have to coalesce the two loops or break one loop in two loops. But one of them contains one parallel loop and the other one two parallel loops. Therefore, we need a more accurate measure of the parallelism found. We present such a measure in the next section.

5.7.2 A Formal Definition

We make the hypothesis that the parallelization algorithms we consider know nothing of the loop nest $\mathcal{L}$ to be parallelized but its reduced dependence graph. The parallelism sought is thus the intrinsic parallelism of the RDG and not of the loop nest. To define our optimality notion we need some preliminary definitions. The first is the definition of the theoretical latency [9] of a parallelized loop nest.

Definition 31 (Latency) *We define the latency* $\mathcal{T}(\mathcal{L}_t)$ *of the transformed loop nest* $\mathcal{L}_t$ *as the minimal number of clock cycles required to execute* $\mathcal{L}_t$ *if:*

- *we have an unlimited number of processors;*

- *we need a single clock cycle to execute any instance of any statement; and*

- *any other operation is costless (needs zero clock cycle to be executed).*

The latency as computed by Definition 31 will obviously not be equal to the actual execution time of $\mathcal{L}_t$. This is just an evaluation of the sequentiality of the loop nest $\mathcal{L}_t$. Nevertheless, this latency enables us to define a notion of *degree of parallelism*, independent from the target architecture that reveals the intrinsic qualities of the parallelized code. Actually, it is necessary, for our study, to use an even more precise definition of the latency, a definition that depends on the statement S that is considered: the S-latency. The *S-latency* has the same definition as the latency, except that only the operations that are instances of statement S need time to be executed (all other operations are executed in zero clock cycle).

We can now define the degree of parallelism detected by a parallelization algorithm, for a given representation of the dependences. However, in order to avoid definition problems such as the one that occurs for the number of parallel loops with loop coalescing, we suppose that we are only trying to parallelize parameterized programs. We also suppose that, in the following definitions, all the RDGs and ADGs (see Sections 5.2.2 and 5.2.3) are described with the same representation of the dependences.

Definition 32 (*S*-Degree of Extracted Sequentiality/Parallelism) *Let* A *be a parallelizing algorithm. Let* $\mathcal{L}$ *be a loop nest and G its RDG. We parallelize G using the algorithm* A. *Let* $\mathcal{D}_S$ *denote the iteration domain of the statement S in* $\mathcal{L}$. *We suppose that* $\mathcal{D}_S$ *contains (resp. is contained in) a hypercube of dimension* n_S *and size* $\Omega(N)$ *(resp.* $O(N)$*), where N is a parameter. The S-degree of extracted*

---

[9]To make the book more uniform, we should use the word *makespan* to mean execution time, but we prefer to keep the terminology introduced in [32], where the word *latency* is used as in the VLSI literature.

sequentiality (resp. of extracted parallelism) of G by A *is then equal to d_S (resp. $n_S - d_S$) where d_S is the smallest nonnegative integer such that the S-latency of the transformed code is $O(N^{d_S})$.*

   Recalls. Let f and g be two functions. $f = O(g)$ if there exists k and N_0 such that $f(N) \leq kg(N)$ for N greater than N_0. $f = \Omega(g)$ if $g = O(f)$. $f = \Theta(g)$ if $f = \Omega(g)$ and $f = O(g)$.

We have supposed that the studied algorithms know nothing about the loop nest to be parallelized but their RDG. Therefore, these algorithms have no knowledge of the domains of the statements and the parallelization does not depend on these domains, i.e., is valid whatever the iteration domains. The hypothesis on $\mathcal{D}_S$ is therefore not restrictive.

The definition we proposed is still far from being perfect; it sees no differences between a purely sequential code and a loop nest including a set of independent computations of size $\log(N)$. Indeed, our degrees of parallelism are all integers. This is natural, because the parallelism found will be expressed with loops and there is always an integral number of loops. But this definition enables us to link the latency with the length of the dependence paths of the ADG, and to link the S-latency with the S-length of the dependence paths of the ADG (the S-length of a path is the number of its nodes that are instances of the statement S). Indeed, any parallelization must respect the dependences. If two operations are linked by an edge of the ADG, they cannot be computed at the same clock cycle. They must be executed one after the other. This is also true for the different operations included in any dependence path. Therefore, the latency of $\mathcal{L}_t$, whatever the parallelization algorithm, must be at least equal to the length of the longest path in the ADG.

   More precisely:

- If an algorithm succeeds in transforming the initial loop nest $\mathcal{L}$ into a nest $\mathcal{L}_t$ whose S-latency is $O(N^{d_S})$ for the statement S, then the S-length of any dependence path is also $O(N^{d_S})$.

- Equivalently, if there exists in the ADG a path whose S-length is not $O(N^{d_S})$, then, whatever the parallelization algorithm, the latency of the transformed code cannot be $O(N^{d_S})$.

This leads us to define some new notions.

Definition 33 (S-Degree of Intrinsic Sequentiality/Parallelism) *Let G be a RDG. We suppose that the iteration domain $\mathcal{D}_S$ contains (resp. is contained in) a hypercube of dimension n_S and size $\Omega(N)$ (resp. $O(N)$), where N is a parameter. Let d_S be the smallest nonnegative integer such that the S-length of any path of* *the ADG is $O(N^{d_S})$. Then the S-degree of intrinsic sequentiality (resp. of intrinsic parallelism) of G is d_S (resp. $n_S - d_S$).*

From Definitions 32 and 33 (and the previous remarks), the S-degree of extracted parallelism of an RDG is always less than or equal to the S-degree of intrinsic parallelism. This is quite natural!

Definition 34 (Optimal Extraction of Parallelism) *An algorithm* A *is optimal for parallelism extraction if for any RDG G and any statement S of G, the S-degree of parallelism extracted from G by* A *is equal to the S-degree of intrinsic parallelism of G.*

To define the optimality of the parallelism detection from the S-latency instead of from the latency, i.e., to consider the performances statement by statement and not globally, enables us to discuss the quality of the parallelization even for statements that do not belong to the most sequential part of the original code.

This definition has the same drawback as Definition 32. It considers sequential a code that does not contain at least one full degree of parallelism. Indeed, let us consider a unique loop of size N whose longest dependence path is of length $\log(N)$. With our definition, to let the original code unchanged is considered optimal even if it is possible to transform it to make it executable in $\log(N)$. However, we will see in the rest of this section that this is not a problem. For approximation of dependences by levels, direction vectors, or polyhedra, if the S-degree of intrinsic sequentiality is equal to d_S, then the length of the longest path is always $\Theta(N^{d_S})$.

Methods to Prove Optimality

With all our definitions, one can prove the optimality of a parallelization algorithm A as follows. Let $\mathcal{L}$ be a loop nest of RDG G for a certain dependence representation, and of ADG G_a. Let d_S be the S-degree of sequentiality extracted from G by A. We have two methods to prove the optimality of A:

1. to build for each statement S a path in G_a whose S-length is not $O(N^{d_S-1})$, e.g., a path in G_a whose S-length is $\Omega(N^{d_S})$.

2. to build a loop nest $\mathcal{L}'$ whose RDG is also equal to G for the same dependence representation and whose *exact dependence graph* contains, for any statement S, a path whose S-length is not $O(N^{d_S-1})$, e.g., a path whose S-length is $\Omega(N^{d_S})$. The new loop nest $\mathcal{L}'$ is called the *apparent loop nest*, because the algorithm that parallelizes $\mathcal{L}$ apparently behaves as if it was parallelizing $\mathcal{L}'$.

Actually, the result of method 2 implies the result of method 1, because the EDG of $\mathcal{L}'$ is a subset of G_a ($\mathcal{L}$ and $\mathcal{L}'$ have the same RDG). Therefore, the result of method 2 proves a stronger result. In particular, the apparent loop nest reveals the intrinsic limitations for the detection of parallelism, of the underlying dependence representation. Indeed, even if there are different amounts of parallelism actually existing in $\mathcal{L}$ and $\mathcal{L}'$ (they can have different EDGs), these two loop nests cannot be distinguished by the parallelization algorithm as they have the same RDG. In other words, any algorithm of parallelism detection (taking as input the chosen dependence representation) will make no differences between $\mathcal{L}$ and $\mathcal{L}'$ and will parallelize them identically. As $\mathcal{L}'$ is optimally parallelized, the parallelization algorithm is considered optimal for the chosen dependence representation. We used this method in Section 5.7.1 to prove that ALLEN-KENNEDY optimally parallelizes Example 21. To prove the same result by the first method, we consider the ADG of Example 21, which is equivalent to the ADG of Example 22 (depicted in Figure 5.35). As before, we see a dependence path containing $\Omega(N^2)$ operations. Thus the S-latency is $\Omega(N^2)$, which establishes the result.

Method 1 establishes a weaker result than method 2, but is simpler. We use this method especially when we think it would be too complicated to exhibit an apparent set of loops. We use it in Section 5.7.5 to prove the optimality of DARTE-VIVIEN. On the contrary, we use the first method in Section 5.7.3 to establish the optimality of ALLEN-KENNEDY. Figure 5.40 recalls the links between the original loop nest $\mathcal{L}$, the apparent loop nest $\mathcal{L}'$, and their respective EDG, RDG, and ADG.

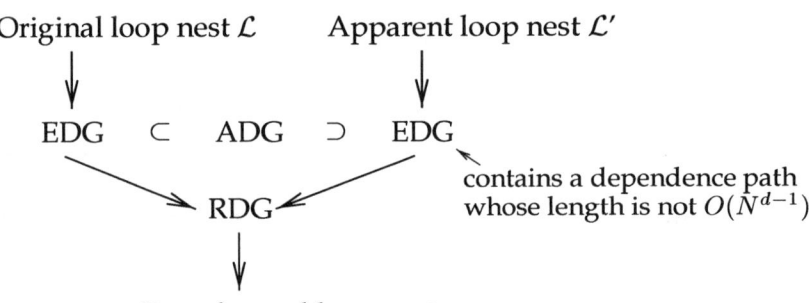

Figure 5.40: Links between $\mathcal{L}$ and $\mathcal{L}'$, and their apparent dependence graphs.

One might think that the latency and S-latency of the transformed code are difficult to compute. Indeed, in the general case, they can only be computed by the execution of the code for a given value of the parameters. Nevertheless, for most parallelization algorithms one can compute the S-degree of extracted parallelism (without knowing exactly the S-latency) by only looking at the structure of the transformed code. This is formalized by Lemma 33. In this case, we come back to the intuitive definition of the S-degree of parallelism as the number of nested parallel loops surrounding statement S.

Lemma 33 *Hypotheses:*

- *The transformed code $\mathcal{L}_t$ includes no control structure other than loops.*

- *Variables and parameters used to compute loop boundaries are not modified by the loop body.*

- *Each statement S of the original loop nest $\mathcal{L}$ appears only once (or a nonparameterized number of times) in the transformed code $\mathcal{L}_t$ and is surrounded by exactly n_S loops in the two loop nests.*

- *The iteration domain $\mathcal{D}_S$ defined by these n_S loops contains a hypercube $\underline{\mathcal{D}}$ of dimension n_S and of size $\Omega(N)$ and is contained in a hypercube $\overline{\mathcal{D}}$ of dimension n_S and size $O(N)$.*

Under these hypotheses, the number of parallel loops surrounding S is equal to the S-degree of extracted parallelism.

Proof Let us consider a statement S of the original code $\mathcal{L}$. To simplify the proof, we denote by $\mathcal{L}_r$ the code obtained when deleting from $\mathcal{L}_t$ everything that does not concern the instances of S. The latency of $\mathcal{L}_r$ is by definition the S-latency of $\mathcal{L}_t$. Furthermore, $\mathcal{L}_r$ is a n_S-deep perfect loop nest containing the unique statement S. Let $\overline{L}$ (resp. $\underline{L}$) be the perfect loop nest containing the unique statement S whose loops describe the iteration domain $\overline{\mathcal{D}}$ (resp. $\underline{\mathcal{D}}$).

As $\underline{\mathcal{D}} \subset \mathcal{D}_t \subset \overline{\mathcal{D}}$, the latency of $\mathcal{L}_r$ is greater than that of $\underline{L}$ and less than that of $\overline{L}$. Furthermore, as $\overline{\mathcal{D}}$ and $\underline{\mathcal{D}}$ are hypercubes of dimension n_S, their latency is easy to compute. The latency of $\underline{L}$ is $\Omega(N^{d_S})$ and that of $\overline{L}$ is $O(N^{d_S})$, where d_S is the number of sequential loops surrounding S. Therefore, the latency of $\mathcal{L}_r$ is $\Theta(N^{d_S})$ and the S-degree of extracted parallelism of $\mathcal{L}_r$ (and thus the S-degree of extracted parallelism of $\mathcal{L}$) is $(n_S - d_S)$, i.e., the number of parallel loops surrounding statement S. ∎

5.7.3 Optimality of ALLEN-KENNEDY

In the original algorithm, the search for parallelism is stopped as soon as at least one parallel loop is detected; after parallelization, each statement is surrounded by at most one parallel loop. It has been proved (see [125, section 7.2.5]) that "the algorithm determines loops whose iterations can be executed in parallel without synchronization and transforms them into doall-loops; if such a transformation is possible at more than one level, then it is performed at the outermost possible level." More precisely, the ith outermost loop surrounding a statement S (with i as small as possible) will be marked as parallel if and only if there is no dependence at level i between two different instances of S.

The particular version of Allen and Kennedy's algorithm that we presented in Section 5.3 is slightly different. The search for parallel loops is done even at levels deeper than the first detected parallel level. Several parallel nested loops can be generated as well as arbitrary sequences of **DOPAR** and **DOSEQ** loops. With the same proof technique as in [125], it is easy to prove that such a strategy leads to an optimality result in the following sense: For each statement, the algorithm determines as many parallel loops as possible if, in the transformed code, the instances of each statement are described with exactly the same loops as in the initial code. This does not prove a general optimality property in the meaning introduced in the previous section. In particular, this does not prove that it is not possible to detect more parallelism with more sophisticated techniques than loop distribution and loop fusion.

In fact, we can prove a stronger result. The technique we use to establish the optimality is the second method presented in the previous section. The loop nest to be parallelized may contain more parallelism than found by ALLEN-KENNEDY. However, it is not possible to detect this parallelism if the only piece of information available is the RLDG. In other words, the EDG corresponding to the original loop nest may contain larger independent sets of operations, but no algorithm can detect this potential parallelism if the only knowledge concerning the dependences between the different statements is the RLDG. Actually, even if the structure of the code, i.e., the way loops are nested, is taken into account, no more parallelism can be detected. To show such a result, we build an apparent loop nest with the same code structure as the loop nest to be parallelized, with the same RLDG, whose EDG exactly contains the amount of parallelism detected by ALLEN-KENNEDY. Because the original loop nest and the apparent loop nest cannot be distinguished either by their RLDG or by their code structure and because since the apparent loop nest can be shown to be optimally parallelized, this proves an optimality property for parallelism detection.

We now show how to build the apparent loop nest. During the recursive calls to the ALLEN-KENNEDY algorithm given in Section 5.3.2, we select some edges that we will consider in a special way when generating the apparent loop nest. This selection is done at step 3a of the algorithm (see Section 5.3.2); one of the edges with level equal to $l_{\min}(C)$ is arbitrarily marked as *critical*. Then the generation of the apparent loop nest is done using the APPARENT_LOOP_GENERATOR algorithm.

Algorithm (Generation of an Apparent Loop Nest for a Given RLDG)

APPARENT_LOOP_GENERATOR(RLDG G):

1. Keep the code structure of the original loop nest, but set all lower bounds to 1 and all upper bounds to N. Let I be the iteration vector.

2. **For each** statement S_i in the original loop nest **do**:

    (a) In the apparent loop nest, define a statement T_i surrounded by the same loop nest as S_i in the original loop nest.

    (b) Declare an array a_i of dimension n_{S_i}, the number of loops surrounding S_i. The result of the computation performed in statement $T_i(I)$ is stored in $a_i(I)$.

    (c) Define the right-hand side of T_i as follows. For each edge e, from S_j to S_i, add a reference to $a_j(J)$ in the right-hand side. J is defined as follows. The components of J are equal to the components of I until level $l(e) - 1$, and the $l(e)$th component of J is equal to the $l(e)$th component of I minus 1, so that the two references $a_j(J)$ and $a_i(I)$ create a dependence at level $l(e)$. Then, if e is a critical edge, all remaining components of J are fixed to N. If e is not a critical edge, the remaining components of J are equal to the components of I until level $\min(n_{S_i}, n_{S_j})$ and equal to N for the last components if any. In this case, if $n_{S_i} = n_{S_j}$, the dependence is uniform.

Lemma 34 proves the validity of this algorithm.

Lemma 34 *Let $\mathcal{L}$ be a set of nested loops with RLDG G. Then G is also the reduced level dependence graph associated to the apparent loop nest built by* APPARENT_LOOP_GENERATOR(G).

Proof Let G' be the RLDG associated to the apparent loop nest $\mathcal{L}'$ generated as earlier. Note that in $\mathcal{L}'$ there is only one *write* for each index vector I and each array a_i; this *write* occurs in statement T_i at iteration I. Therefore, the dependences in $\mathcal{L}'$ that involve array a_i correspond to a dependence between this unique *write* and some *read* on this array. Each *read* on array a_i on the right-hand side of a statement corresponds, by construction of $\mathcal{L}'$, to one particular edge e in the graph G. Therefore, G and G' have the same vertices and edges. One just has to check that the level of all edges is the same in G and G', which is obvious. ∎

Example 14, Continued

For Example 14, we can choose as critical edges the edges depicted as solid lines in Figure 5.41. The corresponding apparent loop nest is given in the same figure. □

```
DO i=1, N
  DO j=1, N
    DO k=1, N
      a₁(i,j,k) = a₁(i,j-1,k) + a₂(i,j-1,N) + a₃(i,j-1)
      a₂(i,j,k) = a₁(i,j,k-1) + a₂(i,j,k-1)
    ENDDO
    a₃(i,j) = a₂(i-1,j,N) + a₃(i-1,N)
    a₄(i,j) = a₁(i-1,j,N) + a₃(i,j) + a₄(i,j-1)
  ENDDO
ENDDO
```

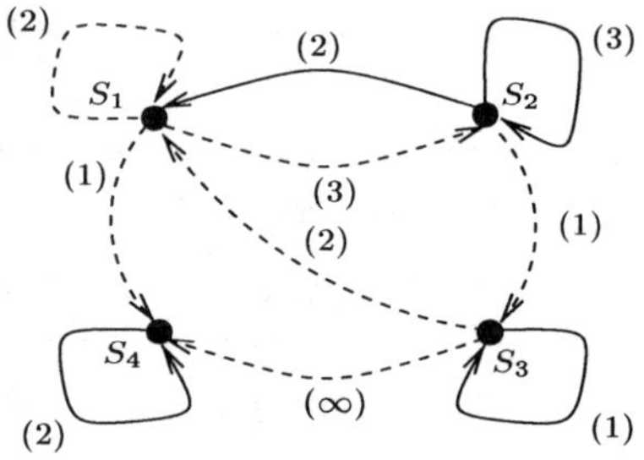

Figure 5.41: Apparent loop nest for Example 14 and its RLDG with critical edges in solid lines.

Let d_S be the number of calls to ALLEN-KENNEDY (the initial call excluded) that concern a statement S, i.e., the number of calls ALLEN-KEN-NEDY(H,k) such that S is a node of H. As we noticed in Section 5.3.2, d_S is also the number of sequential loops that surround S in the parallelized code.

Theorem 34 *Let $\mathcal{L}$ be a loop nest, G be its RLDG, $\mathcal{L}'$ be the apparent loop nest associated to $\mathcal{L}$, and N be the size parameter that defines the loop bounds in $\mathcal{L}'$. Then for each strongly connected component G_i of G, there exists a path in the EDG of the apparent loop nest $\mathcal{L}'$ that visits each statement S of G_i $\Omega(N^{d_s})$ times.*

The proof is long, technical, and painful. Its arguments are similar to those used to establish Theorem 23 (Section 4.4.2). Furthermore, the result is more interesting than the proof itself. Thus we do not prove this result here; we refer curious readers to [32], where they will find the details. The consequence of Theorem 34 is the following.

Corollary 5 (Optimality of ALLEN-KENNEDY**)** *The* ALLEN-KENNEDY *algorithm is optimal for parallelism extraction in reduced level dependence graphs.*

This proves that as long as the only information available is the RLDG, it is not possible to detect more parallelism than found by Allen and Kennedy's algorithm. Even the structure of the code cannot help. Exploiting the shape of the iteration domains, i.e., the definition of the loop bounds, may help, except if all loops are parameterized by unknown parameters, as in the apparent loop nest built earlier. Thus, the only way to detect more parallelism is to use a more accurate representation of the dependences.

5.7.4 Optimality of WOLF-LAM

We have the same type of optimality result for WOLF-LAM than for ALLEN-KENNEDY. But here, our proof is indirect. Indeed, we proved in Section 5.5.6 that the DARTE-VIVIEN and WOLF-LAM algorithms find exactly the same degree of parallelism in a set of direction vectors (thus implicitly considering that the loop nest contains a single statement). In the next section we will prove the optimality of DARTE-VIVIEN for a more general dependence representation: the polyhedral reduced dependence graphs (Theorem 37). These two results together establish the optimality of WOLF-LAM.

Theorem 35 (Optimality of WOLF-LAM) WOLF-LAM *is optimal for the detection of parallelism in a set of direction vectors. In other words,* WOLF-LAM *is optimal for the detection of parallelism in nested loops that contain a single statement when dependences are represented by direction vectors.*

This optimality result cannot be generalized. Indeed, when the loop body contains several statements, WOLF-LAM is not optimal. Figure 5.42 presents a counterexample. The reader can check that ALLEN-KENNEDY can find some parallelism in this example, WOLF-LAM cannot. It fails to find some because of the direction vectors $(1, -, 0)$, $(0, 1, -)$, and $(0, 0, 1)$. To add a step of loop distribution between the recursive calls to WOLF-LAM enables it to find some parallelism here. (But this is not an optimal strategy in general.)

5.7.5 Optimality of DARTE-VIVIEN

To prove the optimality of DARTE-VIVIEN, we compare the makespan of the schedules (i.e., the latency of the parallelized codes) it produces with the longest dependence paths in the dependence graphs it processes. Therefore, we first give an estimate of the length of paths in the apparent dependence graph associated to a given PRDG G. This way, we obtain a lower bound on the sequentiality and thus an upper bound on the parallelism

Example 24

```
DO i=1,N
  DO j=1,N
    DO k=1,N
      S₁: a(i,j,k)=a(i-1,j+i,k)+a(i,j,k-1)+b(i,j-1,k)
      S₂: b(i,j,k)=b(i,j-1,k+j)+a(i-1,j,k)
    ENDDO
  ENDDO
ENDDO
```

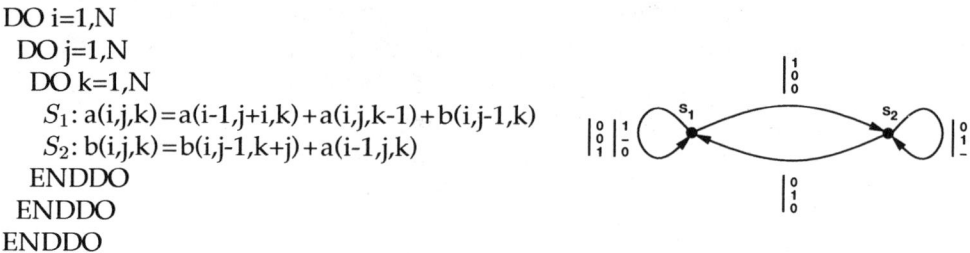

Figure 5.42: Example 24 and its RDG.

contained in the studied representation of the dependences. To do so, we apply to the uniformized graph G_u the theorem on the longest dependence paths that we proved for a system of uniform recurrence equations. Then we transpose the result to the original graph G_o using the results of Section 5.5.2 on the equivalence between paths of G_o and G_u. This way, we prove the same type of result than the one established for SUREs.

Theorem 36 (Longest Dependence Paths of a PRDG) *Let G_o be a PRDG. We assume that the iteration domain of G_o contains a hypercube of dimension n and size $\Omega(N)$. Let d_S be the depth of the node S of G_o for algorithm* DA *(resp. for algorithm* DA**) applied to G_u. Then there exists, for each strongly connected component G_i of G_o, a path in the apparent dependence graph of G_o whose projection on G_o is a cycle that contains $\Omega(N^{d_S})$ occurrences of each node S of G_i.*

Proof   First note that the depth of an *actual* node of G_u is the same for the algorithms KMW (Section 4.4.2) and DA (Section 5.5.3), the former making no differences between actual and virtual nodes. Then, we use Theorem 23 to build, for each strongly connected component G_i of G_u, a path in the apparent dependence graph whose projection on G_u is a cycle that contains $\Omega(N^{d_S})$ occurrences of each node S of G_i. The projection on G_u is a cycle that contains at least one actual node. Thus, we can conclude by using Corollary 4, which gives us a cycle of G_o and ensures us that an actual node has the same number of occurrences in both cycles.   ∎

We did not prove that the paths we built were the "longest," as announced. This result is proved indirectly by the following optimality theorem.

Theorem 37 (Optimality of DARTE-VIVIEN**)** *The schedules built by* DARTE-

VIVIEN *are optimal; if the iteration domain contains (resp. is contained in) a hypercube of dimension n and size $\Omega(N)$ (resp. $O(N)$) and if d is the depth of decomposition of the dependence graph G, then the makespan of the schedule is $O(N^d)$ and the length of the longest dependence path is $\Omega(N^d)$.*

More precisely, if d_S is the decomposition depth of the node S of G then the makespan of the schedule associated to S is equal to $O(N^{d_S})$ and there exists in the apparent dependence graph a path that contains $\Omega(N^{d_S})$ occurrences of S.

Proof   We just have to compare what Lemma 32 and Theorem 36, respectively, state.   ∎

Once again, this optimality result is with respect to the dependence analysis considered, i.e., polyhedral reduced dependence graphs. Indeed, consider the example of Figure 5.43. When approximating the dependences by some polyhedra, we have two self-dependences of weight $(0, 1)$ and two dependences whose polyhedra have a single vertex $((1, 2)$ and $(1, -2)$ respectively), and a single ray $((0, 1)$ and $(0, -1)$ respectively). Then the RDG contains a zero-weight multicycle, and this multicycle includes the two actual nodes. Therefore, DARTE-VIVIEN finds no parallelism in this example. Nevertheless, to compute iteration (i, j) of statement S_1 (resp. S_2) at time $2i + j$ (resp. $i + j$) respects the dependences. Such a schedule exhibits one degree of parallelism that cannot be found by DARTE-VIVIEN. Because of the approximation of the dependences by polyhedra, the loop nest *appears* to be purely sequential. However, if we know the exact dependences, then we can successfully parallelize this example using Feautrier's algorithm.

Example 25

```
DO i=1, N
  DO j=1,N
    S₁: a(i,j) = b(i-1,j+i) + a(i,j-1)
    S₂: b(i,j) = a(i-1,j-i) + b(i,j-1)
  ENDDO
ENDDO
```

Figure 5.43: Example 25 and its RDG.

5.7.6   Suboptimality of FEAUTRIER

On one hand, we proved that FEAUTRIER was a generalization of DARTE-VIVIEN when looking at polyhedral reduced dependence graphs (Theorem 33, Section 5.6.4). On the other hand, we have proved in the previous section that DARTE-VIVIEN was optimal for this representation of the dependences. These two results put together establish the following theorem.

Theorem 38 (Optimality of FEAUTRIER for PRDGs) *The schedules built by* FEAUTRIER *are optimal: if the iteration domain contains (resp. is contained in) a hypercube of dimension n and size $\Omega(N)$ (resp. $O(N)$) and if d is the depth of decomposition of the dependence graph G, then the schedule makespan is $O(N^d)$ and the length of the longest dependence path is $\Omega(N^d)$.*

More precisely, if d_S is the decomposition depth of the node S of G then the makespan of the schedule associated to S is $O(N^{d_S})$ and there exists in the apparent dependence graph a path that contains $\Omega(N^{d_S})$ occurrences of S.

Limitations of FEAUTRIER

The previous theorem does not deal with the general case of affine dependences. In fact, Paul Feautrier proved in his original article [40, 41] that his algorithm was not optimal for parallelism detection in static control flow programs. His counterexample is given next.

Example 26

The FEAUTRIER algorithm finds no parallelism in the following code:

```
DO i=0, 2n
  x(i) = x(2n-i)
ENDDO
```

Indeed, this code contains a single loop that is not already parallel. The problem here is that we are looking for a transformation that is conservative in the number of loops. If we break the loop into several loops, i.e., cut the iteration domain into several subdomains, we can find an equivalent code that is fully parallel:

```
DOPAR i=0, n
  x(i) = x(2n-i)
ENDDOPAR
DOPAR i=n+1, 2n
  x(i) = x(2n-i)
ENDDOPAR
```

If all instances of the statement are scheduled the same way, i.e., with the same affine function as in Feautrier's algorithm, we cannot derive such a code. Extending FEAUTRIER with index set splitting (i.e., cutting a domain into subdomains) is considered in [52]. □

5.7.7 Conclusion

For all classical dependence representations, we thus have an "optimal" algorithm for parallelism detection, except for affine dependences: ALLEN-KENNEDY is optimal for an approximation of dependence distances by dependence levels, WOLF-LAM is optimal for an approximation of dependence distances by direction vectors (and all statements considered as a single block), and DARTE-VIVIEN is optimal for an approximation of dependence distances by polyhedra, but FEAUTRIER is not optimal for affine dependences, even though it is the most general algorithm. It is still an open question whether there exists a polynomial-time algorithm that can generate a parallel code of bounded size (i.e., not dependent on the parameters) and that exhibits parallelism optimally (in the meaning of Definition 34).

5.8 Bibliographical Notes

In this chapter, we chose to present the algorithms that use loop transformations for parallelism detection and not the loop transformations themselves. Our presentation is thus mainly inspired by the original papers of Allen and Kennedy [4], Lamport [75], Wolf and Lam [117], Darte and Vivien [33], and Feautrier [41], and by [32] and [34] for the optimality study. Nevertheless, these algorithms have only emerged after some particular loop transformations had been identified as useful and studied in a more specific manner, in particular at Rice University and the University of Illinois at Urbana-Champaign. We cannot refer here to all the transformations proposed in the past, we rather refer once again to the books by Zima and Chapman [125] and Wolfe [121], and to the surveys by Bacon, Graham, and Sharp [12], and Banerjee, Eigenmann, Nicolau, and Padua [14].

As already pointed out, detecting parallelism is only a subproblem of the whole parallelization process. In particular, we mentioned but did not address two other problems for which the research is still very active, namely, the tiling problem and the mapping/alignment problem.

Tiling (also known as loop blocking or loop partitioning) is a technique whose objective is to increase the granularity of computations, the locality of data references, and the computation-to-communication ratio of fully permutable loop nests. The iteration space is divided into hyper-parallelepipeds (tiles), whose size and shape are optimized according to some optimization criteria. Seminal papers on tiling include [63, 109, 116, 101]. Further references are [17, 1, 20, 86, 58, 8].

Lately, a large research effort has focused on another technique: aligning and mapping arrays and computations onto distributed memory machines. Several methods and tools have been presented since the reference papers of Li and Chen [81, 82], who have studied the problem of aligning arrays to minimize communication. We refer the reader to the survey paper of Ayguadé, Garcia and Kremer [9] on mapping methods and tools. Further references include [70, 54, 7, 15, 42, 67, 35, 78].

5.9   Exercises

Exercise 5.1 (Dependence level and the ALLEN-KENNEDY **algorithm)**

- Give a set of perfectly nested loops, with uniform dependences, such that the reduced dependence graph by level (RLDG) is exactly the graph of Figure 5.44.

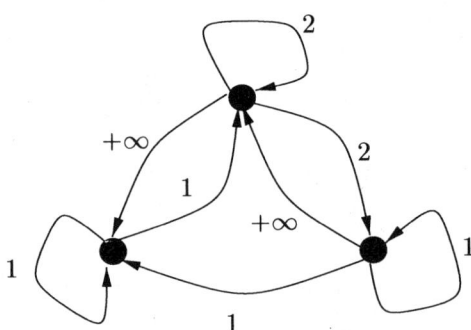

Figure 5.44: RLDG for Exercise 5.1.

- Give a set of (nonperfectly) nested loops for which the RLDG is Figure 5.44 and such that each statement is surrounded by the smallest number of loops.

- Same question with the additional constraint that the result of each statement is stored in an array of the smallest dimension.

- Apply ALLEN-KENNEDY on one of these three codes.

Exercise 5.2 (Dependence analysis)

Consider the following code:

```
DO i=1, n
 DO j=1, n
   a(i+j) = b(j,i-1)
   b(j,i) = a(i-1+j) + b(i,j)
 ENDDO
ENDDO
```

- Compute the exact dependences of this code.

- Give an approximation of the distance vectors by direction vectors, then by level. Give a parallel version of the code.

Exercise 5.3 (A sequential example)

Consider the following code:

```
DO i=0, n
 DO j=i, n
   a(i,j) = a(i,j-1) + a(i+1,j-i)
 ENDDO
ENDDO
```

- Analyze the dependences of the loop nest. Describe the expanded dependence graph (EDG) and the reduced dependence graph (RDG). In the RDG, express the dependence vectors in the language $(\mathbb{Z}, +, -, *)$.

- Give the constraints that should be satisfied if a linear schedule exists. Show why there is no such schedule.

- Give a (nontrivial) lower bound for the length of the longest dependence path in the EDG. Conclude.

- Nevertheless, give a way to parallelize the code. Explain why the transformation you used is not so easy to apply in general.

Exercise 5.4 (A uniform loop nest with a single statement)

Consider the following code:

```
DO i=5, n
 DO j=1, n
  a(i,j) = a(i,j-1) + a(i+1,j) + a(i+1,j-1) + a(i-5,j+4)
 ENDDO
ENDDO
```

- Give the reduced dependence graph.

- Give an optimal linear schedule, i.e., a linear schedule for which the number of sequential steps (the makespan) is minimized. What is its makespan? Check that there does exist a dependence path in the expanded dependence graph of equivalent length.

- Rewrite the code to make the parallelism explicit.

- Using an additional array, show that this is possible to reduce the makespan. Give an example (similar to the preceding code) for which the elimination of anti dependences does not change the minimal makespan.

Exercise 5.5 (A uniform loop nest with several statements)

Consider the following code:

```
DO i=0, n
 DO j=0, n
  S₁: a(i+1,j+1) = a(i+1,j) + b(i,j+2)
  S₂: b(i+1,j) = a(i+1,j-1) + b(i,j-1)
  S₃: a(i,j+2) = b(i+1,j+1) - 1
 ENDDO
ENDDO
```

- Give the reduced dependence graph for the code, and specify the type (flow, anti, or output dependence), the dependence vector, and the level corresponding to each dependence.

- Use ALLEN-KENNEDY to parallelize the code. What is the makespan (number of sequential steps) of the resulting code?

- Find the linear scheduling with minimal makespan. Find the shifted-linear scheduling with minimal makespan (i.e., a common vector and a possibly different constant for each statement). What are the respective makespans of these two schedules? Give an equivalent (function of n) for the length of the longest past in the expanded dependence graph. Exhibit such a path.

The reduced dependence graph here is strongly connected. This property is not true anymore if one of the anti dependences is removed.

- Show how to transform the code, with the introduction of one new array c, so that the reduced dependence graph now has two strongly connected components, one with S_3 alone.

  Note: Don't forget the initialization of the array c and the output in the original array.

- Show that we can now break the code in two pieces, one for iterations on S_1 and S_2, and a completely parallel code for S_3.

- For the first part involving S_1 and S_2, give the linear scheduling and shifted-linear scheduling with minimal makespan. What are their respective makespans? Give an equivalent (function of n) for the length of the longest past in the expanded dependence graph. Exhibit such a path.

Exercise 5.6 (The LAMPORT algorithm and some variants)

Consider the following code:

```
DO i=1, n
 DO j=1, n
  a(i,j) = b(i-1,j) + a(i-1,j)
  b(i,j) = a(i,j-1)
 ENDDO
ENDDO
```

In this exercise, we consider only perfectly nested loops with uniform dependences. For all examples, we will consider the preceding code.

- Give the uniform dependences of the code.

- Recall the linear scheduling technique, i.e., explain why we impose the constraint $X.d \geq 1$ for each dependence vector d when trying to schedule the computations of iteration $I = (i, j)$ at time step $X.I$, i.e., $xi + yj$ if $X = (x, y)$.

- Parallelize the code with the linear scheduling technique. Parallelize the same code with ALLEN-KENNEDY.

We will now try to extend the linear scheduling method to retrieve the result obtained by ALLEN-KENNEDY (and even more). We now try to schedule the operation $S(I)$ – iteration I of statement S – at time step $X.I + \rho_S$ where ρ_S depends on S.

- Show that the constraint is now $X.d + \rho_{S'} - \rho_S \geq 1$ for each dependence vector d from S to S'. Show that such constraints are equivalent to the constraints $X.d(C) \geq l(C)$ for each cycle C in the dependence graph where $d(C)$ is the sum of dependence vectors along C and $l(C)$ is the length of C. Show how we can retrieve by this technique the result obtained by ALLEN-KENNEDY.

- We now choose even weaker constraints. We impose only $Xd(C) \geq 1$ for each cycle C in the dependence graph, but we restrict to integral solutions X. Explain what happens. Show that we can always deduce from X a valid scheduling, possibly by changing the textual order of the statements. Retrieve again the previous result.

- Show that the following code is also a parallelized version of the code. How did we find it? Discuss the advantages and disadvantages of this solution compared to the previous ones.

```
DOSEQ i=1, n
 DOPAR j=1 to N+1
  IF (j > 1) THEN
    a(i,j-1) = b(i-1,j-1) + a(i-1,j)
  ENDIF
  IF (j < n+1) THEN
    b(i,j) = a(i,j-1)
  ENDIF
 ENDDOPAR
ENDDOSEQ
```

Bibliography

[1] A. Agarwal, D. A. Kranz, and V. Natarajan. Automatic partitioning of parallel loops and data arrays for distributed shared-memory multiprocessors. *IEEE Transactions on Parallel and Distributed Systems*, 6(9):943–962, 1995.

[2] A. Aiken and A. Nicolau. Perfect pipelining: A new loop optimization technique. In *1988 European Symposium on Programming*, volume 300 of *Lecture Notes in Computer Science*, pages 221–235. Springer-Verlag, 1988.

[3] V. H. Allan, R. B. Jones, R. M. Lee, and S. J. Allan. Software pipelining. *ACM Computing Surveys*, 27(3):367–432, Sept. 1995.

[4] J. Allen, D. Callahan, and K. Kennedy. Automatic decomposition of scientific programs for parallel execution. In *Proceedings of the Fourteenth Annual Symposium on Principles of Programming Languages*, pages 63–76, Munich, Germany, Jan. 1987.

[5] J. R. Allen and K. Kennedy. PFC: A program to convert Fortran to parallel form. In *Proceedings of IBM Conference on Parallel Computing and Scientific Computations*, 1982.

[6] J. R. Allen and K. Kennedy. Automatic translation of Fortran programs to vector form. *ACM Transactions on Programming Languages and Systems*, 9(4):491–542, Oct. 1987.

[7] J. M. Anderson and M. S. Lam. Global optimizations for parallelism and locality on scalable parallel machines. *ACM SIGPLAN Notices*, 28(6):112–125, June 1993.

[8] R. Andonov and S. Rajopadhye. Optimal orthogonal tiling of two-dimensional iterations. *Journal of Parallel and Distributed Computing*, 45(2):159–165, 1997.

[9] E. Ayguadé, J. Garcia, and U. Kremer. Tools and techniques for automatic data layout: A case study. *Parallel Computing*, 24(3-4):557–578, 1998.

[10] W. Backes. *The Structure of Longest Paths in Periodic Graphs*. PhD thesis, Universität des Saarlandes, Saarbrücken, July 1993.

[11] W. Backes, U. Schwiegelshohn, and L. Thiele. Analysis of free schedule in periodic graphs. In *SPAA'92, Fourth Annual ACM Symposium on Parallel Algorithms and Architectures*, pages 333–342, San Diego, 1992. ACM Press.

[12] D. F. Bacon, S. L. Graham, and O. J. Sharp. Compiler transformations for high-performance computing. *ACM Computing Surveys*, 26(4), 1994.

[13] U. Banerjee. *Dependence Analysis for Supercomputing*. Kluwer Academic Publishers, Norwell, MA, 1988.

[14] U. Banerjee, R. Eigenmann, A. Nicolau, and D. A. Padua. Automatic program parallelization. *Proceedings of the IEEE*, 81(2):211–243, 1993.

[15] D. Bau, I. Kodukula, V. Kotlyar, K. Pingali, and P. Stodghill. Solving alignment using elementary linear algebra. In K. Pingali, U. Banerjee, D. Gelernter, A. Nicolau, and D. A. Padua, editors, *Languages and Compilers for Parallel Computing, Seventh International Workshop*, volume 892 of *Lectures Notes in Computer Science*, pages 46–60. Springer-Verlag, 1994.

[16] A. J. Bernstein. Analysis of programs for parallel processing. *IEEE Transactions on Electronic Computers*, 15:757–762, Oct. 1966.

[17] P. Boulet, A. Darte, T. Risset, and Y. Robert. (Pen)-ultimate tiling? *Integration, the VLSI Journal*, 17:33–51, 1994.

[18] P.-Y. Calland, A. Darte, and Y. Robert. Circuit retiming applied to decomposed software pipelining. *IEEE Transactions on Parallel and Distributed Systems*, 9(1):24–35, Jan. 1998.

[19] B. W. Char, K. O. Geddes, G. H. Gonnet, M. B. Monagan, and S. M. Watt. *Maple Reference Manual*. Springer-Verlag, 1988.

[20] Y.-S. Chen, S.-D. Wang, and C.-M. Wang. Tiling nested loops into maximal rectangular blocks. *Journal of Parallel and Distributed Computing*, 35(2):108–120, 1996.

[21] P. Chrétienne. Task scheduling with interprocessor communication delays. *European Journal of Operational Research*, 57:348–354, 1992.

[22] P. Chrétienne, E. G. Coffman, Jr., J. K. Lenstra, and Z. Liu, editors. *Scheduling Theory and Its Applications*. John Wiley & Sons, 1995.

[23] P. Chrétienne and C. Picouleau. Scheduling with communication delays: A survey. In P. Chrétienne, E. G. Coffman, Jr., J. K. Lenstra, and Z. Liu, editors, *Scheduling Theory and Its Applications*, pages 65–89. John Wiley & Sons, 1995.

[24] E. G. Coffman, Jr. *Computer and Job-Shop Scheduling Theory*. John Wiley & Sons, 1976.

[25] E. Cohen and N. Megiddo. Strongly polynomial-time and NC algorithms for detecting cycles in dynamic graphs. In *Proceedings of 21st Annual ACM Symposium on Theory of Computing*, pages 523–534, 1989.

[26] T. H. Cormen, C. E. Leiserson, and R. L. Rivest. *Introduction to Algorithms*. The MIT Press, 1990.

[27] A. Darte. On the complexity of loop fusion. In *International Conference on Parallel Architectures and Compilation Techniques (PACT'99)*, Newport Beach, CA, Oct. 1999.

[28] A. Darte and G. Huard. Loop shifting for loop compaction. In U. Banerjee, D. Gelernter, A. Nicolau, and D. A. Padua, editors, *The Twelfth International Workshop on Languages and Compilers for Parallel Computing*, Lecture Notes in Computer Science. Springer-Verlag, San Diego, CA, Aug. 1999.

[29] A. Darte, L. Khachiyan, and Y. Robert. Linear scheduling is nearly optimal. *Parallel Processing Letters*, 1(2):73–81, 1991.

[30] A. Darte, G.-A. Silber, and F. Vivien. Combining retiming and scheduling techniques for loop parallelization and loop tiling. *Parallel Processing Letters*, 7(4):379–392, 1997.

[31] A. Darte and F. Vivien. Revisiting the decomposition of Karp, Miller, and Winograd. *Parallel Processing Letters*, 5(4):551–562, Dec. 1995.

[32] A. Darte and F. Vivien. On the optimality of Allen and Kennedy's algorithm for parallelism extraction in nested loops. *Journal of Parallel Algorithms and Applications*, 12(1-3):83–112, 1997. Special issue on Optimizing Compilers for Parallel Languages.

[33] A. Darte and F. Vivien. Optimal fine and medium grain parallelism detection in polyhedral reduced dependence graphs. *International Journal of Parallel Programming*, 25(6):447–497, Dec. 1997.

[34] A. Darte and F. Vivien. Parallelizing nested loops with approximation of distance vectors: A survey. *Parallel Processing Letters*, 7(2):133–144, June 1997.

[35] M. Dion, C. Randriamaro, and Y. Robert. Compiling affine nested loops: How to optimize the residual communications after the alignment phase? *Journal of Parallel and Distributed Computing*, 38(2):176–187, 1996.

[36] H. El-Rewini, H. H. Ali, and T. G. Lewis. Task scheduling in multiprocessing systems. *Computer*, 28(12):27–37, 1995.

[37] H. El-Rewini, T. G. Lewis, and H. H. Ali. *Task Scheduling in Parallel and Distributed Systems*. Prentice Hall, 1994.

[38] P. Feautrier. Parametric integer programming. *RAIRO Recherche Opérationnelle*, 22:243–268, Sept. 1988.

[39] P. Feautrier. Dataflow analysis of array and scalar references. *International Journal of Parallel Programming*, 20(1):23–51, 1991.

[40] P. Feautrier. Some efficient solutions to the affine scheduling problem, Part I: One-dimensional time. *International Journal of Parallel Programming*, 21(5):313–348, Oct. 1992.

[41] P. Feautrier. Some efficient solutions to the affine scheduling problem, Part II: Multi-dimensional time. *International Journal of Parallel Programming*, 21(6):389–420, Dec. 1992.

[42] P. Feautrier. Towards automatic distribution. *Parallel Processing Letters*, 4(3):233–244, 1994.

[43] P. Feautrier and N. Tawbi. Résolution de systèmes d'inéquations linéaires: mode d'emploi du logiciel PIP. Technical Report 90-2, Institut Blaise Pascal, Laboratoire MASI (Paris), Jan. 1990.

[44] J. A. B. Fortes and F. Parisi-Presicce. Optimal linear schedules for the parallel execution of algorithms. In *International Conference on Parallel Processing*, pages 322–328, 1984.

[45] M. R. Garey and D. S. Johnson. *Computers and Intractability: A Guide to the Theory of NP-Completeness*. W. H. Freeman and Company, 1991.

[46] F. Gasperoni and U. Schwiegelshohn. Generating close to optimum loop schedules on parallel processors. *Parallel Processing Letters*, 4(4):391–403, 1994.

[47] A. Gerasoulis, J. Jiao, and T. Yang. A multistage approach for scheduling task graphs on parallel machines. In P. M. Pardalos, M. G. Resende, and K. Ramakrishnan, editors, *Workshop on Parallel Processing of Discrete Optimization Problems*, volume 22 of *DIMACS Series in Discrete Mathematics and Theoretical Computer Science*, pages 81–103. American Mathematical Society, 1994.

[48] A. Gerasoulis and T. Yang. A comparison of clustering heuristics for scheduling DAGs on multiprocessors. *Journal of Parallel and Distributed Computing*, 16(4):276–291, Dec. 1992.

[49] A. Gerasoulis and T. Yang. On the granularity and clustering of directed acyclic task graphs. *IEEE Transactions on Parallel and Distributed Systems*, 4(6):686–701, 1993.

[50] G. Goff, K. Kennedy, and C. W. Tseng. Practical dependence testing. In *Proceedings of ACM SIGPLAN'91 Conference on Programming Language Design and Implementation*, Toronto, Canada, June 1991.

[51] M. Gondran and M. Minoux. *Graphs and Algorithms*. John Wiley & Sons, 1984.

[52] M. Griebl, P. Feautrier, and C. Lengauer. On index set splitting. In *International Conference on Parallel Architectures and Compilation Techniques (PACT'99)*, Newport Beach, CA, Oct. 1999.

[53] D. Grunwald. Data dependence analysis: The λ test revisited. In *Proceedings of the 1990 International Conference on Parallel Processing*, 1990.

[54] M. Gupta and P. Banerjee. Demonstration of automatic data partitioning techniques for parallelizing compilers on multicomputers. *IEEE Transactions on Parallel and Distributed Systems*, 3(2):179–193, 1992.

[55] C. Hanen and A. Munier. An approximation algorithm for scheduling dependent tasks on m processors with small communication delays. In *ETFA 95: INRIA/IEEE Symposium on Emerging Technology and Factory Animation*, pages 167–189. IEEE Computer Science Press, 1995.

[56] C. Hanen and A. Munier. Cyclic scheduling on parallel processors: An overview. In P. Chrétienne, E. G. Coffman, Jr., J. K. Lenstra, and Z. Liu, editors, *Scheduling Theory and Its Applications*. John Wiley & Sons, 1995.

[57] High Performance Fortran Forum. High Performance Fortran Language Specification. Technical Report 2.0, Rice University, Jan. 1997.

[58] K. Högstedt, L. Carter, and J. Ferrante. Determining the idle time of a tiling. In *Principles of Programming Languages*, pages 160–173. ACM Press, 1997.

[59] T. C. Hu. Parallel sequencing and assembly line problems. *Operations Research*, 9(6):841–848, 1961.

[60] F. Irigoin, P. Jouvelot, and R. Triolet. Semantical interprocedural parallelization: An overview of the PIPS project. In *Proceedings of the 1991 ACM International Conference on Supercomputing*, Cologne, Germany, June 1991.

[61] F. Irigoin and R. Triolet. Computing dependence direction vectors and dependence cones with linear systems. Technical Report ENSMP-CAI-87-E94, École des Mines de Paris, Fontainebleau (France), 1987.

[62] F. Irigoin and R. Triolet. Dependence approximation and global parallel code generation for nested loops. In *Proceedings of the International Workshop on Parallel and Distributed Algorithms*, Oct. 1988.

[63] F. Irigoin and R. Triolet. Supernode partitioning. In *Proceedings of the Fifteenth Annual ACM Symposium on Principles of Programming Languages*, pages 319–329, San Diego, CA, Jan. 1988.

[64] B. Joinnault. *Conception d'algorithmes et d'architectures systoliques*. PhD thesis, Université de Rennes I, 1987.

[65] R. M. Karp, R. E. Miller, and S. Winograd. The organization of computations for uniform recurrence equations. *Journal of the ACM*, 14(3):563–590, July 1967.

[66] W. Kelly, V. Maslov, W. Pugh, E. Rosser, T. Shpeisman, and D. Wonnacott. *New User Interface for Petit and Other Interfaces: User Guide.* University of Maryland, June 1995.

[67] W. Kelly and W. Pugh. Minimizing communication while preserving parallelism. In *Proceedings of the tenth ACM International Conference on Supercomputing.* ACM Press, 1996.

[68] K. Kennedy and K. S. McKinley. Typed fusion with applications to parallel and sequential code generation. Technical Report CRPC-TR94646, Center for Research on Parallel Computation, Rice University, 1994.

[69] S. J. Kim and J. C. Browne. A general approach to mapping of parallel computations upon multiprocessor architectures. In *International Conference on Parallel Processing*, volume 3, pages 1–8, 1988.

[70] K. Knobe, J. D. Lukas, and G. L. Steele. Data optimization: Allocation of arrays to reduce communication on SIMD machines. *Journal of Parallel and Distributed Computing*, 8:102–118, 1990.

[71] X. Y. Kong, D. Klappholz, and K. Psarris. The I test: A new test for subscript data dependence. In D. A. Padua, editor, *Proceedings of 1990 International Conference of Parallel Processing*, Aug. 1990.

[72] S. R. Kosaraju and G. F. Sullivan. Detecting cycles in dynamic graphs in polynomial time (preliminary version). In A. Press, editor, *Proceedings of the Twentieth Annual ACM Symposium on Theory of Computing*, pages 398–406, May 1988.

[73] V. Kumar, A. Grama, A. Gupta, and G. Karypis. *Introduction to Parallel Computing.* The Benjamin/Cummings Publishing Company, Inc., 1994.

[74] M. S. Lam. Software pipelining: An effective scheduling technique for VLIW machines. In *SIGPLAN'88 Conference on Programming Language, Design and Implementation*, pages 318–328, Atlanta, GA, 1988. ACM Press.

[75] L. Lamport. The parallel execution of DO loops. *Communications of the ACM*, 17(2):83–93, Feb. 1974.

[76] P. Le Gouëslier d'Argence. *Contribution à l'étude des problèmes d'ordonnancement cyclique multidimensionnel.* PhD thesis, Université Paris VI, Jan. 1996.

[77] P. Le Gouëslier d'Argence. Affine scheduling on bounded convex polyhedric domains is asymptotically optimal. *Theoretical Computer Science*, 196(1-2):395–415, 1998.

[78] P.-Z. Lee. Efficient algorithms for data distribution on distributed memory parallel computers. *IEEE Transactions on Parallel and Distributed Systems*, 8(8):825–839, 1997.

[79] C. E. Leiserson and J. B. Saxe. Retiming synchronous circuitry. *Algorithmica*, 6(1):5–35, 1991.

[80] T. G. Lewis and H. El-Rewini. *Introduction to Parallel Computing*. Prentice-Hall, 1992.

[81] J. Li and M. Chen. Index domain alignment: Minimizing cost of cross-referencing between distributed arrays. In *Frontiers 90: The Third Symposium on the Frontiers of Massively Parallel Computation*, College Park, MD, Oct. 1990.

[82] J. Li and M. Chen. The data alignment phase in compiling programs for distributed-memory machines. *Journal of Parallel and Distributed Computing*, 13:213–221, 1991.

[83] Z. Y. Li, P.-C. Yew, and C. Q. Zhu. Data dependence analysis on multidimensional array references. In *Proceedings of the 1989 ACM International Conference on Supercomputing*, pages 215–224, Crete, Greece, June 1989.

[84] B. Lisper. Linear programming methods for minimizing execution time of indexed computations. In P. Feautrier and F. Irigoin, editors, *International Workshop on Compilers for Parallel Computers*, pages 131–142, MASI, Paris, Dec. 1990.

[85] R. E. Lord, J. S. Kowalik, and S. P. Kumar. Solving linear algebraic equations on an MIMD computer. *Journal of the ACM*, 30(1):103–117, 1983.

[86] N. Manjikian and T. S. Abdelrahman. Scheduling of wavefront parallelism on scalable shared memory multiprocessor. In *Proceedings of the International Conference on Parallel Processing (ICPP'96)*. CRC Press, 1996.

[87] M. Marrakchi. Optimal parallel scheduling for the two-step graph with constant task cost. *Parallel Computing*, 18:169–176, 1992.

[88] J. A. M. McHugh. Hu's precedence tree scheduling algorithm: A simple proof. *Naval Research Logistics Quaterly*, 31:409–411, 1984.

[89] K. S. McKinley and K. Kennedy. Maximizing loop parallelism and improving data locality via loop fusion and distribution. In U. Banerjee, D. Gelernter, A. Nicolau, and D. A. Padua, editors, *The Sixth Annual Languages and Compiler for Parallelism Workshop*, volume 768 of *Lecture Notes in Computer Science*, pages 301–320. Springer-Verlag, 1993.

[90] D. I. Moldovan. On the analysis and synthesis of VLSI systolic arrays. *IEEE Transactions on Computers*, 31:1121–1126, 1982.

[91] A. Munier. *Contribution à l'étude des ordonnancements cycliques*. PhD thesis, Institut Blaise Pascal, Université Paris VI, 1993.

[92] Y. Muraoka. *Parallelism Exposure and Exploitation in Programs*. PhD thesis, Department of Computer Science, University of Illinois at Urbana-Champaign, Feb. 1971.

[93] M. Newman. *Integral Matrices*. Academic Press, 1972.

[94] D. A. Padua and M. J. Wolfe. Advanced compiler optimizations for supercomputers. *Communications of the ACM*, 29(12):1184–1201, Dec. 1986.

[95] J. K. Peir and R. Cytron. Minimum distance: A method for partitioning recurrences for multiprocessors. *IEEE Transactions on Computers*, 38(8):1203–1211, Aug. 1989.

[96] C. Picouleau. Two new NP-complete scheduling problems with communication delays and unlimited number of processors. Technical Report 91-24, IBP, Université Pierre et Marie Curie, France, Apr. 1991.

[97] C. Picouleau. Task scheduling with interprocessor communication delays. *Discrete Applied Mathematics*, 60(1-3):331–342, 1995.

[98] K. Psarris, X. Y. Kong, and D. Klappholz. Extending the I test to direction vectors. In *Proceedings of the 1991 ACM International Conference on Supercomputing*, Cologne, Germany, June 1991.

[99] W. Pugh. The Omega test: A fast and practical integer programming algorithm for dependence analysis. *Communications of the ACM*, 8:102–114, Aug. 1992.

[100] P. Quinton. Automatic synthesis of systolic arrays from uniform recurrent equations. In *The Eleventh Annual International Symposium on Computer Architecture*, Ann Arbor, MI, June 1984. IEEE Computer Society Press.

[101] J. Ramanujam and P. Sadayappan. Tiling multidimensional iteration spaces for multicomputers. *Journal of Parallel and Distributed Computing*, 16(2):108–120, 1992.

[102] S. K. Rao. *Regular Iterative Algorithms and Their Implementations on Processor Arrays*. PhD thesis, Stanford University, Oct. 1985.

[103] B. R. Rau. Iterative modulo scheduling. *International Journal of Parallel Programming*, 24(1):3–64, 1996.

[104] B. R. Rau and C. D. Glaeser. Some scheduling techniques and an easily schedulable horizontal architecture for high performance scientific computing. In *Proceedings of the Fourteenth Annual Workshop of Microprogramming*, pages 183–198, Oct. 1981.

[105] V. P. Roychowdhury. *Derivation, Extensions and Parallel Implementation of Regular Iterative Algorithms*. PhD thesis, Stanford University, Dec. 1988.

[106] Y. Saouter. *A propos de systèmes d'équations récurrentes*. PhD thesis, Université de Rennes 1, Oct. 1992.

[107] Y. Saouter and P. Quinton. Computability of recurrence equations. *Theoretical Computer Science*, 116(2):317–337, Aug. 1993.

[108] V. Sarkar. *Partitioning and Scheduling Parallel Programs for Multiprocessors*. Pitman, 1989.

[109] R. Schreiber and J. J. Dongarra. Automatic blocking of nested loops. Technical Report 90-38, The University of Tennessee, Knoxville, TN, Aug. 1990.

[110] A. Schrijver. *Theory of Linear and Integer Programming*. John Wiley & Sons, New York, 1986.

[111] W. Shang and J. A. Fortes. Time optimal linear schedules for algorithms with uniform dependencies. *IEEE Transactions on Computers*, 40(6):723–742, June 1991.

[112] B. A. Shirazi, A. R. Hurson, and K. M. Kavi. *Scheduling and Load Balancing in Parallel and Distributed Systems*. IEEE Computer Science Press, 1995.

[113] F. Vivien. *Détection de parallélisme dans les boucles imbriquées*. PhD thesis, École normale supérieure de Lyon, France, Dec. 1997.

[114] J. Wang, C. Eisenbeis, M. Jourdan, and B. Su. Decomposed software pipelining. *International Journal of Parallel Programming*, 22(3):351–373, 1994.

[115] M. E. Wolf. *Improving Locality and Parallelism in Nested Loops*. PhD thesis, Stanford University, Aug. 1992.

[116] M. E. Wolf and M. S. Lam. A data locality optimizing algorithm. In *SIGPLAN Conference on Programming Language Design and Implementation*, pages 30–44. ACM Press, 1991.

[117] M. E. Wolf and M. S. Lam. A loop transformation theory and an algorithm to maximize parallelism. *IEEE Transactions on Parallel and Distributed Systems*, 2(4):452–471, Oct. 1991.

[118] M. Wolfe. *Optimizing Supercompilers for Supercomputers*. PhD thesis, Department of Computer Science, University of Illinois at Urbana-Champaign, Oct. 1982.

[119] M. Wolfe. *Optimizing Supercompilers for Supercomputers*. MIT Press, Cambridge MA, 1989.

[120] M. Wolfe. *TINY: A Loop Restructuring Research Tool*. Oregon Graduate Institute of Science and Technology, Dec. 1990.

[121] M. Wolfe. *High Performance Compilers for Parallel Computing*. Addison-Wesley Publishing Company, 1996.

[122] J. Xue. On tiling as a loop transformation. *Parallel Processing Letters*, 7(4):409–424, 1997.

[123] T. Yang and A. Gerasoulis. List scheduling with and without communication delays. *Parallel Computing*, 19:1321–1344, 1993.

[124] T. Yang and A. Gerasoulis. DSC: Scheduling parallel tasks on an unbounded number of processors. *IEEE Transactions on Parallel and Distributed Systems*, 5(9):951–967, 1994.

[125] H. Zima and B. Chapman. *Supercompilers for Parallel and Vector Computers*. ACM Press, 1990.

Index